Local Politics

Local Politics

A Practical Guide to Governing at the Grassroots

Second Edition

Terry Christensen and Tom Hogen-Esch

M.E.Sharpe
Armonk, New York
London, England

Library of Congress Cataloging-in-Publication Data

Christensen, Terry.
Local politics : a practical guide to governing at the grassroots / by Terry Christensen and
Tom Hogen-Esch. — 2nd ed.
  p. cm.
Includes bibliographical references and index.
ISBN-13 978-0-7656-1440-7 (pbk.: alk paper)
ISBN-10 0-7656-1440-5 (pbk.: alk. paper)
 1. Local government—United States. I. Hogen-Esch, Tom, 1968– II. Title.

JS331.C53 2006
352.140973—dc22   2006024579

Printed in the United States of America

The paper used in this publication meets the minimum requirements of
American National Standard for Information Sciences
Permanence of Paper for Printed Library Materials,
ANSI Z 39.48-1984.

BM (p)   10   9   8   7   6   5   4

Contents

Part II Official Decision Makers: Inside City Hall

Part IV Budget Politics, Public Policy, and Regional Government

List of Tables and Figures

Tables

Figures

Preface

When most of us pay attention to politics, it's national or international politics—wars or presidents or electoral contests for high office. Maybe that's because politics at those levels is more dramatic or because the media concentrate on them more. But our daily lives are affected much more immediately by politics in our own communities, from what happens when we flush the toilet to the safety of our neighborhoods, the traffic on our streets, and the air we breathe. Turning our attention to politics at this level can be a revelation: it's *local*—all around us. We can observe it firsthand, without a media filter, learning from the example of our own communities. We see real people participating in the political process and realize that we, too, can do so.

Unfortunately, textbooks about this subject often fail to communicate this immediacy and more often stifle than stimulate interest. Most seem to be written more for professional academics than for undergraduates, often from a wide variety of majors, who are just being introduced to the subject. *Local Politics: A Practical Guide to Governing at the Grassroots* recognizes the diversity of contemporary students of local politics and aims to meet their needs. Designed as a primary text for courses in urban, local, or state and local politics, this book is written with an emphasis on clarity, readability, and accessibility. Every effort has been made to make this a real teaching text, not only through its straightforward organization and style but also by emphasizing the nuts and bolts of local politics and by actively encouraging students to learn about local politics by observing their own communities—while simultaneously stressing comparison and generalization. This practical focus also makes the book a useful resource for participants in local government and politics, as we learned from the positive reaction of practitioners to the 1995 version of *Local Politics*.

Local Politics also moves the spotlight a little bit away from the big, old Frostbelt cities that are the focus of most discussions of urban politics. That's why the title uses the word *local* rather than *city* or *urban* with all the images those words convey. The term *local politics* more readily implies a variety of communities, including small ones, as well as a variety of types of government, including counties, special districts, and school districts. Frostbelt cities remain an important focus here, but suburbia and Sunbelt communities, where a majority of Americans now live, are at the center of this book.

As the subtitle *A Practical Guide to Governing at the Grassroots* states, *Local Politics* takes a practical, or applied, approach to its subject, providing a clear description and analysis of the structure and process of local politics. Rather than treating cities as abstractions and reducing readers to passive observers, *Local Politics* encourages readers to become aware of local politics in their own communities, not only to provide concrete examples of the subject under study, but also to gain a sense that they can participate themselves. As part of the nuts-and-bolts approach, *Local Politics* includes practical "In Your Community" assignments in every chapter. These are projects students can easily undertake to apply the text to their own lives and learn from their own communities.

Our book begins with four chapters that examine the socioeconomic, geographic, demographic, and intergovernmental contexts of local politics—laying the foundation for future chapters. We pay special attention to suburbanization and the movement to the Sunbelt, as well as to immigration, globalization, and the roles of the state and federal governments in local politics. Part II unveils the formal institutions or structures of local governments in terms of their sources, historical evolution, and general workings. We study the movement from political machines to reform and counterreform, and then consider the balance of power among local legislators, executives, and bureaucracies. Part III turns to political forces outside government, such as voters, campaigns, the media, interest groups, and nongovernmental power structures. Part IV examines local politics from the perspective of budgets and selected public policies, concluding with a chapter on metropolitan regional government, a subject that directs our attention to the future of local politics.

Many years of teaching, research, and political involvement have gone into this book. An earlier version, published in 1995, was tested and deemed a success in classrooms and communities, but was sorely in need of updating. A single author, now a senior member of the profession, wrote the first version. A second author, fresh from graduate school, joined the team for this new edition. Besides our passion for local politics, we also have in common extensive practical political experience as consultants and participants as well as researchers. As political scientists, we learn from the scholarly work of our colleagues across the nation and around the world, but we also learn from politicians, journalists, and activists in our communities and, always, from our students, who bring their own practical experience in local politics to our classrooms every day, constantly challenging and adding to our knowledge and understanding. These, then, are the first to whom thanks are due: our students, our professional colleagues, and the journalists and activists with whom we've had the pleasure of working.

For Terry Christensen, a few merit special appreciation. Ahmad Chapman, Chris Schwarz, Peter Tessier, and Caroline Reebs helped with research, often with minimal guidance but always with good will and great ingenuity. Michael D. Coulter (Grove City College), William Laverty (University of Michigan, Flint), David Sturrock (Southwest Minnesota State University), David Redlawsk (University of Iowa), Amy Bridges (University of California, San Diego), Norman R. Luttbeg (Texas A&M University), and Ken Yeager (San Jose State University) all provided support and encouragement for this new edition. Finally, my mom, Ruth Christensen, is the proudest possessor of my collected works and has always supported me in whatever I wanted to do, and Ray Allen and Ziggy patiently tolerated the many I hours spent at the computer working on this project and others, not to mention a frequently messy study. A sabbatical from San Jose State University helped me complete this project, while Tom has surely earned a sabbatical with this work.

Tom Hogen-Esch would like to especially thank Raphael Sonenshein (Cal State Fullerton), a friend and mentor, for his support over the years. I would also like to thank Michael B. Preston and Juliet Musso (University of Southern California) for helping me get started in this profession. Thanks also to all of my colleagues at Cal State Northridge, but particularly professors Matt Cahn, Larry Becker, Martin Saiz, Julie Delgado, and Nick Dungey for their support and good humor. I would also like to thank my parents, Thieo and Cheryl, and my brother, Chris. Their support over the years has been invaluable. Finally, I would like to thank my co-author, Terry, for bringing me onto the project. It has been a great pleasure and honor working with you.

Niels Aaboe and Patricia Kolb at M.E. Sharpe seized on the project with enthusiasm and waited patiently—while prodding gently—for its completion. Makiko Parsons, Angela Piliouras, and Katherine H. Maas brought it to fruition with high professionalism, improving it in countless ways with their meticulous work.

Thanks to all.

Terry Christensen
Tom Hogen-Esch

Local Politics

1 Introduction to the Study of Local Politics
Why We Bother and How We Go About It

You walk into a room where a meeting is in progress. A few of the participants glance at you as you enter; a few are too intent on the business at hand to notice you; most look bored and disinterested; several are reading. A voice is droning on over a loudspeaker. You find a seat and take in your surroundings. If you're in a large, old city, the room may seem a bit like a church, with people sitting in wooden pews facing the front of the room, where some more official-looking people in big chairs sit at desks, perhaps facing one another rather than their audience, which they may outnumber. If you're in a newer city, perhaps in the suburbs or the Sunbelt, the room will be modern and may seem more like a theater, with rows and rows of comfortable seats for the audience and a small group of official types at desks and in padded chairs that swivel, but facing the audience rather than one another.

The official-looking people sitting in the front are mostly men and mostly white. The one who looks most important and official of all sits in the middle and seems to be running the show. Nearby, perhaps below or to one side of the official group, are people shuffling papers or taking notes. Also beneath or to one side of the group is a podium from which a man in a suit is addressing them, his back to the audience. His, you now discern, is the voice on the loudspeaker. Some of the official types seem to be listening to him, but others are whispering to each other, talking on the phone, pouring themselves coffee, reading, or seemingly having an out-of-body experience. The speaker concludes with some ingratiating remarks, and the official in the middle thanks him and calls on one of the paper-shufflers at a nearby desk. Referring to a report of some sort, this person speaks quickly, using many unfamiliar words and phrases. Then one of the important-acting officials mutters something and the presider rattles out, "All-in-favor-all-opposed-motion-approved-the-next-item-is-18c." A few people leave the room looking pleased; others seem to wake up.

Another jargon-spouting official reports, one of the people at the top table gives a mini-lecture, and a succession of people line up behind the podium. You understand that item 18c involves a housing development. The first speakers, all in suits, proclaim its economic benefits and its contribution to solving your community's dire housing shortage. You are sympathetic. Then, one after the other, people who seem to be average citizens speak. They turn out to be residents of neighborhoods near the proposed development. Unlike the earlier speakers, they are nervous. They do not use jargon and they sometimes seem a little vague, but they make clear their worries about the project's impact on traffic, schools, and other local services. Some decry the loss of open space and ask for the land to be made into a park. You are sympathetic until some declare that they fear that the "type of people" who might live in the new housing would decrease property values and lead to the deterioration of their neighborhoods. If the proposed condominiums would really cost $350,000, as their developer announced, you suspect it would be people like your own family who might buy them. When the speakers conclude, the officials debate the issue briefly. One or two clearly play to the audience; others seem indifferent. Another quick vote is taken and the housing is approved. The men in suits leave smiling. The more casually dressed people seem bewildered at first, then straggle out grumbling and frowning, glancing disgustedly back at the officials up front. One comes down to walk out with them, pursing her lips and shaking her head.

"Item 19a," announces the front-and-center official and another paper-shuffler mutters a report, halting abruptly when the doors burst open and a television camera crew sweeps in led by someone in heavy makeup and hair that doesn't move. Blinding lights suddenly bathe the chamber. The person making the report stutters to continue, and all of the important-acting officials now sit up straight and look attentive and concerned. A couple of rumpled-looking people sitting at a table to one side and writing in funny little notebooks smirk. As the made-up person directs the camera, a new set of speakers queues up at the podium. This time they are elderly and gray haired, and you gather that the officials are about to take something away from them. But before they begin their speeches, the bright lights fade, the TV crew sweeps out, and everybody slumps, looking dazed and disappointed. Meanwhile, a group of police officers in uniform enters the room and sits together, right in front.

You've got an early class the next day, so you make your way out, noticing that you could have picked up a printed agenda at the door. You're surprised to find a crowd in the hall. Some people are talking angrily; you recognize them from the housing debate. A couple of men in suits are huddled with one of the important-looking officials. Some average-citizen types are walking in wearing yellow "Save Our" something-or-other pins.

Mulling it over on the way home, you are surprised that although it seemed boring while you were sitting through it, what you observed now seems sort of interesting, even a little exciting. You've just witnessed a bit of local politics at work: a city council or county board with its mayor or chairperson and supporting bureaucracy along with lobbyists and citizens and a reporter or two. The process, the people, and even the room and building (grand and intimidating or comfortable and accessible) reveal a lot about local government and politics. After another meeting or two, you will discern organizational structures and an operating style. You'll figure out which people, interests, and values have clout. If you go to enough meetings, you'll see most of the elements of local politics in action—elected officials, bureaucrats, interest groups and lobbyists, the media, and sometimes even important members of the local business elite. You may sense the abstract presence of the voters or the public, especially around elections. You'll hear talk of taxes and budgets, of economic development, social issues and services, regional problems, and relations with state and federal governments.

Such meetings will not tell you all you need to know about local politics, but they are a pretty good starting place. They can help you generate questions about how your local politics works and can connect the things you learn about in class to the real world. If you study other communities, you'll find that for all their differences, they have much in common with your own.

IN YOUR COMMUNITY

Have you ever been to a city council meeting? (If not, go to one!) What kinds of issues were discussed and what groups were represented? How were the issues resolved?

Why Study Local Politics?

The most practical reason to study local politics is that it affects us all every day, from what happens when we flush the toilet to life in our neighborhoods, to getting along with one another, personal safety, jobs, schools, traffic on our streets, and even the air we breathe. Yet as much as it affects us, few of us understand how local politics works or how to make it work for us.

The foiling of an international terrorist plot receives more media attention and may seem more glamorous, but international or even national politics rarely touch us as immediately or directly as do events at the local level. The glamour of a movie-star governor in California or a cliffhanger presidential election may grab our attention, but since most of us do not live in our state capitals or in Washington, DC, the action is too far away for us to observe in person. Modern media, with cable channels like C-SPAN and with the Internet, are changing that, but for the most part we still have to rely on intermediaries to pass on information and impressions to us. As excellent as they may be, journalists and editors (and even Web bloggers) filter information and interpret it for us. In your own community, however, you can be your own reporter. You can go see for yourself, actually talk to the participants, and learn the ropes of politics by "doing." Sheer proximity makes studying local politics a worthwhile endeavor, and many of the lessons we learn can be applied to all levels of politics. As the saying goes, in a very real way, all politics is local.

At first glance, local matters such as a zoning change may seem mundane, even trivial. Some are. But just as often, the controversies, politics, and personalities surrounding a zoning change can be compelling and dramatic. Either way, they affect us too intimately to dismiss or leave to others. Moreover, acting as individuals or as part of an **interest group**, our ability to influence local politics far exceeds our power to shape events at the state or national level. One of the first surprises for students of local politics is learning how few players actually participate and how easy, with a little *chutzpah*, it is to become one—particularly if you are someone who understands how the game is played. As an informed participant in the local political process, you can develop, in a relatively short period of time, knowledge and expertise on issues that few others in the community have.

We should not, however, fixate on just one community. This is a common pitfall in studying politics at all levels. In studying only one city or "case" there is a tendency to assume that its dynamics will more or less resemble politics elsewhere. This may or may not be true. The solution to this dilemma is fairly simple: compare. The feasibility of such comparison makes local politics an excellent subject of study, in some ways better than national or even state politics, which is limited to only fifty states. In contrast, some metropolitan areas alone contain hundreds of local governments, so you don't even need to go far away to begin making comparisons. The sheer number of local political jurisdictions creates other problems—which we will discuss later—but for now, the basic point is that **comparison** allows us to avoid the "tunnel vision" that comes from studying only one community.

Comparison also enables us to develop generalizations or **theories**, not only about local politics, but about politics and political behavior at all levels. Building theories about human behavior is not easy, but there is a method to the madness. First, researchers make **observations** and then hypotheses (educated guesses) about how and why human events happen. Next, they gather data or evidence to test their hypotheses. If their hypotheses are confirmed, the process moves on to the development of a theory, or a model for explaining how something works. Ultimately, the purpose of theories is to predict what might happen in similar cases. Again, it isn't enough to look at just one community or tell a story about a particular event, as a journalist does. One of our goals is to look at many communities or events and try to discern patterns among them in order to arrive at useful, **predictive generalizations**.

So what kinds of things might we study and begin to make hypotheses about? We can study the relative influence of different individuals and groups and their influence on what issues make it onto the agenda, what alternatives are considered, and, ultimately, how issues are decided and implemented. We might seek to understand why and under what conditions groups form alliances, or **coalitions**, with one another to affect policy decisions. We could also consider the impact of government structures or a city's social psychology, which we will discuss later, in producing a particular political outcome. We might study the impact of age, class, ethnicity, education, or even geography on why groups vote the way they do. Again, whether we are studying power relations, political institutions, voting behavior, or something else, it is through comparison with other cases that the most useful conclusions are reached.

Finally, comparison has a more practical utility as well. In addition to building theories, comparison is also a critical tool in solving practical problems facing urban areas—one of the most important skills we hope you will learn from this book. Whether you are interested in finding ways to save on street maintenance, improve the delivery of services, or more effectively incorporate residents into the decision-making process, comparison opens our eyes to solutions to problems that we might not have thought of on our own. Often called "best practices research," one of the first places to look in solving everyday problems is to study how similar problems have been dealt with in other cities.

In short, the larger goal of comparison is to better understand politics and find better solutions to problems. But your own community is still the best starting point. Think of it as the frog you dissected in biology lab. You cut up one frog, not to learn only about that frog but to learn about frogs and anatomy in general. Your frog was unique, as are all living creatures and communities, but its anatomy had a lot in common with other frogs and creatures, so you learned about them, too. Remember, though, that unlike that frog, the communities we're going to study are very much alive. They may change as we study them. Who knows, the results of your study might even change them!

Know Your "City Limits"

As a budding practitioner of local politics, one of the things that can set you apart is to become one of the few who truly understand "the big picture." In order to practice the art of what is possible in city politics, we need to begin with an understanding of several important limitations that face cities and other local governments. Local politics is somewhat unique in that it is subnational and largely subordinate to other levels of politics and to larger economic and social forces. Although there is significant debate on this point, some analysts think that these larger forces have now overwhelmed local politics, making them trivial or even irrelevant. Obviously, local politicians and many citizens disagree.

Subordinate Governments

For most of human history, there was no such thing as "a city." Until the advent of agriculture, human societies were transient, hunter-gather groups that followed food sources as they migrated or the weather changed. Early agricultural techniques changed everything, allowing societies to form more permanent settlements. As those settlements grew, they became what we think of today as cities, and those cities eventually became the center of political life. Some, like Athens or Rome, expanded and came to dominate great empires. Many others functioned as **city-states**—that is, as tiny, independent countries. Each was "sovereign," governing itself, making its own foreign policy, and raising an army to defend itself and its surrounding territory. Massive walls were essential to the defense of city-states. (That's why a lot of the ancient cities you may have visited in your travels had walls around them.) But when cannons were invented, the walls fell and so did the city-states. The modern equivalent of the city-state survives in a few places such as Singapore, San Marino, and maybe Hong Kong, but most of the great city-states of history have been absorbed into more economically efficient and militarily powerful "nation-states" that emerged in the past few centuries. In recent decades, a similar process has been underway in absorbing those nation-states into larger political and economic entities such as the European Union.

Like nations, politics in cities is therefore no longer self-contained, if it ever truly was. Rather, it is subnational and subordinate—dependent instead of independent. Some cities, like Rome, are older than the nations of which they are a part, yet they derive their right to exist from these now-superior authorities. In most countries, governmental authority is highly centralized, and local governments are essentially administrative agencies for the national or state government, where all real power lies, where the money comes from, and where most policy is made. In such countries, local politics is usually about choosing who gets to carry out national or provincial programs.

The United States is not nearly so centralized, making the study of politics in this country both interesting and somewhat unique. In the United States, power, authority, and responsibility for different programs and policies are divided between the national and state governments through our **federal system**. State governments, in turn, delegate some of their authority and responsibility to implement programs to city, county, and other local governments. States may delegate to local governments the power to police communities, decide land-use issues, tax, spend, decide on governmental structure, and much more—or less. The state's delegation of power may be broad and generous or narrow and restrictive, depending on state politics and the influence of local governments within it. Many local governments feel constrained by their subordinate and dependent status, yet despite this, local governments in the United States enjoy much greater autonomy, or **home rule**, than local governments in most other countries.

The history of the ebb and flow of local autonomy is quite interesting. The U.S. Constitution makes no mention at all of the status of local governments. Thus, until the early twentieth century, cities in the United States were largely left to their own devices to address their problems, and the decisions they made rarely had much significance outside their boundaries. At the end of the nineteenth century, as cities struggled mightily to cope with the tremendous challenges posed by **industrialization**, events at the local level began to assume wider economic and political importance. It soon became clear that cities required at least some greater regulatory authority to deal with complex issues such as sanitation, transportation, and other problems. British political writer James Bryce, observing the unfolding chaos in American cities in the late nineteenth century, famously observed: "The governance of its cities is the one chief failure of American democracy."[1] Initially, state governments began to grant local governments powers such as taxation and bonding authority to deal with the new challenges. However, those new powers also came with strings attached. It wasn't until the Progressive Era of the early 1900s and later events such as the Great Depression, World War II, and the postwar economic boom that state and federal governments began making more laws or programs that superseded or constrained those of local governments. In other words, if cities were going to have more power and influence, their corresponding state governments—largely dominated by rural interests—were going to make sure they were keeping the emerging power of cities in check.

Despite the general trend toward the erosion of home rule, in the early twentieth century the U.S. Supreme Court nonetheless gave cities the power to regulate land use. Also known as **zoning**, land-use decisions are still a primarily local power, but in the past few decades a plethora of state and federal environmental, planning, and other laws have eroded even this power, further limiting local authority. As a nation founded on principles of self-government, though, the American people cling tightly to their tradition of home rule.

Nevertheless, the trend toward state and federal intervention has clearly been in the other direction. Local governments have now joined citizens in complaining about state and federal red tape and bureaucracy. Even the hiring or firing of their own employees is sometimes dictated by state and federal regulations on civil rights and affirmative action. Since the 1980s, local governments have been virtually stripped of most federal financial assistance. In some cases, state officials have literally raided the tax base of local governments to deal with crippling state budget crises. Aside from the usual political resistance to raising local taxes, state laws often restrict what kind and how much tax local governments can raise. In particular, the trend in some states toward funding local government operations with sales taxes rather than the more stable property tax has meant that when the national or state economies catch a cold, the locals catch pneumonia.

Besides these legal and fiscal constraints, state and federal politics and politicians often steal the spotlight. Their actions and their campaigns are seen as more glamorous and dramatic and often push local politics off center stage and sometimes right out of the theater. The decline, consolidation, and displacement of local media, with fewer newspapers and the dominance of television, have only added to this.

Capital Mobility

The power of economic forces, in particular **capital mobility**, places another important limit on the practice of local politics. Businesses provide jobs and tax revenues for communities. Without a viable local economy, communities can literally wither and die. Economic interests have therefore always exerted great influence on local politics. Often, alliances emerge between business and political leaders in the shared interest of economic development. Business leaders are often well represented in local office and usually have a major say in the organization of local governments, their powers, tax structures, and programs. The power of business interests comes from their wealth and their command over employees and associates, but it also comes from their prestige in a capitalist society and the manifest need of communities for the jobs and taxes they provide. When business speaks, government listens, and local government, with all of its constraints, pays the closest attention of all. Some analysts, such as Paul Peterson in his influential book *City Limits*,[2] believe that this economic logic best explains why keeping business happy is the predominant concern of local governments.[2]

Like the relationship between local, state, and national governments, relations with business have changed in recent years, and usually not to the advantage of local governments. Bigger government of the 1930s and 1960s was partly a response to bigger business and the emergence of a corporate capitalist economy. But businesses, even big ones, were once locally owned and operated. Their proprietors lived locally and were usually influential in local politics, even if they rarely held elected office. But today, the biggest businesses in most communities are now branch plants of national or multinational corporations. Except in the cities that host corporate headquarters, their owners (now usually shareholders rather than individuals or families) do not live locally. The company is represented by a CEO who probably has little connection to the community. These businesses usually take less interest in local politics than their home-grown predecessors, but when they do, their power is even more heavy-handed because their commitment to the community is clearly not as great.

Threats to move their plants to Mississippi, Mexico, or Malaysia if they don't get what they want are taken seriously. They probably wouldn't be in a particular community in the first place if they hadn't been promised just what they wanted. Local governments desperate to retain jobs and tax revenue often feel as much or more constrained by the decisions of large corporations as by those of state and federal governments. In the face of capital mobility, cities must leverage any and every advantage, such as location, climate, a skilled workforce, or even culture in bargaining with business, as urbanist Richard Florida argues.[3] Much like business corporations themselves, local governments have been forced to find creative strategies to carve out an economic niche in an increasingly competitive marketplace. Quite often, those strategies are centered around catering to the interests of increasingly mobile businesses.

IN YOUR COMMUNITY

List the advantages and disadvantages of your city. Think in terms of what is attractive to both business and residents.

Residential Mobility

As with the mobility of capital, cities must also remain attentive and responsive to the mobility of their residents. As a nation of immigrants, the American people have always been more mobile than, say, Europeans. In the past it was common for people to live cradle to grave in one community, working, raising families, going to school, shopping, and socializing. But most Americans don't live like that anymore. Like corporations, we'll go from city to city and state to state, in search of better jobs, schools, weather, or a particular quality of life. We even hop from city to city in our daily lives, living in one, working in another, and shopping and socializing in still others. We've become virtually temporary residents of our communities—if the places where we live even deserve that term—and have become more like consumers in an increasingly connected regional, and now global, economy. This isn't necessarily our fault, nor is it necessarily a bad thing—it's simply a fact of life in a modern corporate economy. As with strategies to retain, expand, or attract businesses, cities must promote policies and provide services that appeal to their residents. If the quality of life or services in a city drops below a certain level, as with businesses, residents may chose "exit" over "voice" or "loyalty"[4] by moving to the next town (or state) where things are better. As with the need to cater to business, cities must also pay close attention to the needs of their residents. Thus, a key element of city politics is in striking the proper balance between providing for the needs of business and residents.

Urban Fragmentation: Governing the "Crazy Quilt"

The pattern of our daily lives—pursuing different activities in different parts of a metropolitan area with different local governments—points to still another way that local politics is limited. Communities were once geographically separated from one another, each with its own government, self-contained and responsible for solving its own problems. As metropolitan areas have grown, communities now run into one another, and literally hundreds of local governments may operate in the same urban area, forming what many have called a "**crazy quilt**" of overlapping jurisdictions. One problem this creates is that while problems such as environmental contamination, traffic congestion, and housing shortages pay no heed to political boundaries, solutions to these problems require local governments to cooperate. It's a topic that we will return to in chapter 4 and again in the final chapter, but for now it's enough to know that the central problem this creates involves competition. In the chase for tax revenue or status, local governments compete with one another for industry, residents, or even professional sports franchises in ways that may not benefit the larger social good. Communities from well beyond a single urban area also join such competitions, further weakening local cooperation and undermining the stability and autonomy of local governments. In sum, the combined effects of the erosion of home rule, increased capital and **residential mobility**, and urban fragmentation pose tremendous challenges for American local governments.

What's Left for Local Governments?

All these "**city limits**" would seem to add up to a pretty gloomy picture. "The very heart and soul of local politics has surely died,"[5] laments political scientist Mark Gottdiener. Reduced to "form without content," he continues, "local politics has long since passed over into the hands of professional managers, multinational corporations, local capital caught in a predatory jungle of small business competition, provincial politicians making do on dwindling party resources, and certainly not least, federal interventions promulgated by the long series of crises befalling the country since the 1960s."[6]

Other analysts, such as Clarence Stone, strongly believe that local politics still matters and assert that the rigid economic determinism implied in the writings of Peterson and Gottdiener is overstated. Stone recognizes the impact of all the "structural constraints," such as state and federal laws, economic forces, and urban fragmentation, but insists that policy outcomes "are mediated through political arrangements," including the institutions and actors in local government. In other words, in Stone's view, cities and their politics still very much matter.[7]

Obviously, if we didn't agree that cities can still shape their future in meaningful ways, we wouldn't have bothered writing this textbook. But we also think it is more important than ever for practitioners of local politics to understand the nature and scope of the legal, economic, and institutional environment in which local governments must operate. In recognizing these important constraints, however, we also want to emphasize that local governments have a number of tools at their disposal to respond to political events, problems, and changing environments. In other words, despite constraints, cities still have choices. Will a city's police force behave like an occupying army or will it practice community policing? Will a city go for growth at all costs or risk losing some economic benefits to preserve its environment? Will a city provide services for the homeless or shuttle them out of town? Will it welcome economic, ethnic, and other forms of diversity or seek to be up-scale and exclusive? Will it cater to the automobile or promote alternative modes of transportation? And so on.

On these and other matters, local governments still make choices, which is what politics is all about. These choices may be diminished, narrowed, even trivialized or marginalized, but they still make a difference in how people live their daily lives, how they feel about where they live, and even whether or not they participate in community life and local politics. Even if only little things are left to the locals, these "little things" are often critical to a city's quality of life. But local governments still make big decisions, too, ranging from building subway systems and stadiums to schools and policing. Many of these decisions are bitterly fought over (albeit by a minority of residents), which is the best evidence of all that local politics still matters, at least to the locals.

Prophets of the city limits perspective do not necessarily disagree with this. They do not argue that local politics should be forsaken or ignored. But for our purposes, finding a definitive answer to whether local politics "matters" is less important than in understanding the larger political and economic environment in which twenty-first-century cities now operate. Moreover, the reasons for studying local politics discussed earlier, including its effects on us, its accessibility, and its utility as a learning lab, still stand.

A Practical Approach

We have chosen to approach the study of local politics from a practical perspective. We begin in Part I by considering the geographic, socioeconomic, demographic, and intergovernmental environment of local politics. We move on in Part II to the formal institutions, structures, and political process of local government. In Part III, we turn to system inputs, including voters, elections, the media, and interest groups. We also focus our attention on community power structures as a summary of all we studied before. Part IV takes us to some of the policy outputs of the political system, including local taxing and spending and public policy issues such as education, welfare, crime, transportation, and growth. Finally, we critically consider several proposals to reform America's large metropolitan regions with their multiple, overlapping local governments.

A few themes will run through our study. You can probably already guess what they are. One is power; another is the politics of growth, which is discussed more in the next chapter, which also introduces another recurrent theme: the distinctions, conflicts, and competition between central cities and suburbs and between communities in the Sunbelt and those in the Frostbelt. Above all, however, our approach will be practical, emphasizing the nuts and bolts of local political institutions and procedures. Our goal is for you to gain an understanding of politics in your own community, both as a student and as someone with a stake in the community. You should use your community and the others around you as a learning laboratory, testing what this book says against what you observe there and vice versa. You should also gain practical knowledge that will help you as a citizen participant in the politics of your own community. Remember, though, that our aim is not just to learn about local politics where we live, but to learn more generally, so that we know what questions to ask in order to understand local politics wherever we happen to live or visit.

Essential Terms

interest group
comparison
theories
observations
predictive generalizations
coalitions
city-states
federal system

home rule
industrialization
zoning
capital mobility
crazy quilt
residential mobility
city limits

On the Internet

- Go to your city and county websites and peruse them. When is the next meeting? What issues seem to be important to your community?
- www.statelocalgov.net/index.cfm has a comprehensive list of Internet sites relating to state and local government.
- www.cyburbia.org/directory/ provides a clearinghouse for information on a wide range of urban policy areas.

Notes

1. Nathan Glazer and Irving Kristol, eds., *The American Commonwealth, 1976* (New York: Basic Books, 1976).

2. Paul E. Peterson, *City Limits* (Chicago: University of Chicago Press, 1981).

3. Richard L. Florida, *The Rise of the Creative Class: And How It's Transforming Work, Leisure, Community, and Everyday Life* (New York: Basic Books, 2002).

4. Albert O. Hirschman, *Exit, Voice, and Loyalty: Responses to Decline in Firms, Organizations, and States* (Cambridge, MA: Harvard University Press, 1970).

5. Mark Gottdiener, *The Decline of Urban Politics: Political Theory and the Crisis of the Local State* (Newbury Park, CA: Sage, 1987), pp. 13–14.

6. Ibid., p. 14.

7. Clarence Stone, "The Study of the Politics of Urban Development," in *The Politics of Urban Development*, ed. Clarence N. Stone and Heywood T. Sanders (Lawrence: University Press of Kansas, 1987), pp. 4, 12, 16, 17.

Part I

The Environment of Local Politics: Characteristics of Urban Places

"Demography is destiny" is an old saying that's often applied to local politics. While undoubtedly an overstatement, there is much truth to the implication that most problems facing urban areas correspond to a city's demographic factors, whether they are related to ethnicity, class, age, housing, or so on. We'll get to local government structures and to the political process, including mayors, council members, bureaucrats, lobbyists, voters, media, and others, in later chapters. But the physical and demographic environment in which these structures and actors function has such an important influence on them that we need to start there. Without a proper understanding of these basic underlying factors, it is impossible to fully understand urban politics, or to formulate solutions to problems that arise.

The environment of local politics isn't just air, water, land, trees, and squirrels, although the physical setting is important. The environment of local politics includes much more—anything, really, which might have an impact on the political process. In Part I, we concentrate on three broad influences: the physical setting, demographic and economic factors, and the intergovernmental environment of local politics. Chapter 2 delves into the physical setting, including such factors as location, climate, proximity to water, and transportation links. The discussion includes such factors as population size and density, ethnic diversity, and economic structure. In chapter 3 we'll consider the historical processes of urbanization, suburbanization, and the rise of the Sunbelt. Then, in chapter 4, we'll become more explicitly political and turn to the intergovernmental context of local politics, developing the points introduced in chapter 1 about the erosion of local autonomy and the relationship of local governments to each other and to state, national, and international influences.

Studying these factors will help us understand what goes on in local politics. Variation in these characteristics, which social scientists call **variables**, may explain why local politics differs from place to place. Some social scientists even think they can predict local political phenomena such as voter turnout and public spending on the basis of these characteristics, which we will refer to again in later chapters on government structures and the political process.

Most analysts agree that local politics is influenced, perhaps even determined, by its geographic, demographic, cultural, historical, and intergovernmental environment. But as in any system, influence works both ways. Local politics, at least to some extent, shapes its own environment. Policies developed by local governments also affect their physical and socioeconomic setting, and local political actions have an impact on state and national politics. The components of the system are interdependent, although that doesn't mean their influence is equal. If there is one set of factors in local politics that outweighs the others and that is overlooked in practical, day-to-day politics, it is surely these environmental factors, which impose upon cities both constraints as well as opportunities.

Essential Term

variables

2 The Environment of Local Politics
The Geographic, Demographic, and Economic Contexts

We begin with the most basic elements of the environment of local politics, the broad and sometimes nebulous physical, social, and economic characteristics of communities. The physical setting, size, density, diversity, social psychology, and economic structures of places significantly shape their politics, providing both constraints as well as opportunities that communities must try to transcend or capitalize on. Although each of these socioeconomic characteristics will be discussed separately, we should bear in mind that they are interrelated, impacting not only local politics but one another as well. We should also think of them as variables that, in their variation from one locality to another, help us explain and understand why elements of local politics such as government structure, voter turnout, and interest group activity differ from place to place. We will refer to these characteristics in more detail in chapters to come.

The Basics: Setting, Size, Density, and Diversity

The most basic characteristics that distinguish localities are what we will call setting, size, density, and diversity. If we put these on a continuum, at one end would be a hermit's cabin in the woods and at the other would be the great cities of the world, large in population and dense and diverse. In between would be rural villages and towns, small cities and suburbs, and then larger and larger cities. We need not concern ourselves with the hermit, but our interest in local politics should direct our attention to all the others, at least to some extent. The chapters that follow concentrate on large cities and their suburbs, which is where most Americans live. But while these are clearly urban rather than strictly rural places, urbanism is a matter of degree, defined, at least initially, by the variables of setting, size, density, and diversity.

Setting: Physical Geography

As the old saying goes, there are three important factors in real estate: "Location, location, location." The same goes for cities. The most basic and perhaps most important factor influencing a city is its physical or **geographic setting**. It's no coincidence that most of the great—and even many not so great—cities of the world developed on sites with geographic advantages, such as rivers, natural harbors, or major trade routes. These and other physical attributes presented natural advantages in terms of connecting a city to regional, national, or international markets. At a more basic level, rivers and lakes provided access to fresh water, not only for drinking water and irrigation, but also as a de facto sewage system. Of course as the contamination of waterways created new health and economic problems, cities were forced to find technological solutions such as modern sewage-treatment plants.

Some cities thrived by combining geographic advantages with proximity to a valuable natural resource, such as coal, iron, or oil. The city of Pittsburgh, for example, would never have developed a powerful steel industry were it not for its proximity to Pennsylvania's coal mines and its intersection of the Allegheny and Monongahela Rivers. In more recent times, tourist cities such as Santa Monica, California, have flourished largely because of a mild climate, location on the Pacific Ocean, and proximity to an international airport and a large and interesting urban area. The basic point is that every city is located where it is for a reason—usually relating to its geography and, at a very basic level, its access to fresh water.

In some cases, cities that did not possess a particular geographic advantage simply went about creating them. In these "imperial cities,"[1] city officials overcame nature by building huge, often publicly funded construction projects to lay the foundation for growth. For example, in 1880, the city of Los Angeles was just another California desert pueblo with a population of about 10,000. By 1980, the city had boomed to a population of nearly three million and was the nation's second largest municipality. How did this happen? In short, ingenuity and will-power. City "boosters" went about making up for the area's lack of natural advantages by building both a protected deep-water harbor and a 250-mile aqueduct. The former made the city a player in international sea commerce, while fresh water from the Sierra Nevada Mountains set the stage for the city's initial population explosion between 1915 and 1930. Of course, the city possessed other advantages, such as oil and sunshine, which allowed the region to develop important petroleum and entertainment industries. But those industries would never have flourished the way they did without access to water, courtesy of the city government.[2]

Other cities have overcome their isolation by orchestrating transportation advantages. For example, mining and other industries flourished in Denver, Colorado, because city boosters were instrumental in wooing the railroads during the late nineteenth century. During the mid- to late twentieth century, freeways and airports assumed these same functions, connecting cities to far-flung markets. With the Internet, some now question whether locational advantages will play as important a role in determining a city's future. With information a key part of the twenty-first-century economy and now easy to transmit, it may not matter whether your firm is located in Chicago, or Butte, Montana—or Timbuktu for that matter.[3]

A caveat to this is that workers, particularly highly educated workers, may prefer to live in an area with more cultural opportunities, or an area with a better climate. Richard Florida argues that in the Internet age, successful cities will attract creative and affluent residents by becoming "cool." Florida says that cities able to cultivate the "three T's," **technology, tolerance, and talent**, will be able to attract highly educated residents critical to the promotion of economic growth in growth industries such as high technology, entertainment, multimedia, and other creative forms of production.[4] In such cities, such as San Francisco, Austin, and Seattle, city officials promote arts and culture, exciting nightlife, and tolerance toward gays and lesbians. Either way, location still determines much about what is, and what is not, possible for a city.

But geography can be limiting, too, as the ghost towns of the world attest. The resource that helped build up a city may be depleted or a transportation mode may become exhausted or obsolete. Physical barriers like mountains and oceans or limited resources like water or gold may restrict economic expansion, as may an area's susceptibility to natural disasters such as fires, floods, tsunamis, hurricanes, tornadoes, or earthquakes. After the devastating hurricane seasons of 2004 and 2005, many residents of Gulf Coast communities seriously questioned whether they would continue living in such hurricane-prone areas.

Even smog, partially a function of geography and meteorology, is a serious threat to the quality of life in regions such as Los Angeles, Houston, and Denver. In these regions, mountains can trap air particles and pollution and, along with wind patterns and sunlight, can form nasty "inversion layers" that can blanket cities in a choking brown haze. Over time, exposure to air pollution can pose serious health risks to residents—particularly children—making an area less attractive to business and people. Because air pollution is a regional (as opposed to local) issue, regional governments have formed and have emerged as major sites of conflict between clean air activists and proponents of economic growth.

Geography can also cause other practical problems for local governments. Sheer size may make the delivery of government services more difficult. For example, policing an area like the city of Jacksonville, Florida, which is 758 square miles— geographically the largest city in the lower forty-eight states—may require more and different resources than policing San Francisco's comparatively tiny forty-eight square miles. Sprawling geography can also make political participation more difficult, leading to alienation, frustration, and ultimately a tenuous legitimacy for city government. Residents of the island borough of Staten Island, New York, and the peninsula community of West Seattle, have long felt alienated from their city governments, in part due to physical separation from the rest of the city. Some authors have even critiqued the pattern of single-family settlement known as **urban sprawl** for fostering the economic dependence and social isolation of women.[5] In short, a city's setting or location is a basic, but nonetheless critical, variable in understanding its politics.

IN YOUR COMMUNITY

Make a list of your community's locational advantages and disadvantages. How do they impact local politics where you are?

Table 2.1

Twenty Largest Cities in the United States, Ranked by 2003 Population

New York City	8,085,742	Detroit	900,198
Los Angeles	3,819,951	Indianapolis	783,438
Chicago	2,869,121	Jacksonville	773,781
Houston	2,009,960	San Francisco	751,682
Philadelphia	1,479,339	Columbus	728,432
Phoenix	1,388,416	Austin	672,011
San Diego	1,266,753	Memphis	645,978
San Antonio	1,214,725	Baltimore	628,670
Dallas	1,208,318	Milwaukee	586,941
San Jose	944,857	Fort Worth	585,122

Source: U.S. Census Bureau, Statistical Abstract of the United States, 2003.

Population: Size, Density, and Diversity

In addition to geographic size, **population size** also helps to define a community's politics. In general, more people mean more complexity, more problems, more politics, more opportunities, and more government. (See Table 2.1 for the largest cities in the United States.) Of course, larger cities also tend to be densely populated and more ethnically diverse, adding to their complexity. Whether large or small, however, communities of the same size are not all equally dense or diverse. These characteristics are related but may also vary independently, which is why we need to consider them separately.

Larger populations usually mean more politics and government because, like geographic size, greater population increases the potential for conflict over resources, and managing this conflict requires organization. You've seen it in a group you belong to or perhaps on a reality TV show. Three or four people may get along well without leadership or structure; with thirty or forty a greater diversity of opinions will emerge and so will the potential for conflict. Some people want power; others want a leader; some just want problems solved. Often, somebody steps in to set up rules or tell people what to do; some may follow, while others may build alliances with others to advocate for a different course of action. Once one group gets power, others may compete for it. In a nutshell, that's politics, and a lot of it—including the need for government—stems from increased size.

The Social Psychology of Density

If increased population precipitates politics and government, density makes them imperative. **Density** refers to the spatial or geographic concentration of population—in other words, more people living closer together. (See Table 2.2 for some sample densities of U.S. urban areas.) Much of local politics is about either creating, maintaining, or preventing density, and interest groups have their own ideas about what

Table 2.2

2000 Population Density per Square Mile, U.S. Urban Areas

Urban area	Density
Los Angeles-Long Beach-Santa Ana	7,068
San Francisco-Oakland	7,004
San Jose, California	5,914
New York-Newark	5,309
New Orleans, Louisiana	5,102
Davis, California	4,845
Vallejo, California	4,682
Honolulu, Hawaii	4,660
Tracy, California	4,622
Las Vegas, Nevada	4,597
Galveston, Texas	4,528
Oxnard, California	4,460
Miami, Florida	4,407
Fairfield, California	4,356
Stockton, California	4,218

Source: U.S. Census Bureau, Census 2000.

kinds of density are desirable. For example, some homeowner groups (discussed in chapter 10) view multi-family dwellings (particularly low income) as the ultimate land-use nightmare. Conversely, those same homeowners might welcome density in the form of upscale retail shops, cafes and restaurants, or other amenities that cater to their tastes. The point is that *what type* and *where* density goes are among the most important and contentious issues in urban politics.

Higher densities have a number of potential advantages, again, depending on your perspective. First, without higher density, we wouldn't have cities. Density puts enough people close together to create jobs and educational opportunities, as well as rewarding social and cultural interactions that take place at cafés, universities, symphonies, bars, sporting events, and gyms. Social interaction in cities can also provide the well-spring for social movements, such as those for civil rights, women's rights, and gay rights as well as for scientific and technological advancement. Without the opportunity for intellectual and social collaboration fostered by density, many of the technological innovations and societal changes that we take for granted would likely not have occurred.

But higher density can also be the source of social and economic problems, such as conflict over traffic, noise, and pollution as well as disputes over land and property. If everybody lived far enough apart, perhaps these problems would not arise, but then neither would cities. With density comes the potential for increased social conflict. In rural areas, isolated residents probably can't hear a neighbor's noisy party, and they very rarely vent their anger on total strangers if only because they rarely see them. But in urban places with higher densities, disputes resulting from noise, crime, and violence are more likely. But even the most serious problems such as violent crime vary over time. For instance, despite increasing public concern over crime, in part stoked by increased media coverage, during the 1990s and early 2000s violent crime in most American cities dropped to historic lows.[6]

Small or rural communities may be spared many of these "urban ills," but small town life can easily be romanticized. In many rural areas people must drill their own wells to provide water for irrigation or drinking. But unlike in most cities, people may become sick from exposure to waste from latrines or septic tanks that often leak or from groundwater contamination from the use of pesticides and other chemicals. Moreover, in some rural communities, access to services like health care, police, and fire protection is often limited or non-existent. In such cases, people may be forced to form volunteer fire departments. But even these organizations are often too strapped for cash to provide adequate services, exposing residents to many risks associated with isolation from others. In the end, neither high- nor low-density settlement can be said to be objectively "better." A lot depends on the kinds of trade-offs you are willing to make in order to live a lifestyle you prefer.

IN YOUR COMMUNITY

How would a volunteer fire department work in your neighborhood? Are there other examples in your area of volunteer organizations solving problems that governments might also solve?

Coping With Density

Intruding on one another's lives is a natural result of density, but social discord is not inevitable. Scientists experimenting with rats living in overcrowded (high-density) conditions observed increased antisocial behavior, such as fighting, sexual deviance, and eating their young. But when equally dense rat colonies were better designed, with plenty to eat, one-way paths, and more nest holes, antisocial behavior decreased. The problem was not density per se but how the density was organized.

The same principle applies to human communities, some of which organize and manage density better than others. Sometimes this is done informally through cultural norms. Expectations of personal space (the distance from strangers at which people feel comfortable) are lower in most urban cultures and vary from society to society. Most Americans expect at least two or three feet of social space, while Europeans tolerate less, and people in many parts of Asia even less, partly because higher densities have taught—or forced—people to do so. Some people in dense communities learn to establish their personal space by avoiding eye contact with strangers in crowded places. When car-crazy Los Angeles opened a new mass transit system, riders accustomed to the privacy of their own automobiles were given lessons on maintaining personal space in public. Other informal customs also help. In some places, people wait in line for buses, trains, or tickets to movies. It's a way of a crowd managing itself, and violators are usually informed that they're breaking the line. In many large cities, people on escalators stand on the right and walk on the left, so that those in a hurry can get by. Small signs directing people to do this are posted on most escalators, but strangers learn the rule quickly either from observation—or from an icy glare from someone in a hurry. Sharing a table in a crowded restaurant or a taxi at rush hour are other common ways of dealing with density.

IN YOUR COMMUNITY

When you ride in a crowded bus or subway, what are some of the ways you observe that people cope with density?

But when cultural controls alone don't suffice, just as when private latrines and volunteer fire fighting become inadequate, the burden of organizing density and mitigating social conflict falls on government. Police departments were among the first agents of social control established by local governments during the late nineteenth century as city populations swelled due to industrialization. Police officers will readily tell you that they deal not only with crime but with all sorts of social and antisocial behavior. If you think about it, teachers and social workers perform some of the same socializing functions. Traffic management, from stop signs and traffic lights to one-way streets, pedestrian crossings, and bike lanes, is another way governments try to manage density.

So is **land-use planning**. In fact, city planning is a field devoted largely to solving density-related problems in cities. Early planners such as Frederick Law Olmsted argued for the creation of city parks such as New York's Central Park, in part to serve as places where industrial workers could go to relax and recreate, thus mitigating the class tensions emerging from the industrial economy. Depending on the goal, planners can devise strategies to reduce conflict over, say, parking, by either requiring more parking spaces, or requiring *fewer* spaces, thus providing an incentive to take public transit. Strategies along the lines of "**smart growth**" have become increasingly popular among planners and local officials in recent years. The general idea is a reversal of decades of planning that valued automobile-dependent suburban living. This smart growth paradigm argues that jobs, businesses, and residences should not all be separated by miles of pavement and a car, but rather integrated into a single interconnected community. By encouraging people to drive less and walk or bicycle more, local governments can devise strategies that encourage positive social interactions and healthier lifestyles. As will be discussed later, convincing Americans to give up their yard and detached house, an ideal deeply rooted in American cultural traditions, has not been easy.

Diversity

The complexities introduced by population size and density are augmented by a third associated variable: **diversity**. Although things are rapidly changing, historically, rural communities tend to be populated by people who are more or less alike in terms of race, ethnicity, and culture. But as population increases, so does diversity. Just as communities vary in geography, size and density, so they vary in diversity, from **homogeneous** (similar) to **heterogeneous** (mixed). Besides race, ethnicity, and culture, variables of diversity may include class, occupation, age, sexual orientation, religion, political attitudes, and more. Diversity is what makes cities so exciting, with so many different people to watch and cultures to experience, including a choice of shops, restaurants, and entertainment. But like size and density, increased diversity complicates social life, and communities have to find ways of managing it.

For a variety of reasons, some people have difficulty dealing with others unlike themselves. Their intolerance may lead to distrust, hostility, conflict, and possibly violence. The cultural ways of dealing with density discussed earlier may break down when diversity increases because new people with different cultures can be slow or reluctant to learn and follow the norms of the established culture. Immigration, especially when the immigrants are unlike those who arrived earlier, often causes social strain. Hostility toward the new arrivals may also be compounded by established residents' fears of competition for scarce jobs and low-cost housing, or political fears about immigrants "taking over."

For example, cultural tensions between recent Korean immigrants and established blacks in Los Angeles surfaced prior to the 1992 riots. When the violence was triggered by the not-guilty verdicts in the trial of four Los Angeles Police Department officers, rioters in South Los Angeles disproportionately targeted Korean-owned businesses. Although many factors were involved, the vast cultural gap in interpreting daily social interactions between blacks and Koreans was an important one. Traditional Korean culture views social exuberance and prolonged eye contact with strangers as a sign of disrespect. In dealing with Korean business owners, many black customers interpreted the reserved demeanor of Korean store clerks as offensive and rude. Following the riots, leaders in both communities have made efforts to foster mutual cultural awareness and understanding. As conflict increases, so does the need for this kind of informal conflict management. Obviously, government has a role in managing conflict, not only through appropriate policing, but also in fostering cultural awareness and recognizing and promoting cultural holidays and events.

Local Governments and the Management of Diversity

The term **segregation** carries many negative connotations from its association with Jim Crow laws in the American South following the Civil War. While there are still many negative aspects, segregation—whether voluntary or mandatory—is another common way of reacting to diversity. Known as "self-segregation," it is common for groups of people to choose particular neighborhoods for comfort and convenience, to be near people who share their ethnicity, religion, or language, or to avoid confrontation with others unlike themselves. We all know of cities with a Chinatown, a Little Italy, or sections of cities that contain predominantly Persian, Irish, Jewish, Polish, or Guatemalan residents. Cities can also be sectioned off by sexual orientation, such as San Francisco's Castro District, or even by age as groups of young singles, retirees, and families tend to form clusters. For a number of reasons many people simply prefer to live with others like themselves—and it's not necessarily a bad thing. Without at least some self-segregation, there would be no Chinatowns or Little Italys.

In the past, though, racial and ethnic groups were segregated by law. These laws have been repealed, although the patterns of segregation they created continue in many places. More perniciously, subtle and informal racial discrimination still exist and maintain segregated settlement patterns. For example, **racial steering** occurs when minorities are purposely "steered" to certain neighborhoods by real estate agents. **Redlining** occurs when mortgage lenders refuse loans in certain neighborhoods. And minorities are still rebuffed by some landlords and home sellers. All these forms of discrimination are illegal, but cases are often hard to prove and expensive to litigate. While great progress has been made to stamp out such forms of illegal discrimination, the persistence of discrimination suggests that there is more to be done.

Contemporary segregation results not only from the preferences of groups of people and from discrimination, but also from a city's management of its housing stock. Local governments zone different areas for certain kinds of housing. Some sections are designated for high-density apartments, others for single-family homes with yards, still others for grand estates. Although the law may technically allow anyone to live in these neighborhoods, the price of housing keeps many people out. This results in **segregation by class**, but since the average income of minorities lags behind that of whites, it translates, some say unintentionally, into what is effectively segregation by race. Thus, in our society, only the rich have complete choice about where they live.

Class segregation is reinforced by the way urban areas in the United States are broken down into many local governments. We will return to this subject in the next two chapters, but for now it will do to understand that instead of one government encompassing an entire urbanized area, most urban areas have one large city and many smaller surrounding ones. These governments inevitably act to provide a particular quality of life for their residents—and often this means protecting the ethnic and class homogeneity of their communities. In short, one way residents of urban areas cope with diversity is by forming many independent governments, resulting in what urban historian Philip Ethington terms "segregated diversity"[7] whereby urban areas are simultaneously diverse as well as segregated, often by political boundaries. Thus, in urban areas, many residents confront diversity only when they drive past it on the freeway.

Even if we want to, however, most of us who live in urban areas can't insulate ourselves completely from people unlike ourselves. As with density, we have to learn ways of coping with diversity. One way is **tolerance**. In fact, we have no choice. If we as city dwellers yelled insults or ran away every time we saw somebody who was different—in color, looks, dress, manner, language, or whatever—we'd wind up institutionalized. Instead, we learn from experience that the vast majority of "different" people are going about their own business just like us. Research shows that exposure to diversity makes most of us more, not less, tolerant. The more we learn about other cultures, the less we tend to find diversity strange or to fear it. This process leads us to recognize diversity not as negative and threatening but as positive and stimulating, even to taking pride in friendships with people and cultures unlike our own.

Some cities in the United States are among the most diverse in the world, which makes coping with diversity both more important and more difficult. Tolerance, segregation, and government agents of social control such as police can be overwhelmed, especially if other pressures, such as accelerated immigration and economic recession, are added to the mix. Urban societies can break under the strain, exploding into riots like those in Los Angeles in 1965 (Watts) and 1992 (South Central), Miami (Overton) in 1980, or Cincinnati (Over-the-Rhine) in 2001. Such strains and explosions usually lead to calls for more government action, thus taking us back to politics.

But diversity adds something to politics besides a need to cope, something more positive. To begin with, when diversity increases tolerance, it enhances democracy. We are more willing to accept the rule of the majority in elections and to protect the rights of minorities—both essential elements of democracy—when we do not fear or hate our fellow citizens. Diversity usually also acts as a stimulant to local politics, as it does with so much else in urban life. As founding father James Madison famously argued in the *Federalist Papers*, in small, homogeneous places, one group or faction often dominates. As communities grow, however, other groups emerge, organize, and demand their rights and privileges. Seeing the benefits these groups have gained—jobs, elective offices, a community center, a special holiday—leads other new or previously unorganized groups to mobilize and demand their share. Organization and participation stimulate more organization and participation.

As a consequence, politics in heterogeneous communities is usually more competitive and interesting, with more participation by individual voters and organized groups than in homogeneous places. Power tends to be more broadly distributed, too. This could, and often does, mean more conflict, which can become nasty or result in gridlock. But conflict at least means different interests are being expressed and people have some choice. Homogeneous communities tend to be in general agreement or consensus about political matters, which usually brings low levels of participation and competition, the suppression of some interests, and limited choices. For all the problems that accompany diversity (mostly due to intolerance) it also brings excitement, vitality, stimulation, and greater participation to community life and politics.

S^2D^2: Setting, Size, Density, and Diversity

Although these four characteristics or variables have been considered separately, they are closely associated elements of community life. Large cities are usually great not only in geographic size but also in population, density, and diversity; small communities, conversely, are frequently of lesser size, density, and diversity. The impacts of these factors vary accordingly in large and small communities and in those that fall between the two extremes. Their politics vary similarly, as we will see.

The Political Economy of Urban Places

As mentioned, there is a symbiotic relationship between setting, size, density, and diversity, with each factor to some extent influencing the others. In this section, we explore the ways in which the economic structure of communities varies and affects local politics. Rural economies are relatively simple, based mostly on agriculture and a limited number of other activities. Urban economies are far more complex, with elaborate specialization, a high degree of interdependence, massive concentrations of wealth and power, and a far more nuanced class structure. Politics in rural and urban places vary accordingly, as do politics in urban places with varying degrees of economic development and vitality. Most urban scholars agree that economic forces are the reason for the existence of modern cities, and, as discussed in chapter 1, some political economists argue that economic growth is the key to understanding how local politics works.

Specialization and Interdependence

In the most undeveloped rural societies, people take care of most of their own needs, clearing land, building their homes, growing their food, making their clothing, and entertaining themselves. In order to survive in these societies, individuals need to cultivate expertise in a number of essential tasks. Of course, complete self-sufficiency is rare even in the most isolated parts of the United States today, but overall, rural residents are more self-sufficient than urban dwellers. Urban residents specialize in trades and professions and depend on one another to exchange goods and services. By and large, city residents do not build their own homes, grow their own food, or make their own clothes. In fact, the more affluent one is, the more one leaves to others to do. Almost none of us—perhaps with the exception of scavenging street people—is even remotely self-sufficient.

The more sophisticated the urban economy, the more "**postindustrial**" it becomes, meaning production techniques rely less on machines and factories and more on the development and dispersal of technology and information. **Specialization** is a hallmark of both industrial and postindustrial societies as workers concentrate on mastering specific and narrow tasks, a strategy that improves overall economic efficiency. People do what they do best or what is available for them to do, and, hopefully, they earn enough money to buy housing, food, clothing, and services from others. Specialization requires a diversity of people to provide and use the different specialties. When your sink breaks, sure, you could read a plumbing manual, buy the necessary tools, and (eventually) learn the skills to fix the problem. But most people simply hire a plumber, making the rational calculation that going to all that trouble is not an efficient use of their time. Restaurants, shops, businesses of all kinds, and services from resume writing to house cleaning all need to find their clienteles, and the more people there are in an area, the more likely it is that there will be enough demand for their skills to support themselves. As generations of sociologists have observed, the trend toward economic specialization is intrinsic to all cities.

Specialization is a major source of the diversity of urban places and thus of the delights of urban life. It affects local politics by multiplying the interests that may organize and demand their say. But specialization also affects community life by increasing our **interdependence** or need for one another. In a highly specialized economy, we need one another for the day-to-day exchange of goods and services, but we also need one another for the overall viability of the local economy. Environmentalists who demand local limits on growth almost always win public sympathy until somebody points out that limiting growth will mean fewer jobs in the construction and real estate industries. Perhaps only a small percentage of the population would be directly affected, but the other workers and businesses who serve them would soon feel the pinch, too. In a specialized, interdependent economy, what happens in one sector has a ripple effect on others. Individuals and communities thus rally to protect local industry, even at the expense of their own environment or, sometimes, other communities.

The Specialization of Cities

Like individuals, cities were once relatively self-sufficient, producing most of what they needed in conjunction with surrounding rural areas. Cities began to specialize long ago, however, and the greatest cities achieved their stature by trading the products of their specialization with others. The industrial revolution and modern transportation and communication technology only accelerated the trends toward specialization and trade. As a consequence, few cities remain completely self-sufficient, even in combination with nearby agrarian areas, and most fulfill some economic niche to a certain degree. Detroit made cars, Pittsburgh made steel, Seattle made airplanes, New York has Wall Street, Los Angeles has film and television industries, San Jose (Silicon Valley) makes computers, Washington, DC, has government, and so on. Cities may be so dominated by a single industry that they are literally called "company towns." Their identities as places are inextricably tied to the collective identity, often showing up in the names of professional sports teams such as the Pittsburgh "Steelers" and Green Bay "Packers."

Specialization is a two-edged sword, however. A successful specialty can bring economic boom and well-being, but, if a specialty falls out of favor, a boomtown can quickly become a ghost town. Detroit (cars), Pittsburgh (steel), Akron, Ohio (rubber), and New England (textiles) all put too many eggs in a single basket, resulting in prolonged economic crises when circumstances changed. These cities have since all tried, with varying success, to prevent or soften future economic downturns by diversifying their economies. But since the location of industry is decided more by private companies than local government, their ability to do this is limited. With the accelerating trend toward global competition, diversification becomes both more important for a city's economic survival and more difficult to achieve.

Cities of California's Silicon Valley became victims of both trends when the dot-com bubble burst in the late 1990s. These cities' overreliance on high-tech industries left them vulnerable to high unemployment rates and even higher rates of underemployment. City revenues declined, services suffered, and residents fled. Worse yet, the "bust" came at a time when companies had more freedom to relocate, often with lavish enticements and subsidies from competing local, state, or national governments. Many of Silicon Valley's technology jobs have reemerged in countries such as India, which produces large numbers of highly educated and skilled workers willing to work for less money than American workers are. Not only must cities attempt to diversify their economic portfolios while retaining specialized industries, but they must remain ever-vigilant about catering to the needs of industry if they want to keep what they have.

As cities specialize in order to compete in a global market, they also become more interdependent on one another as markets for their goods and services. They need one another to exchange what they make and do; they need one another to survive. But unlike individuals, cities rarely function in communities and almost never rally to protect another's interests. More often, they simply compete with one another, partly due to tax structures imposed on them by states and partly due to their own internal politics. Thus, one of the great challenges for urban areas in the twenty-first century is to overcome political fragmentation and to devise regional strategies to facilitate economic cooperation.

Wealth, Class, and Power

For reasons that will be explored later, Americans are not a particularly class-conscious people. But that doesn't mean that economic classes don't exist or that we can't enhance our understanding of urban politics by examining class structures. Urban economies are characterized by great concentrations of wealth and elaborate class structures, both of which have their impact on politics and power. Karl Marx's writings are among the early analyses of class structures, and it's no coincidence that his writings reflect economic trends he witnessed emerging in the industrializing cities of Europe.

Historically, concentrated wealth in rural places was mainly in the form of land ownership, and a two-tiered class structure comprised mostly landowners and workers, with owners of small farms, shops, and a few professionals such as doctors and teachers constituting a small middle class. Until relatively recently, the economy of the American South, save a few large cities, resembled this traditional, almost feudal, class structure. In recent years, the decline of family-owned farms and the rise of corporate farming have reinforced this traditional structure, hollowing out a crucial part of the rural middle class. Immigration to rural areas, mostly from Latin America, has introduced a new segment of the workforce, at once allowing moribund industries to remain competitive, while simultaneously raising issues of citizenship, participation, and exploitation. Although there is some evidence that small towns—particularly in the Sunbelt—are again becoming destinations for young, middle-class families, overall, the rigid class structure of agrarian economies appears to be a pattern that will only continue in the near future.

The great traders and merchants—department store owners such as Sears and Macy and industrialists such as Carnegie and Rockefeller—historically stood atop the class structure of large cities, often replacing the leadership of more established families. More recently, the land development industry has produced a new oligarchy in many cities. In urban places, land is a valuable and limited commodity making ownership and control over its development an important and lucrative endeavor. Indeed, much local political activity is devoted to increasing land values. In addition to developers, multinational corporations have increasingly overshadowed traditional ruling families in large cities. But unlike established families, corporate CEOs such as Microsoft chairman Bill Gates are probably less concerned with what happens at Seattle city council meetings than at meetings of the World Trade Organization or trade decisions made by Congress and the president. Whether industrialist, developer, or corporate CEO, when these individuals live in the communities where their businesses operate, if they choose to, they almost invariably exercise disproportionate power.

Such massive **concentrations of wealth** affect local politics because they alter the distribution of power. The great economic interests often agree on political issues, for example, generally supporting growth. But as economies develop and diversify, the number of economic powerhouses may grow and their interest on some issues may diverge. Landowners, the building industry, retailers, manufacturers, and the service industries, not to mention locally owned and branch-plant operations, have slightly different interests that may affect local politics. Local landowners, for example, may be prepared to accept tax increases to pay for better services, while corporate branch plants threaten to leave town. Downtown high-rise developers and retailers fight new suburban shopping malls. Manufacturers push for better planning to provide more affordable housing and better transportation for their workers, while landowners and developers push for unbridled growth. These differences might be small, but there are no differences at all in communities dominated by a single major landowner or industrialist.

Growth and economic expansion alter not only communities' ownership of wealth, but also their class structures. These, too, become much more elaborate. Whereas the class structure of a simple rural society or company town might amount to little more than owner and workers, sophisticated urban economies comprise many strata. At the top, the wealthiest may be several cuts above land and factory owners. At the bottom, the street people and urban underclass rank well below the working class. Most significantly, the class in between is usually large and is itself diversified to include lower-middle, middle, and upper-middle classes. These are the office workers, teachers, government workers, small business operators, managers, lawyers, doctors, and others, shading upwards into the bottom echelon of the upper class. Out of these classes come neighborhood, environmental, and other groups that may challenge economic elites, particularly developers, since they do not perceive themselves as being dependent on economic growth.

The elaborate **class structure** in large urban places creates a basis for many political conflicts. Although class-consciousness is low in the United States, classes sometimes perceive and express differing political interests. The segregation of urban areas by class is one expression of these interests, and class conflict in cities is most visible when neighborhoods defend themselves against outsiders or other neighborhoods, invariably of a class lower than their own. During the nineteenth and early twentieth centuries, unionized workers challenged the capitalist upper class in some cities. In others, the political dominance of the old Yankee upper class was displaced by the immigrant working class organized by political machines, which were, in turn, deposed by a reform movement that mobilized the burgeoning urban middle class. In both cases, these classes gained advantages, although major economic interests were accommodated by both machines and reformers. In recent years, class has been a factor in the battle to control growth in some communities. The 1980s' surge in homelessness and the 1992 riot in Los Angeles, which were about both class and race, are other recent reminders of both class structure and politics.[8] In many cities, as ethnic and national identification recede, some believe that class conflict between those who own property and those who rent it is emerging as an important political fault line.[9]

The Hourglass Economy

In addition to class structures within cities, it is also important for students and policy makers to understand the way in which urban economies themselves fit into the emerging global economic structure. **Globalization** can be defined as the increasing worldwide interdependency of capital and labor markets. There is no single date one can point to as the "start" of globalization; in some sense globalization has always been going on. But most scholars argue that, since the 1970s, there has been an accelerated degree of interconnectedness of the world's economies as a result of better trade infrastructure and flow of information and a reduction of trade barriers due to international trade agreements. Moreover, since the 1970s, as the mobility of capital has increased, so has the mobility of labor, though to a lesser extent. Passed by Congress in 1965, the Hart-Cellar Act did away with preferences for immigrants from Northern Europe and instituted a system based on a wider variety of national origins, particular skills needed in the American economy, and family unification. Preferences for immigrants from communist nations such as the USSR, Vietnam, and Cuba were also instituted. The 1985 Immigration Act further boosted immigration by permitting millions of undocumented residents to apply for U.S. citizenship, further boosting immigration. During the presidential campaign of 2004, several proposals were floated by both major political parties to make it easier for non-citizens to apply for citizenship, in part as an attempt by both parties to woo Latino and other immigrant votes. No matter how it is ultimately decided, the issue of immigration is key to understanding how urban and rural economies are changing.

The impact of greater capital and labor mobility has been felt most strongly in cities. Cities have been the primary sites of much of the economic activity of globalization, and thus the economies of cities have been greatly impacted—both positively and negatively—by global economic forces. The resulting economic structure that has emerged in many American cities has been described metaphorically as an "**hourglass economy**." As seen in Figure 2.1, at the top of the hourglass are high-tech jobs in computer, multimedia, engineering, biotechnology, defense and other high-skilled industries. Also making up the top of the spectrum are jobs and skilled professions such as law, medicine, accounting, dentistry, and so on. At the bottom of the hourglass are poorly paid service industry jobs such as gardeners, janitors, and restaurant workers, as well as low-skilled manufacturing jobs in industries like furniture, textiles, and food processing. Over the past several decades, job growth in service sector has far outpaced that of growth in other sectors.

Figure 2.1 **Hourglass Economy**

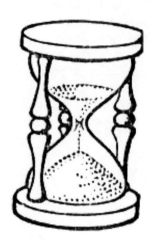

- High Tech/Professions

- Small business,
  government, non-profit

- Service/Manufacturing

The hourglass metaphor powerfully illustrates the decline of the middle economic stratum and in particular the nation's manufacturing industries such as defense and steel and auto production, among many others. Because the costs of manufacturing (particularly labor costs) are far lower in Latin America and Asia, many of the nation's high-paying manufacturing jobs have been forced to leave in order to remain competitive. What remains of manufacturing sector jobs is being pushed down to low-end, often non-unionized industries such as meatpacking, apparel, and other industries that often do not offer health insurance. These jobs pay relatively low wages in comparison to, say, the auto industry jobs of the 1960s and rely increasingly on cheap, exploitable, immigrant labor. Working conditions in these jobs are among the harshest of any industry. In the hourglass economy, government workers, such as teachers, policemen and other bureaucrats, non-profit employees, and small business owners make up the bulk of what is left of the shrinking middle class.

Naturally, the hourglass metaphor does not perfectly capture all of the complexities. For instance, not all service jobs are at the low end of the pay scale. Many financial service jobs, such as financial advisers and mortgage brokers, are well paying. Also, the hourglass metaphor may give the false impression of relative equality between the number of jobs at the top and bottom. A pyramid shape might better illustrate the inequality in new economic structure. Nor is the news all bad. Small-business creation remains one of the bright spots for the U.S. economy in terms of retaining a stable and secure middle class. In many cities, immigrant communities are important engines of small business growth. On the whole, though, the metaphor is a good way to think about the impact of globalization on urban economies. The ominous flow of the sand downward represents a trend that will likely only get worse.

What does the hourglass economy mean for cities? Why should anyone care? For one, it leads to increasing gaps between rich and poor. History tells us that the most stable societies are ones with a relatively large middle class. A class structure with a wide gap between rich and poor has historically been a recipe for social unrest and sometimes even violent revolution. Some even connect rising inequality with the explosion of gated communities in the United States.[10] A related impact on cities has been increased rates of immigration, particularly from Latin America and Asia, to fill positions at the low end of the job market. While sometimes strengthening local economies, the dependency on importing cheap labor may also leave urban econo-mies susceptible to competition from even cheaper labor in other countries. Another problem that immigration creates for local and state governments is that increasing competition for limited jobs at the top means that access to education—particularly higher education—becomes all the more critical, at a time when public schools and universities are facing severe budgetary constraints. Finally, because government jobs are some of the few remaining middle-class jobs, increasing conflict between ethnic groups for government jobs can be expected to manifest itself in city elections, in conflict between city workers and city government, and in power struggles within city bureaucracies. We will continue our discussion of immigration in chapter 3.

Ultimately, many observers fear that widening gaps between rich and poor will result in greater social, political, and economic instability. Certainly, the subject has drawn the attention of politicians at the highest levels, who may or may not be in a position to make meaningful changes without fundamentally upsetting the global economy. Urban regions, meanwhile, are largely helpless to impact these trends, again underscoring the notion of "city limits." Because of political fragmentation, seeking regional solutions would be almost impossible, even if local governments were inclined to cooperate. Even though New York, Los Angeles, and Chicago are identified most frequently as American "global cities," it is clear that these are not the only global American cities. Places such as Miami, San Diego, Seattle, San An-tonio, and many others are also being fundamentally reshaped by their transnational economic, cultural, and political ties. When we add to the mix the recent flow of immigrant labor into American rural communities, it is safe to say that no American community remains completely untouched by the forces of globalization.

IN YOUR COMMUNITY

Discuss whether, and how, your community has been impacted by globalization.

The Growth Imperative: The City as a Growth Machine

Given the important role of economic forces, it is not surprising that scholars have placed economic growth at the center of their explanations of urban politics. Soci-ologist Harvey Molotch argues that "the political and economic essence of virtually any given locality, in the present American context is growth."[11] According to Molotch, local "land-based" business elites seek "exchange values" (profits) "through the in-creasing intensification of land use" and "governmental authority, at the local and nonlocal levels, is utilized to assist in achieving this growth at the expense of com-peting localities."[12] Molotch terms the alliance between business and government elites—frequently joined by public employee unions and minority groups—a **growth machine**. The promise of jobs and housing often wins public and governmental support for growth, and local government has its own vested interest in growth as a means of increasing tax revenue. Of course, others also engage in local politics in pursuit of their own interests. In particular, Molotch identifies homeowner and environmental groups as potential adversaries of the growth machine. The groups are primarily driven by the desire to protect their quality of life but also the property value of their homes.

But while these and other interests are active, and growth is not the only issue in local politics, virtually every community is and must be concerned about its economic viability. Localities act as growth machines because of the political power of local economic interests and the inevitable competition among communities for economic well-being. And state governments add to the growth imperative through the structures of taxation and regulations they impose on local governments.

In sum, in order to fully understand issues that face urban places, we need to first be aware of the broader economic context of local politics, including specialization, interdependence, the concentration of wealth and class structures, and global forces and the hourglass economy. Although Molotch's summarizing conception of localities as growth machines is somewhat limited, it is nonetheless useful as shorthand for understanding the centrality of the economic growth imperative in urban politics, a theme that will recur in the chapters that follow.

The Social Psychology of Urban Life

A final factor to consider in understanding the way people relate to one another and to their society, and the way they think about themselves in relation to society, is social psychology, which has its own impact on local politics. Urban sociologists such as Louis Wirth look at society in terms of primary and secondary social groups. The former are predominant in rural societies and small towns, while the latter exist in more urban settings.[13]

Primary Groups

Primary groups center on the family—not just the nuclear families of parents and children that most of us are accustomed to, but also extended families that include parents, children, grandparents, aunts, uncles, and cousins. Such extended families are most commonly found in rural societies, villages, and small towns, where people know not only their own family but everybody else. Here, people depend on one another, with several family members working together on a farm or in a small business. Even when people in such societies specialize, they know one another not only in terms of their economic roles (as farmer, landowner, merchant, teacher, or student), but as complete people, members of the community with family ties.

Such places have a strong **sense of community** and identity, of warmth and intimacy. People feel they belong and they know who they are. They always greet one another, and when they ask, "How are you?" they may really want to know. They keep an eye on one another's kids. They care for each other and take care of members of the community who need assistance. Helping an elderly person carry something is not an anonymous act of goodwill, but a favor to a classmate's grandmother—not helping will mean a lecture on manners. The person passed out on the street isn't an anonymous alcoholic to be stepped around, but the familiar town drunk—the father or uncle of somebody known. Instead of avoidance, people are more likely to help such a person. Members of the community with mental disabilities may also be accepted and assisted rather than institutionalized. Small communities may only have one town drunk or one developmentally disabled person to cope with, which makes it easier, but knowing them as members of the community rather than reducing them to stereotypes based on their disability is even more important.

This idyll has its darker side, however. Such communities can be oppressive and conformist. Everybody knows everybody, and they mind one another's business. Kids don't skip school without their parents hearing about it. The old lady up the road sits on her front porch all day watching traffic—and reports speeders or even loud music to whoever will listen. The way you dress, your haircut, the company you keep, and your behavior will all be observed and commented upon. If you step out of line, the whole town will know. Strangers are noticed, warily watched, and welcomed only if they have a local connection and fit in. Such informal social control reduces the need for government, which may be good, but it also oppresses people who don't follow all the rules or who are misfits. The alcoholic mentioned earlier doesn't need a social worker or a halfway house, but he won't get therapy, and the community's disapproval will be made known. They put up with him only because he was born there. Others, such as loners, homosexuals, women who want careers, men who don't want to go into the family business, people with different political views—anybody who doesn't fit the cozy norm—are shunned and often isolated. The power of this disapproval and isolation is greater because of the tight-knit nature of the community. People who fit in feel happy and complete; those who do not tend to be miserable or leave.

Cities of Strangers

When societies urbanize, primary groups break down. In the more developed economies of cities, people are not as dependent on one another as they were on the family farm or business. Thanks to specialization, individuals get jobs and support themselves; they rent apartments and get away from the family home. In cities, the extended family shrinks to the nuclear family, and even that may break up. Family members spread out through an urban area or even further. They lose the sense of community and identity of rural places, but they also escape the pressure to conform. People no longer meddle in their lives. Instead, people ignore them. They are free, but often alone.

Economic specialization makes the freedom possible and the sense of isolation inevitable. We don't spend our days with our families and other people who know us but with strangers who, despite the occasional "Have a nice day," do not treat us as whole human beings but as roles: students, teachers, customers, check-outs, bosses, workers, passersby. We aren't greeted by everyone on the street; no one really wants to know how we are; we step around drunks and ignore old ladies carrying their groceries. We don't want to get involved; we're all strangers. In a notorious 1991 incident in Los Angeles, a Korean shopkeeper shot and killed a young black woman, Latasha Harlins, in a dispute about whether the woman was shoplifting a can of soda. Besides the clash of cultures, these were strangers dealing with one another in an impersonal and unfriendly city, a situation that likely wouldn't arise between two residents of a small town.

"Great cities," urbanist Jane Jacobs once observed, "are not like towns, only larger."[14] They differ from towns and suburbs in basic ways, and one of these is that cities are, by definition, full of strangers. In small settlements everyone knows your affairs. In the city everyone does not—only those you choose to tell will know about you. This is one of the attributes of cities that is precious to most city people. Many of us thrive on this freedom and privacy and would feel stifled in a small town. Others feel alienated from the society around them—lost, lonely, unloved, sad, even angry.

Secondary Groups

Secondary groups are a response to these urban social conditions. Whereas people are born into primary groups, they join secondary groups on a voluntary basis because of some shared interest. You can think of them as similar to the interest groups we discussed earlier. Such groups may be economic (a union, chamber of commerce, or a network of professional women, for example), or they may be ethnic, religious, cultural, political, or athletic. They can be anything that interests any two or more city dwellers, and one of the nice things about cities is that they are big and diverse enough to supply people who share almost any interest. These groups give people an identity, a sense of belonging and community to replace the primary-group connection they've lost, but membership is voluntary, not a passive birthright. People can choose—to join, quit, or join another group—but they must act. Cities let people blossom, not only because they are freer, but also because they can develop their own interests, whatever they may be unless, of course, they are too overwhelmed by alienation to act, as many people are.

The Search for Community, Social Capital, and Increased Government

The loss of primary group connections is also expressed in a restless **search for community**. People attach their identities to places, such as particular neighborhoods, small towns, or outlying suburbs, hoping to reclaim some of the benefits of small-town life. Some groups, such as street gangs, even attach place significance to telephone area codes. Both urban neighborhoods and suburban places often call themselves "villages" or "towns," and people often say they are "from" these places rather than from the larger urban entity of which they are a part. Fierce loyalties and rivalries sometimes develop and may be expressed in competition between schools and sports teams. Urban neighborhoods and suburban places, however, often deliver less sense of community than their residents hope for because they are never as intimate as small towns. People do not spend all their time in such places—they work, shop, and visit friends and relations elsewhere—and they don't get to know one another as well as people do in small towns. Some urban areas nevertheless develop a sense of community, especially if they have common meeting places, such as a park, shopping area, or bar, or if lots of people walk or take public transportation together and get to know one another that way. Neighborhood newspapers or newsletters also help, and many neighborhood groups consciously work to build community to increase their political efficacy. Some neighborhoods and suburbs may thus offer a good compromise between the oppressive intimacy of the small town and the isolation of urban places. People know one another well enough to pay attention to one another without intrusively minding each other's business.

Often, the identity of neighborhoods and suburbs is a result of segregation, an almost universal response to the alienation of living among strangers. As noted in our discussion of segregation as a way of dealing with diversity, most people seem to prefer to be among others like themselves. Persistent racial and economic discrimination have made segregation a serious problem, but this phenomenon is not unique to United States. "Segregation by neighborhoods," declares urbanist Mark La Gory, "is universal in modern societies because it is, in some sense, functional. It maintains order in a potentially disorderly society, . . . makes everyday life more predictable for the city dweller, . . . minimizes the risks of conflict, and promotes social solidarity."[15] Equally, it can be discriminatory, oppressive, and a source of social conflict. La Gory's point is not to defend segregation, but to understand its near inevitability.

The concept of "**social capital**" offers another way to look at communities. As defined by Robert Putnam, "social capital" consists of "connections among individuals —social networks and the norms of reciprocity and trustworthiness that arise from them."[16] Greater social capital means greater civic engagement in communities, from voting to activity in community organizations. Better-educated and more affluent individuals tend to have higher levels of social capital, as do communities of such individuals. "Social capital is inevitably easier to foster within homogeneous communities,"[17] Putnam observes, because people more readily trust and associate with others like themselves. As social capital increases, residents become citizens engaged in the life of their communities and, in effect, caring for their communities and one another. With higher social capital and greater civic engagement, it follows that citizens' involvement in their own communities—through volunteerism, voting, and membership in all sorts of community organizations—is greater in small and middle-sized, homogeneous communities—usually suburbs—rather than big, diverse central cities. This isn't universally the case, however. Communities with more varied class and ethnic interests—large, diverse cities—sometimes have more vital group activity, for even though the poor and minorities are less likely to organize than the affluent and well educated, they sometimes do so and, faced with competition, those normally likely to organize assuredly do.

Where social capital and sense of community are weak, another response to the breakdown of primary groups in urban places may be increased government. In rural areas and small towns, much social control is informal, carried out by the community itself. People watch out for and help one another, keeping each other in line and providing protection from outsiders. But in a city of strangers, these mechanisms break down. People don't know one another and don't want to get involved; they don't know who belongs and who doesn't. Many behaviors that would be castigated in small towns are ignored in cities, so people are freer. But some behaviors are unacceptable even in cities, so formal or governmental agents of social control, such as police, social workers, teachers, truant officers, and health and safety inspectors replace at least some of the informal controls of smaller communities. Alcoholics, the elderly, or the mentally ill are institutionalized or left to wander the streets rather than cared for by their families or communities. Urban social connections have grown so weak that we sometimes don't even know our own neighbors, leaving it to police to organize neighborhood watch programs, introducing neighbors to one another and asking them to exchange phone numbers and keep an eye on one another's homes.

The paradox is that as cities free us from the social oppression of closed rural societies and small towns, they often leave us feeling lonely, without the protection and sense of community and belonging of small-town life. These differences are the result of size, density, diversity, and economics of urban places, yet they have their own impact on local politics, stimulating the formation of interest groups, the search for community, segregation, and reliance on government as an agent of social order.

IN YOUR COMMUNITY

How would you rate your community's "sense of community"? What criteria will you use? What are the important secondary groups that exist to help people establish and maintain community connections?

The Environment of Local Politics

Setting, size, density, and diversity are good places to start in attempting to analyze problems that face local governments. Additional variables, such as the economic and class structure of cities, as well as the impact of globalization, can be added to the analysis. Finally, we looked at how the social psychology of place can be added to the mix to explain social relations. Variation in these characteristics helps explain why local politics differs from place to place. All of these characteristics are related, however, usually varying not independently, but in concert with each other. We also found that urbanism is a matter of degree, with communities ranging from rural to suburban and urban, from villages and towns to small, middle-sized, and great cities. See "A Glossary of Places" that follows for definitions of terms that describe communities. Each place is unique, yet all share some characteristics and some are distributed among the different sorts of communities in clear patterns. Demography may not be "destiny" in a strict sense, but we think you'll agree that its implications for urban politics are fundamentally important.

In the chapters that follow, we will refer to these characteristics and patterns as we discuss the formal institutions of local politics, as well as its informal participants, from interest groups to voters and the media. First, however, we will examine some of the major historical trends that have impacted cities and what sorts of people live in various sorts of places today.

A Glossary of Places

Rural: People live in relative isolation in the countryside, with farming the primary activity.

Urban: A large, diverse population living close together with a highly specialized and interdependent economy; describes a social, economic, and cultural, but not necessarily governmental, entity.

Suburban: A smaller, less diverse population living in lower densities on the periphery of big cities and traditionally dependent on them; more urban than rural.

Central city: The dominant city in an urban area—the largest, oldest, and most diverse. It is also self-governing and is the economic center of the region.

Neighborhood: A part of a city with its own distinct identity, but not self-governing.

Suburb: A community adjacent to a central city with less urban characteristics (suburban) and its own local government (as distinct from a neighborhood).

Town: A relatively self-contained community with a population of a few thousand, separate from other communities and probably, but not necessarily, with its own government; in some northeastern states, it is also a unit of local government equivalent to a city or municipality.

City or Municipality: A legal or incorporated local government, created by citizen petition and state recognition (see chapter 4). Primary functions include police, fire protection, land use, streets and traffic, public works, parks, and libraries. Suburbs or towns are technically cities or municipalities if they are incorporated.

County: A form of local government created by states to carry out specific functions, usually including elections, justice, welfare, health, and transit, and limited services such as police, fire protection, parks, and libraries for rural areas. Counties may contain several cities (see chapter 4).

Urban area or Metropolitan region: An urbanized area with many cities and often more than one county, but usually without a single government of its own (see chapter 14).

Essential Terms

geographic setting	smart growth
technology, tolerance, and talent	diversity
urban sprawl	homogeneous
population size	heterogeneous
density	segregation
land-use planning	racial steering

redlining
segregation by class
tolerance
postindustrial
specialization
interdependence
concentrations of wealth
class structure
coping with density

globalization
hourglass economy
growth machine
primary groups
sense of community
secondary groups
search for community
social capital

On the Internet

- The U.S. Bureau of the Census website (www.census.gov) is a great place to find detailed demographic data about your community.
- The Census Bureau website (www.census.gov/hhes/www/housing.html) also has a number of links to various topics relating to housing.
- www.urban.org/ is a good website for finding research materials relating to urban economic and social policy.
- www.gdrc.org/uem/ is a good website for learning about urban environmental management.
- The Department of Commerce website (www.economicindicators.gov/) has detailed statistics on housing, construction, and other economic indicators.
- The Bureau of Labor Statistics website (www.bls.gov/) has a wealth of information on employment and other economic indicators.

Notes

1. Kevin Starr, *Material Dreams: Southern California Through the 1920's* (London: Oxford University Press, 1991).

2. Robert M. Fogelson, *The Fragmented Metropolis: Los Angeles, 1850–1930* (Berkeley: University of California Press, 1993).

3. Joel Kotkin, *The New Geography: How the Digital Revolution Is Reshaping the American Landscape* (New York: Random House, 2000).

4. Richard L. Florida, *The Rise of the Creative Class: And How It's Transforming Work, Leisure, Community, and Everyday Life* (New York: Basic Books, 2002).

5. Robyn Dowling, "Suburban Stories, Gendered Lives: Thinking through Difference," in *Cities of Difference*, ed. Ruth Fincher and Jane M. Jacobs (New York: Guilford Press, 1998).

6. See for example, Barry Glassner, *The Culture of Fear: Why Americans are Afraid of the Wrong Things* (New York: Basic Books, 1999).

7. Philip J. Ethington, "Segregated Diversity: Race-Ethnicity, Space, and Political Fragmentation in Los Angeles County, 1940–1994" (final report to John Randolph Haynes and Dora Haynes Foundation, July 20, 2000). See Gary A. Tobin, ed., *Divided Neighborhoods: Changing Patterns of Racial Segregation*, Urban Affairs Annual Review 32 (Newbury Park, CA: Sage, 1987).

8. Although racial conflict precipitated and pervaded the Los Angeles riot, businesses were often targets regardless of who owned them, and the rioters' resentment of business owners as people of privilege was clear.

9. Matt A. Barreto, Mara Marks, and Nathan Woods, "Homeownership: Southern California's New Political Fault Line?" (paper presented at the annual meeting of the Western Political Science Association, Portland, OR, March 11–13, 2004).

10. Edward J. Blakely and Mary Gail Snyder, *Fortress America: Gated Communities in the United States* (Washington, DC: Brookings Institution Press; Cambridge, MA: Lincoln Institute of Land Policy, 1997).

11. Harvey Molotch, "The City as a Growth Machine: Toward a Political Economy of Place," *American Journal of Sociology* 82, no. 2 (September 1976): 310. See also Stephen L. Elkin, *City and Regime in the American Republic* (Chicago: University of Chicago Press, 1987); and Paul E. Peterson, *City Limits* (Chicago: University of Chicago Press, 1981).

12. Molotch, "The City as a Growth Machine," p. 309.

13. See the classic Louis Wirth, "Urbanism as a Way of Life," *American Journal of Sociology* 44, no. 1 (July 1938): 1–24.

14. Jane Jacobs, *The Death and Life of Great American Cities,* rev ed. (New York: Random House, 2002), p. 126.

15. Mark La Gory, "The Organization of Space and the Character of the Urban Experience," *Publius* 18 (Fall 1988): 77.

16. Robert D. Putnam, *Bowling Alone: The Collapse and Revival of American Community* (New York: Simon and Schuster, 2000), p. 20.

17. Ibid., p. 400.

3 The Evolution of Urban Places
Where People Live and Why

The characteristics of urban places discussed in the last chapter are not evenly distributed among localities. Some are larger, denser, more diverse, and more economically complex than others. In this chapter, we will examine historical patterns of human settlement, as well as more recent population trends. We will focus on three historical population movements and consider how and why people live where they do. The first, running through the eighteenth, nineteenth, and twentieth centuries, is urbanization, the movement from the farm to cities. The second, occurring mostly in the twentieth century, is suburbanization, the movement to the urban periphery. The third, a phenomenon of the latter half of the twentieth century, is the move away from the Northeast and upper Midwest to the southern and western states of the "Sunbelt." Two recent population trends, the "return to the city" movement and immigration from abroad, will also be discussed. Each has its own causes and its own unique social and economic arrangements, and each has its own impact on local, state, and national politics.

Urbanization: The Move to the Cities

Urbanization, or the movement of people from rural areas to cities, is an ancient phenomenon. Humans have been drawn to cities for protection from enemies or a hostile environment, for economic and intellectual opportunities, and for the freedoms described in the last chapter. Cities have long been centers of trade, government, religion, education, and culture, as they are today. For centuries, urbanization was slow, however, because economies were based on agriculture, and the vast majority of people in most countries worked on farms. Growth in international trade accelerated urbanization in some countries such as England in the seventeenth and eighteenth centuries, but it was technological change and the industrial revolution in the nineteenth century that gave impetus to urbanization and produced the cities we live in now. In 1790, only 5 percent of the U.S. population was urban. In 2000, after two centuries of urbanization, 80 percent lived in what the U.S. Census classifies as "urban." Much of the growth was the result of internal migration, as Americans left the countryside for the city for economic reasons. But U.S. urbanization has been also greatly and uniquely augmented by the arrival of millions of immigrants from other countries seeking both economic and political opportunity.

Changes in rural areas and economies spurred by technological advances made urbanization possible and even necessary. Cities depend on farms in the country-side for food. As cities developed, subsistence-level farmers in outlying areas increasingly participated in markets to provide food for city dwellers. The eighteenth and nineteenth centuries brought early scientific farming techniques and increased production, but the huge agricultural surpluses needed for massive urban growth were given even greater stimulus by the industrial revolution, itself an urban phenomenon. The manufacture of farm machinery such as tractors and a variety of industrial techniques facilitated more intensive and productive agriculture. Additionally, the canals and railroads of the industrial revolution opened new markets because agricultural products could be shipped further, faster. Finally, the development of refrigerated rail cars in the late nineteenth century meant that meat and produce could be grown in areas farther from the city and still make it to market without spoiling.

Mechanized agriculture allowed greater farming productivity but with fewer workers, even as America's rural population grew due to high fertility and declining death rates. The western frontier, which had provided a safety valve for excess rural population to homestead small farms, began to fill up in the nineteenth century. Much of the West was too arid and/or mountainous to cultivate while others, such as California, were parceled out in large land holdings rather than small homesteads as in the East and Midwest. These trends, combined with increased economic opportunity in cities and expanding immigration from abroad, caused urban populations to swell.

Industrialization

Much as people may have preferred life on the farm or in small towns, technological advancements began to revolutionize where people could live. **Industrialization**, a process to improve economic efficiency by substituting relatively inefficient human labor with machine labor, greatly impacted the growth of cities. Taking place first in Europe and gradually in the United States during the nineteenth century, the increased use of mechanized agriculture, for example, led to a surplus of farm labor, literally pushing workers into cities. Simultaneously, industrial techniques created millions of new job opportunities, pulling people into cities and rapidly swelling their populations. Single men, women, and even whole families began to stream into America's industrial centers. Initially, workers needed to be near the workplace, which led to higher urban densities. Improved sanitation and construction techniques that allowed for taller buildings also made such densities possible. Transportation advances in the form of electric trolleys, railroads, and buses eventually provided access for workers living farther away, enabling cities to expand.[1] In addition to economics, cities also exerted a powerful cultural pull. All through history, people have been drawn to cities to be free of the oppression and conformity of rural life and to pursue their own interests, including economic opportunity. "Every major urban area is a magnet," says former Seattle Mayor Norm Rice. "Some people come in hope, some to hide."[2] The key point is that without technological advancements such as mechanization and transportation, cities as we know them could not exist.

Defining Urban Places and Metropolitan Statistical Areas

The economics and geography of urbanization have changed over the years, as growth shifted to the edges of cities and then to the postindustrial cities of the South and West, but Americans have continued to concentrate in ever-greater numbers in urban areas. By 1920, over half of all Americans lived in what the Bureau of the Census calls **urban places**. This figure was viewed as a little misleading, however, because the bureau defines urban places as geographic areas with populations of more than 2,500. Some of these are really villages, not cities, and even isolated places with larger populations would be thought of by most people in the United States as towns rather than cities or urban places. In 2000, the Census Bureau attempted to address this issue by distinguishing "**urbanized areas**," which it defined as having more than 50,000 people, from what it calls "**urban clusters**" of between 2,500 and 49,999 residents.

The Census Bureau also uses a fairly complex classification system to describe densely populated metropolitan areas. The bureau has instituted several recent changes to its classification system. As of 2004, the Census Bureau uses the term **Core-Based Statistical Area (CBSA)** to describe a county or counties with at least one core of 10,000 or greater population, including any adjacent counties with a high degree of social and economic integration with the core city. A CBSA with an urban cluster of 10,000 to 49,999 is defined as a **Micropolitan Statistical Area** while a CBSA with an urbanized area of 50,000 or more, and whose suburbs are relatively integrated with a core city, is classified as a **Metropolitan Statistical Area (MSA)**. In addition, the Census now uses the terms "Metropolitan Division" to refer to the county or group of counties within an MSA that has a population core of at least 2.5 million. The term **Combined Metropolitan Statistical Areas (CMSAs)** is the largest designation, representing two or more MSAs. The previous terms, "Consolidated Metropolitan Statistical Area" and "Primary Metropolitan Statistical Areas," are still used by government agencies but will eventually become obsolete.

All of this is another way of saying that it is not as easy as it might seem to distinguish between areas that are "urban" from those that are "rural" or even "suburban." Although we all probably have some intuitive sense of what these terms mean, in practice, even experts have a hard time coming up with clear-cut, agreed-upon definitions. At some point in your studies, you may find yourself confronted with these terms, and so it is important to have some understanding of what they mean.

Urbanization and Early Immigration

Industrialization and urbanization proceeded apace in the United States after the Civil War. Much of the immigration to industrial centers can be considered **internal migration**—migrants from within the United States. The experience of African Americans from 1910 to 1930 is particularly noteworthy, as more than a million blacks migrated to northern and midwestern cities in order to escape poverty and social repression. In addition to internal migrants from rural areas in the United States, immigrants flocked to American cities from all over the world, creating both a unique pattern of urbanization and ethnically diverse cities. Their arrival and the emergence of an industrial working class also produced dramatic political change. Between 1870 and 1890, about 8 million foreign immigrants arrived, mostly from southern and eastern Europe, and most went straight to the great cities of the Northeast, the epicenter of the industrial revolution in the United States.

External immigration peaked with an additional 8.8 million newcomers between 1901 and 1910, then declined during World War I, and then was reduced to a trickle in the 1920s, following public backlash to immigration that resulted in the passage of federal laws establishing strict immigration quotas. During the economic crisis of the 1930s, only half a million immigrants arrived. Big cities continued to grow, however, because of continued internal migration of rural whites, as well as some overseas immigration from U.S. colonies like Puerto Rico and the Philippines.

The mass northern migration of African Americans also continued during this time. As large-scale, mechanized farming replaced labor-intensive sharecropping in the South, southern blacks left for jobs in factories and ports of the North and West, in what has been termed the "Great Migration." Facing virulent racism and a system of legalized segregation known as "Jim Crow," millions of blacks fled the states of the former Confederacy, particularly as jobs were being created by World War II. By 1990, 30 percent of all African Americans were living in New York, Chicago, Philadelphia, or Detroit. Chicago, Oakland, and Los Angeles were also popular destinations for black Americans. Recent immigration trends and their impact on cities and rural areas will be discussed later.

The Postindustrial City

Together, industrialization and immigration built the great U.S. cities of the early part of this century. Then, facing international competition after World War II, U.S. manufacturing industries began to decline. As early as 1956, white-collar office workers and professionals outnumbered blue-collar industrial workers. In the decades that followed, economic growth was greatest in the service-dominated economies of **postindustrial cities**, which specialized in finance, insurance, government, communications, entertainment, tourism, and trade. As discussed in chapter 2, new technologies, especially in communications, data processing, and transportation, facilitated the development of postindustrial cities, many of which were in the South or West rather than the traditionally urban Northeast.

Suburbanization: The Move to the Periphery

As we have seen, urbanization does not necessarily mean movement to big cities. Although Americans have been flocking to metropolitan areas for two centuries, except in the South and West, population growth has been greater in suburbs than in central cities since the 1940s. **Suburbs** are communities adjacent to big cities, often with their own independent local governments. As their name implies, they are usually something less than, or "sub," urban—smaller, less dense, and less diverse. Traditionally, they have been primarily residential and automobile dependent, with inhabitants commuting to a large, central city for jobs, shopping, and entertainment, although in contemporary metropolitan areas this, too, has changed. Despite being less than urban, they are an integral part of urban areas, self-sufficient in some ways and dependent in others. As with urbanization, population shifts to the suburbs have been dramatic. By 1966, more Americans lived in suburbs than in central cities. Today, about half of all Americans live in suburbs alone, and their political power has grown in proportion. The causes of **suburbanization** are many and complex, and its impact on local politics has been monumental.

Anti-city Attitudes

A basic reason for suburbanization can be summed up in one short sentence: Americans prefer it. For decades, public opinion surveys have reported big majorities preferring to live in suburbs or small towns over cities. A 1989 Gallup poll reported only 19 percent of Americans saying that they would prefer to live in a city.[3] Why is this so? Many scholars trace American **anti-city attitudes** and preference for country living to the nation's founding cultural values. "The country life," William Penn wrote, "is to be preferred, for there one sees the works of God, but in cities little else but the works of men."[4] Thomas Jefferson, too, condemned the "degeneration" and "mobs of great cities," which he declared "penitential to the morals, the health, and the liberties of man."[5] For these early writers, the moral and economic independence that came with land ownership was critical to the proper function of any democracy. Property ownership was seen as so critical that the founding fathers declared it a requirement for voting. As a nation first established by independent farmers, Americans have always been ambivalent about the transformation to industrial society and have in turn romanticized the country life.

In contrast, industrializing cities freed Europeans from harsh conditions and rigid class distinctions of feudal economies. European welfare states such as Sweden or France, with their generous social benefits, are in place at least in part to mitigate historical class disparities. This may be one reason why Europeans usually have far more positive views of city life than do Americans.[6] Cities freed Europeans from a feudal class structure, and during the twentieth century, socially progressive central governments made sure that wide economic disparities did not reemerge.

According to historian Kenneth T. Jackson, the design of the typical single-family home, with its yard, trees, water, pet animals, and sometimes even crops, is essentially a model of a miniature farm.[7] These attitudes even show in the way we tend to harken back to nature in the naming of our cities, neighborhoods, and even streets. Today, many Americans still attach contrasting values to someone from the country (honest, hardworking) with someone from the city (the fast-talking "city slicker"). Aside from such moralistic views, U.S. cities are relatively young, so we lack the long and positive urban history of some other countries with their great cities. Frontier, rural, and small-town traditions remain a vivid part of America's collective memory and contribute to our anti-city bias. Ask most Americans to free-associate with the words *city* or *urban*, and they will respond with negatives such as dirty, crime, poverty, racial conflict, smog, concrete, traffic, noise, and perversion. Suburban, on the other hand, may conjure up words like clean, safe, quiet, homogeneous, and affluent.[8]

As noted in chapter 2, racism and intolerance have also been factors in our national preference for suburbia. In 1910, 91 percent of blacks lived in rural areas; by 1980, 85 percent lived in central cities. As blacks migrated to cities, whites moved to suburbs, partly due to racism, in a phenomenon called dual migration or, more revealingly, **white flight**. The concept of dual migration applies to class as well as race, however. In racially homogeneous areas, middle- and upper-class people escaped to the suburbs as poor and working-class people migrated to the central cities.

Suburbanization provided a new mechanism for the segregation of people by race and class because state laws allowed suburbs to declare their political independence from the central city through a process called **incorporation** (see chapter 4). Urban analyst Mike Davis calls this "homeowner separatism," aimed at "putting the more permanent barriers of independent incorporation and exclusive land-use zoning between themselves and non-white or non-homeowning populations."[9]

But despite the retreat from diversity, suburbs have never been all alike. Some are rich, some are middle class, others are working class or even poor; most are white, but some are black, Asian, or Hispanic; in those where the races mix, classes do not. These and other characteristics of suburbs vary considerably, but however much they may differ from one another, most suburbs are internally homogeneous, so if people find the right one, they gain the security of living with their own kind. They insulate themselves from urban diversity and create segregated metropolitan areas. This is accomplished partly through individual choices, but also by economics and discrimination.

There are also many practical reasons why Americans prefer suburbs. Like small towns, suburbs are generally cleaner and safer than cities, offering more space, bigger houses, and more sense of community. Suburbanites often seek the psychological reassurance of being around others like themselves. Cities are also viewed as (and often are) dangerous places; suburbs as safe. Although often exaggerated—suburban crime rates have risen more rapidly than those of some central cities—the difference is still real, and it is particularly important to families. While many singles, childless couples, and the elderly live in the suburbs, families have traditionally predominated, and most people say "for the kids" when asked why they moved to the suburbs. Not only are suburbs cleaner and safer, houses there have extra bedrooms and yards for the kids. Perhaps most importantly, suburbs are seen as places to escape crowded and chronically underfunded public schools in central cities. Overall, suburban schools are newer, better funded, and more homogeneous.

Moreover, as discussed in chapter 13, like city boundaries, school district boundaries legally define which populations will benefit from a district's wealth and success. As we will see, local politics in affluent single-family suburbs often centers on the interrelated goals of improving the reputation of the area's public schools, limiting or altogether preventing apartment construction, maintaining ethnic and class homogeneity, and increasing community safety. Just as people build fences around their homes or gates around their neighborhoods, suburbs construct political fences around their communities to wall in their social and economic advantages, while keeping larger social problems at bay. The combination of open space, safety and security, and better schools is a powerful reason why many Americans prefer suburbs.

But while record numbers of Americans have been able to attain some form of the suburban dream—home ownership exceeds 65 percent nationally—it is not accessible to all. Many cannot afford the price of admission that involves, in most cases, the purchase of a house and one or more cars. For those who can afford it, however, suburbs may be the perfect compromise—"a reasonable reconstruction of our heritage,"[10] according to political scientist Robert Wood—with the feel of a small town but with ready access to an urban economy. Many suburbs are too urban to deliver on the promise of small-town life, but that doesn't keep Americans from pursuing the dream. Besides, many of us would find small towns smothering if we really wound up in one. Despite criticisms of suburbia as bland and monotonous, with cookie-cutter communities, suburbs appear to offer a package of amenities that Americans simply cannot resist.

And the dream is not only American. Other nations have also bought into the suburban dream, though none so much as the United States. Most are not yet affluent enough to afford the cars, highways, land, and houses required. Some have proud urban traditions and cultural traditions that prefer cities and disdain suburbia. The countries of western Europe, for example, are rich enough to indulge in suburbanization and have increasingly done so, but not nearly as much as the United States. Even Canada and Australia, which come closest to the U.S. model, have not suburbanized as much as we have.

But race and class homogeneity, anti-city attitudes, and political independence only partially explain suburbanization in the United States. In particular, our preferences for suburban living have been reflected in—some would say caused by—local, state, and federal government policies in areas such as transportation, housing, taxes, and the economy.

Suburbanization and Transportation Policy

The first U.S. suburbs date back to the early nineteenth century, when they were made up of the country homes or summer "cottages" of the rich. Only the upper class could afford them and the private horse-drawn carriages necessary to get to them. Working- and middle-class people stayed in the cities, to be near jobs and cheaper housing. Even rich businessmen spent most of their time in town to be near their banks and factories.

As technology advanced, more and more people gained access to the suburbs. Horse-drawn and later electric trolleys or sometimes trains enabled the professional classes to move to the suburbs after the turn of the century. Houses and lots grew a little smaller to accommodate them. Still the "streetcar suburbs" of the late nineteenth century were mostly an upper-class phenomenon, just edging into the upper middle class.

The technological development that made modern suburbia possible was the invention and mass production of the automobile. Cars were cheap and readily available by the 1920s, but it wasn't until after the Depression and World War II that auto ownership soared. But cars don't get you far without roads, so suburbanization couldn't have happened without the massive state and federal **highway construction** that followed World War II. Government highway spending was justified by expected economic benefits, more efficient commerce, and, in the case of the federal government, by defense needs (this was just after World War II and the Cold War was tense). But political support for highways was also massive. The driving (and voting) public wanted them. So did cities and local businesses hoping for growth. Land speculators and developers wanted highways to provide access to the new communities they planned. They joined the powerful highway lobby made up of auto manufacturers, tire makers, oil companies, construction firms, and others, resulting in the National Defense Highway Act of 1956, which dramatically increased the federal role in funding highway projects.

No wonder government built highways. The political support was immense, and for many years there was virtually no opposition, except the occasional neighborhood or farmer's objection to a particular route. The negative impact of highways on the environment and on central cities came to be widely realized only in the 1960s, and, although opposition is now more common, the highway lobby remains formidable.

Suburbanization and Housing Policy

Along with easy access, the other essential ingredient for suburbanization was affordable housing. Here, too, federal programs were essential. Because of the Great Depression and World War II, many young couples had delayed purchasing homes, so by the late 1940s, an enormous demand for housing had built up. During the war, with men unable to spend their service pay and many women working, many couples had saved considerable nest eggs, and the postwar baby boom made ownership even more desirable. But having families meant that the sort of home they wanted—a house with a yard and not an apartment—was in limited supply.

Cities weren't built that way and the price of city land was too high to make such single-family dwelling units economically feasible. Mortgage policies also made buying a home almost impossible for most families. Before the Depression, lending institutions required down payments of 40 to 50 percent of the house price, and loans were typically for less than ten years, so big monthly payments were necessary. When home building dropped off during the Depression, the Federal Housing Administration (FHA) was set up to stimulate the economy, encourage construction, and help people obtain housing. Through this and later other **housing programs** (such as Veterans Administration home loans under the GI Bill after World War II), the federal government stepped in to purchase or guarantee home mortgages, either lending the money itself or insuring loans to make banks more willing to lend (since they couldn't lose money). Government-sponsored mortgages required down payments of as little as 5 percent or less and for the first time allowed thirty years for payment.

The combination of pent-up demand and favorable mortgages created a booming housing market. In addition, a home-building "industry" emerged, providing cheaper housing through mass production. Instead of relatively expensive and unique individual houses constructed one at a time, builders bought huge tracts of land and threw up hundreds of identical houses. As with the automobile, factory production methods made **tract housing** ownership accessible to the masses.

But why was this housing built in suburbs rather than in central cities? We've already considered consumer preferences for the single-family housing of the suburbs and the frontier fantasy of small-town lifestyles. But suburbia was also vigorously sold to Americans through extensive advertising by developers and the highway lobby from the late 1940s onward. Movies and television helped, too. Hollywood portrayals of urban life emphasized crime and social disorder, while tales of suburbia were usually situation comedies that idealized suburbia, such as *Father Knows Best*, *Leave It to Beaver*, and *The Brady Bunch*, and more recently shows like *The OC*. Even Lucy and Ricky of *I Love Lucy* started the show in a New York City apartment, but ended up in suburban Connecticut. Were they reflecting the move to suburbia or encouraging it?

Suburbia did not need a hard sell, however, because there was usually no alternative. Little affordable housing was being built in most central cities outside the South and West. The high cost and limited availability of land in central cities raised the price of what was built and imposed higher densities than families with children wanted. And as the sparkling new suburbs were built, central cities deteriorated, with rising crime and poverty, racial conflict, decaying housing, and little government investment in renewal. To add insult to injury, lending institutions **redlined** entire urban neighborhoods, refusing mortgages for home purchases in central city neighborhoods, and federal mortgage assistance, readily available for the purchase of suburban homes, was almost impossible to obtain for central city homes until well into the 1970s. Until the 1960s, the Federal Housing Administration pursued policies that explicitly furthered ethnic and class segregation in the belief that neighborhood homogeneity was necessary to maintain social order.

Suburbanization, Land, and Taxes

Cars and highways were essential to suburbia only because they provided access to cheaper land on the urban periphery. Tract housing required big parcels of land, which were generally unavailable in well-developed central cities where land was also expensive, precisely because it was central. Builders thus went to the outskirts, buying up big areas cheaply, which helped keep the price of houses down so that more people could afford to buy.

But changes to federal tax code and other tax incentives beckoned. In the postwar period, the federal government allowed homeowners to deduct mortgage interest payments and even their property taxes from their federal income tax liability. Lower local government taxes were also an incentive to suburbanize. Local governments depend heavily on property taxes on buildings and land for their revenues. Suburban property taxes were often lower than those in central cities because property values were higher, and the costs of providing services in new, safe, low-density, healthy suburban communities were lower than in aging, crowded, sometimes-dangerous central cities. To meet higher service needs, many central cities imposed a variety of taxes in addition to the property tax, including taxes on sales, utilities, businesses, and sometimes even a local income tax. Most of these taxes could be avoided in the suburbs.

State and federal subsidies for highway building and other infrastructure needs, like sewage treatment facilities, also helped keep suburban taxes low, but the key to lower taxes was the political independence or autonomy of the suburbs. If the new tracts had been developed on the edges of the central city and then absorbed by it, residents would have paid the same taxes as other central city neighborhoods. But permissive state laws allowed suburbs to set up their own governments through the process of incorporation and thus levy their own taxes. In some cases, such as California's "Lakewood Plan" cities of the 1950s, state law allowed cities to incorporate cheaply by contracting with their county government for essential services such as police and fire.[11] Given these incentives, it's no wonder that many central city residents pulled up stakes and headed for the suburbs. Moreover, with ready access to cultural and economic benefits of the central city, but with few of the costs, suburbs were an attractive alternative to central city living, and not only for residents.

The Suburbanization of Jobs

The residents of traditional **dormitory suburbs** commute to the central city for jobs and amenities, such as shopping and entertainment. But some of the same things that made the suburbs attractive to individuals also attracted businesses (and thus jobs), which, in turn, attracted more people. Today, although many suburbs remain dormitory or "bedroom" communities, others are major centers of employment, competing with and envied by the central city.

As early as the 1950s, retailers started moving to the suburbs to be closer to their middle-class consumers. Industry followed. As with housing, land and taxes were major factors in the suburbanization of business. Plenty of cheap land meant that instead of costly high-rises with structural steel, elevators, and escalators, businesses could build low, inexpensive buildings. Outside the costly central city, they could even supply the parking that their auto-dependent customers and workers clambered for. Then, retailers discovered the shopping mall, almost completely abandoning downtown business districts. Industry built modern facilities in open fields and left central city factories to decay. Profits were increased by low suburban taxes, which could be as much as 40 to 50 percent less than in central cities. Retailers, manufacturers, and eventually service industries also discovered that the women of suburbia were a ready source of reliable, low-wage, nonunion, unskilled workers. Eager to attract these businesses for their jobs and taxes, suburban local governments helped with infrastructure improvements and special tax breaks, while the state and federal governments built highways to ensure ready access.

For all these reasons, businesses suburbanized. Between 1947 and 1957, the sixteen oldest and largest cities in the United States "lost an average of 34,000 manufacturing jobs each, while their suburbs gained an average of 87,000."[12] From 1960 onward, more new retail and industrial facilities located in suburbs than in central cities. In the 1970s, new communications technology enabled offices and service industries to join the migration to the suburbs. By the 1980s, well over half of all jobs within metropolitan areas were in suburbs rather than in central cities, their traditional home. By 1990, two-thirds of all the office space in the United States was in the suburbs.[13] The trend has only continued.

New development and the shift in employment to the suburbs have transformed U.S. urban regions so that instead of a traditional single, dominant central city surrounded by a constellation of suburbs, today many metropolitan areas have multiple centers made up of the old central city and other, newer concentrations that have been labeled **edge cities**.[14] Sprouting along freeways, often with gleaming, glass-enshrouded high-rises, edge cities cluster office employment and retail trade in a suburban rather than central city style, with shopping centers, office complexes, landscaping, and lots of parking. People feel safe in edge cities, not only because they provide high-profile security, but because only people who belong there go there. "They don't have to put up with the insecurity and disorder of public spaces," writes journalist William Schneider, because unlike such spaces in traditional cities, these have been "privatized. The difference between a mall and a downtown is that a mall is a private space, a secure environment."[15] Some edge cities are homogenized by race, class, and lifestyle. Some have housing, but workers often live elsewhere, commuting from suburb to edge city without ever going to the central city. In some places, the old commuting pattern from suburb to central city and back to suburb has been replaced by "bumper to bumper traffic in both directions."[16]

Jobs, which once drew people to cities, now draw them to the suburbs. As *Edge City* author Joel Garreau writes, "First, we moved our homes out past the traditional idea of what constituted a city. Then we moved our marketplaces out to where we lived. Today, we have moved our jobs out to where most of us have lived and shopped for two generations."[17] Some would substitute *they* for *we* since many central city residents do not have ready access to these jobs, but no one disputes the big change. "Suburbs," political scientist Carl Abbott declares, "are increasingly self-sustaining as economic entities to generate their own jobs"[18]—often at the expense of the central city.

The Suburban Imperative

Suburbanization is a nearly universal phenomenon. Even in a communist country like China, American-style automobile suburbs began popping up on the periphery of large cities such as Beijing during the 1990s, signaling their residents' rising social status and economic achievement. Wherever they can afford it, people seem to prefer the low-density housing, automobiles, privacy, and homogeneity of suburbia.

But in the United States, greater affluence, a rural past, vigorous marketing, racial intolerance, and economics all propelled suburbanization. So did politics, for these forces resulted in federal transportation and housing programs and state laws of taxation and incorporation that made suburbanization public policy in the United States. Suburbanization, in turn, reshaped local politics in the nation's urban areas.

The Impact of Suburbanization: Segregation and Inequity

Despite the increasing diversity among suburbs, the outstanding characteristic of U.S. metropolitan areas is the separation, isolation, and virtual segregation of population groups by race and class. Central cities concentrate racial minorities, the poor, the untrained, the unemployed, the old, the uninsured ill, people without cars, and aging, decaying housing. In suburbs, people are predominantly white, wealthier, better educated, employed, younger, healthier (and insured); they own cars and their housing is newer and better.

These **central city/suburban distinctions** are real, and in some places, they are increasing, especially in the older metropolitan areas of the Northeast and Midwest. A good illustration of the pattern can be found in Philadelphia. In greater Philadelphia, America's fifth largest metropolitan area, 85 percent of the richest families live in the suburbs while Philadelphia itself houses 80 percent of the region's poorest families. The city's 1990 population was 40 percent African American, while the region's was half that. Between 1953 and 1982, the city lost 18.5 percent of its population, 24.9 percent of its jobs, and 35.2 percent of its businesses, mostly to the suburbs. Between 1970 and 1990 alone, the city's population declined from 2 million to 1.5 million. The city's 2003 estimated population of 1.47 million suggests the trend has somewhat abated, at least for now.[19]

Philadelphia's pattern is fairly typical of the aging cities of the Northeast and Midwest. In contrast, most southern and western central cities have continued to grow and prosper, although even these cities are poor compared to their own suburbs. They also host large minority populations that, in many cities all over the country, are no longer in the minority. In 1990, minorities had become the majority in most of the largest U.S. cities and in 51 of the 200 cities with more than 100,000 people. Much of the change was due to immigration by Asians and Hispanics, as well as continued black migration, while whites continue to move from central cities to suburbs. The differences between central cities and suburbs are relative, of course. Suburbs are themselves diverse and central cities are internally diverse almost by definition, with people of all races and classes. The extremes between these groups is usually even greater within the central city than between the central city and the suburb, as bag-ladies harass fur-wearing shoppers getting out of limousines and street people sleep in cardboard boxes far below skyscraper penthouses. Nor are central cities completely integrated. Race and class groups are generally separated into different neighborhoods and districts. But the diversity of the central city is part of one larger entity, while diversity between the central city and the suburbs or between suburbs is isolated in politically separate and independent units. This political independence, achieved through state laws allowing communities to incorporate or form their own government, includes land-use powers and a tax structure that make segregation possible, generally legal, and perhaps even inevitable.

How Metropolitan Areas Are Segregated

Historically, a number of formal and informal mechanisms have been used to foster ethnic and class segregation in the United States. In the early part of the twentieth century, the homogeneity of suburbs was guaranteed by zoning laws as well as by local laws and restrictions written by developers into property deeds called **restrictive** (or racial) **covenants**. These restrictions forbid the sale of homes to members of designated racial and ethnic groups (most commonly African Americans and Jews, but also Latinos and Asians). Although the American South had its Jim Crow laws, urban areas in the rest of the country used racial covenants with much the same effect. Lending institutions and government agencies that guaranteed loans, including the FHA, reinforced these arrangements not only by accepting restrictive covenants but also by refusing loans to minorities who wanted homes in white suburbia.

The civil rights movement challenged housing discrimination beginning in the 1940s and gradually changed segregationist public policy. The U.S. Supreme Court banned the use of restrictive covenants for purposes of racial discrimination in 1948 (they can still be used to control such things as house size or height or fences). In the 1960s, President Kennedy banned housing discrimination in all federal programs by executive order, Congress prohibited racial discrimination in housing with the Fair Housing Act, and the Supreme Court made discrimination even in private home sales illegal. Most states passed similar legislation. By the time these laws were passed, however, suburban patterns of segregation were well established. Open housing laws helped break down these patterns to some extent and blatant racial discrimination is less common today, but many studies reveal the persistence of segregation in U.S. cities.

More subtle forms of racial discrimination, which may be hard to prove in law, are still around, however, even in the most tolerant communities. Besides the racist attitudes of some realtors and home sellers, minorities still have trouble getting mortgages. Repeated studies show that whether their incomes are low or high, African Americans and Hispanics are more likely than whites with similar incomes to be turned down for home loans. No wonder segregation persists.

Local control of land use is another mechanism of segregation and suburban homogeneity. When local governments are created through state incorporation laws, they are granted land-use, or **zoning**, powers to decide exactly what sort of development they want and where. This, along with the tax advantages already noted, impelled suburban developers and residents to form their own local governments rather than accept absorption by adjacent central cities. Besides lower taxes, they gain control of what happens within their boundaries, so the central city can't build hospitals or low-income housing on their doorsteps. Through their land-use powers, cities establish the class of their residents by the sorts of houses they allow. Such **exclu-**

sionary (or "snob") **zoning** may require large houses on large lots at specified distances from one another. Some cities zone their residential areas entirely R-1, meaning that only single-family, detached units are allowed, effectively banning multifamily or attached units such as condos.

Class segregation follows, not by outright banning of working- or middle-class people, but by pricing them out of the community. The rich can buy anywhere; others cannot. And because minority groups, on average, have lower incomes than whites, they are excluded from many areas.

Hence the segregation of suburbia. Exclusionary zoning has been challenged in state and federal courts, but in general it has been allowed except where it can be clearly proven that its discriminatory effects are intentional—an extremely high legal standard that is difficult to attain. In a series of famous 1970s and 1980s rulings known as the *Mount Laurel* decisions, the New Jersey Supreme Court ruled such exclusionary zoning unconstitutional and declared that new developments should include housing at varied prices. Although significant, these rulings were weakened in implementation by the state and its local governments.

Exclusionary zoning is not merely the result of prejudice, however. The structure of local land-use decisions makes it rational and almost inevitable. Imagine you are a council member in a suburban community. A landowner wants to develop a ten-acre property and offers the city a choice of ten houses on one-acre lots worth $2 million each or 100 townhouses at ten per acre priced at $200,000. Which would you choose? However much council members may worry about housing shortages, even the most progressive minded will usually opt for the big houses. Why? As noted above, the property tax is a major source of local revenue and its proceeds are based on property values. In this case, both developments would generate exactly the same tax income, but council members have to consider that the 100 homes will surely cost much more to service with police, fire protection, school, sewage treatment, and parks than the ten. The city might actually make more money in taxes on the ten than it costs to provide services, but could well lose money on the 100. To help the council decide, a group of people who live near the property are at the meeting to testify. Although their own homes are worth considerably less than $2 million, they support the expensive project and condemn the townhouses for their expected effect on congestion, parking, traffic, and the value of their own properties. No one is present to advocate the lower-cost homes.

This example is oversimplified, but a council in similar circumstances would have little choice. The resultant zoning might be considered exclusionary and would produce class and race segregation, yet given the relationship between zoning and taxes, the decision is economically rational, not necessarily prejudiced. The rules of the game of local governance, established by state government, provide various incentives. It should not surprise us when local governments use the tools at their disposal to the benefit of their community.

The same structural factors create the local growth machines discussed in the preceding chapters, impelling suburban local governments to pursue shopping centers, offices, and industry for the taxes they will generate, competing with one another and with the central city. Designating land for such developments is called

fiscal zoning because land use is determined by expected revenues rather than the need for a particular project or its impact on the environment, transportation, or regional balance. As with exclusionary zoning of housing, fiscal zoning creates tax-rich pockets of wealth within metropolitan areas. "Whether led by affluent homeowners or business factions," writes Mike Davis, "the ensuing maximization of local advantage through incorporation and fiscal zoning . . . inevitably produce[s] widening racial and income divides."[20]

In Your Community
Debate the merits of segregation by ethnicity and class. What are the costs and benefits of segregated urban areas?

Suburbanization and the Separation of Needs and Resources

The political autonomy, land-use policies, and tax structures of suburban local governments have created a general pattern of segregation and isolation in metropolitan areas, with affluent residents and economic prosperity in successful suburbs, and undesirable industry and large poor and minority populations concentrated in many declining suburbs and central cities. But the problem is not just the segregation and isolation of social groups, it is also the **separation of needs and resources**. The central city has the greater need, while the suburbs have the greater resources. Central city populations are more dependent on government services such as welfare, health care, transportation, housing, education, and police as well as recreation programs that they cannot privately afford. Willing workers often cannot find employment because jobs have moved to suburbs that many central city residents cannot reach. Half of the minority households of Boston, New York, and Philadelphia, for example, do not own automobiles.[21] The cost of operating, maintaining, and insuring a car can be prohibitive for somebody earning minimum wage. In contrast, suburbanites are generally economically secure and need fewer public services. They buy their own homes and cars and some join private clubs for recreation and even employ private security. But while the need is in the central city, the tax resources that might pay for the services are greater in the suburbs.

With higher home and property values, industries, shopping centers, and edge city office complexes, suburbs have a rich financial base that they can tax lightly because of lower needs or demands for services. Central cities still contain valuable property and prosperous businesses, but these must be taxed heavily to provide the higher service levels needed for large, dependent populations. Central cities are older, too, and their aging infrastructure, including roads and sewers, costs more to maintain. "Big suburban commercial and industrial projects are putting all the tax-base growth in places that don't share the central city's costs in terms of maintaining an older infrastructure or caring for the elderly, the poor, and the sick,"[22] says the mayor of Fort Worth, Texas, a relatively well-off central city. Although some states have moved to equalize spending for education, nationally, per-pupil spending in central city school districts is lower than in most suburban districts.

Whatever the policy area, the combination of greater resources and less need enables suburbs to tax lightly and still provide good services. Central cities, with declining resources and greater need, must tax heavily just to try to keep things from growing worse, but they are caught in a vicious circle because their heavy taxes drive away industry and commerce and increase the tax burden on the already overburdened poor. This needs/resources separation results from the political independence of the suburbs, which naturally act to maintain and expand their tax bases. They also seek to protect property values for their home-owning constituents and to preserve the racial and class homogeneity of their communities.

Thus, central cities are stuck with a declining tax base and older infrastructure, as well as large numbers of people who need public services. Ironically, many of the people in need come from the surrounding suburbs where, for various reasons, they are unable to stay. They may be old or ill, or alcoholics or drug addicts, or bad economic times may have made them homeless. Most suburbs do not welcome such people or help them stay. Suburban police forces usually instruct the homeless to "move along" or risk being arrested. Instead, they are absorbed by more tolerant central cities, which then must provide the needed services even as their tax resources trickle away to the suburbs.

Suburbanites go to central cities for entertainment, sports, and tourist attractions. They go to the central city to work and shop (though in smaller numbers than in years past) and expect public services to ease and make safe their commute and their presence. From the standpoint of central cities, as a mayor of Pittsburgh once stated bluntly, "The people in the suburbs use our facilities but won't pay for them."[23] In short, neither suburbs and nor central cities can stand alone; they are socially and economically interdependent. As the mayor of Louisville, Kentucky, said in the early 1990s, "You can't be a suburb of nowhere."[24]

But despite their social and economic interdependence, metropolitan areas are politically fragmented due to the multiplicity of local governments. In some other countries, however, both central cities and suburbs are part of one large governmental entity. In this situation, suburbs, which are still homogeneous, are considered neighborhoods within the larger city rather than being politically independent. Taxes and service needs are shared.

In most of the United States, however, metropolitan areas are divided into small, autonomous units. This results not only in the separation of needs and resources but also in the fragmentation of government in urban regions, a topic that we will explore further in chapter 14. The average metropolitan area has ninety local governments, which may be "democratic," but which makes solving regional problems like air pollution and transportation almost impossible because nobody is in charge. (See Figure 3.1 for an example of extreme fragmentation.) Only a few central cities, such as Charlotte, San Antonio, and Houston, have managed to avoid this fragmentation by annexing their suburbs, thus retaining a more diversified population and a stronger tax base.

Political **fragmentation** is taken for granted in most metropolitan areas, but it is

Figure 3.1   **Urban Fragmentation: Los Angeles Metropolitan Area**

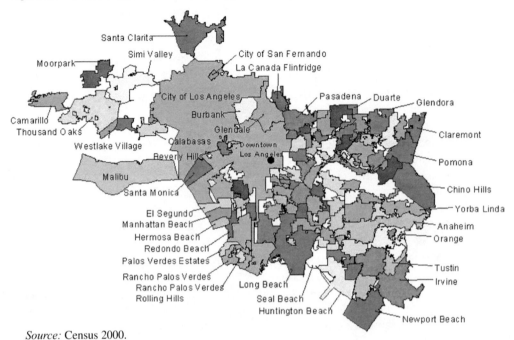

Source: Census 2000.

not inevitable. It is important to remember that segregation, unequal services and taxes, and fragmentation are the results of politics and public policy choices. The multiplicity of local governments, and their land-use and taxing powers all come from the state and reflect the formidable political power of suburban residents and economic interests.

Today's Suburbs: Exclusion and Diversity

Although the traditional dormitory suburb survives—and in many places still thrives—suburbia in the United States has undergone several important changes in recent years. Today's suburban areas are far more likely to be poorer and more ethnically diverse than suburbs thirty years ago. Today, only about a third of all suburbs are exclusively residential, while a third mix housing and jobs, and a third are mainly **employing suburbs** or edge cities. Much of the employment in such places is in services and offices, but some older suburbs still host manufacturing industries as well. The important point is that as suburbia changes, our notions of suburbia need to change with it.

Once dominated by families with small children, today's suburbs house many singles, working couples without children, and empty-nesters who still live in the family home after their children have grown up and moved away. Residential suburbs as a whole have become more diverse in terms of class and ethnicity, although the diversity is usually greater between suburbs than within a single suburb. A majority of residential suburbs are, broadly speaking, middle class, although this

Table 3.1

Ten Most-Segregated Metropolitan Areas, Blacks and Whites, 2000

Metropolitan area	Index of dissimilarity
Detroit, Michigan	85
Milwaukee, Wisconsin	82
New York, New York	82
Chicago, Illinois	81
Newark, New Jersey	80
Cleveland, Ohio	77
Cincinnati, Ohio	75
Nassau-Suffolk, New York	74
St. Louis, Missouri	74
Miami, Florida	74

Source: Lewis Mumford Center for Comparative Urban and Regional Research, 2001.

covers a considerably wide income range. The best-known American suburbs in most areas are still the richest, with multimillion-dollar homes, excellent schools, private security systems, and gated communities. Indeed, data from the 2000 Census show that the number of "rich" suburbs is increasing, mirroring increasing class divisions of the larger society over the past couple of decades.

But most American suburbs now defy traditional notions of suburban affluence. Recent data suggest an accelerating **suburbanization of poverty**, as many suburbs now contain significant numbers of working poor. In hundreds of American suburbs, a majority of residents have incomes below the poverty level, including Florida City (outside Miami), Camden, New Jersey (near Philadelphia), Bell Gardens (Los Angeles), Ford Heights (Chicago), and East St. Louis. Roughly 14 million poor Americans now live in suburbs, only slightly less than the number of poor who live in cities.[25]

There is also evidence that some American metropolitan areas became less ethnically segregated during the 1990s. According to a Brookings Institution study of America's largest metropolitan areas, "the number of predominantly white neighborhoods fell by 30 percent during the 1990s."[26] Black Americans also became less segregated by 2000, although they continue to be more segregated than other ethnic groups.[27] Table 3.1 shows the top ten most-segregated metropolitan areas for blacks and whites, as measured by the **index of dissimilarity**, a standard measure of segregation. With the exception of Miami, all of the cities are in either the Northeast or Midwest.

On the other hand, Hispanics and Asians became somewhat more segregated during the 1990s, although much of that segregation was due to sheer population growth. Census data also show that Asians are more likely to live among whites, while Hispanics are more likely to live among blacks. Clearly, the image of suburbia has changed and is now far more complex. Still, the data from Census 2000 may reveal a new reality. At least for America's largest metropolitan areas, "a striking new level of racial and ethnic mixing occurred in the nation's major metropolitan areas during the 1990s."[28]

Despite continuing segregation, the data also show that many minorities are living the American dream in suburbs. In the 1970s, African Americans and later Hispanics and Asians started moving to the working- and middle-class suburbs in greater numbers. During the 1990s, Joel Garreau pointed out that 40 percent of the African American families in Atlanta are suburbanites and estimated that one-third of the black population of the United States was "largely suburban middle class."[29] Altogether, minorities make up about 27 percent of the suburban populace, up from 19 percent in 1990. Still, significant differences remain. Seventy-two percent of whites live in suburbs, whereas the rate is 49 percent for Hispanics and only 39 percent for blacks.[30] But while contemporary suburbs are becoming racially diverse, they are not necessarily integrated. With a few exceptions, many are examples of what UCLA population geographer James H. Johnson calls "suburban ghettoes"[31]—concentrations of poverty that are overwhelmingly minority.

Immigration (which will be discussed later) has also changed the face of suburban America. As of 2000, astonishingly, more immigrants were living in suburbs than in the nation's central cities. Although some of the new immigrants are highly skilled, such as Asian Indian engineers or Chinese scientists, as we saw in chapter 2, most of the growth of immigrant suburbs is supported by jobs at the low end of the service and manufacturing sectors. In some cities such as Los Angeles and Chicago, entire industries now rely almost exclusively upon immigrant labor.

In sum, the overall picture of America's new suburbs has changed radically since the 1950s. Yet, many of the reasons people move to suburbs remain the same: a house they can afford, a community where they fit in and feel safe, better schools for the kids, a job. Recent data underscore the fact that popular stereotypes of suburbia as uniformly wealthy, conservative, and white—although those places still exist—are increasingly outdated. The key point is that the movement to suburbs appears to be a nearly universal aspiration of Americans. Although our suburbs will probably never be completely integrated in terms of ethnicity and class, for most people, homeownership in the suburbs continues to embody the American dream.

Suburbanization and Local Politics

Finally, in addition to its impact on the distribution of needs and resources, suburbanization also has an effect on the internal politics of communities. The differing populations of central cities and suburbs predictably lead to different policy priorities, although as suburbs change, their priorities may begin to align more with central cities. In general, however, central cities worry about decaying infrastructure, public transportation, welfare, AIDS, homelessness, drugs, gangs, and the urban underclass. Suburbs worry about streets, highways, taxes, growth control, and maintenance of their quality of life. Both, however, fret about their tax base and schools, although the latter is a particular obsession of suburbia. The increasing concentration of poverty and large numbers of recent immigrants has prompted some observers to note that growing pains resulting from increased strain on schools, health services, and other infrastructures are now increasingly felt also in suburbs.[32]

The nature of politics, political participation, and institutions differ, too. In homogeneous suburbs, where everybody is more or less alike, people agree on most issues. Politics is low key and often consensual, with little conflict or competition. Big cities, in contrast, are heterogeneous. All sorts of different people with all sorts of different interests engage in politics, which is often both competitive and conflictual. With such differences in political behavior, suburbs and central cities often opt for different governmental structures and institutions, as we will see in chapters 5 and 6.

The Move to the Sunbelt: New Urban Forms

Even as suburbanization transformed U.S. metropolitan areas, a third great population movement was under way: the population shift from the Frostbelt to the **Sunbelt**. By the 1970s, the old central cities of the Northeast and Midwest were losing population and growth because people were moving not just to different parts of urban areas but to different parts of the country—in particular the South and West—where both central cities and suburbs were growing by leaps and bounds. Although there is no universally agreed-upon definition, the Sunbelt is generally assumed to be the band of states that runs across the southern United States from Virginia down through Florida and west to Colorado, Utah, Arizona, and California. If we also include the less sunny states of Oregon and Washington, this area of the United States has grown the fastest in the past three decades. In 1960, 54 percent of the U.S. population lived in the Frostbelt states of the Northeast and Midwest, while 46 percent lived in the South and West. By 1990, those figures had been more than reversed, with 44 percent in the Frostbelt and 56 percent in the Sunbelt.

Between 1990 and 2000, the population of United States grew by nearly 33 million people, the largest census-to-census increase in American history, surpassing even the post–World War II population boom of the 1950s. But unlike in the 1950s, the bulk of the population growth took place in the South and West. Out of the total 2000 population of 281,421,906, more than 100 million—36 percent of Americans—lived in southern states, an explosion of nearly 15 million residents since 1990. Sixty-four million residents, or 23 percent of the total population, resided in the Midwest, an increase of more than 4.7 million people during the 1990s. Sixty-three million Americans, or 22 percent of the nation, lived in western states, while just 53 million, or 19 percent of Americans, lived in the Northeast. All indications point to continuing immigration to the Sunbelt states of the West and South.

Although the Northeast actually lost population during the 1970s, for most of the 1990s the total metropolitan population of the Frostbelt increased slowly. This growth, however, was almost exclusively in the suburbs, with populations in some central cities shrinking, sometimes dramatically. For example, between 1950 and 1990, Philadelphia and Chicago each lost 23 percent of their populations—a total of 1.3 million people! Chicago's population has rebounded somewhat, gaining 112,000 people between 1990 and 2000, while Philadelphia continued its slide. Between 1980 and 1990 alone, Detroit lost 20 percent of its population, and an additional 3 percent by 2000, and has since fallen out of the top ten most populous cities (see Table 2.1). According to the U.S. Census, former manufacturing powerhouses Cleveland, Cincinnati, and Flint, Michigan, were all among many Frostbelt cities that bled population during the 1990s and early 2000s.

Meanwhile, Sunbelt cities boomed, growing at more than double the national rate. San Jose, California, for example, grew tenfold, from less than 95,000 people in 1950 to nearly 950,000 in 2005. Between 1990 and 2000 alone, Las Vegas, Nevada, grew by 83 percent; Naples, Florida, by 65 percent; Yuma, Arizona, by 50 percent; and so on. By 2005, seven of the nation's ten largest cities were west of the Mississippi River (see Table 2.1). Unlike the central cities of the Frostbelt, which had become geographically "boxed-in" by surrounding independent suburbs, the relatively young central cities of the Sunbelt were able to grow by expanding their boundaries by annexing adjacent areas.

By the 1990s, however, the incorporation of independent cities on the urban periphery was also bringing the territorial expansion of Sunbelt central cities to a halt. Most continued to grow in population, but more slowly, even as growth in their suburbs took off. Mesa, Arizona, a suburb of Phoenix, grew by 89 percent in the 1980s, reaching the sizable population of 288,091 in 1990, and expanding to roughly 450,000 residents by 2005. During the 1980s, Rancho Cucamonga, a Los Angeles suburb, doubled in population from 55,250 to 101,409, and to more than 160,000 by 2005. Bellevue, a suburb of Seattle that had a 1990 population of 87,000, grew to more than 117,000 by 2005. Some of these places are better described as edge cities than suburbs, as are booming Sunbelt areas such as Orange County, California, which has no central city at all.

One of the more interesting population trends reported by Census 2000 was a "reverse" migration of African Americans to southern states during the 1990s. Most of the people who moved to the South during the 1990s were white, but African Americans also began returning in droves. Recall the "Great Migration" of the first half of the twentieth century, in which racism and economic deprivation drove many blacks from the South to northern cities like Chicago and New York, as well as to western cities such as San Francisco and Los Angeles. During the 1990s, however, those same cities experienced the greatest out-migration of blacks. Southern states such as Georgia, North Carolina, and Florida and metropolitan areas such as Atlanta, Dallas, and Charlotte were the largest recipients of black immigrants. Demographers explained the population reversal as partly the result of younger professional blacks reestablishing cultural and familial connections to the region, as well as the return of empty-nesters and retirees, many of whom had left the South in their youth. Researchers also cited improved race relations, cheap housing, and economic opportunity as reasons for the "New Great Migration."[33] Some are now wondering whether the hurricanes Katrina and Rita of 2005 have sparked a permanent large-scale out-migration of blacks from devastated communities in and around New Orleans.

During the 1990s and early 2000s, Mexican Americans and Mexican immigrants also settled in Sunbelt cities, especially in California and Texas, where a majority of all U.S. Hispanics reside. Florida also has a large population of Hispanics, most of whom are Cubans who fled there after the 1959 Cuban Revolution and settled in Miami. In recent years, Florida has seen increasing numbers of immigrants from Colombia, Venezuela, the Dominican Republic, and other Latin American and

Caribbean nations. Asians have also been drawn to the Sunbelt, especially after the Vietnam War, as well as more recently. Today over half of all U.S. Asians live in just three states—California, New York, and Hawaii.[34]

Some parts of the Sunbelt, particularly the South, enjoyed spectacular growth during the 1990s. However, not all Sunbelt states grew at a rapid clip. "Cold" Sunbelt states such as Oklahoma, Mississippi, and Arkansas saw only tepid growth, whereas "hot" Sunbelt states Florida, Texas, and Arizona witnessed extremely rapid growth.[35] By the 1990s, growth had leveled off in once-booming California, with new arrivals (mostly Asian and Hispanic) barely equaling those (mostly whites) who were leaving. Nor did all cities in the Frostbelt shrink; in the 1980s and 1990s, some states such as New Hampshire and Vermont even enjoyed modest growth. As a general trend, though, Sunbelt growth continues to put that of the Frostbelt in the shade.

IN YOUR COMMUNITY
How did your community fare during the 1990s in terms of population growth? What were the driving factors?

Why the Sunbelt Grew

The obvious reason for the Sunbelt boom was its climate, but good weather wasn't new to the region; other factors were even more important. World War II, for example, introduced millions of Americans to the Sunbelt on their way to the war in the Pacific. Many liked it and resolved to return. In addition, post–World War II affluence enabled more Americans to take vacations, and tourism, aided by Walt Disney and other legendary promoters, became a mainstay of some Sunbelt economies. Increased affluence along with social security and Medicare programs also meant that there was a larger and healthier elderly population, many members of which chose to retire in warmer climates. Natural resources, including oil, uranium, and agricultural land irrigated by federal projects built from the 1930s onward, gave Sunbelt growth further impetus.

Tourism, retirees, and natural resources primed the pump, but real growth was stimulated by economic and technological developments. Foremost among these were the electronics, aerospace, and defense industries. These were burgeoning industries, free to build new facilities where the economic advantages were greatest—in the Sunbelt. In contrast to the Frostbelt, Sunbelt workers were underemployed, lower-wage, and, for the most part, not unionized, while cheap housing and good weather continued to draw more workers from other regions. Land was cheap and plentiful, so companies could build inexpensive low-rise plants, and start-up costs were low. Energy was also cheap and plentiful, and warm weather reduced heating costs. The new industries relied on highways and air transportation and on electronic communications, so they did not need to be physically close to the transportation network of ships, barges, and railroads that were the backbone of heavy industry in the Northeast and Midwest.

As with suburbanization, the federal government aided the shift to the Sunbelt with its highway and home loan programs, but other federal spending also disproportionately benefited the Sunbelt. The 1960s and 1970s saw "a massive flow of wealth from the Northeast and Midwest to the fast-growing Southern and Western Regions," led by **defense spending**.[36] With around 10 percent of the U.S. population during these years, California alone raked in as much as 25 percent of the nation's defense expenditures. In addition, aerospace funding went mostly to California, Florida, Texas, and Washington. The new electronics industries of the Sunbelt grew in association with these industries and as a result of federal contracts of their own. These lucrative deals were not, however, the cause of industrial expansion in the Sunbelt. Rather, new and expanding industries—particularly high tech—located in the region for its economic advantages. Like powerful magnets, industry attracted both government and private investment, fueling further growth.

The cities of the Sunbelt were not passive or accidental beneficiaries of these developments. Local growth machines were in high gear, aggressively wooing industry and actively hustling federal spending. Their leaders were confident, probusiness, progrowth, can-do people. They were boosters and their boosting became the stuff of legend. Federal, state, and local funds provided the infrastructure —roads, sewers, water systems, sewage treatment plants, and air and water ports— needed by industry. Virtually new cities were built, and built to suit. Meanwhile, the cities of the Northeast and Midwest, saddled with aging infrastructures, relatively expensive land and labor, high taxes, increasingly dependent populations, and competition from their own suburbs, could not adapt to the needs of the new industries. They soon began to stagnate.

New Urban Forms: Suburban Edge Cities

The Sunbelt phenomenon involved not only a shift in population, but a **new urban form**, a shift, according to Robert Fishman:

> toward urban areas that had been "born decentralized" and organized on new-city principles. The new city lacks what gave shape and meaning to every urban form in the past: a dominant single core and definable boundaries. At most, it contains a multitude of centers, or "edge cities," more-or-less unified clusters of malls, office developments, and entertainment complexes that rise where major highways cross or converge . . . Without anybody intending it . . . decentralization washed over America . . . The single center had lost its dominance [and was no longer able] to monopolize the life of a region.[37]

The concept of edge cities, almost exclusively a suburban phenomenon in the East, characterizes even central cities in the Sunbelt. In short, Sunbelt cities are suburbia writ large. For the most part economically self-sustaining and lower in density and diversity than their Frostbelt equivalents, the lifestyles and even politics of some Sunbelt central cities are more like those of traditional suburbs than big cities. In addition to decentralization, Sunbelt central cities share with suburbs the attributes of predominantly single-family housing, high rates of homeownership, almost total dependence on automobiles for transportation, commuting workers (often to suburbs), and concerns about coping with growth rather than decay. Political priorities differ as well, and local politics is often more consensual than conflictual, although this too is changing as these areas attract more diversity. Accordingly, voter and interest group participation is often lower than in Frostbelt cities, and government structures vary as well. These differences arise partly because Sunbelt cities are new and their political systems have not kept up with their rapid growth. Some still operate with the same institutions and even players as when they were smaller cities, forcing some cities to adapt their political institutions to a new demographic environment.

In the 1980s and 1990s, cut off from further expansion by surrounding suburbs that were outpacing growth in the central city, many big Sunbelt cities found themselves confronted with problems long familiar to those of the Frostbelt: racial conflict, infrastructure decay, homelessness, crime, drugs, gangs, and AIDS. In some cases, traffic congestion and smog were even worse, as auto-dependent Sunbelt cities usually lacked mass-transit alternatives. Then in the early 1990s, seemingly out of nowhere, the federal bounty they had enjoyed for so long suddenly stopped. With the collapse of the Soviet Union in 1989, the Cold War was declared over, resulting in massive cuts in federal defense and aerospace spending. The Los Angeles region alone lost more than 100,000 such jobs. By 1991, unemployment there was higher than in Pittsburgh or Philadelphia. This pattern was not consistent across the Sunbelt and Frostbelt, as many Frostbelt cities even enjoyed a mild revival, partly because their previous decline had again made them economically attractive to industry, and partly because Sunbelt cities were beginning to price themselves out of the market. They also found themselves competing with and envious of their own suburbs and facing growing central city/suburban disparities in class, race, and needs and resources.

Although the Frostbelt pattern has asserted itself in the Sunbelt, cities there are still unique and so are their problems. They contend more with rapid growth and providing services, like suburbs elsewhere, while Frostbelt cities struggle to reverse decay and decline. Compared to Frostbelt cities, they remain well off, growing rather than shrinking, with lower taxes and greater resources. The disparities between Sunbelt and Frostbelt cities are almost as great as those between Frostbelt central cities and their suburbs, underscoring the fact that the needs/resources dichotomy operates on a national scale. Frostbelt cities have sought federal aid to help redress the balance, but until recently, the Sunbelt has benefited disproportionately from federal support.

By the 1990s and 2000s, the megatrends of urbanization, suburbanization, and the move to the Sunbelt continued to transform politics both nationally and locally. As the suburbs and the Sunbelt grew in tandem, so did their political influence in Congress and in state legislatures. Certainly, population growth in the Sunbelt almost certainly will continue to shift the balance of power west and south. In particular, suburbanization and growth of the Sunbelt looked set to continue through the latter half of the 2000s.

Population Trends in the 1990s and 2000s

We now know that suburbs, particularly those in the Sunbelt, continue to experience rapid growth. We learned that the process of urbanization took off during the nineteenth and twentieth centuries, particularly as a result of industrialization and technological change. We then learned of the reasons for the rise of suburbs, including our cultural values and government subsidy. But what has happened to the nation's large cities?

During the 1990s and early 2000s, two important, and somewhat interrelated, trends emerged: (1) a back-to-the-city movement, and (2) substantial immigration from abroad. Both trends—particularly where they reinforced one another—served to dramatically alter the landscape of urban America.

Reviving Central Cities

In some parts of the country, a process of re-urbanization took hold in the 1990s and proceeded through the 2000s, as metropolitan areas continued growing, especially in the Sunbelt and along both coasts. Many central cities became re-colonized, and in a sense rediscovered, by urban professionals and some businesses. In their book *Comeback Cities*, authors Paul S. Grogan and Tony Proscio documented the resurgence of central cities such as Boston, Cleveland, Milwaukee, and Houston, all of which had witnessed serious economic decline at some point during the 1960s, '70s, and '80s. As the authors show, in a sense, these cities' decline sowed the seeds for their resurgence. Rising house prices and wages in the suburbs, along with traffic congestion, drove some industries back to the central core. The authors also credit municipal privatization strategies and public-private partnerships as reasons for these cities' revival.[38]

Indeed, downtown redevelopment, usually as part of a tourism-based strategy, has become all the rage. Older cities such as Baltimore and Boston have capitalized on their historic cores to re-create functional downtown public space while generating redevelopment dollars. In many cases, older and sometimes even abandoned buildings in the downtown core have been brought back to life as artists' lofts, office space, or residential units. In addition, other demographic factors such as immigration and the rising number of singles and couples without children also stimulated reinvestment in some central cities. As middle-class professionals, artists, gays, singles, and others moved into attractive, if slightly run-down, older neighborhoods near the center, investors began renovating the housing stock, revitalizing business districts, and improving the central city tax base.

But the trend of downtown revitalization brought negative consequences for some. **Gentrification**—the displacement of lower-income residents as a result of outside investment, usually with the middle class—raised downtown property values and rents, reducing housing availability for low-income residents, in many cases displacing them entirely from their neighborhoods. Progressive cities such as New York, Los Angeles, and Berkeley, California, have for years employed "rent control" policies limiting the amount landlords can raise rents in an attempt to combat the displacement of low-income residents. Increasingly, progressive-minded cities are also using "inclusionary zoning," which requires developers to build a minimum number of low-income units along with market-rate units, in order to provide incentives for the construction of low-income housing. Still, the poor will always be far more vulnerable to displacement than affluent residents.

No one knows for sure whether the "back-to-the-city" movement is temporary or something more permanent. In any case, the revitalization of American downtowns during the 1990s and 2000s was a welcome reversal of, in some cases, decades of stagnation and decline.

Recent Immigration Trends

In addition to the back-to-the-city movement by former suburbanites and young professionals, a second important trend has emerged to alter American metropolitan areas even more. The population of many central cities also grew significantly from immigration from abroad. The foreign-born population of New York City alone, for example, grew from 2.1 million in 1990 (already an impressive figure) to 2.9 million in 2000—and it continues to grow. The period since 1990 represents a decade and a half of unprecedented levels of immigration to the United States. In raw numbers, immigration levels far surpassed those of the decades of the late nineteenth and early twentieth centuries. Although it is too soon to predict whether immigration levels will continue, level off, or decline, it is clear that immigration from abroad has fundamentally reshaped urban America.

According to the 2000 U.S. Census, 11 percent of the nation's population was foreign born, second only to the 1900 Census, which counted 14 percent of the population as foreign born. Since 1990, the foreign-born population has increased by 57 percent, from 19.8 million to 31.1 million in 2000.[39] In particular, immigration from Latin America and Asia increased dramatically. By 2000, more than 52 percent of the total foreign-born population in the United States was from Latin America, with another 26 percent coming from Asia.[40] According to Table 3.2, Mexicans represent by far the largest portion of foreign born in the United States, followed by immigrants from China (including Taiwan and Hong Kong), and the Philippines. Although the numbers have undoubtedly changed since 2000, Latin America and Asia continue to be the main sources of immigration to the United States.

According to Census 2000, more than half of the nation's foreign-born population lived in just three states: California, New York, and Texas. California alone contained more than a quarter of the nation's total foreign-born population. Table 3.3 shows the top ten large American cities in terms of percent foreign born in 2000. In addition to important "post–World War II gateway" destinations such as Miami and Los Angeles, cities such as Atlanta, Dallas, and Washington, DC, functioned as new "emerging gateway" cities for immigrants.[41] Immigration fundamentally reshaped both the central core as well as the surrounding suburbs of these and other gateway cities. Suburbs such as Hialeah, Florida, and Glendale, California, are examples of two cities that have seen a tremendous influx from abroad in recent years. Hialeah has been transformed by immigrants mostly from Cuba, while Glendale has seen a tremendous rise in its Armenian and Latino populations. The examples underscore the degree to which immigration's impacts extend well beyond the nation's central cities. According to a Brookings Institution study, "by 2000, more immigrants in metropolitan areas lived in suburbs than in cities."[42]

Rural areas, many of which had almost no foreign-born populations as recently as

Table 3.2

Top Ten Countries of Foreign Born in the United States, 2000

Country of birth	Number	Percent of foreign-born population
Mexico	9,177,487	29.5
China[a]	1,518,652	4.9
Philippines	1,369,070	4.4
India	1,022,552	3.3
Vietnam	988,174	3.2
Cuba	872,716	2.8
Korea[b]	864,125	2.8
Canada	820,771	2.6
El Salvador	817,336	2.6
Germany	706,704	2.3
Total	18,157,587	

Source: U.S. Census Bureau, Census 2000, Summary File 3.
[a]Includes Taiwan and Hong Kong.
[b]Includes North and South Korea.

1990, have also witnessed dramatic changes as a result of immigration. According to Census Bureau analyses by geographic region, the South saw its number of foreign born increase by 88 percent during the decade of the 1990s, while the Midwest (65 percent) and Northeast (38 percent) also saw dramatic increases. Many of these immigrants ended up in rural, or what the Census calls "non-metropolitan," areas. According to Census 2000, rates of Hispanic growth exceeded 60 percent in rural counties during the 1990s, far higher than any other ethnic group. Hispanics filled not only low-paying seasonal jobs in agriculture, but also jobs in manufacturing, meat packing, construction, mining, and service industries. In many cases, immigration served to staunch communities' population losses, propping up fledgling industries and creating new ones. As always, with change came growing pains, as long-time residents, many of whom are themselves descendents of previous waves of European immigration, expressed anxiety over the loss of community cohesiveness.

Latin-American Immigration

By far the largest increase in foreign immigration to the United States during the 1990s and 2000s has come from Latin America, and in particular Mexico and Central America. During the decade of the 1990s, the Hispanic population grew by 58 percent, to 35.3 million. As of 2004, the U.S. Census estimates that 1 in 7 residents—41.3 million people—is "Hispanic." Table 3.4 shows the fifteen states with the largest Hispanic populations. Not surprisingly, states such as California, Texas, New Mexico, New York, and Florida that top the list have more established Hispanic populations, but the fastest growth is taking place in states such as North Carolina, Georgia, and Pennsylvania, where **Hispanic immigration** is a relatively recent phenomenon.

Table 3.3

Ten Places of 100,000 or More Population with the Highest Percentage of Foreign Born, 2000

Place and state	Total population	Percent foreign-born
Hialeah, Florida	226,419	72.1
Miami, Florida	362,470	59.5
Glendale, California	194,973	54.4
Santa Ana, California	337,977	53.2
Daly City, California	103,621	52.3
El Monte, California	115,965	51.4
East Los Angeles, California*	124,283	48.8
Elizabeth, New Jersey	120,568	43.9
Garden Grove, California	165,196	43.2
Los Angeles, California	3,694,820	40.9
Total United States	281,421,906	11.1

Source: U.S. Census Bureau, Census 2000, Summary File 3.
*East Los Angeles is a Census-designated place and is not legally incorporated.

Table 3.4

Fifteen States with Largest Hispanic Populations, 2000

State	Hispanic population*	Percent Hispanic
California	10,967,000	32.4
Texas	6,670,000	32.0
New York	2,868,000	15.1
Florida	2,683,000	16.8
Illinois	1,530,000	12.3
Arizona	1,296,000	25.3
New Jersey	1,117,000	13.3
New Mexico	765,000	42.1
Colorado	736,000	17.1
Washington	442,000	7.5
Georgia	435,000	5.3
Massachusetts	429,000	6.8
Pennsylvania	394,000	3.2
Nevada	394,000	19.7
North Carolina	379,000	4.7

Source: U.S. Census Bureau, Census 2000.
*Population rounded.

The sheer pace of Hispanic population growth during the 1990s, a combination of immigration and higher birth rates, caught some demographers by surprise. Census 2000 revealed that Hispanics had surpassed African Americans as the nation's largest ethnic minority, a milestone many experts had anticipated would arrive somewhere around 2005. In some circles, leaders worried that issues of concern to African Americans would be pushed to the back burner, underscoring the extent to which immigration and ethnic politics remain politically charged.

It is important to note that the U.S. Census does not consider Hispanics, also referred to as "Latinos," to be a separate racial group. The U.S. Census asks respondents to choose among the following six racial categories: 1) White, 2) Black or African American, 3) American Indian or Alaska Native, 4) Asian, 5) Native Hawaiian and Other Pacific Islander, and 6) Some Other Race. Census 2000 marked the first time that respondents could select more than one race, including a seventh separate category: "Two or More Races." Latinos, therefore, frequently choose between the categories of "white" and "other," with roughly 48 percent identifying themselves as "white," and approximately 42 percent selecting "Some Other Race." The number of Hispanics or Latinos can be ascertained because the Census, in addition to race, asks respondents to also identify whether they are of Hispanic origin.[43]

The issue of whether Latinos are "white" is not just semantics. Sociologists and historians tell us that the ability of immigrants to assimilate into "whiteness" directly impacts on an immigrant group's economic status in society. "Whiteness" is a status for which almost all immigrant groups to the United States have had to struggle.[44] One of the important questions of the twenty-first century will be whether Latinos will follow the path of assimilation of earlier white ethnic groups such as the Irish, Italians, and Jews, or whether Latinos will maintain a separate ethnic identity, or something in between.

Asian/Pacific Islander Immigration

Since 1990, the second-fastest-growing immigrant group in United States has been Asians/Pacific Islanders. From a population of about 1 million in 1960, Asians/Pacific Islanders increased to more than 12 million by 2005, roughly 4.2 percent of the total U.S. population.

As with Hispanics, the U.S. Asian/Pacific Islander population is extremely diverse in terms of language, culture, and length of residency in the United States. For example, more established communities of Chinese, Japanese, and Filipino Americans trace their origins in the United States to the late nineteenth and early twentieth centuries. Invariably, these groups were both "pushed" by harsh economic conditions and/or war in their home country and "pulled" by economic opportunity in labor-intensive industries such as mining, railroad construction, and farming. Like other immigrant groups, Asians faced widespread discrimination and were systematically denied basic citizenship rights until well into the twentieth century. Asian immigrant groups such as Vietnamese, Laotians, Cambodians, and Hmong immigrated more recently, also as a result of war and economic instability.

Increases in **Asian/Pacific Islander immigration** during the 1980s and 1990s

Figure 3.2 **Diversity Among Asian Subgroups, Census 2000**

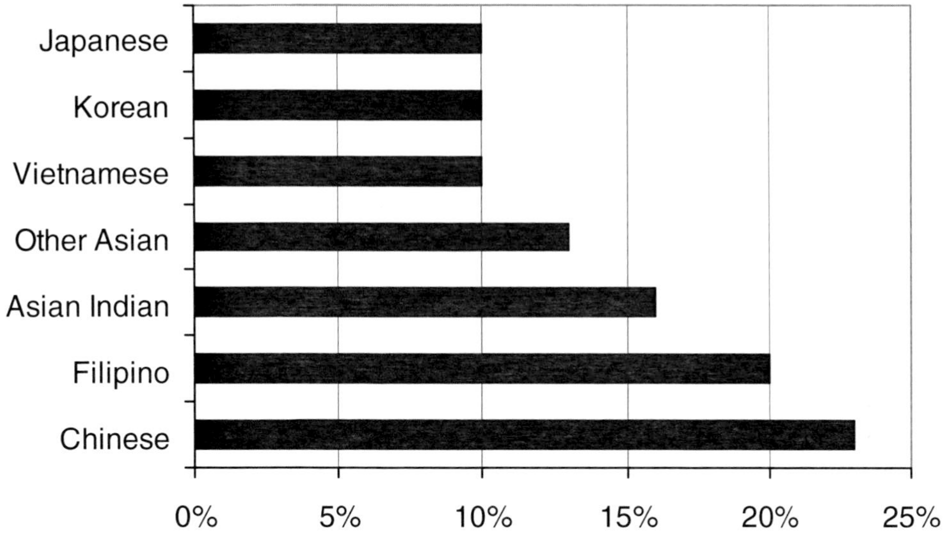

Source: U.S. Census Bureau, 2000.

were a direct result of provisions of the 1965 Hart-Celler Act favoring immigrants fleeing communism and policies favoring family reunification, as well as policies favoring highly educated and skilled immigrants. Figure 3.2 shows the diversity among Asian/Pacific Islander subgroups reported in the 2000 Census. Counting respondents who identified themselves as either "Asian alone" or "Asian in combination with another race," Chinese Americans are the most numerous, accounting for roughly 2.7 million persons, followed by Filipinos with roughly 2.3 million persons, and Asian Indians at roughly 1.9 million residents.[45] Even more than with Hispanics, this diversity means that there is no monolithic Asian culture or political ideology.

Geographically, Asians/Pacific Islanders have tended to settle in the western United States, particularly California (4.2 million) and Hawaii (700,000). Increasingly, Asian immigrants are also settling in places such as New York, Texas, New Jersey, and Washington. Hawaii is the only state where Asians are a majority, with 58 percent as of 2000. As seen in Table 3.5, at 68 percent, Honolulu's Asian population is by far the largest in any large American city. The next nine large cities with significant Asian populations are all in California.

IN YOUR COMMUNITY
Go to the Census website at www.census.gov and find the percentage of foreign-born residents in your community. How have the numbers changed since 1990? Why?

Table 3.5

Ten Places of 100,000 or More with Highest Percentage of Asians, Census 2000

Place	Percent
Honolulu, HI	68
Daly City, CA	54
Fremont, CA	40
Sunnyvale, CA	34
San Francisco, CA	33
Irvine, CA	32
Garden Grove, CA	32
Santa Clara, CA	31
Torrance, CA	31
San Jose, CA	29

Source: U.S. Census Bureau, Census 2000.
Note: Includes Pacific Islanders.

Immigration: Causes and Consequences

The causes and consequences of immigration are numerous and complex and are still being debated. Scholars cite a number of reasons for accelerated rates of immigration over the last twenty years or so, including changes in federal immigration law—in particular the 1965 Hart-Celler Act, which abolished a system of racial preferences for northern Europeans established in the 1920s—and our geographic proximity to Latin America. But perhaps the most fundamental reason is economic—the increasing interconnectedness (or globalization) of the world's capital and labor markets. Economists tell us that capital and labor markets seek out equilibrium in which job availability will attract those with the skills and willingness to work those jobs. In other words, immigrants come for jobs, particularly when there are few economic opportunities in their own countries. But as we will see, that does not mean that the changes that result do not have important consequences for communities. As with earlier periods of immigration during the early twentieth century, such dramatic changes over a relatively short period of time created both numerous challenges and opportunities.

How has immigration manifested itself in the political arena? During the 1990s in California, a backlash to immigration resulted in the passage of several voter initiatives aimed at recent arrivals. In particular, the passage of Proposition 187 in 1994—intended to deny government services such as health care and education to undocumented immigrants—underscored the polarizing impact that immigration can have. Although Proposition 187 was later ruled unconstitutional by a federal court, the debate left a political climate of bitterness, and the surrounding hyperbole in many ways prevented a more rational discussion of immigration reform.

Also during the 1990s, in Garden Grove, California (see Table 3.3), a second controversy erupted over the election of Democrat Loretta Sanchez to Congress. Republican Robert ("B-1 Bob") Dornan, who had represented the Orange County suburb for years, attributed his loss to Sanchez to votes allegedly cast by illegal immigrants in an exceedingly close election. Although the charges were never definitively proven, the controversy highlighted tensions over ethnic change and Latino political power.

Rapid immigration has also created many practical challenges for local governments. According to a 2005 Public Policy Institute of California study, immigrants may have a difficult time making their voices heard in local government. The study recommends several measures, including dedicating the efforts of staff members to coordinate outreach to increase communication between cities and their immigrant residents.[46] Cities such as Boston and Los Angeles also use neighborhood-level governments—which do not require that participants be citizens—to connect city government to the concerns of immigrant communities. Other cities allow noncitizens to serve on boards and commissions, and a few communities even allow noncitizens to vote in school elections. The issue of undocumented immigrants' participation in local politics raises all sorts of interesting questions about the meaning of democracy and citizenship and is an issue that will be closely followed and debated heatedly in coming years.

Weighing the Costs and Benefits of Immigration

America is a nation of immigrants and for the most part, the public generally views immigration positively. But after a decade and a half of unprecedented foreign immigration, its relative costs and benefits continued to be debated, particularly with regard to illegal immigration. In 2004, the Pew Hispanic Center estimated that the nation's undocumented population at roughly 10.3 million, most of whom had arrived since 1990.[47]

Is illegal immigration good or bad? Some argue that as a nation of immigrants, the United States should welcome those willing to work, even if they are undocumented immigrants. They argue that these migrants are critical to the growth of the American economy because they are willing to take low-paying jobs in such sectors as agriculture, construction, and manufacturing that more established ethnic groups shun. Supporters and immigrant rights groups say that the vast majority of undocumented immigrants are hard-working, law-abiding, and taxpaying individuals. Moreover, supporters of liberal immigration policies note that immigration has revived the economies of many urban and rural communities, while enriching the cultural diversity of many neighborhoods.

On the other hand, opponents of illegal immigration typically argue that immigrants undercut wages and displace American workers. They also argue that, unlike for previous generations of immigrants, the American economy is no longer producing the kinds of low-skilled, yet still middle-class jobs that allow for generational upward mobility. Opponents also point to increased service demands on local governments, especially education and health care, increased competition for jobs, and the depression of wages. Advocates of tougher immigration enforcement also cite increased potential for "Balkanization"—ethnic tensions that may lead to political instability and violence—and the emergence of a "permanent underclass." As Congress again debated immigration reform in spring of 2006, massive pro-immigrant demonstrations took place in cities all across the United States. Because reaching consensus among disparate interest groups and the two major political parties is nearly impossible, is difficult to predict what form immigration reform will take, if at all.

Who's right? Well, that depends on your perspective. One of the problems in assessing immigration's costs and benefits is that much of the scholarly work in this area is being done by think tanks, many of which have ideological biases that slant their findings one way or the other. Most nonpartisan researchers see both positives and negatives to immigration. Whether immigration is "good" or "bad" for a particular community frequently depends on who you ask and how you measure the positives and negatives. The fact that the United States continues to be the destination of choice for millions around the world seeking better opportunities suggests that immigration is, at the very least, good for immigrants.

Finally, one of the critical questions in any discussion of immigration has to do with the issue of **upward mobility**. The notion of climbing the economic ladder is deeply rooted in our national mythology. For many earlier immigrant groups, such as the Irish, Italians, Slavs, Greeks, and Jews, upward mobility has more or less been the norm. There is substantial evidence showing that many Asians/Pacific Islanders are following the traditional path of upward mobility. According to the 2000 Census, median household income for Asians/Pacific Islanders was $51,205—higher than any other racial group. In addition, Asian/Pacific Islander poverty and unemployment rates are well below the national average.[48] In contrast, a 2002 study by the Pew Hispanic Center showed that the jobless rate for second-generation Latinos—those who are American born and educated, with at least one immigrant parent—was *higher* than for first-generation immigrants from Latin America. According to Robert Sainz, Executive Director of the Los Angeles Youth Opportunity Movement, "we've got this huge labor pool that doesn't have the training and education to go where the good jobs are."[49]

Rather than upward mobility, some scholars are noticing a disturbing trend toward *downward mobility* among second- and third-generation Latinos in places like Los Angeles. As competition has increased for a dwindling number of relatively high-paying, low-skilled manufacturing jobs, some workers are becoming dissatisfied with their prospects or are opting out of traditional job markets altogether. Clearly, in the information-age economy, access to adequate education may be the single most important factor in facilitating mobility up the economic ladder. Here again the statistics for Asians and Hispanics diverge. Studies show that Asian educational attainment continues to exceed that of all other racial groups, in large part accounting for their economic success. In contrast, Latinos suffer from high dropout rates and lower college attendance rates. Although it is crucial to remember that there is variation within each group, evidence suggests that Asians and Latinos, as distinct groups, may be on very different paths in terms of upward mobility, the consequences of which will be borne by the entire society.

The Evolution of Urban Places

Urbanization, suburbanization, Sunbelt migration, back-to-the-city, and immigration trends discussed in this chapter are important elements in our understanding of local politics. A firm grasp of these processes helps explain the sorts of people who live in a community and how they shape its politics and policies, its needs and resources. One thing to keep in mind from our discussion is that urban areas are in constant flux, usually as a result of dramatic economic or technological change. And as communities change so do their politics. We will return to these factors, along with the others considered in the previous chapter, throughout the rest of this book.

Essential Terms

urbanization	redlined
industrialization	dormitory suburbs
urban places	edge cities
urbanized areas	central city/suburban distinctions
urban clusters	restrictive covenants
Core-Based Statistical Area (CBSA)	zoning
Micropolitan Statistical Area	exclusionary zoning
Metropolitan Statistical Area (MSA)	fiscal zoning
Combined Metropolitan Statistical Areas (CMSAs)	separation of needs and resources
internal migration	fragmentation
external immigration	employing suburbs
postindustrial cities	suburbanization of poverty
suburbs	index of dissimilarity
suburbanization	Sunbelt
anti-city attitudes	defense spending
white flight	new urban form
incorporation	gentrification
highway construction	Hispanic immigration
housing programs	Asian/Pacific Islander immigration
tract housing	upward mobility

On the Internet

- Go to www.census.gov and click on "American FactFinder." From there, you can type in your city or county's name, plus the state, and discover a treasure trove of up-to-date census demographic data about your community.
- The U.S. Bureau of the Census website (www.census.gov/population/www/socdemo/foreign.html) will guide you to a number of recent Census Bureau reports about foreign-born populations in the United States.

- The Lewis Mumford Center for Comparative Urban and Regional Research (www.albany.edu/mumford/) has a wealth of interesting research and a number of reports on comparative urban research.
- The Brookings Institution (www.brook.edu/) is an independent think tank that does excellent research on metropolitan issues.
- The Center for Urban Policy Research at Rutgers University (policy.rutgers.edu/cupr/) conducts basic and applied research on policy issues such as land use, housing, infrastructure, and historic and environmental preservation.
- www.h-net.org/~urban/ offers research as well as online discussion of comparative international urban history.

Notes

1. Sam Bass Warner, *Streetcar Suburbs: The Process of Growth in Boston, 1870–1900*, 2nd ed. (Cambridge, MA: Harvard University Press, 1978).

2. Quoted in Jon Bowermaster, "Seattle, Too Much of a Good Thing," *New York Times Magazine*, January 6, 1991, p. 24.

3. William Schneider, "The Suburban Century Begins," *Atlantic Monthly* 270, no. 1 (July 1992): 34. See also Daniel Bell, *The Coming of Post-Industrial Society: A Venture in Social Forecasting*, anniversary ed. (New York: Basic Books, 1999).

4. Quoted in James A. Clapp, *The City: A Dictionary of Quotable Thought on Cities and Urban Life* (New Brunswick, NJ: Center for Urban Policy Research, 1984), p. 191.

5. Ibid., p. 129.

6. Kenneth T. Jackson, *Crabgrass Frontier: The Suburbanization of the United States* (New York: Oxford University Press, 1985).

7. Ibid.

8. Robert M. Fogelson, *The Fragmented Metropolis: Los Angeles, 1850–1930* (Berkeley: University of California Press, 1993).

9. Mike Davis, *City of Quartz: Excavating the Future in Los Angeles* (New York: Verso, 1990), p. 164.

10. Robert Coldwell Wood, *Suburbia: Its People and Their Politics* (Boston: Houghton Mifflin, 1958).

11. Gary J. Miller, *Cities by Contract: The Politics of Municipal Incorporation* (Cambridge, MA: MIT Press, 1981).

12. Robert Fishman, " Megalopolis Unbound," *Wilson Quarterly* 14, no. 1 (Winter 1990): 36.

13. John Lichfield, "No Particular Place to Live," *Independent on Sunday* (London), November 15, 1992.

14. Fishman, "Megalopolis Unbound," p. 28; and Joel Garreau, *Edge City: Life on the New Frontier* (New York: Doubleday, 1991).

15. Schneider, "The Suburban Century Begins," p. 37.

16. Garreau, *Edge City*, p. 7.

17. Ibid., p. 4.

18. Carl Abbott, *The New Urban America: Growth and Politics in Sunbelt Cities*, rev. ed. (Chapel Hill, NC: University of North Carolina Press, 1987), p. 188.

19. *Economist*, December 1, 1990, p. 25; May 9, 1992, p. 21.

20. Davis, *City of Quartz*, p. 169.

21. John D. Kasarda, "Economic Restructuring and America's Urban Dilemma," in *The Metropolis Era*, ed. Mattei Dogan and John D. Kasarda, vol. 2, *Mega-Cities* (Beverly Hills, CA: Sage, 1988), p. 74.

22. Quoted in the *New York Times*, February 23, 1991.

23. Mayor Pete Flaherty, quoted in Clapp, *The City*, p. 83.

24. Quoted in Katherine Barrett and Richard Greene, "American Cities," *Financial World*, February 19, 1991, p. 36.

25. Peter Dreier, "Poverty in the Suburbs," *The Nation*, September 20, 2004.

26. David Fasenfest, Jason Booza, and Kurt Metzger, *Living Together: A New Look at Racial and Ethnic Integration and Metropolitan Neighborhoods, 1990–2000* (Washington, DC: The Brookings Institution, April 2004).

27. Roderick J. Harrison, "Moving Out When Minorities Move In," *American Demographics*, June 1, 2002, pp. 23–24.

28. Fasenfest, Booza, and Metzger, *Living Together*, p. 1.

29. Garreau, *Edge City*, pp. 140, 150.

30. William H. Frey, *Melting Pot Suburbs: A Census 2000 Study of Suburban Diversity* (Washington, DC: The Brookings Institution, June 2001).

31. Quoted in *San Jose (CA) Mercury News*, April 9, 1991.

32. *The Economist*, March 13, 2004.

33. William H. Frey, *The New Great Migration: Black Americans' Return to the South, 1965–2000* (Washington, DC: The Brookings Institution, May 2004).

34. Jessica S. Barnes and Claudette E. Bennett, *The Asian Population: 2000*, Census 2000 Brief (U.S. Census Bureau, February 2002).

35. Robert E. Lang and Kristopher M. Rengert, "The Hot and Cold Sunbelts: Comparing State Growth Rates, 1950–2000," Fannie Mae Foundation Census Note 02 (Washington, DC: Fannie Mae Foundation, April 2001).

36. "Federal Spending: The North's Loss Is the Sunbelt's Gain," *National Journal*, June 26, 1976, pp. 878–91.

37. Fishman, "Megalopolis Unbound," pp. 28, 36–37.

38. Paul S. Grogan and Tony Proscio, *Comeback Cities: A Blueprint for Urban Neighborhood Revival* (Boulder, CO: Westview Press, 2000).

39. Nolan Malone, Kaari F. Baluja, Joseph M. Costanzo, and Cynthia J. Davis, *The Foreign-Born Population: 2000*, Census 2000 Brief (U.S. Census Bureau, December 2003).

40. Audrey Singer, *The Rise of New Immigrant Gateways* (Washington, DC: The Brookings Institution, February 2004).

41. Ibid.

42. Ibid, p. 1.

43. Elizabeth M. Grieco and Rachel C. Cassidy, *Overview of Race and Hispanic Origin: 2000*, Census 2000 Brief (U.S. Census Bureau, March 2001).

44. Noel Ignatiev, *How the Irish Became White* (New York: Routledge Press, 1995).

45. Mary C. Dickson, *Asians and Pacific Islanders in America: A Democratic Profile* (Washington, DC: Population Resource Center, December 2001).

46. S. Karthick Ramakrishnan and Paul G. Lewis, *Immigrants and Local Governance: The View from City Hall*, no. 101 (Public Policy Institute of California, June 2005, www.ppic.org).

47. Nicole Gaouette, "Illegal Population Flows to Southeast," *Los Angeles Times*, June 15, 2005, p. A13.

48. Marla Dickerson, "Latino Job Seekers Find 'Born in USA' Not Enough," *Los Angeles Times*, April 3, 2002, p. A1.

49. Ibid.

4 The Intergovernmental Environment of Local Politics
Creatures of the States and Supplicants of the Federal Government

The social, economic, demographic, and historical forces discussed thus far greatly influence what goes on in local politics, but before we get down to the nuts and bolts of local government, that is, politics and power, another primary element affecting local politics must be considered. That element is the intergovernmental environment of local politics. Local governments sometimes cooperate with, but mostly compete with and cause problems for, one another. We have already examined some of the impacts of suburbanization and fragmentation; in chapter 14, we will study this further in the context of models for regional or metropolitan governance. The federal government also plays a direct role in local politics, although less today than at some times in the past. By far the most important intergovernmental influence is state government.

Local governments are often referred to as "creatures of the state"—and rightly so. They are created by the state and may be abolished or altered by the state. States limit their organization, powers, finances, and most responsibilities, sometimes generously and sometimes not. Their relations with adjacent or overlapping local governments are also structured by the states, which formulate the whole complicated system. Many of the tools at the disposal of both individual local governments and regional multiplexes of governments have their source in state politics. In this chapter, we attempt to understand the major types of local governments, how they are created, what powers and constraints they have, and what they can and cannot do. As we mentioned in the opening chapters, local governments in the United States have significant political autonomy. Yet, as with sovereignty disputes between the federal government and the states, local government autonomy operates within the confines of a state's constitutional framework, thus providing one of the enduring tensions of American local government.

Types and Tasks of Local Government

Although it is sometimes hard to distinguish among them, at least six types of local government operate in the United States, with each state making its own choice as to which ones it will have, what they will do, and what they will be called. The division of responsibilities among these governments can be complex and varies greatly from state to state.

Counties

According to the National League of Cities, there are 3,069 county governments in the United States.[1] Except for geographically small Connecticut and Rhode Island, all states have counties, which are called "parishes" in Louisiana and "boroughs" in Alaska. States subdivide themselves into **counties** for administrative purposes, and their close connection to state government is what makes counties distinct from other local governments. The entire territory of a state is divided into counties, whereas other local governments cover only parts of the state, never all of it. Moreover, as administrative agencies for the states, much of what counties do is carry out state programs. That's why they must cover the entire state and that's also what distinguishes them from other local governments, which administer more of their own programs. Counties are particularly important in rural and unincorporated areas, where they are the primary local government. Their significance has declined in many urban areas, where their duties are duplicated or have been taken over by cities (municipalities), although in some states, mostly in the Sunbelt, counties continue to provide crucial urban services.

As the principal local government for rural areas, counties usually oversee public health; provide agricultural advice; build and maintain roads; keep records on births, marriages, and property transactions; administer voter registration and elections; carry out tax assessment and collection; and operate the state criminal justice system, with a sheriff, jail, and courts.

Counties also furnish many services that we sometimes associate with cities. Counties are responsible for land-use planning for areas that are not part of any city and often provide fire protection for these areas. Some counties also oversee parks and libraries. In many states, especially in the West, counties administer state and federal social programs, including welfare, mental health, and public hospitals. Some urban counties even operate transit systems. Counties tend to be weakest in the New England states, where older cities handle most of these functions.

IN YOUR COMMUNITY
Go to your county's website. What services does your county provide?

Municipalities

What most people think of as local government is, in legal terms, the municipality. In some states, municipalities are called cities, boroughs, towns, or even villages, and the 2002 Census of Governments counted 19,429 municipalities across the United States. Cities are the primary, but not exclusive, local governments of urbanized areas. In many states, municipalities have more wide-ranging responsibilities and powers than other sorts of local governments, although their authority is still constrained by state law. Nevertheless, municipalities are the most ubiquitous and significant form of local government, and will be our primary focus. Although we refer to **municipalities** and **cities** interchangeably in this book, keep in mind that they may be of any size and are not necessarily large, urban places.

Cities operate within counties and are created from county territory through a process known as incorporation. In many states, the county continues to provide services such as administration of elections, record keeping, tax assessment, courts, and jails, while the city takes over responsibility for police and fire protection and land-use planning. Cities may also handle streets, parks, libraries, sewers, garbage collection, and sometimes other services they choose (but are not obliged) to provide. As mentioned, some large, older cities also manage state and federal welfare, public health, and school programs.

The U.S. Census Bureau identifies thirty-three **consolidated city-county** governments across the country (see Table 4.1). Counties commonly contain multiple municipalities, but in these communities, the county and one or more cities have been combined into one governmental entity for efficiency and, sometimes, social equity. Such consolidations seek to solve the problem of metropolitan fragmentation, although most cover too little territory to do so meaningfully. Virginia has six such city-county consolidations, but an additional thirty-five Virginia cities operate outside county boundaries and provide both county and municipal services.

IN YOUR COMMUNITY
Go to your city's website. What services does your city provide?

Towns and Townships

In twenty states, mostly in the Northeast, local governments called **towns or townships** perform some of the functions of cities and counties. As of 2002, there were 16,504 designated towns or townships in the United States. A few in New England still have the sorts of town meetings Americans like to reminisce about, although most are governed by an elected board. Towns in Connecticut and Rhode Island, which have no counties, and in Massachusetts, Michigan, New Jersey, Pennsylvania, and Vermont, function very much like municipalities. In the remaining thirteen states (with 85 percent of all townships), towns are mostly a vestige of frontier America, existing on paper while their functions have been taken over by municipalities or counties. Some of these towns, however, are still working local governments, and some operate as administrative subdivisions of counties.

Special Districts

The most numerous, yet least well known, of all local governments are **special districts**. The federal government counted 35,052 in 2002. Unlike cities, counties, and some townships, which perform varied functions, special districts usually provide

Table 4.1

Designated City-Counties by State, 2002

City–county consolidation	Year	State
New Orleans–Orleans Parish	1805	Louisiana
Nantucket Town–Nantucket County	1821	Massachusetts
Boston–Suffolk County	1821	Massachusetts
Philadelphia–Philadelphia County	1854	Pennsylvania
San Francisco–San Francisco County	1856	California
5 Boroughs of New York	1890s	New York
Denver–Denver County	1902	Colorado
Honolulu–Honolulu County	1907	Hawaii
Baton Rouge–East Baton Rouge Parish	1947	Louisiana
Hampton–Elizabeth City County*	1952	Virginia
Newport News–Warwick County*	1957	Virginia
Chesapeake South Norfolk–Norfolk County*	1962	Virginia
Virginia Beach–Princess Anne County*	1962	Virginia
Nashville–Davidson County	1962	Tennessee
Jacksonville–Duval County	1967	Florida
Juneau–Greater Juneau County	1969	Alaska
Carson City–Ormsby County*	1969	Nevada
Indianapolis–Marion County	1969	Indiana
Columbus–Muscogee County	1970	Georgia
Sitka–Greater Sitka County	1971	Alaska
Lexington–Fayette County	1972	Kentucky
Suffolk–Nansemond County*	1972	Virginia
Anchorage–Greater Anchorage County	1975	Alaska
Anaconda–Deer Lodge County	1976	Montana
Butte–Silver Bow County	1976	Montana
Houma–Terrebonne Parish	1984	Louisiana
Lynchburg City–Moore County	1988	Tennessee
Athens–Clarke County	1990	Georgia
Lafayette–Lafayette Parish	1992	Louisiana
Augusta–Richmond County	1995	Georgia
Kansas City–Wyandotte County	1997	Kansas
Hartsville–Trousdale County	2001	Tennessee
Louisville–Jefferson County	2001	Kentucky

Source: National Association of Counties, Research Division, www.naco.org/Content/ContentGroups/Publications1/Research_Briefs1/Questions_and_Answers_on_Consolidation.htm.
*Denotes independent cities which are historically city-county consolidations.

only a single or "special" service, ranging from street lighting to flood control to cemeteries. According to the U.S. Census Bureau over 90 percent of the nation's special district governments perform a single function. They are created when citizens or governments want a particular job done, but do not want an existing agency either to take on new responsibilities or to provide service to an area outside the boundaries of a given city or county. Sometimes special districts serve only a part of a city (for example, an industrial zone or downtown). Sometimes special districts are formed when cities, usually small ones, combine resources to provide fire protection, sewage, or other services that they collectively lack. Sometimes special districts cover more than one county, usually for services such as mass transit, air pollution, mosquito abatement, or water quality.

Proponents of special districts argue that they provide specific services that general-purpose governments do not. Supporters say that such districts are more "fair" because a customer's tax burden is often in direct proportion to services received. Critics, however, argue that these agencies add considerably to the complexity of urban governance because their jurisdictions and services overlap those of other local governments. They also argue that special districts are created to benefit special interests and are insulated from popular control.[2]

IN YOUR COMMUNITY
Go to the website of your state's association of special districts. What kinds of services do special districts provide in your area?

School Districts

Contrary to popular belief, the vast majority of **school districts** operate independently of city or county politics. Currently, Hawaii, Alaska, Maine, and New Jersey are the only states in which the public school system is entirely a state function. In 2005 the National League of Cities counted 13,506 independent school districts in the United States. Some states consider them as special districts, while in most others they represent a distinct category of local government. Their autonomous status is derived from the theory—popularized by Progressive reformers during the early twentieth century—that school governance could be insulated from politics, particularly political parties. In practice, school politics are often the subject of some of the most contentious battles in state and local politics.

Historically, the systematic unequal funding of school districts has been one of the most controversial issues. Because most districts are funded by local property taxes, there can be huge funding disparities between affluent and poor areas. In 1973, the U.S. Supreme Court ruled in *San Antonio v. Rodriguez* that such funding disparities were not unconstitutional. However, some states, such as California and Hawaii, have attempted to equalize funding, with only limited success and many unintended consequences. Racial integration of public schools, mandated by the 1954 U.S. Supreme Court decision *Brown v. Board of Education*, which ended legalized segregation, has also been politically charged. During the 1970s and '80s state and federal courts finally began taking a more proactive role in ordering the integration of America's public schools by mandating school busing. The fifty-year anniversary of the overturning of the principle of "separate but equal" in the *Brown* decision was marked in 2004. Looking back on the legacy of the *Brown* decision, many civil rights advocates wished they had focused less on "separate" and more on "equal." In other words, many wish more emphasis had been placed on ensuring adequate funding of minority public schools.

Although primarily independent governments, most school districts operate with substantial state oversight in areas such as curriculum, governance, and funding. Districts are governed by the state education code, often a highly detailed manual stipulating what schools can and cannot do. A state board of education is often the chief policy-making body, and the state department of education in charge of policy implementation, usually under the direction of a state superintendent of public instruction. The No Child Left Behind Act (2001), which mandated standardized testing for students and greater accountability for teachers, among other reforms, represented a major departure from the federal government's historically "hands-off" role in public education. Prior to 2001, education had been almost exclusively a state and local issue, with the exception of a handful of federal nutrition and disability programs. Many states and local school districts have criticized the No Child Left Behind Act as an expensive, unnecessary, and in some ways counterproductive intrusion into local affairs. In particular, classroom teachers cite increased pressure to "teach to the test," which they say may increase test scores, but emphasizes rote memorization at the expense of critical thinking. We will return to school politics in chapter 14.

Community Development Corporations

Sometimes called **redevelopment** agencies, **community development corporations (CDCs)** represent yet another quasi-independent layer of local government. Their purpose is to attract and spur private investment into an area—usually commercial or industrial land—in need of improvement. CDCs are created by cities and counties to improve areas deemed "blighted." Unlike other local governments, they set up their own boundaries and governing boards and, once constituted, operate as a separate and legally independent entity. City councils often act as the CDC's governing board, although some boards are appointed.

Redevelopment agencies have tremendous, some would say unaccountable, powers and a sometimes inglorious history. Many minority communities, such as Boston's Roxbury community, still cringe at the mere mention of the word "redevelopment," having been targets of the City of Boston's Redevelopment Authority over the years for "slum removal." In some instances, community leaders felt that redevelopment efforts had intentionally replaced affordable housing with expensive market-rate housing, displacing many low-income minorities. Typically, redevelopment agencies are able to acquire land through a power known as **eminent domain**. In most states, CDCs use a strategy known as **tax increment financing** to capture a portion of the increase in property tax revenue generated within a redevelopment area. Once a tax base is set and redevelopment begins, the agency captures the increased portion of tax revenue—the "tax increment"—generated in the area. In some states, such as California, redevelopment agencies are required to set aside a certain percentage of their revenues—usually around 20 percent—for affordable housing. CDCs may also have authority to issue **bonds**, without voter approval, to pay for redevelopment projects, infrastructure improvements, housing, and even public art, usually repaid with money received from tax increment financing.

Often criticized as lacking public oversight and too often reflecting the needs of business leaders and developers, these agencies are controversial, albeit effective, tools that cities and counties can use to facilitate economic redevelopment. In a closely watched 5–4 decision in June, 2005, the U.S. Supreme Court ruled that redevelopment agencies can use eminent domain to seize private property in order to promote economic development—without approval from property owners. The surprising ruling lifted a long-standing requirement in some states that such "takings" of private property were legitimate only if they served some "public interest," such as the construction of a freeway or new school. Under the new standard, a redevelopment agency may be able to take private property in order to build a tax-generating shopping mall. In the wake of the ruling, it is likely that redevelopment agencies will play an increasingly important—and controversial—role in local economic development politics.

IN YOUR COMMUNITY

Go to your city's website to see if your city uses community development corporations. What parts of your community have been targeted for redevelopment?

Private Governments

One of the most dramatic developments in local government in recent years has been the rise of private **common interest developments (CIDs)**, sometimes known as homeowner or resident associations. According to political scientist Evan McKenzie, author of *Privatopia*, there are roughly 250,000 CIDs in the United States serving over 50 million residents, and the number is growing.[3] Usually created by developers, membership in CIDs is almost always mandatory. CIDs are not technically governments, yet they now perform governmental functions in condominium and other self-contained developments, usually with an elected governing board. CIDs charge homeowner fees (equivalent to taxes); provide services ranging from security to transportation, gardening, and maintenance; and regulate land use, landscaping, paint colors, and pets. CIDs are not to be confused with their cousins, voluntary homeowner associations, which have also been politically active in many metropolitan areas, typically in protecting communities from unwanted development.

In many parts of the country, **business improvement districts (BIDs)** have also emerged, run largely by business owners in the designated area, although in some cases they do include elected officials on their boards. As with CIDs, BIDs tax themselves to pay for an additional level of security, street cleaning, graffiti removal, or infrastructure improvements. Supporters argue that BIDs fill in important gaps in service delivery that local governments fail to deliver. Proponents say that BIDs have played a major role in retaining and expanding investment in business districts, particularly in urban areas.

Table 4.2

Local Governments in the United States, 2005

Type of government	Number
Counties	3,069
Municipalities	19,429
Towns and Townships	16,504
Special Districts	35,052
School Districts	13,506
Total	87,560

Source: National League of Cities.

However, critics counter that, like other "shadow governments," BIDs represent a retreat from the public sphere, fragmenting and isolating neighborhoods and business districts from one another, and making communities even less willing to participate in—not to mention pay taxes for—solving larger community problems.

Local Governments: Variation Among States

Not counting such associations, the United States had 87,560 recognized local governments in 2002, and the number is growing. As Table 4.2 reveals, the most numerous of these are special districts (especially if schools are included in this category), followed by municipalities. Townships, although numerous, are usually not as significant as the others. But it is important to remember that local government can vary widely from state to state and community to community. The reason is that local government has largely been left up to individual states. A topic not addressed by the federal Constitution, the governance of urban areas has been left up to each state to develop. Thus, we can expect at least some variation from state to state in the way that local governments operate. Finally, keep in mind that there is an ongoing debate over whether metropolitan areas are better served by more or fewer governments. Some criticize the multiplicity of governments in some metropolitan areas as confusing and inefficient, while others defend the multiplicity of governments as enhancements of efficiency and democracy. We will return with a more thorough discussion of this topic in chapter 14.

The types and tasks of local governments vary considerably from state to state, which is why reviewing their functions may be confusing. In general, however, cities have more discretion about what they can do than other local governments do. Although they must supply services mandated by the state, the quality of these services is up to them (subject to their own voters, of course), while counties and special districts are much more constrained by state directives and finance.

Variation among the states is illustrated by the uneven distribution of local governments among them. As Table 4.3 reveals, some states are extremely frugal about creating local governments while others are profligate. As of 2002, Hawaii, where

Table 4.3

Number of Local Governments by State, 2002

State	Number of governments	State	Number of governments
Alabama	1,172	Montana	1,128
Alaska	176	Nebraska	2,792
Arizona	639	Nevada	211
Arkansas	1,589	New Hampshire	560
California	4,410	New Jersey	1,413
Colorado	1,929	New Mexico	859
Connecticut	581	New York	3,421
Delaware	340	North Carolina	961
District of Columbia	2	North Dakota	2,736
Florida	1,192	Ohio	3,637
Georgia	1,449	Oklahoma	1,790
Hawaii	20	Oregon	1,440
Idaho	1,159	Pennsylvania	5,032
Illinois	6,904	Rhode Island	119
Indiana	3,086	South Carolina	702
Iowa	1,976	South Dakota	1,867
Kansas	3,888	Tennessee	931
Kentucky	1,440	Texas	4,785
Louisiana	474	Utah	606
Maine	827	Vermont	734
Maryland	266	Virginia	522
Massachusetts	842	Washington	1,788
Michigan	2,805	West Virginia	687
Minnesota	3,483	Wisconsin	3,049
Mississippi	1,001	Wyoming	723
Missouri	3,423		

Source: U.S. Census Bureau, Census of Governments, 2002.

schools are a state function, had just twenty local governments. At the other extreme is Illinois, with 6,904 local governments. Not far behind are Pennsylvania, Texas, and California. These large, populous states no doubt require more local governments than some, such as Nevada and Alaska, but surprisingly, tiny Kansas ranks fifth in number of local governments. Population has something to do with these numbers, but New York, with a 2003 population of 18.6 million, gets by with half as many local governments as Illinois, with 12.3 million residents. And Florida, with a population of more than 16 million, manages with fewer than Colorado (with roughly a quarter of Florida's population). The survival of many largely vestigial townships in Illinois suggests that the numbers have something to do with history. Pennsylvania also has many townships, although more active ones. But other states at the top of the list have no such excuse.

Table 4.4

Number of Cities by Population Range, 2002

Population range	Number of cities
300,000 or more	58
200,000–299,999	30
100,000–199,999	153
50,000–99,999	364
25,000–49,999	643
10,000–24,999	1,436
5,000–9,900	1,637
2,500–4,999	2,070
1,000–2,499	3,677
Less than 1,000	9,361

Source: 2002 Census of Governments. Volume 1, Number 1, Government Organization. Washington, DC: U.S. Department of Commerce, Bureau of the Census.

Keep in mind that it is hard to generalize from state to state. Because our federal system endows state governments with considerable autonomy with regard to local governments, and because states can differ dramatically in geography, population, cultural values, and so on, it is not surprising that local government would vary from place to place. Table 4.4 shows the number of cities by population range. Notice that the vast majority of cities have small populations—less than 25,000 people. Out of the more than 9,000 cities in the United States, just over 230 of them have populations greater than 100,000 people (see Table 4.4). The statistics tell us something about how and why Americans prefer to be governed, a theme that will be expanded in the next section. Ultimately, the creation of local governments is a reflection of history, need, and, of course, politics.

In practice, these arrangements may be confusing, even to people who work in local government. Many local governments overlap in the complex and administratively fragmented metropolitan areas, thus exacerbating their problems and increasing costs. A single neighborhood is commonly governed by a city, a county, a school district, half a dozen special districts, and possibly a community development corporation. Cities may be responsible for streets, for example, while counties or states are in charge of highways, and a special district builds mass transit or governs air pollution. How is the transportation or air quality system coordinated? Often it is not, but a typical response is to create yet another layer of government to attempt the job.

The Creation of Local Governments

As we have seen, local governments are not mentioned in the U.S. Constitution. Their existence and functions were left to the states to figure out. Counties are created when states divide themselves into units as large or as small as they please, designate them as local governments, and delegate limited authority to them. The states can abolish counties or split existing counties to create new ones by legislative act, by constitutional amendment, or sometimes through a popular vote. Rural parts of urbanized counties sometimes agitate for separation. New counties are rare, however; only five were created in the 1980s, and three of these were in developing areas of Alaska. Townships were created in a similar way, although they sometimes predated states. Today, townships are most likely to fade into disuse and be abolished by states. Special districts are similarly created or abolished by state governments or agencies or, state law permitting, by a pact between local governments, or even a citizen petition, although this is rare. The creation of school districts is also generally determined at the state level, although this responsibility is sometimes delegated to counties or cities. Large-scale regional governments may result from state action or local pacts, sometimes subject to voter approval. But as Nancy Burns argues, the creation of local governments is more than simply a function of population. Rather, she finds that the formation of local governments is ultimately an attempt by interest groups—usually business—to instill private values into public institutions.[4]

Incorporation

Unlike most other local governments, cities are formed through a process of citizen petition and voting called **incorporation**. The term is derived from the Latin word *corpus* (or body) and reflects the citizens' determination to become one body—a municipal corporation—for the purposes of local government. Cities were among the first legal corporations in the United States, and their power to raise money by issuing bonds was used to pay for early municipal services such as road construction, sanitation, and other basic infrastructure. The process for their creation is prescribed in state law, although some old cities predate their states and may have been created by colonial governments. Areas that are not part of any city are governed by counties and thus are considered **unincorporated**. As unincorporated areas urbanize, residents commonly begin to demand more services than most counties can deliver, leading to incorporation efforts. Residents may also wish to form a city to preserve community identity and prevent urbanization, or to avoid being absorbed by some other city. For example, many affluent areas incorporate to protect their tax base from an adjacent big city. Others incorporate in order to ensure a particular quality of life, enhance economic development, or protect ethnic homogeneity.

The process almost always starts with a petition by the community's residents. If the number of signatures required by state law is obtained, the proposal goes forward for review by the county, state, or special state agency created for this purpose. Such reviews are intended to determine whether or not proposed municipalities make sense in terms of tax base, land use, and existing local governments. As we have indicated, the process of local government formation is often highly political, with counties and states responding to the political clout of the incorporating area and making decisions that serve their purposes. In most states, new incorporations were readily approved because counties and state legislatures dominated by rural and later suburban representatives were happy to allow urban areas to fragment rather than to facilitate the expansion and influence of big cities. More recently, concerns about urban sprawl and metropolitan fragmentation have led review bodies to take their mandates more seriously. If the reviewing authority approves the incorporation, the proposal is put to the voters of the prospective municipality. A simple majority must approve. Usually, a city charter (discussed later) is approved and officers are elected at the same time.

The process of incorporation varies considerably from state to state, both in the order of events and in rigor, but the states remain in control of the process and are ultimately responsible for its consequences for metropolitan fragmentation. Sunbelt states, except for North Carolina, Texas, and Hawaii, have tended to be more lax about the process, at least until lately; a few Frostbelt states have been much more strict. Besides, most Frostbelt states aren't growing very fast, so the creation of new municipalities is less of an issue.

IN YOUR COMMUNITY
Research the history of your city's incorporation. What were the main reasons your area became its own city?

How Local Governments Are Organized: Charters

States recognize the existence of local governments by granting them **charters**, which lay out their boundaries, powers, responsibilities, and organization—much as business corporations are "chartered" in each state. Like a governing constitution, these documents enumerate the selection and powers of local officials and the structure of government, along with its basic functions, including taxing and borrowing. The authority and procedures for passing ordinances (local laws) are also in the charter. Depending on the state and the particular type of local government, charters may be narrow and restrictive grants of power or may be relatively generous. The state, however, is ultimately in control.

Special Law Charters

Of the three basic types of charters, the most restrictive is the **special law charter**, enacted by state legislatures for specific cities only. Each city must thus apply for its own charter and must return to the legislature for any changes it wishes to make and often for approval of its ordinances or other actions as well, especially with regard to taxes, but sometimes on far more trivial matters as well. The system is restrictive, inconvenient, and slow. Favoritism and unfairness are likely since some cities will have more effective representation in their state legislature than others. Dating back to colonial times when cities were chartered by monarchs, special law charters were common in the older states of the East and South. Many now have reformed systems, but some cities, mostly in the South, still operate under special law charters.

General Law Charters

Under the most common charter system, that of a **general law charter**, a state grants each type of local government the same basic charter. Counties and special districts almost universally operate under general law charters, as do a majority of cities. General law charters are usually less restrictive than special law charters, and although the state retains control, the problems of inconvenience and unfairness are resolved. Not all cities are the same, however. A one-size-fits-all charter may not suit the needs of the largest and smallest cities in a state equally well, so most states classify cities by size and use different general law charters for different classes of city. As a city's population increases, it may go through a state-specified procedure to move up to the next class of charter, giving it broader powers.

Although general law charters are an improvement, problems arise. The classification scheme can simulate the problem of special law charters if classes are drawn to set apart for special—either negative or positive—treatment. A state law written to apply only to cities of over 1 million, for example, would pertain only to Chicago in Illinois and Philadelphia in Pennsylvania. Another issue is what happens when cities *decline* in population. Prior to 1990, the City of Detroit enjoyed the charter privileges of a city over 1 million, but the 1990 census showed that its population had fallen below that level. Each state must decide its own rules for what happens when cities move up—or down—in class size. Classification may make general law charters restrictive in some states, but in others, an optional charter system makes it even more flexible. Thirty-nine states offer charter options. Under an **optional charter**, cities are allowed to choose their form of government (see chapter 5), including the selection and powers of officials, from a menu set out by the state. They can also change government form within broad limits. California, for example, provides a general law charter system for cities of less than 3,500 people but also gives them the charter option of selecting their form of government. Once California cities grow to have more than 3,500 people they may adopt a home rule charter (described next) granting them broader powers. But California's cities are so satisfied with the state's general law/optional system that although most are larger than 3,500, only 108 of 478 (among them all the state's largest cities) have bothered to exercise their right to home rule.

Home Rule Charters

In the late nineteenth century, cities growing in size and political clout demanded more local authority in order to meet the challenges of rapid urbanization and industrialization. By this time judicial rulings had made it clear that cities were considered legally dependent on states. In response, a movement arose to regain some level of municipal autonomy. Known as the **home rule** movement, which drew strength from American traditions of local self-governance, the effort introduced a system that allowed cities to write their own charters allowing for increased autonomy, within broad limits set by the state. Although the home rule movement dates from the nineteenth century, several states have granted their cities this right fairly recently, including Massachusetts (1965), North Dakota (1966), Florida (1968), Pennsylvania (1968), Iowa (1968), and Montana (1972). In 1970, Illinois gave home rule status to all cities with populations over 25,000 and made provisions for smaller cities to achieve home rule by citizen petition and voter approval. Some form of home rule now operates in over half the states, and two-thirds of cities with populations over 200,000 enjoy home rule, although its meaning varies from state to state. Basically, this broader grant of power allows a local government wider latitude to govern "municipal affairs." In practice, this means cities gain greater leeway over areas such as setting up their own form of government, conducting municipal elections, and other actions not otherwise prohibited by state law. The problem lies in clearly defining whether an issue is of "municipal" or "statewide" concern. Take the issue of affordable housing, for example, which could be construed as either a municipal or statewide concern. Historically, state courts have intervened on a case-by-case (some would say arbitrary) basis to draw these lines.

Needless to say, local governments generally prefer more home rule to less, and the historic trend during most of the twentieth century was toward home rule, at least for cities. In recent years, however, local governments have seen an erosion of their home rule authority, particularly on fiscal matters. Other types of local governments still operate almost exclusively under general law charters or acts of state legislatures, although a modest home rule movement for counties has been under way for some time. Today, thirty-seven states permit counties some form of home rule charter, usually more limited than that for cities. But only about 80 of the nation's 3,086 counties enjoy even such limited home rule. Most of these are large, urban counties; eleven are in California.

Although home rule seems inherently good in terms of democracy and local control, critics point out that it contributes to fragmentation by making small local governments responsible for policies that often have regional implications.[5] Given state fiscal constraints on local governments, home rule may also give them more responsibilities than they can reasonably provide for from their own limited revenues. The ideal of home rule, sacrosanct among local governments and a cherished tradition of American local government, remains in perpetual tension with the notion of local governments as creatures of the states and, as we will see, the need to provide regional solutions to regional problems.

In Your Community

Go to your city's website and find the link to the city charter. Does your city use a home rule, general, or special charter? What do you notice about the structure of your city government?

Changing a Charter

As communities change, charters, like constitutions, may also need to change with the times. Organizational structures that worked well in the last century may not be adequate in this one; systems that functioned smoothly in small, homogeneous cities may break down with growth, economic changes, and increased ethnic and class diversity. City charters are ultimately an expression of the fundamental power dynamics of city government. Thus, political factions seek to institutionalize their authority in city government either by protecting existing power arrangements or creating new ones. The next two chapters describe the different forms of government laid out in city charters and how they have changed over the years. For now, we will focus on the formal mechanisms for changing a charter.

Besides setting out the charter system, state laws (or constitutions) also describe procedures for **charter amendments**. These, too, vary from state to state. In states or cities with special law charters, any change must be approved by the state legislature. In general law systems, some changes must be made by the state legislature or by constitutional amendment. To conform to the basic concept of general law charters, each change should apply to all local governments covered by the system, which may make revision difficult. But many general law systems allow cities to revise their charters when population growth moves them to a new charter classification. Besides a formal procedure specified in state law, voter approval is usually required. In states with the optional charter plan, cities may initiate a limited range of charter revisions subject to voter approval. Home rule cities may change their charters in any way not prohibited by state law, also with voter approval. In all of these cases, local governments usually originate the action, with a vote of the city council or county board. In some states, voters may propose charter amendments and get them on a local ballot through an initiative petition.

The process of drafting or amending a charter is inherently political because charters are not neutral documents. As the following chapters will make clear, charters distribute formal political power in a community, and once enacted, they can freeze power arrangements until sufficient countervailing powers build up to challenge them. In general, special and general law charters reflect the power of the state legislature and the local government interests that influence it, whereas optional and home rule charters mirror the power of more local interests.

Where local governments have the power to draft and amend their own charters, singular changes are usually placed on the ballot by the city council or by citizen initiative. More controversial or sweeping change typically starts with a "blue ribbon" committee whose recommendations are put to a popular vote. Charter review bodies are sometimes elected, but more often city officials appoint them. Typically, they are made up of the community elite: business and civic leaders, along with some interest group delegates and sometimes even academics. Rarely are they completely representative. Charter commission proposals, however, must be submitted to the voters who are generally skeptical about change. Nevertheless, elites often win because of low voter turnout and consensus among community leaders, particularly the local media.

Charters need revision from time to time to adapt to changing communities and priorities. Charters that do not adapt stultify elements of the community and can undermine the legitimacy of local government. For example, in 1999, residents of the sprawling city of Los Angeles approved a wholesale revision of the city's 1920s-era charter, instituting among other changes a system of neighborhood governments and regional planning bodies to better represent the city's diverse communities. In this case pressures for change came from "below," from a coalition of homeowners and business groups in the San Fernando Valley portion of the city that had been agitating for years for more power over issues such as land development. It was only when Valley activists mounted a credible threat to break away from Los Angeles that momentum for charter reform gained steam among elites. In New York City during the 1980s, reform pressures came from "above." Following a U.S. Supreme Court decision invalidating the city's government structure, a Charter Revision Commission recommended abolishing the city's Board of Estimate, replacing it with an expanded City Council.[6] But charter change can become obsessive and get out of hand. San Franciscans, for example, vote on an average of a dozen charter amendments every election. The more they amend their charter, the longer and more detailed it gets, constraining local officials and requiring even more amendments. San Franciscans, however, have little trust in government and rejoice in their hyperdemocracy.

Whether changes are sweeping, as in the case of New York and Los Angeles, or piecemeal, as in San Francisco, the key points to keep in mind are (1) that charters lay out the governing arrangements for cities, (2) that factions within city governments seek to institutionalize their power either by reforming the city charter or maintaining the status quo.

How States Create Local Growth Machines

The discussion of local government structure and charters may seem confusing at first, but there is one underlying theme to all of it: economic growth. The state governments that set up the system and the local leaders who run it have several tools at their disposal in order to promote this economic growth. Cities and counties can grow by intensifying land use within their borders, increasing economic development and diversity. Cities and other local governments can also change their borders, expanding by annexation. The powers for both forms of growth, however, are derived from and encouraged by the states.

Land-Use Planning

Probably the greatest power the states allocate to cities and counties is that of deciding how land can be used. Land-use regulation is one of the few remaining powers that has not been substantially eroded by interference from state government. Land-use decisions can produce great wealth and social stability as well as environmental disasters. Cities exercise land-use powers within their borders while counties regulate land in areas that are not part of a city. As a general principal, counties are supposed to be primarily administrative agencies of the state, rather than agents of economic development. However, in practice, county governments have often been most enthusiastic partners with business interests in promoting economic growth. Some states, such as Oregon and Washington, provide incentives and mandates to direct development to existing urban areas in cities with existing service infrastructures. No wonder cities have been labeled growth machines. The power over land and development is one of the few that is clearly theirs and they are uniquely empowered to address the demands of land-related interests. Profligate use of these powers has, however, caused states to impose some controls, such as state requirements for general plans and environmental impact reports.

As discussed in prior chapters, the mechanisms for regulating growth within cities and counties are **zoning** and general planning. Through zoning, local governments designate areas for specific land uses, ranging from single-family, suburban-style homes to high-rise apartments, corner stores, shopping malls, and industry. Because it limits the rights of property owners, zoning was challenged in the courts, but in 1926 the U.S. Supreme Court ruled it a constitutional use of local power,[7] and the use of zoning spread rapidly. **General plans**, another twentieth-century innovation, aim to rationalize and coordinate all of a community's zones and project comprehensive and sustainable patterns of future development. The need for sewers, streets, parks, and other public facilities are considered. But while general plans are often expressions of future development, opponents of growth will use the documents as a basis for legally challenging particular projects that may not conform to the city's general plan. In general, though, the idea of a general plan is to provide guidelines for future development, although many general plans reflect only what already exists. Exceptions to zoning laws or general plans, known as **variances**, usually sought by developers, keep local governments busy. Often opposed by slow growth interests, variances are yet another tool for controlling—or encouraging—growth.

Local governments can also facilitate growth through capital improvement or infrastructure projects such as roads, storm drains, sewers, and other physical facilities. Without them, growth cannot occur. Private developers can, and increasingly do, pay for such improvements, but local government is charged with seeing that they are provided, one way or another, and it has traditionally done so at taxpayer expense, much to the delight of developers.

Annexation

With land as a primary commodity in urban politics, cities naturally attempt to add to their territory through the process of **annexation**. Only unincorporated areas (not part of any other city) may be annexed; once a city runs up against another city, it can expand no further. Counties have fixed boundaries, however, and cannot annex territory because they are entirely surrounded by other counties or other states (remember, the territory of all but two states is divided into counties). Occasionally, large counties have been divided into two or more smaller counties.

Although unincorporated areas that are already developed may be annexed, most annexations occur when cities want to add land for new development to expand their population and tax base or for major infrastructure development such as air or water ports. Landowners sometimes seek annexation by a city because counties won't allow them to develop their property. Residential areas sometimes request annexation to obtain city services, such as sewers or police protection. Again, it is state law that sets the rules for all boundary changes. In some states, the legislature or the courts must approve annexations. Virginia, for example, requires approval of annexations by a special three-judge panel. In some other states, only the city must approve, but in most, the landowners of uninhabited areas and residents of inhabited places must give their approval as well. Rural landowners are often eager for annexation, but sometimes veto absorption by an expansion-minded city out of fear of higher taxes and loss of community identity.

Growing cities, particularly in the Sunbelt, annexed aggressively from the 1950s to the 1980s, doubling, trebling, and quadrupling their territory in some cases. Between 1990 and 2000, U.S. cities annexed 12,805 square miles. Half of the territory annexed was in the South and one-fourth was in the West, while northeastern cities —largely built out and surrounded by incorporated suburbs—annexed only 250 square miles.[8]

Not all land surrounded by a city is necessarily part of that city, however. In some cases residents resisted or the city avoided annexation. Areas with physical problems (such as toxic waste dumps) or those with poor, minority populations may be skipped over by cities. The unincorporated "pockets" or "islands" left behind will continue to be governed by the county, paying lower taxes, but receiving fewer services and sometimes causing confusion in service delivery. Sometimes unincorporated areas are more than just small pockets. In Florida and Georgia, for example, unincorporated areas contain a majority of the suburban population.[9] Aggressive annexation, especially by Sunbelt cities, has led to sprawling boundaries, competition among cities, and inefficient services in some areas. Strip annexations along a road or even underneath bodies of water, as in the case of the city of San Diego, are sometimes done to ensure access to some desirable land. Some states have prohibited such annexations, while most have introduced stricter reviews of proposed annexations by special agencies or courts to make sure they encourage geographic cohesiveness or otherwise make sense.

Where annexation is relatively easy, however, the problems of **metropolitan fragmentation** are less severe since the central city can absorb emerging suburbs. Thanks to progressive state annexation policy, Charlotte, North Carolina, has been able to do just that. In other areas, emerging suburbs rush to incorporate, forming their own cities to avoid becoming part of the growing central city, which they fear will share its problems with them and raise taxes. Such **defensive incorporation** preserves the racial and class homogeneity of the suburb, but adds to the isolation of the central city and increases metropolitan fragmentation. In general, however, state laws have encouraged fragmentation by making incorporation easy and annexation difficult. Big cities in the Frostbelt long ago found themselves surrounded by incorporated suburbs and thus unable to expand or to capture the tax- and job-generating growth that was moving to the suburban fringes. Lately, some Sunbelt cities and even some older suburbs have hit the same barrier.

Cities can give up territory by a process known as **deannexation**, sometimes referred to as detachment, or "secession," although this is rare. In the past, cities with white majorities fearing domination by a growing minority vote have attempted to deannex minority neighborhoods, but federal courts have firmly rejected such deannexations as unconstitutional. A few cities have given up territory to tidy up irrational borders created by annexation wars dating back to the 1950s. In such cases, states require another city to annex the territory. Both cities and the voters of the area must approve. In some instances, parts of cities threaten to detach for political reasons. During the 1990s, "**secession**" movements emerged in the borough of Staten Island, New York, and the San Fernando Valley portion of Los Angeles, as well as several other cities. Both areas claimed they were shortchanged in services and systematically underrepresented by their city government. Although neither effort was successful, the credible threat of secession forced each city to make political concessions that they might not have made under other circumstances.

Almost as rarely, two or more cities may merge or consolidate, usually when one cannot provide adequate services to its residents. Normally, voters in each city must approve the **consolidation**, as in 2000 when voters in the city of Louisville, Kentucky, voted to consolidate with surrounding Jefferson County. In some cases, state legislatures can impose consolidation, such as New York's 1898 consolidation of the independent jurisdictions of Brooklyn, the Bronx, Queens, and Richmond (Staten Island) with Manhattan to create a five-borough mega-city. A vote is not generally required for school district consolidations, which have been more common. After World War II, for a variety of reasons, many states consolidated school districts through this process, drastically reducing the number of districts from over 100,000 to 13,522.

But despite such realignments, most metropolitan areas, as the preceding chapter noted, are characterized by governmental fragmentation and an inequitable distribution of needs and resources. Again, these are a direct result of state policies governing local boundary change. If a state wants few local governments and less fragmentation, it can make annexation and consolidation easy and incorporation difficult. Instead of many cities in an urban region, one large one will predominate, with needs and resources pooled, enabling government to address problems on a wider scale.

Alternatively, states may encourage fragmentation by making annexation difficult and incorporation easy. Except in a few cases, such as Texas, Missouri, and North Carolina, most states have policies that encourage fragmentation because state legislators have been more eager to please rural and suburban voters than those of big cities. Permissive incorporation statutes have also benefited local growth machines. Critics of metropolitan fragmentation argue that serving the short-term, narrow interests of political and economic elites, however, has exacerbated larger social problems in many metropolitan regions. However, defenders of these arrangements point out that fragmentation provides small-scale, accessible local governments and gives citizens choices. In sum, state laws governing incorporation, annexation and detachment are critical in determining how many local governments will be formed, and in doing so, may go a long way in determining the social and economic policies that follow.

IN YOUR COMMUNITY

Research the history of your city's growth by annexation. What were your city's historical periods of growth, and why?

The States and Local Government Finance

Another critical area of state influence over local government is finance. Local governments depend heavily on the states, not only for direct financial aid, but also because states set the conditions for local taxation, borrowing, and spending.

States control whether a local government can collect sales, property, income, or other taxes. In most states, only specific types of local taxes are allowed, although the generous home rule charters of some states give cities more options. Most, however, are strictly limited to a few types of taxes. Principal among these is the **property tax**, which is levied on land, dwellings, and buildings. The heavy reliance of cities on property taxes (forced on them by states) contributes to their propensity to be growth machines, because growth means new development, higher land values, and increased local revenues.

Tax rates are also usually limited or even set by the state. The **tax rate** is the percent of income, property, or other value collected as a tax. A common rate of **sales tax**, for example, is 5 percent, while a property tax rate might be set at 1 percent of the property's assessed value. States often fix the rate or set an upper limit below which local governments may choose a rate. A few states offer more options. Born of the city's fiscal crisis during the 1970s, the 1975 Financial Emergency Act, which gives New York City the power to levy municipal income and corporate taxes, is set to expire in 2008.[10] Such restrictions constrain the ability of local governments to obtain the revenue they may need and so limit not just tax rates but also spending.

States also set conditions for local **borrowing**, including how much may be borrowed, how and when the money must be repaid, and how it may be spent. Local governments are universally prohibited from deficit spending, with the exception of borrowing for **capital improvement** projects such as roads, buildings, or sewage plants. Under strict state guidelines, local governments borrow money by issuing "**bonds**" to be repaid from local revenues over an extended period of time. State law also sets the total amount a local government may borrow, usually based on the community's total property value since borrowing is ordinarily paid back from property taxes. Some borrowing is paid back by revenues from projects built with the loan, such as redevelopment projects, airports, or stadiums.

State restrictions on tax types, rates, and borrowing are commonly supplemented by requirements for voter approval in **tax referendums**. Super majorities as high as two-thirds of the voters may be required to pass local tax proposals, an amount rarely achieved with today's tax-hostile electorates and one that states rarely require for their own taxes. Local spending is not as constrained by state law as taxation is, but when the states assign different types of tasks (such as police, welfare, education) to the different types of local government, they are, in effect, directing spending. They also **mandate spending** when they require local governments to do such things as filing environmental impact reports (EIRs) on development projects or when they require a specific level of welfare payments but do not supply counties with enough money to meet it. On the other hand, states also help out local governments with grants and shared taxes. About one-third of state spending goes to such **intergovernmental aid**, with up to a third of all local funds and over half of school revenues coming from the states. Much of this money, however, is earmarked for spending on specific services such as welfare and roads. We will add to this discussion in chapter 12 on local government budgets. For now, it is enough to know that financially, as in so many other ways, local governments are truly creatures of the state.

States' Rights: The Bottom Line

Besides the broad powers of states over local governments discussed thus far, states may "preempt" (override) local action in a number of other key policy areas. For example, even where local governments were sympathetic, efforts to unionize public employees were thwarted until state laws were changed in the 1960s and 1970s. Recently, some states have preempted local gun and smoking ordinances with their own laws. "In Illinois," *The Municipal Year Book* reports, "home-rule powers were preempted on matters regarding consumption taxes, cable television, above-ground storage tanks, the pay of police and fire officers injured in the line of duty, and floodplain and floodway zoning."[11] In California during the 1990s, the lobby for apartment owners helped pass statewide legislation preempting local rent control laws. States also set standards for local services. New York State, for example, sets the caseloads of social workers, thus making staffing decisions for its local governments. In California, such mandates became so burdensome that local governments lobbied for and won a state agreement to institute no further mandates without funding.

All these powers of states over local governments are determined by the state legislatures (or sometimes by the voters) in laws or in state constitutions. Laws or statutes are easier to change and so are more flexible, but many states fix the rights and powers of local governments more rigidly in their constitutions, which may not be so easily changed. Entrenchment of their rights in state constitutions is a good news, bad news situation: sometimes it protects local governments from hostile legislatures, but it may also be intended to constrain them.

Local Autonomy and Dillon's Rule

So far, we have emphasized the relationship between state governments and their supplicants, local governments. Several themes have been emphasized. First, local government in the United States has traditionally operated with a fairly high level of autonomy, particularly compared to other democracies. Remember that a strong tradition of local self-government had developed in the American colonies long before there were states. Moreover, the U.S. Constitution says almost nothing about the status of local governments, so much was left to states to determine. In short, the relationship between local and state governments simply had to evolve. On the one hand, local governments in the United States are fairly easy to create and, as we have seen, their powers are fairly substantial, particularly over land development. However, the general trend throughout the nineteenth and twentieth centuries has been toward the erosion of local government autonomy. In particular, the principle of **Dillon's Rule** usurped earlier principles of local sovereignty. Judge John F. Dillon laid out his reasoning in 1872:

> It is a general and undisputed proposition of law that a municipal corporation possesses and can exercise the following powers, and no others: First, those granted in express words; second, those necessarily or fairly implied in or incident to the power expressly granted; third, those essential to the accomplishment of the declared objects and purposes of the corporation—not simply convenient, but indispensable. Any fair, reasonable, substantial doubt concerning the existence of power is resolved by the courts against the corporation, and the power is denied.[12]

In other words, local governments may only do exactly what the states say they may do. They have no inherent rights or constitutional status. When disputes arise, the states win so long as the powers they allocate to local governments have been explicitly stated in the law. Exceptions to this strict interpretation have arisen, however, where states have granted local governments a general police power to see to the community's well-being. Some states even give home rule cities the right to do whatever is not directly prohibited by state law. For most local governments, however, Dillon's Rule translates into state domination. This shouldn't be surprising, given that (in most cases) states came first and then created local governments. Of course, the states did not give away all their power in the process. The home rule movement of the early twentieth century modified this somewhat, but the fact remains that local governments have no inherent right to exist except at the behest of the states, which can in theory alter their power or even abolish them entirely.

It is an axiom of politics that those who have power surrender it only when forced to do so by countervailing power. Although local governments have gained over the years, they have never accumulated sufficient political clout to force states to grant them broad powers. Their best opportunity came when big cities gained enough population to threaten to dominate state elections. By the 1920s, urban residents were becoming the majority in some states and should have gained control of their legislatures. At about that time, however, rural representatives who still controlled some of these legislatures ceased the regular **reapportionment** or redrawing of legislative districts to reflect population change following each census. Over the years, wild population disparities between urban and rural legislative districts grew. The resultant **malapportionment** enabled rural legislators hostile to the expanding, tax-hungry cities to keep the upper hand. In addition, political districts for the upper house of many state legislatures were drawn according not to population, but geography. Members represented counties (just as U.S. senators represent states), often with radically unequal populations, again allowing rural interests to dominate.

Malapportionment and representation by geography were finally ruled unconstitutional by the U.S. Supreme Court in the 1960s on grounds that they denied each person an equal vote ("one man, one vote," was the phrase the Court used).[13] The wave of state-level reapportionment that followed brought equal representation by population to state legislatures. But reapportionment came too late for big cities. By the 1960s, growth was concentrated in the suburbs, so, although cities gained some representation, the suburbs benefited most, and, as we have seen, suburban and urban interests are not always aligned. Suburbs incorporated (under conditions made easy by rural legislators antagonistic to cities) precisely to avoid being absorbed by big cities. Suburban legislators regularly formed alliances with rural representatives, and many state legislatures remained anti-city, limiting taxes and encouraging fragmentation in metropolitan areas by keeping incorporation easy and annexation difficult. "Historically," said former Philadelphia Controller Jonathan Saidel with slight exaggeration, candidates "outside of Philadelphia get elected to the Pennsylvania Senate or House by stating in their brochures, 'I promise never to help the City of Philadelphia as long as I live.'"[14]

But suburban and rural legislators were not the only ones pleased to constrain local government. Political scientist Stephen Elkin argues that Dillon's Rule and other legal limitations on cities were the results of "the remaking of urban government in the later nineteenth and early twentieth centuries . . . [in an] effort to create city governments that suited the political actors who had emerged." These actors included merchants, industrialists, landowners, and builders who were being challenged by social reformers, socialists, and labor unions in many big cities. Dillon's "underlying purposes," Elkin writes, were "to protect private property [from the] kind of democracy developing in cities" through judicial and state controls. Such constraints, he goes on, were "congenial to development interests," including "the requirement of balanced budgets, restrictions on how cities can raise money, strict construction of grants of taxing authority, and restrictions on borrowing for other than capital works."[15] In short, economic interests in the cities used the states and the courts to ensure that cities would be primarily growth machines rather than agents of social reform.

But while the subordination of local governments to the states is well established in the law, its degree varies from state to state. Where local discretion is limited, state legislatures take a very active part in local government, but even where the grant of power is relatively generous, states often intervene. A 1989 study estimated that "about one out of five state measures . . . affected local government," ranging from 3 percent in Hawaii and Mississippi to 67 percent in Alabama.[16]

With so much activity and so much at stake, it should come as no surprise that local governments form alliances to lobby state governments. Representatives from big cities, suburban areas, and rural counties form legislative caucuses to pursue the interests of their constituencies, and many cities and counties hire their own lobbyists in the state capital. Associations of cities, mayors, counties, and school districts are all among the most active lobbying groups in state capitols.

Federal-Local Government Relations

Although less so than states and other local entities, the federal government is another important element in the intergovernmental environment of local politics. Recall that the U.S. Constitution makes no mention of local government and so provides it no rights or status. Indeed, the Tenth Amendment of the Constitution gives emphasis to this absence of status by reserving all the power that is not specifically assigned to the federal government for the states and their citizens—not to cities or counties. Nevertheless, the federal government has played a significant part in local governance throughout its history, although more at some times than at others.

Legal Relations Between the Federal Government and Local Governments

Despite the lack of a direct, constitutional connection between local and national governments, the latter has played a major part in defining the rights and powers of the former, sometimes empowering but more often constraining. The U.S. Constitution and acts of the national government are superior to state and local laws (except for those rights of states and citizens reserved in the Constitution itself). Local acts must therefore conform to these laws. Citizens and interest groups frequently challenge the actions of local governments in court on grounds that their rights have been violated under U.S. law. The **federal courts** hear these cases, and their rulings have greatly affected local governments. In addition to crucial U.S. Supreme Court decisions dealing with zoning and reapportionment, perhaps the most far-reaching U.S. Supreme Court decision upheld Dillon's Rule.[17] *Trenton v. New Jersey* (1923) gave the principal of state preeminence over local government nationwide application.

The federal courts have also frequently acted to protect the rights of minorities in local government, applying the U.S. Constitution and a series of federal civil and voting rights acts to actions by cities, counties, school districts, and other local governments. Civil rights cases have mandated better access for the disabled, banned discrimination in public places such as theaters and swimming pools, forced desegregation of schools, and outlawed housing discrimination, although, as we've seen, not entirely successfully. Federal court rulings in the area of voting rights and minority representation transformed politics in many communities. Some cities and counties have been ordered to change the way they select council members or to redraw council district boundaries when the courts found discrimination against minorities. Deannexations and even some exclusionary incorporations have been carefully scrutinized by the courts and various federal agencies to prevent unconstitutional actions. Local governments must also adhere to federal law in affirmative action and antidiscrimination cases. Local police practices, including reading defendants their rights and monitoring and preventing police abuse have been regulated by federal intervention.

Although courts operate on the basis of precedent (following previous decisions), they sometimes reverse or modify their positions, which may throw local governments into confusion and difficulty. Racially "separate but equal" schools, for example, were approved by the federal courts for a century and then ruled unconstitutional in 1954, with local governments obliged to restructure their entire school systems. Politics can also intervene. Recently, federal courts in areas dominated by justices appointed by Presidents Reagan, George H.W. Bush and George W. Bush have limited enforcement powers of local governments in areas such as the environment, affirmative action, and police practices.

Regulatory Relations

The U.S. Congress makes laws, and federal regulatory agencies make and implement more specific rules that affect local governments, which usually comply without the necessity of judicial intervention. For local governments, federal environmental policy, most of which has been developed since the 1970s, may be most significant. For example, local governments provide for sewage treatment and trash disposal, either of which may pollute water, air, or land, all which are now subject to **federal regulation**. Local governments also plan the distribution of housing and transportation systems, both of which affect the use of automobiles and thus air quality, also subject to federal regulations. Local airports are federally regulated for both air and noise pollution. Federal standards for safe drinking water have also been imposed. All of these are surely good, but to local officials, who must respond to both federal and state regulators who implement federal law, the erosion of their authority is not.

Policy Impacts

As our discussion of suburbanization and the move to the Sunbelt revealed, federal programs not directly aimed at local governments may still affect them. Suburbanization and the decline of central cities were greatly stimulated by federal housing and highway programs. These policies also facilitated Sunbelt growth, along with disproportionate federal spending on aerospace and defense in that region. Conversely, changes in defense expenditures during the 1990s and 2000s devastated the economies of hundreds of communities as military bases closed and defense spending was either cut or redirected.

Federal fiscal policies also touch local governments when they cause the economy to expand or contract. Like families, cities suffer from high inflation rates (goods and services cost more) and unemployment (more people on welfare or on the streets) and, when recession hits, their tax revenues decline. National tax policy on mortgages, interest rates, local government bonds (borrowing), and many other fiscal matters influence local economies. Even the national income tax rate borne by citizens may set a political feasibility limit on the taxes that local governments can impose, even when allowed by the states.

Federal Aid

Most of the federal impacts on local government discussed thus far are limiting and not particularly welcome locally. Federal programs, however, are popular with local governments when they bring in money. **Federal aid** to local governments dates back to the early days of the republic, when land grants rather than money were given to localities to be used for schools or sold to pay for roads, bridges, harbor dredging, or other transportation or communication improvements. In the twentieth century, as it ran out of land to give away, the federal government initiated cash grants-in-aid. Relatively little money was involved until the 1930s when President Franklin D. Roosevelt, elected with strong support among urban voters, sought to stimulate the economy and bring the nation out of the Depression through federal spending programs, many of which were directed to cities. Urban growth after World War II brought an expansion of federal highway and other programs intended to facilitate suburbanization. The 1960s saw another burst of activity during the presidency of Lyndon B. Johnson. Johnson's Great Society initiatives such as the Fair

Housing Act of 1968, which outlawed discrimination in housing markets, and the Model Cities Act of 1966, which focused redevelopment dollars on needy urban areas, represented an increasing commitment to establishing a coherent national urban policy. The Department of Housing and Urban Development (HUD) was created in 1965 and coordinates most federal urban programs.

One common form of federal aid begun in the 1930s and later expanded is the **categorical grant** in which Congress designates projects (airports, libraries, and so on) and allocates funding for a specific purpose. State and local governments then apply for the funds. If their application fits the project standards set by Congress, they may win a grant. Some local contribution, called matching funds, may be required, but the main task of the local government is to carry out the project according to federal specifications, which include rules on minority hiring and sometimes the participation of citizens in decision making. Federal departments monitor and audit local implementation of all grants. For the federal government, such grants-in-aid are a fast, economical, and handy way of getting what it wants done and of pumping money into the economy without having to create new bureaucracies. For struggling local governments, grants are a way to get money, even if they mean inconvenient paperwork and spending on projects that are not high local priorities. Still, local governments do complain about red tape, and critics have asserted that money is wasted on projects that aren't really needed just because the grants are available. Small and middle-sized cities also have grumbled about **grantsmanship**, the way grants seem to go to big cities that play the game best because they have more representatives and effective lobbyists in Washington.

Criticism has led to reform, although politics is always a factor. Urban grants-in-aid are usually more generous when Democrats are in power, not only because Democrats tend to favor government solutions to problems such as poverty, but also because big cities—the primary grant recipients—generally vote Democratic. Republican presidents Nixon, Ford, Reagan, and George H. W. Bush and George W. Bush, all conservatives with predominantly rural and suburban supporters, scaled back urban grants. One reform was a formula-based distribution of some grant funds based on population, tax effort, income, or the like. All local governments get a share, so red tape and grantsmanship are eliminated. The money has to be spent on a specified range of programs, but communities can choose their own particular projects. Another reform consolidated groups of grants dealing with a particular policy area, such as transportation or housing, into **block grants** under which local governments gained more discretion about how to spend the money within the block category. Although amounts are set by formula, local governments still have to apply for them. The federal government briefly tried revenue sharing, distributing money by formula to states, cities, and counties with no applications required and no strings attached. Local governments liked getting their checks in the mail (who wouldn't?), but the program was ended by the federal government's own budget problems. Despite reforms, grants-in-aid to state and local governments grew in number from 130 in 1960 to 539 in 1981, including programs for airports, transit, roads, housing, sewers, libraries, parks, flood control, law enforcement, water and air quality control, disaster relief, urban renewal, and many more.[18]

The Coming of New Federalism

Although begun under Nixon, the approach known as "**new federalism**" did not take hold until 1981, the year Ronald Reagan became president. The election was a watershed in American politics as the nation dramatically shifted away from its faith in government solutions to social problems. Reagan's conservative revolution—continued under George W. Bush—sought to "return power to the states" and cut federal spending on domestic programs in general and urban projects in particular. Public backlash to big government helped Reagan and many conservative Democrats and Republicans merge some programs into block grants and abolish others, reducing the number of grant programs to around 400, and decreasing funding for such grants for the first time in their history. According to *The Municipal Year Book,* "direct grant assistance declined at a 5.3 percent annual rate between 1980 and 1989."[19]

Some areas were cut more than others. The budget of the Department of Housing and Urban Development, for example, was slashed from $31.9 billion to $15.4 billion under Reagan and the construction of new public housing projects ground to a halt—even as homelessness in the United States skyrocketed. According to *Financial World,* total federal grants to cities alone were "$10.8 billion in 1978–1979. Had that aid grown proportionately to the rise of city expenses, [by 1991] it would [have totaled] over $22 billion. In fact, it totaled just a third of that—a scant $7.3 billion in 1988–1989."[20] In Philadelphia alone, federal aid fell from $250 million in 1980 to $54 million in 1990. In Los Angeles—the site of the worst urban riots in U.S. history in 1992—federal aid for subsidized housing dropped by 82 percent between 1981 and 1992; for job training and employment by 63 percent; and for community development programs by 40 percent. During those years, big city budgets, on average, doubled while the federal contribution declined from 17 to 6 percent.[21]

Under Reagan, federal mandates requiring state and local action on air quality and other environmental issues also added to local costs, again without funding. Local governments turned to the states, which took up part of the slack from their own budgets. Some states sought alternative revenue sources for local governments or assumed greater responsibility for traditionally local concerns such as education. In 1989, President George H. W. Bush continued Reagan's general approach, although he appointed Jack Kemp, a political moderate and advocate of market-oriented redevelopment strategies. But Bush soon became distracted by foreign matters and a nasty recession, and eventually lost the presidency to Democrat Bill Clinton.

With Clinton, hopes for a revival of federal aid to local governments rose, especially among big city mayors, most of whom had supported his candidacy. His appointment of two dynamic individuals, former Denver mayor Federico Pena as Secretary of Transportation and former San Antonio mayor Henry Cisneros as Secretary of Housing and Urban Development, encouraged them, as did the promise of welfare and health care reform, which would especially help big cities. But the massive federal deficit inherited from prior administrations precluded a major refunding of federal aid programs, although money for housing, transportation, community policing, and education was modestly increased. Perhaps more importantly, Clinton ran and governed as a "New Democrat," meaning that he would not seek major expansions of federal urban programs.

Rather, Clinton, who once declared in a State of the Union speech that "the era of big government is over," championed a strategy known as "reinventing government," which sought to streamline government efficiency and eliminate waste. The approach models government functions on the operations of business, much as Progressive Era reformers of the early 1900s had sought to do. Clinton also signed the 1996 Welfare Reform Act, which replaced the 1930s program Aid to Families with Dependent Children (AFDC) with a program known as Temporary Assistance for Needy Families (TANF). TANF provides states with annual block grants and, most importantly, places a five-year lifetime limit on welfare benefits. Although many were forced off of public assistance and into entry-level jobs during the economic boom of the late 1990s, prolonged recession and sluggish economic growth could mean more job layoffs and homelessness in cities. In sum, Clinton's strategy to aid urban areas, including his support of **empowerment zones** that offer tax breaks to encourage urban redevelopment, illustrated something of a hybrid approach of government spending and free-market incentives.

So far, the administration of George W. Bush (2001–present) has focused very little attention on urban issues. Prioritizing foreign affairs during most of his presidency, George W. Bush has emphasized free-market strategies and even "faith-based initiatives" in dealing with urban issues. Through the White House Office of Faith-Based and Community Initiatives, the Bush administration has sought to remove the barriers that had prevented religious organizations from gaining access to federal dollars, in order to help solve issues such as homelessness, poverty, HIV/AIDS, and other social problems. The approach harkens back to the pre–New Deal Era when private philanthropic organizations performed the bulk of charity work in the United States. In his 2006 budget, Bush proposed cutting by 35 percent funding for a program known as Community Development Block Grants (CDBGs). The proposal drew heavy criticism from officials in most of the nation's large cities where CDBG money is relied upon to fund local redevelopment and affordable housing initiatives. But concerns over terrorism and the Iraq war have overshadowed every initiative targeted toward cities. The Bush administration has required cities to respond to security concerns in the wake of the 9/11 terrorist attacks, and urban areas such as New York, Los Angeles, Chicago, and Las Vegas have been forced to spend huge sums of their own money preparing for potential terrorist attack.

Federal Urban Policy

Although the United States has been an urban nation since at least 1920, the country has failed to develop or even seriously consider adopting a national strategy for America's urban areas. Instead, federal policy making has followed something of a crisis and response model: the Depression of the 1930s, housing shortages after World War II, drugs and crime in the 1980s, and urban riots in the 1960s and 1990s, although the latter produced little but hand wringing. Some federal policies, such as those that encouraged suburbanization and the move to the Sunbelt, actually exacerbated the problems of big cities. Even federal urban renewal programs ended up displacing many of the people the programs were supposed to benefit. The contradiction between these two approaches—urban renewal for central cities and policies that stimulate suburbanization—probably reflects the political power that suburbs and rural areas wield over federal policy. Taking into consideration federal subsidies for wealthy and middle-class homeowners such as the home mortgage interest deduction, property tax deduction, and the exclusion of home sales profits from capital gains taxes means that affluent and middle-class Americans are subsidized by government to the tune of more than $100 billion per year. In contrast, money for direct assistance programs such as Section 8 housing, a federally funded voucher program to help poor people pay rent, totaled just over $32 billion in 2000. Thus, it appears that Americans are not averse to government subsidies in theory, but rather to the idea that government spending to support the poor will encourage dependency on government rather than individual initiative.

As we have seen, in the intergovernmental context of American politics, local governments are sometimes reduced to virtual beggars, making their case in federal court, in the lobbies of Congress, or in the regulatory agencies and panhandling the departments that administer federal programs, all on a piecemeal basis. Members of Congress assist the cities and their constituencies in these efforts, although many local governments employ professional lobbyists in Washington, and big city mayors lobby individually and through the U.S. Conference of Mayors. As we have seen, state constraints on their taxing and spending powers have forced local governments to turn to the federal government, which, in recent decades, has been turning away from them.

The Intergovernmental Context of Local Politics

The home rule movement, beginning in the nineteenth century, struggled to wrest power and authority back from the state governments. But the big story of the late twentieth and early twenty-first centuries has been the erosion of municipal autonomy, particularly in the area of city funding. Home rule has been increasingly constrained by state and federal laws, budget crises, and court decisions, among other reasons. True, higher governments have also devolved more responsibilities to local government, such as ensuring clean water and air and helping to prepare for a terrorist attack, but often without providing adequate funding. Indeed, cities have been hit with something of a double whammy: as federal assistance to local government has contracted, the states (usually by voter initiative) have increasingly dipped into the pockets of locals.

If this picture seems gloomy, we should remember that current circumstances are the result of political choices, which are themselves constrained by a country's history, political events, and ideology. It's easy to forget that local government in most other countries is far more centralized than in the United States or any of its states. The cities of Europe, although they lack American-style home rule, are far more secure in their funding, as national governments pay for a broad range of social programs and other services that Europeans prefer. In contrast, U.S. local governments enjoy a much higher degree of home rule, but are far less secure about where their funding will come from. Moreover, as we have seen, Americans are less comfortable with government-funded social programs. It's a balance between government intervention and free-market capitalism that has largely endured throughout American history, and it's one that Americans seem to prefer, particularly in the era of new federalism, when American cities have been increasingly on their own, and far more is left to them as to whether they will sink or swim.

Essential Terms

counties
municipalities
cities
consolidated city-county
towns or townships
special districts
school districts
redevelopment
community development corporations (CDCs)
eminent domain
tax increment financing
bonds
common interest developments (CIDs)
business improvement districts (BIDs)
incorporation
unincorporated
charters
special law charter
general law charter
optional charter
home rule
charter amendments
zoning
general plans
variances
annexation

metropolitan fragmentation
defensive incorporation
deannexation
secession
consolidation
property tax
tax rate
sales tax
borrowing
capital improvement
bonds
tax referendums
mandate spending
intergovernmental aid
Dillon's Rule
reapportionment
malapportionment
federal courts
federal regulation
federal aid
categorical grant
grantsmanship
block grants
new federalism
empowerment zones

On the Internet

- The National League of Cities organizes national lobbying efforts on behalf of municipalities. Their website (www.nlc.org/home/) is a good clearinghouse of information about cities.
- The National Association of Counties website (www.naco.org/) is a good source of information about counties.

- The Downtown Research and Development Center, an advocacy group, is a good source of information about Business Improvement Districts; its website is www.downtowndevelopment.com/bid.php.
- The U.S. Advisory Commission on Intergovernmental Relations is a permanent, independent, bipartisan intergovernmental agency established in 1959 to study ways to improve intergovernmental efficiency; its website is www.library.unt.edu/gpo/ACIR/Default.html.

Notes

1. National League of Cities, www.nlc.org/about_cities/cities_101/166.cfm (accessed July 27, 2005).

2. Evan McKenzie, *Privatopia: Homeowner Associations and the Rise of Residential Private Government* (New Haven, CT: Yale University Press, 1994).

3. Nancy Burns, *The Formation of American Local Governments: Private Values in Public Institutions* (New York: Oxford University Press, 1994).

4. Ibid.

5. See Sho Sato and Arvo Van Alstyne, *State and Local Government Law*, 2nd ed. (Boston: Little, Brown, 1977), p. 143.

6. Joseph P. Viteritti, "The Tradition of Municipal Reform: Charter Revision in Historical Context," in *Restructuring the New York City Government: The Reemergence of Municipal Reform*, ed. Frank J. Mauro and Gerald Benjamin (New York: Academy of Political Science, 1989), pp. 16–30.

7. *Village of Euclid v. Ambler Realty*, 272 U.S. 364 (1926).

8. Rodger Johnson, Marc Perry, and Lisa Lollock, "Annexation and Population Growth in American Cities, 1990–2000," *The Municipal Year Book* (Washington, DC: International City/County Management Association, 2004), p. 3.

9. Vincent L. Marando and Robert D. Thomas, *The Forgotten Governments: County Commissioners as Policy Makers* (Gainesville: University Presses of Florida, 1977), p. 22.

10. *New York Times*, May 28, 2004.

11. David R. Berman, "State Actions Affecting Local Governments," *The Municipal Year Book* (Washington, DC: International City/County Management Association, 1989), p. 129.

12. John Dillon, *Commentaries on the Law of Municipal Corporations*, 5th ed. (Boston: Little, Brown, 1911), p. 448.

13. *Baker v. Carr*, 369 U.S. 189 (1962); and *Reynolds v. Sims*, 377 U.S. 533 (1964).

14. Quoted in the *New York Times*, October 8, 1990.

15. Stephen Elkin, *City and Regime in the American Republic* (Chicago: University of Chicago Press, 1987), pp. 19, 20–21, 50.

16. Berman "State Actions," p. 55.

17. *Trenton v. New Jersey*, 262 U.S. 182 (1923).

18. U.S. Bureau of the Census, *Statistical Abstract of the United States, 1983* (Washington, DC: U.S. Government Printing Office, 1983), p. 296.

19. Frank Shafroth, "The Reagan Years and the Nation's Cities," *The Municipal Year Book* (Washington, DC: International City/County Management Association, 1989), p. 115.

20. Katherine Barrett and Richard Greene, "American Cities," *Financial World*, February 19, 1991, p. 24.

21. David R. Morgan and Michael W. Hirlinger, *Urban Affairs Quarterly* 29, no. 2 (December 1993): 257.

Part II

Official Decision Makers: Inside City Hall

We now turn from the social, economic, demographic, and intergovernmental contexts of local politics to the content of the charters that create and empower local governments. In the next few chapters, we will examine the structures, institutions, and forms of local government.

Charters set up the structures of local government and allot power formally, but formal power, or authority, is only one kind of power. This sort of power comes with office or position. Its holders may order us to act in certain ways and prohibit other actions with legal sanctions such as fines or imprisonment to back them up. But informal power, such as the influence of political parties, newspapers, chambers of commerce, neighborhood groups, or even single individuals who hold no public office, also operates in every community alongside the formal authority allocated by charter.

The informal structure of power, discussed further in chapter 11, reflects the social, economic, and demographic environment of each community and, in turn, shapes the formal distribution of power in its charter—along with state law, as we saw in the previous chapter. People with informal power seek to institutionalize that power in city and county charters through the formal structures of government they advocate, either in state or local politics. If they succeed—and if they are real power holders, they do—power is frozen for a time, to their advantage, for as we will see, structures of government are not neutral. They give advantage to some and disadvantage others; they affect who has access to positions of power and who gains those positions; they make some more likely to win and others more likely to lose, not only in campaigns for office but on issues; and they influence the substance of public policy, or what government does.

But communities change, and so do their informal power structures. New powers, perhaps economic interests or recently organized minorities, emerge and expect access. If the formal distribution of power is too rigid to absorb them, if they fail to gain attention or office, they may conclude that governmental structures are holding them back and seek to change those structures. If the community and its informal power structure have changed enough—if the new interests are really powerful—such a change will occur, and the formal allocation of power will be brought into line with informal power, at least until the community changes again. This interplay between formal and informal power will be apparent in the following chapters, as we examine three basic forms of city government along with the forces that created them.

5 Forms of Government
From Weak Mayors and Machines to the Beginnings of Reform

The oldest form of local government in the United States is the town or township meeting of all local voters, usually held annually. At these meetings, local officials are elected and laws and taxes are approved. This system, which dates from colonial times, operates only in some New England states and has become rare because few communities are small enough for it to function well, even though it remains an American ideal. When a town gets to be more than a village, more elaborate structures are usually adopted.

Since the days of the town meeting, U.S. communities have grown and developed, increasing in diversity and complexity. The forms of government they adopted also changed. Town meetings were gradually replaced by elected, representative government. In the early days of the republic, the weak mayor system predominated, and it still survives in some communities. But by the mid-nineteenth century, spurred by economic growth and immigration, corrupt political bosses and machines had subverted the weak mayor system and set in motion an urban reform movement. The initial result of reform was the strong mayor form of government, although by the turn of the century, reformers were ready to propose more radical change.

The Weak Mayor Form of Government

The oldest major form of local government in the United States is the weak mayor system, forged by the American Revolution. Having just overthrown an authoritarian monarch, Americans were unwilling to grant their own executive officers much power. At the national level, the Articles of Confederation set up a feeble government with virtually no executive. States and cities at least had governors and mayors, but their powers were strictly and elaborately limited by even more checks and balances than those that would appear in the U.S. Constitution in 1787.

The Mayor. The mayor in the **weak mayor system** is only a nominal chief executive. The city council (the local legislature) and other appointed or elected executive officers also hold substantial power. Initially, the mayor was appointed by the council from among its members and served mainly as a presiding officer. Some weak mayor cities still operate this way, although after 1820, many began to elect their mayors directly. The weakness of the office comes from limits on the traditional executive powers of appointment and administration.

111

Figure 5.1 **The Weak Mayor Form of Government**

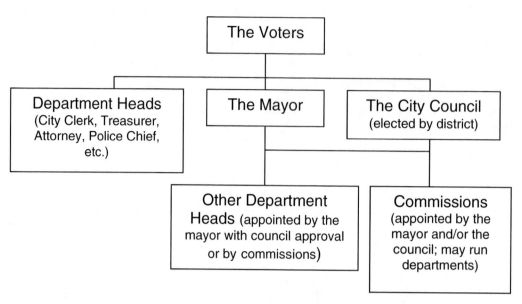

The Council. **City councils** in this form of government also reflect the democratic values of its founders. They tend to be large in size, numbering fifteen to fifty members, and are elected by wards or districts. Each district covers just a part of the city, ensuring every neighborhood its own council member, although in large districts members may represent several neighborhoods. Besides acting as the legislature, the city council in a weak mayor form of government plays a prominent part in the normally executive functions of appointment, administration, and budgeting. Council powers are enhanced by the inability of the mayor to veto or reject its actions. But power is not centralized in the council, either. As the demands on city government became too great for councils to handle, some responsibility was devolved to commissions or boards. Usually with around five members appointed by the council or mayor or both, or sometimes elected, these commissions run certain city departments.

The Long Ballot. In the 1830s, Jacksonian democracy brought the election of the mayor as well as other members of the executive branch, including the city attorney, city clerk, treasurer, and department heads such as the police chief (see Figure 5.1). The **long ballot** resulting from the election of so many officers is highly democratic, but it also fragments executive authority. Even where charters give mayors some responsibility for the operations of the city departments, their administrative powers are severely limited by having to deal with independently elected department heads with constituencies of their own. To compound the problem, other officers, boards, or commissions are appointed by the city council to run departments. The best a weak mayor can usually hope for is the power to appoint some of these officials, often subject to city council approval and rarely with the power to remove appointees from office.

The Weak Mayor System

The weak mayor system, with mayors denied the veto and with their administrative and hiring and firing powers severely constrained, accomplished the political goal of its post-Revolutionary framers, who wanted to avoid dictatorial executives. But the cities they wrote their charters for were small, and their electorates, confined to white male property owners, were smaller, with clearly shared interests. The weak mayor system probably worked well in such circumstances since all its participants were similar and easily agreed on city policy. But cities grew and became more diverse, with expanding populations demanding access to local offices and disagreeing more about what should be done. From the 1820s onward, the ideals of Jacksonian democracy gradually brought wider participation and more elected officials within the basic weak mayor system.

The goal of Jacksonian democracy was greater citizen participation, but unfortunately, the system didn't always function ideally. Power was fragmented, with authority widely distributed among a large number of officeholders, making it hard to get things done and often failing to deliver effective, efficient local government. Political leadership could not surmount this fragmentation because the office of mayor was, by the very nature of the system, little more than titular. No one person was clearly in charge.

Even the democratic values of the system were subverted by the absence of accountability—when things went wrong, the voters didn't know whom to blame. For example, if crime increased in a neighborhood, the voters could go to their district council member, who could claim to have raised the issue only to have been ignored by the police chief, the mayor, and the rest of the council. The police chief and the mayor, representing the same voters, might blame the problem on one another or on an ineffective council representative. Short of throwing them all out, which is difficult for a single neighborhood to achieve, the discontented constituents could only mutter among themselves and bolt their doors.

The weak mayor system works reasonably well in small, homogeneous cities where people are in general agreement and don't expect a lot from their government. When they need something done, informal, personal relationships can cut through the fragmentation. So the weak mayor form works best when local government doesn't need to do much, as was the case at the time of its creation. Industrialization, immigration, and growth put the system under strain, however. Diversity increased and social homogeneity was reduced. Disagreements and conflicts arose as new interests and groups wanted a piece of the action. The informal, personal contacts of small communities no longer function in big cities, where social relations are formal and impersonal. Growth also brings bigger problems, from sewage to traffic and crime, which need action and which a leaderless, fragmented government simply cannot solve. Local growth machine interests often feel that inefficient government is holding them back. For all these reasons, the weak mayor form of government today operates mostly in small, relatively homogeneous cities, mostly in the Northeast and Midwest.

Some large cities, including Atlanta and Chicago, stuck with the weak mayor form of government longer than others, but over time these cities have given their mayors more power and abandoned the weak mayor form. Los Angeles, the second largest city in the United States, is a case in point. Until recently, the mayor of Los Angeles had a high profile, but limited power. Most of the city's sixteen departments, including police and fire, were run by independent commissions that hired the department heads and oversaw their budgets. Commissioners, who served five-year terms, were appointed by the mayor with council approval. In 1991, when the videotaped beating of a black citizen by police officers outraged the city, then-mayor Tom Bradley, an African American and former police officer, was unable to control the city's police department. Even with city council support, the mayor could not fire the city's controversial police chief, Daryl Gates, who had been appointed by the police commission rather than the mayor, and who enjoyed the added protection of civil service rules, a reform adaptation of the weak mayor system. "I cannot conceive of a city like Los Angeles where the mayor does not have the power to appoint or dismiss department heads," said Bradley. "It's a terrible system."[1] A bad situation turned worse in 1992 when the white officers who were videotaped doing the beating were found not guilty by a predominantly white jury and rioting broke out in Los Angeles and elsewhere. Only unrelenting political pressure finally forced the disgraced police chief to reluctantly resign.

Los Angeles voters then revised their charter to limit their police chief to a five-year term (subject to one reappointment by the mayor), and a new, black, community-oriented chief took office. Los Angeles, with urban problems of mind-boggling complexity and 3.7 million people of astonishingly diverse backgrounds (47 percent are Hispanic, 30 percent white/non-Hispanic, 11 percent African American, and 10 percent Asian), is a city that had clearly outgrown a weak mayor charter written by and for a white, business-dominated community in 1924. In 1999, Los Angeles voters approved a new charter increasing the mayor's power to fire department heads, along with some other reforms.

Many other cities, experiencing similar if less dramatic problems, have moved beyond the weak mayor system. But charter change is not the only solution to these problems. Political organization outside the formal structures of government can be an alternative way to make awkward systems work and, in most communities, such organizations preceded structural reform.

Bosses and Machines: Coping with Fragmentation

The weak mayor system created a vacuum in leadership and authority when cities grew large. Sometime in the nineteenth century, local politicians began figuring out a way to fill the vacuum, overcome the fragmentation, and make local government work, although not necessarily efficiently or fairly. All they had to do was fill the multiple offices of the weak mayor system with allies who would cooperate with one another. With many officials elected on long ballots, campaigns and candidates had to be carefully coordinated. This was easy in small, homogeneous cities, but it became difficult when the cities grew large and diverse, with many competing groups.

Slate-Making

Slates, or lists of approved candidates for various offices, from coroner to city council, mayor, governor, and even president, solved the problem. These lists were agreed on by political party activists who cut deals at meetings, in bars, or in smoke-filled back rooms. A single candidate was chosen for each office, and the candidates and their supporters all agreed to support one another. A successful slate would include candidates from different neighborhoods, ethnic groups, and other constituencies, thus pulling together diverse interests to support rather than compete with one another by providing something for everyone. Once the slate was selected, it had to be taken to the voters, and elaborate organizations evolved to do just that.

But what could hold such an organization together? Shared values or ideology might be one way, but, as analysts of political culture tell us, the Americans are more pragmatic than ideological, preferring problem solving and getting things done to philosophical or theoretical debate. The particular responsibilities of local government make a practical orientation even more appropriate at that level than others. After all, local government is about streets and sewers, not war and peace or even economic policy. Besides, the diverse groups that made up the slates probably disagreed about ideological values. Political parties proved a somewhat better unifying force, at least in the past, but Americans are not particularly partisan, often voting for candidates of different parties.

Political Machines

Political parties, provided the emerging urban political organizations with a unifying label, though often it amounted to little more than a front. To sell their slate, organizations needed stronger glue. They found it in greed, combined with the real and serious needs of many recently arrived immigrants in the nineteenth-century industrializing cities. The slate-making organizations distributed rewards to win and hold support. These rewards were, as political scientists Edward C. Banfield and James Q. Wilson have pointed out, "both specific and material."[2] They were specific in that only supporters received these benefits, and material in that they involved jobs, contracts, and other, often minor, favors, ranging from a turkey at Thanksgiving to a drink on election day. These rewards were distributed so efficiently that the organizations came to be called **machines**.[3] Insiders got jobs at city hall and with businesses allied with the machine. Many such businesses also profited enormously from their association with machines. Ordinary citizens could go to the machine for help (although the machine often went to them) when they needed a ticket fixed or had problems with housing or jobs or when the kids needed a new pair of shoes. And the machine could punish as well as reward. Enemies as well as those who merely failed to support the machine were not only denied benefits but often made to suffer. They could lose jobs or contracts for goods or services, be harassed by police or health inspectors, or be subjected to social abuse by neighbors.

The distribution of both rewards and punishments in exchange for support is called **patronage**, or the spoils system, based on the old saying, "to the victor belong the spoils," and the machines exploited it with a vengeance. To them, local government was little more than a way of making money, not in a growth machine sense, but more immediately, out of its daily operations.

IN YOUR COMMUNITY
Research the political history of your community at the local library. Has a political machine ever operated there? What was its base, who was left out, and how long did it last? (If you live in a suburb or other relatively new municipality, pick a large, older city nearby.)

Industrialization and Immigration

In a way, the weak mayor form of government with its vacuum of power made machines inevitable, but other factors were also essential to their success. Machines have operated in homogeneous, small cities and rural communities, but they had their heyday in the growing industrial cities between about 1880 and 1930. Before that, in smaller cities, informal, personal contacts cut through the structural inefficiencies of the weak mayor form of government and Yankee cultural values, disdainful of corruption and selling votes, predominated. But the industrial revolution transformed U.S. cities. Millions of immigrants arrived from all over Europe, often bewildered and in need of help. These urban immigrants supplied the machines with a dependent, manipulable voting base.

Ethnic identity was used as a building block by the machines, many of which were dominated by particular ethnic groups, especially, but by no means exclusively, the Irish and Italians. Saint Patrick's or Columbus Day parades became as much celebrations of political power as of ethnic traditions. Other European ethnic groups were allies, taking their places on electoral slates and enjoying their share of the machine's rewards. Newly arrived immigrants, lonely and far from their native lands, welcomed the solidarity and community the machines shrewdly provided.

How the Machines Helped

But as cynically manipulative as the machines may have been, they provided genuinely needed psychological reassurance and other, more tangible services as well. They helped assimilate the immigrant masses to U.S. society, giving them a sense of belonging to something and teaching them some aspects of U.S. culture. In an immediate and practical sense, the machines were the social workers of their day. Arriving immigrants were greeted by machine operatives who spoke their language and helped them settle into the appropriate ethnic neighborhood—a sort of segregation that was useful to the machine for organizing but was also comforting to the strangers in a strange land. Housing could be found, jobs could be obtained, and the children could be placed in schools, where they quickly Americanized. If the family fell on hard times, the machine stepped in to help.

Organization of the Machines

To accomplish all this, the machines developed an elaborate organizational structure, operating under the aegis of a political party and associated with city government, but not part of it. At the top was the leader, or **boss**, with other party chieftains. These leaders might or might not be elected officials. They didn't need to be officials because their power came not from government but from the machine. Government officials were sometimes merely the machine's carefully selected minions, carrying out orders. City council wards or districts provided the next organizational unit, each with its own constellation of ethnic neighborhoods and its own leader who, like the bosses above him (they were virtually all men), probably was a full-time organizer rather than the district council member. Beneath the ward boss was a network of precinct or block captains who knew everybody in their neighborhood, kept track of supporters, made sure they voted, and distributed the benefits and punishments of the machine. Once called **ward heelers** because of the shoe leather they wore out making their rounds, they were the machine's eyes and ears in the neighborhoods, its enforcers as well as its social workers. More than that, however, they personalized the machines by being part of the communities they organized. They lived in and hung out in the neighborhoods, drinking in the bars, chatting on street corners and doorsteps, going to funerals and weddings. They knew everybody's name, from children to grandparents, and took part in their lives, providing help when it was needed. All they expected in exchange was votes or, in the case of those who got jobs and contracts, a little kickback for the campaign treasury.

For the immigrant poor and working classes, this was not a bad deal. Coming from undemocratic countries, their votes may not have meant much to them, but even if they had, why wouldn't they support the people who helped and nurtured them? For the machines were not just organizations, they were people. The machine's representatives personalized politics and government. They were seen as friends by many of the constituents they helped (and kept in line). Machine supporters got something in return for their votes, which is more than many of today's voters feel they get. Those in need were given assistance and treated with dignity and respect because they had something the machine wanted, while even the most deserving recipients of government services today often feel insulted or humiliated by impersonal, bureaucratic agencies.

In Your Community

Using census data, trace the growth of a large city in your state from 1870 to 1920. What immigrant groups played a significant role in that growth? Was the growth related to the rise of a political machine?

Business and the Machines

Although the poor and working classes supplied the mass voting base for the machines, business interests benefited, too. Lucrative contracts for building city facilities or for goods and services purchased by the city were awarded to machine supporters, usually with an expected kickback. Millions were made and wasted in such deals. Some business allies won highly profitable licensed monopolies, or franchises, as the exclusive operators of gas, electricity, water, or trolley companies. Other businesses, such as gambling, prostitution, and speakeasies (during Prohibition) were protected by the machine, which made sure the police overlooked the operations of their pals and tormented their competitors.

Even businesses less directly connected to the machine willingly accepted its rule and sometimes used its services. Many newspapers were well connected to machines, which could help with (or create) union or distribution problems as well as supply readers. Small businesses, such as restaurants, might appreciate a lax health inspection. Industrialists or merchants might want quick zoning decisions. The machine could cut through the complexities of fragmented government and guarantee results for those who cooperated. With so much money involved, even banks acquiesced.

Urban and Rural Machines

These sorts of machines were most common in the big, industrializing cities of the Frostbelt. Among the most notorious and long-lasting machines were those of New York City, Albany, Boston, Philadelphia, Jersey City, Hoboken, Baltimore, Cincinnati, Indianapolis, and Chicago. Machines were less prevalent in the cities of the Sunbelt states, where industrialization and immigration were slower. Powerful machines nevertheless took root in New Orleans, Memphis, Savannah, Charleston, Augusta, Chattanooga, Montgomery, Jacksonville, Tampa, and San Francisco.

Machines also arose in rural areas and small cities all over the country, suggesting that masses of immigrants were not crucial to their development. The bosses of rural and small-town machines could be just as ruthless and corrupt as their urban counterparts. The most famous of the urban machines were associated with the Democratic Party, but in rural areas and a few big cities, such as Philadelphia, some were Republican. The entire state of California, including big cities and rural counties, was run by a Republican political machine dominated by the state's monopoly railroad company from about 1880 to 1910.

Corruption, Favoritism, and Inefficiency

The machines made government work and provided an important social connection for people who might otherwise have been lost and alienated in the impersonal societies created by rapid urbanization. But their benefits were outweighed by their shortcomings. The machines were notoriously, publicly, even boastfully corrupt. "I see my opportunity and I take it," said a leader of New York's machine.[4] Taxpayers' money was stolen and legitimate business profits were drained away by machines. Local government services such as transit and utilities cost more because the minions of the machine were on the take. And these higher costs were driven even higher by inefficiency. After all, the machine was more concerned that its supporters got jobs and contracts than it was with their performance. Whether an applicant for a job as health inspector knew anything about sanitation or a contractor could build a sound bridge or supply well-made goods at reasonable prices was less important than his loyalty to the machine. This was the glue that held the machine together, but it almost guaranteed inefficient, amateurish, and corrupt government.

Those who benefited directly and personally, even if only occasionally and in small ways, were satisfied, as were those who identified with the machine socially. But others were left out. Some ethnic groups were excluded, either because they wouldn't play the game or because they weren't invited due to prejudice. Ethnic animosities from old country homelands kept some out. Jews were excluded from some machines, but rose to leadership in others. Asians, Hispanics, and African Americans were often spurned, although in cities such as Chicago and Memphis, minority organizations operated as subsidiaries of the dominant machine.

But the largest group that was left out by the machine was the rapidly growing urban middle and upper-middle classes. These included lawyers, merchants, managers, bankers, doctors, teachers, and other professionals. Some individuals among these groups were associated with the machines, at least occasionally, but for most, the machine had little to offer. They didn't want a job at city hall or, with some exceptions, a contract either. Some didn't mind a favor now and then (such as having a ticket fixed or a zoning regulation changed), but most believed that government should take care of its responsibilities fairly and efficiently, not by playing favorites and not by spending tax money on inept city staff and graft. The very principles of the machine violated their professional, middle-class values, and its toleration of gambling, prostitution, and rum-running was an affront to middle-class morality. To the mostly white, Anglo-Saxon, Protestant (WASP) upper and middle classes, the machines didn't seem very American, not only in their values but also in their composition. These classes also disapproved of the way the machines bought votes by handing out favors. As educated professionals, they thought votes should be cast intelligently, for the good of the community rather than for personal benefit. But they were also apprehensive of the machines' immigrant support base, which, unlike their own immigrant forbears, was mostly Irish or eastern or southern European and Catholic. These "foreigners" were taking over their cities. Thanks to assimilation accelerated by the machine itself, some of the children of these foreigners joined the ranks of the middle-class malcontents.

Bigger economic interests also grew discontented at the wastefulness and inefficiency of the political machines, with which most had played along when it suited them. Some businesses wanted a more stable, reliable, and tax-efficient local government and worried about the machine's role as an intermediary with their workers. Local growth machine interests were also discontented with the political machines. Many landowners, builders, and others who sought benefits from more rapid growth concluded that the machines were holding them back. Physical improvements to the cities, such as street lighting and sewers, were not happening fast enough or competently enough. The big financial institutions that loaned cities money (through bonds) for such works were reluctant to do so when cities were notoriously corrupt. Emergent national corporations were unwilling to locate new plants in such places. Growth machines felt stymied and turned against their one-time allies in the political machines.

The Collapse of the Political Machines

Urban political machines went into decline at the beginning of the twentieth century. The most obvious cause of their demise is the reform movement created by the dissatisfied middle class and business interests described earlier. Some of the changes in government structures the reformers introduced wounded the machines deeply, but such reforms could not have been achieved if other changes hadn't made them politically feasible. The reform movement and its agenda will be discussed in the next section and, in greater depth, in the next chapter, but, first, we need to consider other forces that weakened the machines.

The reform movement would never have been possible if demographic change had not enlarged the class base for reform and weakened the machines in other ways as well. The cultural and economic **assimilation** of immigrants made them less willing to accept the values of machine politics because they needed its jobs and help less. Many became middle class; some moved to the suburbs. Ironically, their assimilation and cultural advance was assisted by the machines, which thus contributed to their own decline. To survive, the machines needed a constant influx of needy, new immigrants, but the flow of European immigrants was cut off by national legislation introduced in 1924 by antimachine reformers. Immigrants were still arriving in the cities, but by the late 1920s, these were mostly African Americans from the rural South, who many racist machines refused to include—at their own peril. With a growing middle class and changed patterns of immigration, the demographic base of the machines was shrinking.

Then the Great Depression of the 1930s brought mass unemployment and hardship, slowing the rise of the middle class but not helping the machines. Although they had long exploited such conditions among the urban working class and poor, the Depression expanded the scale of people's needs beyond what the machines could meet. Unemployment in big cities rose to 25 and even 50 percent, far beyond the level for which the machines could provide jobs or other assistance. With the support of urban and rural machines, Democratic President Franklin D. Roosevelt introduced the social welfare programs of the New Deal. But the new welfare system eventually hurt the machines because assistance was taken out of their hands and provided by a new welfare bureaucracy on the basis of objective need rather than political affiliation or loyalty to the machine. Some machines managed to control the new bureaucracies, but over the long run, the new system they helped bring about hurt them all.

Even before the mass unemployment of the Depression, however, other urban problems had grown increasingly complex and beyond the capacity of the corrupt and technically amateur machines to solve. Industrialization and population growth increased both need and demand for improved housing, transportation, public safety, and sanitation, and the expanding middle class called for good schools and for amenities such as parks and libraries. Many machines simply could not cope with it all.

After World War II, other social changes helped finish off the machines. With the economy booming, people needed the machine less, and suburbanization proceeded apace, draining away the third or fourth generations of machine families. Radio and then television kept people indoors and at home, rather than on the stoops and in neighborhood bars and other public gathering places where the machine's operatives could socialize with them. Home visits increasingly meant that favorite TV programs were interrupted or that ward heelers wasted their time silently watching them with the families.

In sum, the machines were weakened by social changes, some of which they helped bring about. The reform movement, which would have been impossible without these changes, merely hastened the process. The strength of the machines, however, is manifested by the fact that their demise took well over fifty years. Like Arnold Schwarzenegger in the *Terminator* movies, political machines kept coming back, surviving waves of change and reform to live, fight, and win again. Some fought their last battles in the 1950s, and Chicago's machine hung on until the death of its boss, Mayor Richard J. Daley, in 1976 (his son, Richard M. Daley is now mayor, but not boss, of Chicago). Although most are now history, the vestiges of machines are still important if not dominant political factions in such cities as Albany, Chicago, and Hoboken. In others, including several cities in New York and New Jersey, their style of favors in exchange for support still operates.

Today, journalists and other people often refer to the "machine" of this or that politician, but usually they only mean the organized backers of an individual, a group that is not like the old machines, either in structure or in strength. The organizations of today's politicians are mostly loyal to a single person, but the loyalty of the old machines was to themselves, whoever the leaders were. Bosses were important, but the machines survived changes at the top. Today *machine* is usually a figure of speech, as in the concept of growth machines introduced in chapter 2.

The First Reform: The Strong Mayor Form of Government

Opposition to political machines is as old as the machines themselves. After the Civil War, crusading journalists, who came to be known as **muckrakers**, exposed corruption and campaigned for change, joined by many upper- and middle-class, often anti-immigrant, citizens. Aroused opponents of the machines soon emulated them, putting together slates of candidates and sometimes successfully winning local office. They rarely gained complete control or stayed in office long, however, because the ideals that held them together were not as binding as the machine's rewards.

The opponents of the machine claimed they just wanted good government, not for themselves personally, but, they insisted, for the community as a whole. Their perception of the public good was often confused with their own class interests, but few seem to have entered politics to gain individual benefits. Unlike their machine counterparts, most did not see themselves as career politicians and expected to go back to their own businesses and professions after a term or two in office. But well meaning as they may have been, they usually found themselves unable to achieve their goals.

The machine was not easily beaten. Its operatives hung on, gaining advantage where they could. Perhaps they could win just a few of the offices on the long ballots. Under the fragmented weak mayor form of government, these offices might be enough to stop the reformers from doing much. Or they would simply outlast the reformers. Maybe it would take an election or two, but the promise of personal reward kept their workers loyal while they waited for the reformers to go back to their businesses, more likely frustrated than satisfied with their accomplishments. One machine politician called the reformers "mornin' glories,"[5] because they bloomed briefly, then wilted. When they did, the machine made its comeback.

Soon the advocates of good government concluded that winning occasional elections was not enough. They needed to change not only the personnel of local government but also its structure. After all, the nation had moved beyond the Articles of Confederacy to stronger government barely a decade after the revolution. Many states had similarly reformed their governments. Now it was the cities' turn.

The **reform movement** was born, and its first product was the strong mayor form of government. The concepts of reform and strong mayor may seem contradictory since the reformers were fighting powerful bosses. But the strength of the bosses came from their command of the machines or party organizations, not the office of mayor. As noted, many bosses never held elective office. The idea of the reformers was to put enough power in the hands of a single, strong executive to get something done once they won an election.

The Short Ballot. Instead of a long ballot with several elected executive officers and department heads, under the strong mayor form of government only one executive, the mayor, is elected. On this **short ballot**, the city council is also usually smaller, so voters elect fewer officials and can more easily hold them accountable. As Figure 5.2 suggests, this much-simplified structure of city government revolves around the chief executive.

The Strong Mayor. In a **strong mayor system**, the office of mayor is modeled on that of the U.S. president. The mayor is elected for a four-year term and can be reelected for unlimited terms (term limits were introduced later in some cities). As chief executive, the mayor formulates the budget, recommends policy, and oversees the day-to-day administration of city programs. The mayor appoints and removes department heads, usually without the approval of the city council, although mayoral appointment of some officials, such as the city attorney and the city clerk, may require council approval or, in some cases, these may still be elected positions. Members of city boards and commissions are also appointed and removed by the mayor, but usually with council consent.

The Council. The city council in a strong mayor form of government is a more purely legislative body with less involvement in administration. Nevertheless, the council must approve the mayor's budget and programs and often some appointments. The mayor, however, may **veto** council actions, with a two-thirds vote by the council required to override the veto. While weak mayors usually preside over council meetings and vote with the council, strong mayors generally do not. As with the national government, the executive branch is clearly separate from the legislature.

The Strong Mayor System

The benefits of the strong mayor form of city government include leadership, clear accountability to the voters, and better-coordinated government more able to deal with complex urban problems. The fragmentation of the weak mayor form of government is resolved—government can govern. Political scientists generally advocate the system for these reasons. Mayors like it, too. But activists in many communities

Figure 5.2 **The Strong Mayor Form of Government**

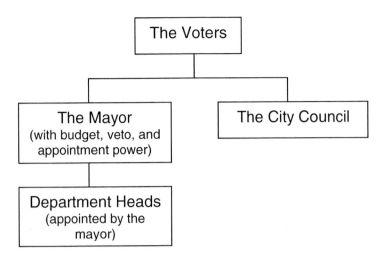

worry about a single individual having so much power (an issue that strangely arises for mayors but rarely for the far more powerful U.S. president). Checks and balances are provided by council approval of the mayor's budget and policy proposals, but some cities have modified the pure strong mayor form of government with additional checks, including term limits and council approval of selected appointments.

Another common concern about the strong mayor system has been that although the chief executive must be a skilled politician to get elected, there is no guarantee that he or she will have the management skills to run a highly complex administrative apparatus (another concern that doesn't seem to arise with the presidency). Mayors who want to stay in office or advance may also pay more attention to winning elections than to mundane matters of administration. To address this problem, most cities with strong mayors have changed their charters to allow the mayor (usually with council approval) to appoint a **chief administrative officer (CAO)**. The CAO is supposed to be a trained administrator, charged with overseeing the technical operations of the city, answerable to the mayor, and under the overall policy direction of the mayor and council. San Francisco introduced the CAO in 1931 and many cities have adopted it since then. Some, including New York and Los Angeles, have more than one of these officials and call them deputy mayors.

Overall, the strong mayor form of government is most commonly found in large cities, including Baltimore, Boston, Cleveland, Detroit, New York, Philadelphia, Pittsburgh, St. Louis, and San Francisco, and mostly in the Northeast and Midwest, where big cities first emerged in the United States. Few cities, however, have systems as pure and simple as the one presented in Figure 5.2. Most have chosen to introduce at least modest limits on executive power. Such limits are the result of the chronic mistrust of executives in local government—a mistrust far greater than that of state and national executives. The bosses and machines created the distrust and went on justifying it, for if the strong mayor system made it easier for reformers to gain control of local government and get things done, it also made it easier for the machines. Their slate making was simplified and their command of government was often more thorough thanks to this reform.

Efforts to make the office of mayor more powerful started in the 1880s and continued through the turn of the century, a time when enough of the social changes described previously had occurred to produce a reform movement but not to destroy the machines. Far from being vanquished, they survived and even thrived under the strong mayor form of government. Their frustrated opponents reacted by escalating their demands for reform.

IN YOUR COMMUNITY
Research the form of government of the largest city in your state. Compare and contrast its form of government with the weak mayor and strong mayor models described in this chapter.

Change and Reform

As we noted, U.S. cities emerged in the nineteenth century, burgeoning with growth brought about by industrialization and immigration. And this growth also brought political change. The old order, the WASP elites, lost control of local politics to the bosses and machines that skillfully organized and controlled the immigrant masses while cutting deals with business interests. Working-class and poor voters benefited from the machine in small, personal ways, but machines never really spoke for their class interests or advocated serious social reform. In fact, it was in the machine's interest to keep its supporters dependent. But change continued to happen, with an emerging urban middle class and, eventually, reduced immigration, the Depression, New Deal social welfare, and suburbanization. The base of the machine started to crumble and the reformers launched their challenge, first electorally and then structurally with the strong mayor form of government. Neither defeated the machine, which lived to fight another day, and often to win. But the reformers were not easily discouraged, and as we will see, history was on their side.

Essential Terms

weak mayor system	assimilation
city councils	muckrakers
long ballot	reform movement
slates	short ballot
machines	strong mayor system
patronage	veto
boss	chief administrative officer (CAO)
ward heelers	

On the Internet

- The American Immigration Home Page (www.bergen.org/AAST/Projects/Immigration/) has a history of immigration to America.
- The U.S. Bureau of the Census website, at www.census.gov, provides online access to current and past census data on immigration.
- The Geostat Center, at www.fisher.lib.virginia.edu/collections/stats/histcensus/, has population and economic information for U.S. states and counties from 1790 to 1960.
- Try Googling "bosses and machines" or "Tammany Hall" (the name for the New York City machine).

Notes

1. *New York Times*, March 31, 1991.
2. Edward C. Banfield and James Q. Wilson, *City Politics* (New York: Vintage, 1963), p. 115.
3. For studies of political machines, see John M. Allswang, *Bosses, Machines, and Urban Voters*, rev. ed. (Baltimore: Johns Hopkins University Press, 1986); Alexander B. Callow, Jr., ed., *The City Boss in America: An Interpretive Reader* (New York: Oxford University Press, 1976); Harold F. Gosnell, *Machine Politics: Chicago Model*, 2nd ed. (Chicago: University of Chicago Press, 1968); Milton Rakove, *Don't Make No Waves—Don't Back No Losers: An Insider's Analysis of the Daley Machine* (Bloomington: Indiana University Press, 1975); Mike Royko, *Boss: Richard J. Daley of Chicago*, rev. ed. (New York: Plume, 1988); and J. T. Salter, *Boss Rule* (New York: McGraw-Hill, 1935).
4. William L. Riordan, *Plunkitt of Tammany Hall: A Series of Very Plain Talks on Very Practical Politics . . .* , rev. ed., introduction by Terrence J. McDonald (Boston: Bedford Books of St. Martin's Press, 1994), p. 3.
5. Ibid., pp. 17–20.

6 Reform Politics
The City-Manager Form of Government and Beyond

The reform movement that emerged in the 1880s and 1890s picked up steam at the turn of the century and won many victories through the 1920s, when it became less prominent, perhaps because much of its agenda had already been enacted and also because the Depression and World War II were more pressing concerns. But although reform has not occupied center stage in most communities since the 1920s, it does continue to play a part in local politics. Vestiges of reform organizations endure in many places, just as vestiges of machines survive in some, albeit as endangered species. The influence of the reformers also survives in the mind-set or culture of local politics. More significantly, however, the reform movement left in place governmental structures that shape politics in most communities today, nearly a century after they were first enacted. In some cases, these reform institutions had effects that were not intended; in others, the intended effects have frustrated elements of the communities and have been challenged by a new and different generation of reformers.

The Reformers and Their Agenda

The municipal reformers were predominantly middle and upper class, with the former providing the votes while the latter took the lead in most communities. Upper class, however, is a relative term, here referring not to the mega-rich we read about or see on TV today but to local elites, such as prominent lawyers, department store owners, manufacturers, bankers, landowners, automobile dealers, and even undertakers. These were the people who formed blue-ribbon committees to campaign for good government. Some had held their noses and gone along with the machines when they had to, but when the potential antimachine constituency grew large enough, they grabbed the opportunity to overthrow the inefficient and corrupt machines and increase their profits. They were often joined by the more middle-class clergymen, academics, and journalists. In many communities, women were also prominent in the reform movement, which coincided with the national campaign for women's suffrage.

Conservative Reform

Although women activists gave it a social conscience, the municipal **reform movement** was essentially conservative, seeking to protect and advance the interests of its upper-class leaders and middle-class supporters. The movement scored a public re-lations coup when it seized the reform label, which to most Americans is a positive term meaning change and improvement. The reformers did bring change and im-provement, but mainly for themselves and not for the urban poor or working class.

Machines, however, were also essentially conservative political institutions. Al-though they relied on the votes of the poor and working class, they reciprocated only with small, personal favors (nevertheless appreciated by those in need) and not with more sweeping social reforms that might have benefited their constituents more in the long run but also made them less dependent on the machine itself. The working class was carefully controlled and contained.

In some places, however, the attack on the machines focused on what political scientist Stephen Elkin calls the casualties of the industrial city, demanding more radical **social reform**.[1] Concerned about slums, poverty, crime, appalling working conditions, and other issues, the social reformers, including socialists and radical labor leaders, attacked big business, local economic elites, and machines. Around the turn of the century, they elected mayors in Cleveland, Detroit, and a few other cities and tried to improve living conditions, provide better and cheaper local ser-vices, and raise taxes on business. In most communities, however, social reformers were denounced as dangerous radicals, isolated, and edged out by the more conser-vative municipal reformers described earlier.

Social reformers nevertheless remained a factor in local and national politics through the 1930s. Along with the conservative municipal reformers, they were part of the national **Progressive movement** that helped to elect presidents Theodore Roosevelt, Woodrow Wilson, and, later, Franklin D. Roosevelt. The Progressives successfully campaigned for state and national regulations on monopolies (trusts) and corporations, and for improvements in industrial working conditions, including child labor laws, compensation for work-related accidents, and safety inspections. These programs re-flected the agenda of the social reformers, but conservative municipal reformers were more enthusiastic about the Progressives' **limits on immigration**, which they saw as a way of cutting off the voting base of the machines. Some labor unions also supported immigration controls, to keep out cheap competitors for their jobs. Earlier, racism had led to limits on Asian immigration, but in the 1920s, Congress passed laws setting strict limits on other immigrants as well, especially those from southern Europe. An average of half a million immigrants a year had arrived between 1870 and 1920, mostly going to cities, but the new laws allowed just 150,000 per year. By cutting off the lifeblood of the machines, the ethnocentric WASP elite had struck a significant blow against the machines—and immigrant minorities.

IN YOUR COMMUNITY

Research the political history of your community at the local library. Has it had a reform movement? What reform structures were introduced? Who were its lead-ers? What were their occupations (your local librarian can help you find out)? Were they like the reformers described in this chapter? (If you live in a suburb or other relatively new municipality, pick a large, older city nearby.)

The Municipal Reform Agenda

But long before immigration controls took hold, the municipal reform movement had concentrated its attention on the inefficiency, corruption, and backwardness of the machines. The upper-class reformers condemned the machines for delivering poor services at high cost, thus inhibiting growth and hurting business. The machines, they asserted, took advantage of both ignorant immigrants, whom some reformers disdained as foreigners, as well as the outmoded structures of local government.

The municipal reform movement that resulted from these criticisms of machine politics was based on three essential beliefs, each of which is open to question. First, the reformers postulated that the job of local government was to serve the common good or public interest—not the self-interests catered to by the machines. All would benefit, not just a few, and politics would be based on agreement or consensus, not conflict and selfishness. Pursuit of the common good is a worthy goal, but it is easier to state than to achieve. The very concept of a common good assumes that people and their needs are similar enough to reach a consensus on the responsibilities and services of local government, but, at least in large cities, they are not. As we know, diversity is part of the very nature of urbanism. If people and their needs are not the same, they are unlikely to agree on the common good. For the upper- and middle-class reformers, for example, the public interest meant cheap, efficient local services such as streets and sanitation, but the poor and working classes might have preferred social programs and protection from exploitative employers. In fact, the reformers confused their own interests with the common good; to the extent that others accepted their view, they won another public relations victory.

The second basic belief of the reformers was that they could get politics out of government. They wanted to replace machine politicians operating in their own interests with skilled administrators and technicians running local government on the objective principles of "**scientific management**." The business of local government, the reformers argued, was to provide basic services, such as street maintenance, garbage collection, and sanitation. To the reformers, these were not essentially political matters. "There is no Republican or Democratic way to pave a street," they liked to say, insisting that local government could be run like a well-managed business, with party politics and even politics in general extracted. Their thesis had great appeal (and still does) but, in fact, politics cannot be taken out of government any more than it can be taken out of life. Even the simplest decisions allocate benefits and costs—whose street is to be paved first? Who pays? Does paving come before parks, housing, or schools? Government constantly makes choices, and while the reformers' insistence that such choices be made objectively is a worthy goal, politics always plays a part.

And, finally, the reformers thought they could achieve their aims and transform politics and power by changing the structures of government, by replacing the weak or strong mayor systems with more efficient and incorruptible institutions. (They succeeded to some extent, although they also learned that changing structures doesn't solve problems unless the politics and power in a community also change.) Basing

Table 6.1

The Municipal Reform Package

	Before reform	After reform
Elections	Caucus or Convention	Primaries, Runoffs
	Partisan	Nonpartisan
	District	At-large
	Long ballot	Short ballot
	Concurrent	Isolated
	Representative Democracy	Direct Democracy
Executive	Mayor	Manager
Personnel	Patronage (spoils)	Civil service
Contracts	Patronage (spoils)	Competitive bidding

their actions on these beliefs, they proceeded with considerable political skill to campaign for and enact an astonishing array of structural reforms. Virtually no community was untouched by their efforts.

Reforming Elections: The Pursuit of the Common Good

The reform movement focused on changing municipal charters, the constitutions of local government discussed in chapter 4. In some cities, sweeping reform packages amounting to virtually new charters were proposed by blue-ribbon commissions dominated by the reformers themselves. In others, reforms were introduced piece by piece in individual charter amendments. In either case, the voters had to approve and usually did. Sometimes, however, the reformers took the battle to the state level, pushing through laws or constitutional amendments that imposed changes on every city in the state. These statewide changes usually concerned elections, while the structures of the local government themselves were left to be determined locally.

The full extent of the reform package is outlined in Table 6.1, with the structures and institutions that preceded reform listed in the middle column and those that were part of the reform in the column on the right. The most ardent reform cities enacted the full reform package; others adopted only selected elements; and those most resistant to reform accepted only what the states imposed. Table 6.1 can be seen as a sort of menu from which cities make choices, suiting their own needs and tastes—but not necessarily in any particular order. The components of the reform package were conceived at different times (some as early as the 1890s, some as much as two decades later), so many cities proceeded with reform bit by bit. Only after about 1910 could they contemplate the full package, and many did.

Initially, reform at both state and local levels concentrated on the electoral systems the machines so skillfully manipulated. The reformers sought to break the slate-making power of the machines by altering the way candidates were nominated, removing political parties from local elections, isolating local elections from state and national politics, and more. Although they were the most widely adopted of all the reform ideas, these electoral innovations had a less devastating effect on the machine than the reformers expected, and they also had negative consequences that were probably not anticipated.

The Direct Primary

Before reform, candidates for state and local office were chosen by political parties in caucuses of leaders or in conventions (somewhat larger gatherings of party activists). Power was wielded in infamous "smoke-filled rooms," as bosses cut deals to agree on slates of candidates. This control was essential to machine politics, but left voters a narrow choice between the slates of two parties, one of which was usually dominant. In short, the real choices were made by bosses in backroom deals. The reformers therefore introduced **direct primary** elections in which the voters of each party—not just the bosses—select the nominees themselves in elections held weeks or sometimes months before a final or general election. Anyone who collects a few signatures and pays a small fee can run for a party's nomination for any office. Voters choose among the candidates and the one who gets the most votes becomes the party nominee for a particular office, running against the nominees of other parties, also chosen in primaries. Direct primaries make elections more democratic and weakened the slate-making capacity of machines. The survival capacity of the machines was formidable, however. They were soon cutting their deals in time to ensure victory for their candidates in the primaries.

Nonpartisan Elections

The reformers escalated their attack on party machines by moving to eliminate parties from local elections altogether, forbidding party recruitment and endorsement of candidates and banning party labels from local ballots. In **nonpartisan elections**, candidates are listed on the ballot only by name and sometimes occupation, with no indication of party affiliation. Some cities with nonpartisan elections have primaries to narrow the field of candidates and ensure that whoever is elected has a majority. If one candidate wins more than 50 percent of the primary vote, he or she is declared elected. Otherwise, the top two vote-getters face each other in a **runoff election**.

Nonpartisan elections are perhaps the most widespread of all reforms—with 72.6 percent of all U.S. cities and 94 percent of those in the West having nonpartisan elections. The system is least popular in the Northeast, where nonpartisan elections are used by only 21 percent of the cities—and where the machines lasted longest and were perhaps most powerful. Alaska, California, Idaho, Minnesota, New Mexico, and Wyoming give cities no choice: nonpartisan local elections are required by state law. Only a few states impose nonpartisan elections on counties (including Wisconsin and California, the two states where the Progressive movement was most powerful), but 85 percent of all school board elections are nonpartisan.

The job of the machine was made more difficult by nonpartisan elections because the party couldn't officially select or formally endorse candidates, and machine voters were denied the useful cue of party labels on ballots, but many machines figured out ways of instructing their voters. City council elections in Chicago, for example, are nonpartisan, yet the last vestiges of America's most notorious and long-lasting political machine survive there even now, particularly in white ethnic neighborhoods. In 1989 they were an important part of the coalition that helped elect Mayor Richard M. Daley thirteen years after the death of his father, Richard J. Daley, one of the most powerful bosses in U.S. history. Between the Daleys, reform politicians such as Harold Washington, an African American, won the office of mayor, but they never completely vanquished the machine.[2]

At-Large Elections and Short Ballots

The Progressives also attacked the machines' organizational structure by changing the way city council members were selected. The existing system was by wards or districts, with each member representing a specific area of the city. The reformers saw wards as the building blocks of the machines and also argued that district representation was narrow and parochial, ignoring the needs of the city as a whole. Instead of the common good, reformers believed council members articulated only the interests of the neighborhoods and the ethnic groups in their districts, resulting in conflict, obstruction, and deal making. To break down the machines' neighborhood organization and lessen the parochialism of local politics, the reformers instituted **at-large elections**, through which the whole city elects all members of the council. In some at-large systems, all candidates run against one another for half the council seats in each election and the top vote-getters win, creating a sort of free-for-all that is an advantage for well-known or well-financed candidates and that can be confusing to voters.

To provide better focus, other cities give at-large council seats numbers, and candidates select which one they will run for (and thereby who they will run against); usually, if no one gets more than 50 percent of the vote, the top two face a runoff election. A few cities, recognizing that neighborhood connections have some merit, require that candidates for particular at-large seats live in specified districts of the city; sometimes the primary election is conducted in the district with the city as a whole choosing between the top two candidates in a runoff.

Whatever the details, the reformers felt at-large elections wouldn't work with the large city councils common in the nineteenth century because each voter would be expected to select all members of the council, which could number fifty or more. The reformers therefore reduced the size of city councils to, on average, five to seven members. Districted councils are usually at least twice as large (for example, the Los Angeles city council has fifteen members, while Chicago's has fifty and New York City's has fifty-one). Besides making at-large elections feasible, reformers expected less conflict and more agreement on smaller councils. The **short ballots** resulting from electing fewer council members and other city officials also gave the machines fewer positions for their slates and thus fewer ways to pay off allies.

Today about 60 percent of U.S. cities elect their council members at-large and another 27 percent elect some at-large and some by district. Most large cities, however, especially in the Northeast and Midwest, elect council members by district, as do counties. School boards, however, are mostly chosen at-large.

At-large elections and shortened ballots made it harder for machines to organize ethnic groups and neighborhoods and to make slates. They also somewhat shifted the focus of city councils to broader, citywide issues and lessened conflict since each member represented the same constituency. But adept machines coped with this reform, too; some even found that it simplified their tasks.

Isolated Elections

The reformers also worried about the influence of state and national campaigns on local politics. With balloting for all three levels held at the same time through **concurrent elections**, candidates for local office sometimes won on the coattails of their popular allies for governor or president, even though what motivates voters in state and national races may have nothing to do with local issues. Reformers thought this distorted local politics and aided party machines, so they moved to separate local elections from state and national contests by holding them on different dates. With **isolated elections** the reformers hoped to concentrate voter attention on strictly local concerns. More than 60 percent of U.S. cities and most school districts use isolated elections, which may focus more on local issues, but which also result in lower voter turnout because the stimulus of state and national campaigns is removed. Those who do vote tend to be less representative of the community as a whole, with higher proportions of affluent, conservative voters (the same constituency that supported reform). Machines were thus weakened not only because they couldn't coordinate local campaigns with those for higher office but also because their supporters were less likely to vote.

Direct Democracy

Just in case the machines survived all these reforms, the reformers introduced **direct democracy** as a sort of insurance. Instead of leaving policy making to elected representatives, citizens were given the right to make laws by the **initiative** process. If a specified number of voters sign an initiative petition, a proposed law is put on the ballot and is enacted if it wins a majority. Through the **referendum**, another form of direct democracy, citizens may petition to revoke an act of the council; referendums are also required for charter amendments or borrowing money. Finally, if voters grow discontented with their representatives before they come up for reelection, they can petition for a **recall** election through which the representative may be removed from office.

Direct democracy thus provides a means of expressing the public interest other than through elected representatives. It also allows citizens to make policy and remove corrupt officials when the machines managed to win elections despite all the reforms, as they often did. Indeed, while the machines were temporarily weakened by this astonishing array of electoral reforms, many reconciled themselves to change and endured; some even thrived. The reformers proved equally resilient, however.

Despite their social conservatism, they were nothing less than radical about structural change. Even before completing their transformation of local elections, they were experimenting with innovative forms of government.

Taking Politics out of Government: The City-Manager System

As we saw in the last chapter, the early reformers endeavored to replace the weak mayor form of government with the strong mayor system and the shortened ballot. But when they saw the bosses and machines taking advantage of that modification, they sought more fundamental change.

The Commission Form of Government

When the city government of Galveston, Texas, seemed incompetent to guide rebuilding after a catastrophic hurricane hit the city in 1900, a group of business leaders more or less took over. They persuaded their state legislature to approve a new charter with a radically different form of government for Galveston. Instead of a traditional executive and legislature, Galveston combined both functions in one body—a commission. Voters elected just five commissioners; together they acted as the city council, but each also headed a specific department, such as public safety, public works, parks and libraries, or finance. This streamlined system worked well for Galveston and was soon adopted elsewhere. Before 1920, nearly five hundred cities adopted the **commission form of government**, usually along with at-large, nonpartisan elections and direct democracy.

But the disadvantages of the commission form soon became apparent. Some commissioners proved better at getting elected than at administering their departments. Commissioners tended to compete with one another and to protect the interests of their own departments, but the system provided no leadership to overcome these tendencies. Because of these problems, it soon lost popularity. Houston gave it up in 1942; San Antonio in 1951. Even Galveston gave it up. Today, commissions govern less than 2 percent of U.S. cities. Most of these cities are small. The largest city still using the commission form of government is Portland, Oregon, where it has been adapted to include a mayor. In 2003, voters in Sioux City, Iowa, rejected reverting to a commission system. In 2005, Cedar Rapids, Iowa, switched from the commission system to a council-manager form of government.

The Council-Manager Form of Government

The commission form of government may also have fallen into disfavor because another new system was even more appealing—the council-manager form of government. First introduced in Sumter, South Carolina, in 1912, by 1920, the new system had been adopted by more than a hundred cities, and today it is the most popular form of city government. The **council-manager form of government** was modeled on modern business practices, with the voters equivalent to corporate stockholders,

Figure 6.1 **The Council-Manager Form of Government**

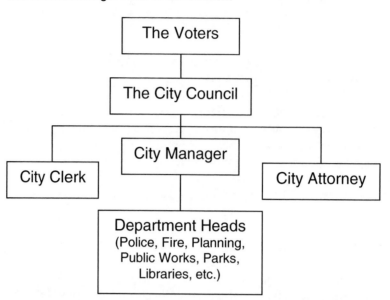

the council to the board of directors, and a professional manager responsible for operations (see Figures 6.1 and 6.2). This innovative arrangement couldn't have suited the reform mentality better.

The City Council

On the ultimate short ballot, with nonpartisan, at-large, isolated elections, voters choose only a small **city council**, usually numbering five to seven members. Initially, the system had no mayor at all, but now mayors are elected or chosen by the council from among its members in most council-manager cities. The mayor's role, however, consists largely of presiding over council meetings. Council members are expected to serve only part-time, linking the public to its government and defining broad policies that the city manager and administration implement. The most important task of the council is appointing the city manager to oversee the operations of the city. The council may also appoint the city attorney, who gives the council legal advice; the clerk, who keeps its records; and the auditor, who checks city finances. With nonpartisan, at-large elections and administration in the hands of a professional manager, the influence of parties and the parochial interests of neighborhoods or ethnic groups are as far removed from government as possible, and the pursuit of the "public interest" proceeds unhindered. In the ideal council-manager system, politics stop with the council, although reform electoral structures limit politics even there.

The City Manager

Based on the reform theory that the business of local government is to provide basic services of a technical nature and should therefore not be political, the council-manager

Figure 6.2 **From the City Charter of Galveston, Texas**

Section 1. The City Manager. The Council shall appoint a City Manager, who shall be the chief administrative and executive officer of the City. The City Manager shall be chosen by the Council solely on the basis of administrative and executive training, experience and ability. The City Manager shall reside and be domiciled in the City no later than 90 days after the effective date of hire and shall continue to reside and be domiciled in the City while serving as City Manager. The City Manager may either be appointed for an indefinite term and be removed by majority vote of the entire membership of the Council, or at the Council's discretion may be appointed or contracted for a definite term not to exceed two (2) years. Provided, however, that the City Manager shall not be appointed nor awarded a contract sixty (60) days before or after any City Council election. The action of the Council in suspending or removing the City Manager shall be final but the City Manager may demand written reasons for removal and the right to be heard thereon at public meeting of the Council. The compensation for the City Manager shall be fixed by the Council. No member of the Council shall, during the time for which the member is elected or for two (2) years thereafter, be chosen as City Manager.

Section 2. Powers and Duties of the City Manager. The City Manager shall be responsible to the Council for the proper administration of all the affairs of the City. The City Manager shall have power and shall be required to:

(1) Appoint and remove any officers or employees of the City except those officers appointed by the Council as otherwise provided by law or this Charter.

(2) Prepare the budget annually, submit it to the Council for approval, and be responsible for its administration after adoption.

(3) Keep the Council advised of the financial condition and administrative activities of the City, and make such recommendations as may seem desirable.

(4) Perform such other duties as may be prescribed by this Charter or required of the City Manager by the Council, not inconsistent with the provisions of this Charter.

system is at the heart of the reform effort to take politics out of government. The political element of the system, the council, hires and fires the manager, usually by majority vote. In doing so, the council is expected to make its decisions on the basis of the technical, administrative competence of the candidates, not on their political views or connections. **City managers** are expected to be neutral, skilled professionals —experts in administration who can efficiently carry out policies set by the council. Unlike political leaders, managers can come from outside the community. In fact, outsiders are often preferred since their lack of local connections would enhance their objectivity.

Where are such individuals to be found? When the system was first introduced and on into the 1920s and 1930s, the pool of professional candidates was small. Communities often subverted the system by hiring locals. Many of the first city managers were engineers, but eventually a national pool of professional administrators grew. Council-manager cities now advertise job openings widely and get applications from all over the country. To hire locally is considered bad form (with political overtones), and professional managers advance their careers by moving from city to city, with the largest council-manager cities at the top of the ladder.

As chief executive, the manager appoints department heads, including police, fire, public works, planning, parks and recreation, and others. The department heads, under policy directives from the council and supervision by the manager, oversee the delivery of city services. The council plays no formal part in hiring, firing, or disciplining department heads and may be forbidden from communicating with them except through the manager, to whom they answer. The manager is also responsible for the budget, a crucial role in shaping city services, although the council must approve the manager's budget proposals.

The council-manager system, so modern sounding and so consistent with reform theory, spread quickly. California's reformers made it that state's general law form of government, and it still operates in all but a few of its 477 cities. In Virginia, state law requires the council-manager form of government for all cities. Almost half of the cities in the United States with a population of more than 25,000 now use the system, but the only large cities that employ it are Dallas, Phoenix, San Antonio, and San Jose.

Like all reform nostrums, the manager plan has its drawbacks, tending to insulate government from the public and to prevent the expression of legitimate differences of opinion. Nor does it truly remove politics from government since administrators have views and biases of their own and may still be susceptible to some political influence, usually that of business elites. More alarming for the reformers, machines adapted even to this innovation. The Pendergast machine continued in Kansas City,[3] for example, and in Asheville, North Carolina, the local boss merely had himself appointed manager.

Civil Service

Another important reform associated with the council-manager form of government was the introduction of **civil service**, or merit hiring, first instituted in New York in 1883, but not widely adopted until after 1920. Workers had previously been hired and retained on the basis of loyalty to the machine rather than their qualifications or performance on the job. When control of city hall changed hands in elections, a whole new set of workers would be hired. This patronage, or spoils, system provided rewards for supporters of the machines, but resulted in inefficient and amateurish city services. To increase competence among city staff and strike a blow at patronage, the reformers initiated a hiring system based on ability to do the job rather than party loyalty.

All city employees except the department heads appointed by the manager (or the mayor in a mayor-council system) are in the civil service system, although managers, mayors, and department heads sometimes may appoint a few deputies. In a civil service or merit system, personnel departments set specifications for jobs. Educational qualifications, written exams, and interviews then sort out job applicants, with the top candidates (not the relatives and friends of current staff) winning employment. Once hired, workers go through a probationary period and, if they perform their job well, gain job security through a form of tenure, and can be fired only for proven incompetence at the job—not just because a new mayor and/or council are elected.

The system protects workers from political interference on the job, and it dealt a serious blow to the machines, although some adapted even to this reform, merely taking over the system and manipulating it by fixing exam results or selling passing scores. Today, many people worry that civil servants have so much job security that they don't have to pay attention to their clients (the taxpayers) or even to do their jobs well to keep them. It is important to remember, however, that their job security was intended to solve the even more serious problems of political interference and incompetence.

Competitive Bidding

The corrupt and inefficient doling out of contracts for city purchases, services, and construction projects to the machine's allies was another part of the spoils systems the reformers attacked. Their solution was **competitive bidding**, a system by which professional administrators set and advertise the specifications or requirements for a purchase or project and any interested company can put in a formal, sealed bid for it. The lowest bidder who meets the specifications wins the contract—not the boss's pals. Selection of any but the lowest bid must be justified. Under some competitive bidding arrangements, stipulations requiring locally based companies, union employers, or minority businesses may be applied, and small contracts are generally excepted from the process.

Naturally, the machines found ways to cheat. They manipulated specifications so only certain companies could qualify, leaked competitor's bids, or accepted artificially low bids and allowed cost overruns later. The system has been widely adopted, however, especially on large projects, and although sometimes imperfect in operation, it dealt a serious blow to the machines. Competitive bidding and civil service hiring take away the major components of the spoils system. In cities where they function as intended, traditional political machines have never revived, whatever other reform structures are adopted (or revoked).

IN YOUR COMMUNITY
Study your city's charter (available from the city clerk). Can it be characterized as reformed or unreformed? Which elements of the charter are reformed? Which are not?

The Consequences of Reform: The Bias of "Good Government"

From the turn of the century to the 1950s, few cities were immune to the reform movement, although it struck at different times in different places and with varying degrees of success. The reform movement was strongest in the South and Southwest, as many small and middle-sized cities grew and matured. The movement was also strong in the Midwest, but in the Northeast, reform was patchy. Overall, however, the tide had turned against the machines, as immigrants assimilated, new immigration from abroad was curtailed, a new welfare system was set up, and the middle class expanded. The machine's power base shrunk and a constituency for reform developed, readily endorsing the movement's good government rhetoric featuring the public interest, professionalism, and getting politics out of government. The structural reforms imposed on city government altered it radically, but despite the lofty ideals, reform institutions (like all institutions) have a bias. Not surprisingly, the **bias of reform** favored the reformers themselves.

Weak Parties and At-Large Elections

The direct primary and nonpartisan, at-large, isolated elections hurt the machines, but they also weaken political parties, lower voter turnout, change the composition of the electorate, and make it easier for some sorts of people to get elected. Direct primaries reduced the ability of bosses to control the nomination of candidates and increase democracy, but because anybody can run for and win the party nomination, personalities count more than policies do, and parties may end up with unwanted candidates who do not agree with their programs. Such independence has its merits, but it dilutes the meaning of the party label and makes it harder for voters to know what candidates stand for and to hold them accountable. Nonpartisan elections enhance this tendency. They also cut off the lower rungs of the party ladder, so candidates for higher office are less likely to serve apprenticeships in local politics.

However vague the platforms of U.S. political parties are, most voters believe a party label gives them clues about candidates. But no such clues are provided in local government primaries and nonpartisan elections, so how do people decide? Some choose which candidates to vote for by the ethnicity of their names (would you be more likely to vote for a candidate with a really foreign-sounding name or one with a name a little more familiar?). Some choose by the candidate's occupation (business people, teachers, and police officers usually do well). Other clues may include well-known family names, religion, military service, or status as a local sports hero or media star. These characteristics tell voters something, but not much. Party labels tell more, including whether candidates are inclined to be liberal or conservative. They are especially useful for candidates who are a little outside the mainstream because they may reassure voters that even though the candidates are not quite like them (male/female; majority/minority; heterosexual/homosexual), they are okay because they are Democrats or Republicans.

Parties are more than labels, however. They are also campaign organizations. When they are absent from campaigns, other elements gain influence. Incumbents or anyone whose name is well known do better. Newspapers gain importance because they can make candidates well known or ignore them. Campaign contributors become more influential because they can pay for the campaigns previously provided by the parties. Candidates who are white businessmen usually do best because the traditional voting majority is comfortable with them and also because they can more easily raise campaign funds and count on newspaper support. Women, minority, and working-class candidates have a harder time selling themselves to voters, campaign contributors, and newspaper publishers.

At-large elections increase the structural bias against these candidates. Instead of running in a district made up of a few neighborhoods, they have to run citywide. Such races cost more, which hurts those candidates, especially minorities, without ready access to contributors. Minority candidates also have a tougher time precisely because they are members of minority groups and will need to win votes from whomever makes up the city's majority, whereas in district elections their own group might be enough to elect them. In big cities, women are sometimes hindered by at-large elections, too, mainly because their community work tends to focus on neighborhoods and schools, so they have weak citywide connections. Women have done well in at-large elections in small and medium-sized communities, however. And despite the disadvantages of the system, many minority and women candidates have managed to win at-large races in recent years,[4] thanks to their own hard work and declining racism and sexism among some voters.

Low Voter Turnout

Voter turnout is also affected by reform electoral structures, declining precipitously with nonpartisan, isolated elections. The parties aren't actively hustling voters, and local elections separate from state and national balloting often get little publicity and stimulate little interest. Having an appointed manager instead of an elected mayor also leads to decreasing voter interest. On average, 30 percent of voters participate in such elections, less than half the turnout in cities with partisan, concurrent elections. In California, for example, voter turnout in cities that held elections at the same time as national or statewide elections is 21 to 36 percent higher than in cities with isolated elections.[5] Reformers don't worry about lower turnout, however, because they assume (with some justification) that those who do not vote are not well informed about local matters anyway. But the electorate is not only smaller under reform, it is different and less representative of the city as a whole. Those most likely to vote are better educated, older, more affluent, and more conservative; they elect people like themselves. Minority and working-class people are least likely to vote or to be elected, except where they are themselves the majority.

The Winners

In most communities, reform election structures increase the electoral chances of white (or WASP) businessmen and decrease those of others. The primary beneficiaries of these reforms are the very people who were the reform movement. As political scientist Amy Bridges observes, they "wrote the rules to win the game."[6] Did they intend to institute such bias? In a way, they did. In their view, the system they replaced had been biased against them and helped ethnic, working-class candidates. Many reformers were hostile to such people, although most were more concerned about the corruption of the machines. In attacking the machines, however, they also lessened the participation and electability of some of their constituents. For the most part, this was probably not intentional, and most reformers would say the system is open and fair to all. They are reluctant to acknowledge that it works best for people like them—and that everybody isn't like them.

When the reformers won elections, what sort of person did they appoint as city manager? And what policy guidance did reform councils give? What sorts of standards were set for civil servants, and what sorts of people were employed? Again, the reformers created a system in their own image, with middle- and upper-class professionals getting elected and hiring other, similar professionals. They homogenized city government and actually made it less representative of their communities as a whole and more representative of themselves. Those not like the reformers—the ethnic immigrants and working class in the machine age and later, African Americans, Hispanics, and Asians—have little chance of winning elections or even attention. Council members can ignore minorities and their neighborhoods as long as the predominant, usually middle-class, voting majority of a city is satisfied. City managers answer to the council, not the voters. They are careful not to alienate majorities but may ignore minorities with impunity. Modern civil servants have job security and insulation that protects them from political interference, but that also enables them to ignore public pressure. They need not rush to please their clients or, it sometimes seems, even bother to be courteous.

Majority Rule

The reformers didn't take politics out of government; they only made it less responsive to the interests of those other than the majority in any community. The common good or public interest turned out to be nothing more than what the majority wanted. Majority rule is democratic, of course, but it isn't always good government if it means some people and some interests—those not consistent with the majority—are left out. Reform dogma failed to recognize that people are not all alike and that they might want different things from city government. Working-class neighborhoods, minority groups, or other components of urban diversity often have very different needs and interests than those of the majority, yet under reform structures, these are almost inevitably ignored. However, those who are unrepresented are not always working-class or racial minorities. In some cities, these groups have become the majority, and white, middle-class people find themselves left out, because the reform system is biased in favor of any group that constitutes a majority and against any group that is a minority.

Besides strengthening majority rule, reform also gave advantage—or spoils?—to the upper class and business elites who were its leaders. Reform structures, with low voter turnout and council members and professional administrators who thought like themselves, suited businessmen and their interests very well. They wanted low taxes and efficient city services, with social programs put on a back burner (or left to the state and federal governments). But more, they expected reform governments to bring progress through growth, generating jobs, profits, and taxes. Through the reform movement, business interests narrowed the focus of local government to basic services and growth, guided by business-oriented professionals.[7] The growth machine replaced the party political machine.

Counterreform: Back to the Future

Eventually, however, disenchantment with the narrowness and unresponsiveness of reform structures brought a counterreformation in many cities. Like the reform movement itself, the challenge to reform was brought about by changes in the cities themselves. As we saw in chapter 3, by the 1920s, the primary immigrants to large cities were minorities, first black, then Hispanics, and later Asian. After World War II, white flight to the suburbs started eroding the reform constituency of big cities, even as minorities approached majority status there. By the 1960s, a critical mass of people who felt excluded from city politics was emerging. The black civil rights movement showed the way, demanding voting rights and full participation for all. The federal government responded with civil and voting rights legislation and by funding community organizing through the War on Poverty and related programs. Hispanics emulated African Americans in organizing and demanding their rights. Then the women's movement took hold, followed by the political mobilization of gays and lesbians. In the 1970s, a neighborhood movement swept the cities, with groups forming not only in minority neighborhoods but in others as well. Many complained that they had no direct council representation and were shocked to learn that a majority of at-large council members lived in just one part of town (usually a rich neighborhood with high voter turnout). All these interests felt that local governments dominated by white, upper-middle-class males (from managers and mayors to council members and civil servants) neither represented nor responded to them. At about the same time, environmentalists and antigrowth campaigners began criticizing city development policies and a deeply antibureaucratic tax revolt took hold.

Like the "morning glory" reformers before them, these dissatisfied groups first put up candidates and attempted to win office. Some were successful, and by the late 1960s, most city councils had at least token women, minority, and environmentalist representatives. Unfortunately, these candidates, driven by the need to win majority support to be elected, sometimes alienated their own initial constituencies. More often, they found they could change little in city government when they managed to get elected. To the critics of reform, white elected officials and bureaucracies protected by the civil service system (especially the police) continued to be insensitive to the needs of minorities, women, and neighborhoods. The growth machine ground on, ignoring social needs, neighborhood services, and environmental concerns.

Like the earlier reformers, those who felt excluded sought to change the structures of local government. The primary goals of the **counterreform** movement were to make government more representative and more responsive. They wanted more participation. They wanted local government to pay more attention to all of its constituents. They wanted more sensitive and better-controlled local bureaucracies. Rejecting the basic assumptions of the earlier reformers, they argued that there could be no single public interest in communities because people are not all alike. Varied needs and views should be represented in local government, not only by elected officials but also in bureaucracies. They accepted the inevitability of political conflict that such representation would bring, insisting that reform structures had only artificially created consensus by suppressing different points of view. To accomplish these goals, they went back to the future, selectively reviving or adapting traditional political structures and introducing a few new ones.

District Elections

By the 1970s, women, blacks, and, in some places, Latinos were having more success winning at-large elections. The federal Voting Rights Act of 1965 increased black voter registration and greatly increased the success of black candidates in the South. At the time of the Voting Rights Act there were 300 black elected officials in the entire country; by 1992 there were 5,000 in the South alone.

Besides voter registration, the counterreformers saw the at-large system of council selection as a major barrier to the success of women and minority candidates and sought to replace it with good, old-fashioned **district elections**. Each part of the city would gain direct representation, they thought, and responsiveness to neighborhoods, many of which had never had direct representation on their city councils, would improve. Minorities, if they were concentrated in particular districts, would be more likely to win an election. So would women and working-class people, because their networks tended to be localized rather than citywide. District elections would also cut campaign costs, the counterreformers thought, and thus enhance the electoral prospects of all these groups.

Although most big cities in the Frostbelt had never changed from district elections, many growing Sunbelt cities, including Albuquerque, Dallas, Houston, Phoenix, San Antonio, San Diego, and San Jose, went back to districts in the 1970s and 1980s. In some, the change was wrought by community organizations forcing a referendum or initiative (devices made available by the earlier reformers). In others, including Dallas and Birmingham, the reform was imposed by federal courts that concluded that at-large elections denied minority representation under federal voting rights legislation.[8] According to Sunbelt author Carl Abbott, "One-third of the cities in the Confederate South with significant black populations" had shifted back to district elections by 1986.[9] The at-large systems of many communities have been successfully challenged in the courts since then, including some cases brought by white minorities.

In many cities where district elections have survived or been revived, more minorities, women, and neighborhood candidates have been elected and these groups are more satisfied with city government than under the at-large method.[10] Political scientist Amy Bridges studied southwestern cities that made the change from at-large to district elections and found that "the personnel of city councils changed," becoming "more racially diverse than the city councils of big-city reform." District elections, she writes, "changed the face of local politics . . . and introduced issues of equity into political debate."[11] Neighborhood as well as minority representation played a major part in the movement for district representation in southwestern cities, as did efforts to control the sprawling growth of cities in that region.

But the record is mixed. "The use of district rather than at-large elections has no impact on representation of minorities," asserts political scientist Norman R. Luttberg. Increased minority representation results more from growth in minority populations than from changes in government structure, he found.[12] Anecdotal evidence from many cities, along with Bridges' study of southwestern cities, suggests otherwise, but this may reflect the initial impact of the change in method of selecting city council members. We should also remember that such change would not have occurred if the minority population had not grown to sufficient size and mobilized politically to bring it about.

Opponents of districting worry about conflict, parochialism, and a lack of attention to citywide issues, but Luttberg found that the system of representation made no difference in the policies approved by council members.[13] Other studies suggest that while district representatives are more oriented to neighborhoods and basic services than their at-large counterparts, they are still (disappointingly for some) sensitive to citywide concerns.[14] But beyond actual policy outcomes and changes in the composition of city councils, district elections provide a powerful and reassuring political symbol that all citizens and all areas of the city are represented.

Other Reforms

District representation was the primary goal and outcome in many cities that experienced counterreform, but in some, other changes were also advocated and implemented, including the further empowerment of city councils, strengthening mayors, concurrent elections, and efforts to limit the power of civil service bureaucracies.

Empowering Councils

To confront the power of bureaucracies, city managers, and mayors, some counterreformers recognized that the more representative councils they had wrought with district elections would need to be more powerful. Reform council members had been expected to be part-time and were paid accordingly. But the counterreformers and some traditional reform groups such as the League of Women Voters advocated raising council salaries enough to allow representatives to do the job on a full-time basis; higher salaries would also broaden the range of candidates who could run for office since only the affluent or certain sorts of professionals such as lawyers could afford to take on the job for only token wages.

In some large cities, **empowering councils** meant that council members were also allowed to hire a personal staff so they wouldn't have to rely exclusively on what their executives and bureaucrats told them and so they could respond more efficiently to constituent concerns. Some councils were allowed to hire budget analysts or auditors to advise them as a group, again to counterbalance the executive branch and bureaucracy.

Stronger Mayors

Mayors gained power in the urban counterreform movement, too. The council-manager system had initially omitted mayors altogether, although most cities soon changed their charters to allow the council to designate one of its members as mayor to preside over meetings and perform some ceremonial functions. Eventually, some cities realized that councils were too fractious and managers were too bureaucratic to provide the sort of political leadership that was often needed. As a consequence, 65 percent of council-manager cities now elect their mayors. Just being elected doesn't really give a mayor much power, of course, but being the focus of public and media attention, as mayors are, does bring power to those who know how to use it. Many cities have also taken other actions to achieve **stronger mayors**, including higher salaries, much-expanded personal staffs, and, more substantive, budgetary and appointment power.

Concurrent Elections

To buttress council representativeness and mayoral leadership, some reformed cities returned to concurrent elections because they could save money by sharing election costs with higher levels of government and because isolated elections depressed and biased voter turnout. This little shift vastly increased voter participation and representativeness. Nonpartisan elections also came under attack, but, because they are usually enshrined in state constitutions, change proved difficult. In California, however, counterreformers challenged nonpartisanship in the courts and won a 1989 U.S. Supreme Court ruling (based on freedom of speech) allowing parties to endorse candidates as community groups could.[15]

Controlling Bureaucracy

The insulation and unresponsiveness of civil service bureaucracies were also concerns for the counterreformers. They tried **controlling the bureaucracy** by allowing elected officials mayoral and council staffs, auditors, and policy analysts, as well as special budgeting systems. They also demanded affirmative action hiring to ensure that a broader cross section of people would gain employment with local government—not just the white males that the white male bureaucracy seemed to hire. If hiring was biased, the counterreformers argued, so were city services because an unrepresentative bureaucracy could not be sensitive to its diverse constituency.

Some cities tried to assuage the discontent of those who felt excluded by increasing direct citizen participation in local government through boards, commissions, and committees. Cities such as Boston and New York attempted to break down their rigid bureaucracies and increase responsiveness by decentralizing local government through neighborhood city halls or more formal community control of some services by neighborhood representatives. More recently, Los Angeles gave some land-use and planning powers to area planning commissions and created a system of neighborhood councils.

Bureaucracies have generally proven resistant to such reforms, but where demographic change has given minorities greater political clout, they have gained jobs in the civil service and even came to dominate some departments.

Growth Control, the Tax Revolt, and Term Limits

Minorities, women, and working-class neighborhoods were in the forefront of counterreform as discussed so far, but in the 1970s, other antagonists to the status quo appeared. Middle-class neighborhoods and environmentalists supported the counterreformers on some issues, such as district elections, but their primary concern was controlling growth to assure better local services. Their challenge to the growth machine was supplemented by a broader tax revolt that set strict limits on local revenues and thus, to some extent, on growth. Unlike the counterreformers, the homeowners who dominated the tax revolt were conservative and fundamentally antigovernment. In the late 1980s, they campaigned for **term limits** to restrict the number of times mayors and council members could be reelected. More turnover, they asserted, would prevent these officials from succumbing to the values of the status quo, lobbyists, and bureaucrats.

Continuing Counterreform

The counterreform of local government structures is still under way in many cities, but it has already transformed community politics in some. Many more women, minorities, homosexuals, and working- and middle-class people have been elected, and bureaucracies, while retaining most of their power, have been changed. Diversity is more widely recognized and accepted; local government is more representative and responsive. The antigrowth movement and the tax revolt have also made their mark.

IN YOUR COMMUNITY
Check with your city clerk on any revisions in your city's charter since 1960. Would they be characterized as reform or counterreform?

The Distribution of Forms of Government

The institutions of local government have evolved over two centuries of history and change, through industrialization, immigration, urbanization, suburbanization, and the move to the Sunbelt, from the mayor-council form of government to reform and the council-manager system and beyond. Some cities have gone through all these changes; others have experienced only a few. This variation accounts, in part, for the current use of different forms of government by different cities today, although other factors also shape the **distribution of forms of government**. Historical development, region, size, and demography all play a part.

Table 6.2

Distribution of Forms of City Government

Size of city	Number of cities	Mayor-council (%)	Council-manager (%)	Commission (%)	Town meeting (%)
Over 1,000,000	4	50	50	0/0	0/0
5,000–1,000,000	8	88	13	0/0	0/0
250,000–499,999	23	52	48	0/0	0/0
100,000–249,999	104	28	72	0/0	0/0
50,000–99,999	226	27	71	1	1
25,000–49,999	487	34	62	*	3
10,000–24,999	996	33	56	2	7
0–9,999	2,395	42	47	1	8
By region					
Frostbelt (Northeast)	2,337	44	41	2	12
Sunbelt (South and West)	1,907	31	68	*	*

Source: The Municipal Year Book (Washington, DC: International City/County Management Association, 2003).

Note: Data are based on a survey of cities. Percentages may not add up to 100 because of rounding and cities not responding.

*Denotes less than 0.5 percent.

The mayor-council system is most common in the Northeast and Midwest, where cities developed in the nineteenth century when that form of government predominated. Table 6.2 reveals that larger cities, whether in the Frostbelt or the Sunbelt, use the mayor-council form, not just because they are older cities but because of the need for political leadership in such diverse places. Note that the table does not distinguish between weak mayor and strong mayor systems. At least one study has demonstrated that cities with large ethnic minority and working-class populations are more likely to use the mayor-council form.[16] Large cities in the Frostbelt incline to the strong mayor form, and big Sunbelt cities tend to restrict mayoral authority. Surprisingly, a majority of cities with a population of less than 10,000 also use the mayor-council form. Mostly in older, Frostbelt states (except New England), they seem content with their original weak mayor systems. Unlike large, diverse cities, these small, homogeneous communities experience less political conflict and few complex problems, so they can get by without strong mayoral leadership and executive authority.

The council-manager form is most common in cities that matured after the turn of the century, especially in the Sunbelt and most of all in the western United States, where the reform movement was strongest and where political parties were, and remain, weakest. Suburbs, again especially those in the Sunbelt, also incline strongly to the council-manager system. Reflecting this, a substantial majority of middle-sized cities use the manager form (see Table 6.2). These communities tend to be

Table 6.3

Method of Election of City Councils

City size	Percent at-large	Percent district	Percent mixed
Over 500,000	33.0	44.0	22.0
250,000–499,999	20.0	28.0	52.0
100,000–249,999	40.2	22.0	37.9
50,000–99,999	48.6	13.9	37.5
25,000–49,999	53.9	16.8	29.2
10,000–24,999	59.6	16.1	24.5
0–9,999	65.0	17.0	18.0
All cities	60.9	16.8	22.3

Source: The Municipal Year Book (Washington, DC: International City/County Management Association, 1998).
Note: Data are based on a survey of cities.

relatively homogeneous, so political consensus is easy to reach and fewer people feel left out by the majority-oriented reform system. When reform cities grow, they become more diverse and political conflict increases. Professional administrators such as city managers are often unable or unwilling to respond to the increasing demands placed on them. As a result, most large Sunbelt cities have strengthened their mayors and altered other institutions as well.

Besides the basic forms of government, associated structures and institutions are similarly distributed. District elections, for example, are more likely to be found in larger cities and in the older cities of the Northeast and Midwest, while at-large council representation is more common in smaller and middle-sized cities and in the Sunbelt and suburbia (see Table 6.3). The regional pattern is also evident in use of nonpartisan elections, with only 21 percent of northeastern cities as compared to 94 percent of western cities requiring nonpartisan elections.[17] Although the number of cities adopting the council-manager system with its associated reform structures has risen steadily since it was first introduced, as cities grow, they generally find that increasing diversity and conflict necessitate stronger leadership and broader representation, and adapt accordingly.

As a consequence, fewer and fewer cities can easily be categorized as weak mayor, strong mayor, council manager, reformed, unreformed, or re-reformed. Most have adapted their systems to particular needs at particular times, picking and choosing the electoral or governmental structures that suit them and that satisfy the political forces of the moment. Each form and institution has advantages and disadvantages; none is best in the abstract. Mayoral systems, for example, bring better leadership and accountability and are more democratic. They probably work best in large, diverse cities with conflictual politics and a need for leadership and conciliation. But a manager system seems to work well in small or middle-sized homogeneous cities with clear, consensual majorities. The manager form is also thought to be best for professionalism and efficiency, although at least one statistical study found "no apparent difference in the efficiency levels of the two [major types of] municipal struc-tures."[18] In many council-manager cities where counterreformers or others have ex-pressed the need for stronger and more accountable leadership, mayors have been increasingly empowered so that the system is best thought of as **mayor-council-manager**, a sort of hybrid of the council-manager and mayor-council systems.

In fact, such hybrids have already become the dominant form of city government in America today. According to H. George Frederickson and colleagues,

> Beginning in the 1950s, the most prominent features of council-manager government such as a professional executive and merit civil service, were being widely adopted in mayor-council cities. The most prominent features of mayor-council government, such as a di-rectly elected mayor and some council elected by districts, were being widely adopted in council-manager cities. By the 1990s, the fusion of these two models had resulted in the dominant form of American local government: the adapted city.[19]

For Frederickson and his colleagues, communities using the council-manager sys-tem are "administrative cities" and those using the mayor-council system are "politi-cal cities." But as the former seek to be more responsive to citizens and the latter strive to function more efficiently and professionally, they adopt components of each other's systems—adapting to changing populations, needs, and conditions. "Most American cities are now best described as adapted," they write.[20]

We'll discuss the **adapted city** further in the next chapter but for now it's a useful concept to remind us that no particular form of government is "best." Rather, the needs of each city determine which form of government is best for that city. By mixing elements of the different systems, cities can refine their forms of govern-ments to their own needs. Nevertheless, it is important to remember that the different forms are never neutral. Those who have power at a particular time choose the form of government that gives them advantages. Others may feel unrepresented and ig-nored, but if they organize and increase their own power, they may challenge and sometimes change the system.

Counties, School Districts, and Other Local Governments

Most of our discussion in this and the preceding chapter has focused on forms of city government. Government in counties, schools, and special districts varies much less and has changed less over time.

While city government has gone through the changes described earlier, county government has mostly remained as it began, something like the weak mayor form of government without the mayor (see Figure 6.3). Typically, a three- to five-member legislative body called the **county commission** or **board of supervisors** is elected by districts on a long ballot that includes from three to over a dozen depart-ment heads. The county commission or board appoints additional department heads. The legislative body dominates and, as with the weak mayor form of government, the county system tends to result in fragmented government and unclear account-

Figure 6.3 **County Government**

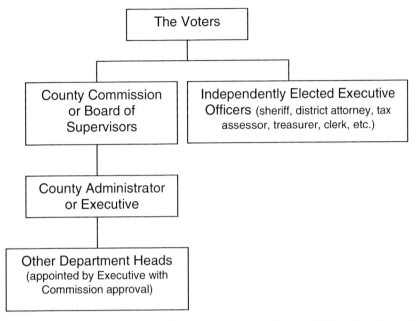

ability for the voters, especially when the number of directly elected executive officers is great. Even where only a few executives are elected, the multiple membership of the county board or commission can result in conflict and deadlock rather than leadership.

This anachronistic system survives because, as we learned in chapter 4, counties, even more than cities, are creatures of the state. Unlike cities, they function as administrative agencies of the state, carrying out its programs and policies. As such, the states keep tighter control, in most cases dictating the structure of county government through general law charters applying to all the counties in the state equally. Only about 5 percent of counties across the country have been granted home rule charters through which they can adapt their government structures to their own needs.[21] As administrative agencies of the state, home rule is probably less urgent, however, than in big cities, and fragmentation is less of a problem. Moreover, in many states, counties are primarily responsible for local government in rural areas with homogeneous populations that make few demands—a little like the cities of the early United States, when the weak mayor form of government worked well enough.

Bosses and machines ruled counties just as they ruled cities. In fact, rural counties with few immigrants may have had the strongest and most ruthless machines of all. The reform movement rarely gained momentum in the counties, however, perhaps because of the power of their machines, but more likely because of the absence of a middle-class constituency for reform. Some reforms were introduced, but with counties so closely controlled by the states, the battleground was usually the state legislature rather than the county government.

But while a majority of the nation's counties continue to operate with the traditional elected board or commission and an assortment of elected department heads, fully 40 percent of the 3,069 counties have moved away from that traditional form by providing for an elected or appointed executive.[22] Among those that elect executives, including Denver, San Francisco, New Orleans, and New York, several are consolidated city and county governments, but some traditional counties have also seen the need for an executive leader chosen by election. The states of Arkansas, Kentucky, and Tennessee now mandate elected executives for their counties, although other states, like Texas, provide no such option. A more common change in county systems—especially in urban counties—has been the addition of a professional **county administrator** or executive similar to a city manager.[23] Often recruited from the same pool as city managers, they are appointed by the county commission or board of supervisors and bring technical and management expertise to the increasingly complex business of county government. Like city managers, they have difficulty when political conflict is great and leadership is needed. With the addition of county administrators, we can see that counties are also adapting their form of government to a changing world.

School districts adapted somewhat less. Most are governed by elected or sometimes appointed boards of five to seven members who hire a professional manager or superintendent of schools to oversee school operations. The system is similar to a council-manager form of government, but school superintendents tend to be even more powerful than city managers because school board members are often less professionally knowledgeable or politically astute than council members and rarely have as much time to devote to their duties. When disagreement arises, the most common response is to replace the administrator, although sometimes the governing boards are replaced instead, either by recall or through normal elections.

Special districts operate in a similar fashion, with powerful administrators and often amateur, part-time board members. Their boards, however, are usually appointed by governors, mayors, or other elected officials, so they are not subject to regular elections or recall. The public thus has little control over these agencies—and most citizens don't even know they exist.

Filling the Forms

The structure of local government is influenced and sometimes dictated by state law as well as by the changing characteristics of the communities themselves. Those who have power mold the structures which, in turn, shape access to government as well as public policy. But while institutional structures have their biases, nothing is absolute in politics. Within any of these forms of government, the balance of power among mayors, managers, city councils, bureaucracies, and voters may change, altering not only the form of government, but also the way it works. Moreover, real people occupy the positions and offices we've discussed. The way they are chosen affects the sort of people they are, and who they are affects what they do, as we will see in the next chapter.

Essential Terms

reform movement
social reform
Progressive movement
limits on immigration
scientific management
direct primary
nonpartisan elections
runoff election
at-large elections
short ballots
concurrent elections
isolated elections
direct democracy
initiative
referendum
recall
commission form of government

council-manager form of government
city council
city managers
civil service
competitive bidding
bias of reform
counterreform
district elections
empowering councils
stronger mayors
controlling the bureaucracy
term limits
distribution of forms of government
mayor-council-manager
adapted city
county commission or board of supervisors
county administrator

On the Internet

- The International City/County Management Association (ICMA) (www.icma.org) is a national organization for professional local government administrators.
- Check individual city websites (including your own) for information about elected officials, government structures (charters), census data, and so on.
- The Eagleton Institute of Politics (Rutgers University) (www.eagleton.rutgers.edu/e-gov/e-politicalarchive-Progressive.htm) has information on women's role in the reform movement.
- The League of Women Voters (www.lwv.org) is a nonpartisan reform group; check for state and local chapters.

Notes

1. Stephen Elkin, *City and Regime in the American Republic* (Chicago: University of Chicago Press, 1987), p. 28.

2. Robert T. Starks and Michael B. Preston, "Harold Washington and the Politics of Reform in Chicago: 1983–1987," in *Racial Politics in American Cities*, ed. Rufus P. Browning, Dale Rogers Marshall, and David H. Tabb (New York: Longman, 1990), pp. 88–107.

3. Alfred Steinberg, *The Bosses* (New York: Macmillan, 1972).

4. See Susan A. MacManus and Charles S. Bullock, "Minorities and Women Do Win At Large!" *National Civic Review* 77, no. 3 (May–June 1988): 231–44; and Susan Welch and Timothy Bledsoe,

Urban Reform and Its Consequences: A Study in Representation (Chicago: University of Chicago Press, 1988).

5. Zoltan L. Hajnal, Paul G. Lewis, and Hugh Louch, *Municipal Elections in California: Turnout, Timing, and Competition* (Public Policy Institute of California, March 2002, www.ppic.org). See also Amy Bridges, *Morning Glories: Municipal Reform in the Southwest* (Princeton, NJ: Princeton University Press, 1997), pp. 133, 179.

6. Bridges, *Morning Glories*, p. 24.

7. See Clarence N. Stone and Heywood T. Sanders, eds., *The Politics of Urban Development* (Lawrence: University Press of Kansas, 1987).

8. See for example, *Rogers v. Lodge*, 458 U.S. 613 (1982); *Thornburgh v. Gingles*, 106 S. Ct. 2752 (1986); and Susan A. MacManus and Charles S. Bullock, "Racial Representation Issues," *PS: Political Science and Politics* 18 (Fall 1985): 759–69.

9. Carl Abbott, *The New Urban America: Growth and Politics in Sunbelt Cities*, rev. ed. (Chapel Hill: University of North Carolina Press, 1987), p. 255.

10. See Peggy Heilig and Robert J. Mundt, "Changes in Representational Equity: The Effect of Adopting Districts," *Social Science Quarterly* 64, no. 2 (June 1983): 393–97.

11. Bridges, *Morning Glories*, pp. 200–1.

12. Norman R. Luttberg, *The Grassroots of Democracy: A Comparative Study of Competition and Its Impact in American Cities in the 1990s* (Lanham, MD: Lexington, 1999), pp. 145–46.

13. Ibid., p. 124.

14. Welch and Bledsoe, *Urban Reform*, pp. 77–78.

15. *Eu v. San Francisco County Democratic Central Committee*, 489 U.S. 214 (1989).

16. Thomas Dye and Susan MacManus, "Predicting City Government Structure," *American Journal of Political Science* 20, no. 2 (May 1976): 257–71.

17. *The Municipal Year Book* (Washington, DC: International City/County Management Association, 1988), p. 17.

18. Kathy Hayes and Semoon Chang, "The Relative Efficiency of City Manager and Mayor-Council Forms of Government," *Southern Economic journal* 57, no. 1 (July 1990): 176.

19. H. George Frederickson, Gary A. Johnson, and Curtis H. Wood, *The Adapted City* (Armonk, NY: M.E. Sharpe, 2004), pp. 6–7.

20. Ibid., p. 18.

21. National Association of Counties, www.nac.org.

22. Ibid.

23. Vincent L. Marando and Robert D. Thomas, *The Forgotten Governments: County Commissioners as Policy Makers* (Gainesville: University Presses of Florida, 1977), pp. 30, 33.

7 Legislators and Executives
The Balance of Power

The forms of government discussed in the preceding chapters substantially determine how local governments operate and what sorts of people gain positions of power. In each form, power is shared. In city halls and county courthouses across the nation, legislators and executives grapple for control of programs and policies, sometimes cooperating, sometimes in confrontation, sometimes even in gridlock. Formal authority, such as the veto or power of appointment, gives the protagonists advantages or disadvantages and is therefore itself sometimes the subject of power struggles. But most of the time, legislators and executives play by the rules of the game, using whatever political resources they command. These include not only the formal powers granted to them in charters, but also calling on allies, manipulating the media, or rallying the public to their personal causes, if they have any (most are content to maintain the status quo). Their own personalities and political styles also affect their power and how they play their roles. Go to a meeting of your city council or county commission and see for yourself.

IN YOUR COMMUNITY

Go to at least two meetings of your city council and write a short essay on your observations, testing some of the generalizations made in this book. Consider the roles played by council members, administrators, citizens, and interest groups as well as relationships among the council members themselves. Does anyone seem to dominate the process? Are decisions made at council meetings after careful deliberation or do they appear to have been made in advance? Why?

Legislators and executives are not the only players, however. Bureaucrats are significant participants, as are committees and commissions appointed by councils and mayors to advise them and sometimes to exercise independent authority. Voters, interest groups, and powerful individuals outside government also greatly influence what happens in city hall. All these may be allies for legislators or executives in their power struggles, while the division of power within local governments gives these other elements a way around a resistant council, mayor, or manager.

Besides the clash of policies and personalities, local politics is also about the way governments operate and the values they emphasize. In the first half of the twentieth century, the reform ideals of professionalism and efficiency predominated, but since the 1960s, the counterreform goals of responsiveness, accountability, representativeness, and leadership have come to the fore. These two sets of values are not mutually exclusive, of course, and both are desirable. Communities must seek their own balance between them, but this process itself injects another layer of tension in local governments, for the outcome of the contest can subtly or substantially shift the balance of power.

Local Legislators: Representation Without Power?

Today's **city councils** tend to be small, part-time, poorly paid, and dependent on the executive branch for information and guidance. This hasn't always been the case, however, and in many communities, councils have become more assertive in recent years, gaining greater influence, although still at a disadvantage in relation to the executive.

For much of the nineteenth century, councils dominated city politics. City charters gave them substantial budgetary and appointment powers and kept the executive branch feeble and fragmented under the weak mayor form of government. Early councils were large, numbering fifty or more members in some big cities, and many were bicameral, with an upper and lower house like the U.S. Congress. With **district elections** and small constituencies, representation and responsiveness were ensured, but these unwieldy bodies were not strong on leadership, much less on efficiency or professionalism. Bosses and machines solved some of these problems by amassing the diffuse powers of the weak mayor system so that action was possible, although the city councils often remained the focal point of local politics. Decisions were made by **logrolling**: you support my boondoggle and I'll support yours. Brokerage politics—making deals—was a way of life. Those who supported the machine were assured representation, responsiveness, accountability, and leadership. Those not aligned with the machine were left out, however, and professionalism and efficiency were beyond the pale.

Many of the reforms that followed focused on city councils. Bicameralism was eliminated, and councils were reduced in size to an average of just five to seven members chosen in at-large, nonpartisan elections. The reformers also took away some logrolling resources by introducing civil service hiring and competitive bidding and shifted the balance of power toward the executive, with the strong mayor and council-manager forms of government. As part of their quest to get politics out of local government, they restricted the powers of what they saw as its most political element, the legislature. City council members were expected to serve part-time, providing policy guidance and leaving administration to experts. The reforms increased efficiency and professionalism but often at the expense of representation, responsiveness, and accountability.

At-Large versus District Elections

Smaller councils make agreement easier, but the associated reform of **at-large elections** also helps build consensus and has probably affected who gets elected to city councils and how they behave more than any other reform. Over 60 percent of U.S. cities elect council members at-large, while 14 percent use district elections and 21 percent mix the two systems (see Table 6.3).[1]

Reformers hoped at-large elections would shift the focus to citywide rather than parochial interests and help achieve consensus, since every council member would be elected by the same constituency—usually a majority of the city's voters. The system does work well in small or middle-sized, homogeneous communities, where people are pretty similar to one another and are in general agreement on what the city should do. In large, diverse cities with lots of political conflict and competition, at-large elections often leave minorities underrepresented and frustrated. Detroit, Seattle, and Austin are among the few large cities that continue to use at-large elections, while most other big cities never implemented this reform. As other cities, such as Atlanta, Phoenix, San Antonio, and Laredo (Texas), have grown large, they have returned to district elections under political pressure from minorities and neighborhoods. Some have done so when federal courts ruled that their at-large systems denied minority representation. This group includes small cities such as Watsonville, California; middle-sized ones such as Springfield, Illinois; and large ones, such as Dallas. In 1987, the white minority in Birmingham won district representation in a court case.

Several cities mix at-large and district elections in hopes of retaining a citywide perspective while increasing representativeness and responsiveness. Rochester, New York, for example, elects four council members by district and five at-large. Atlanta went from at-large to district elections and then to a mix of twelve district council members with three, including the mayor, elected at-large. Denver, Houston, and Oakland use similar combinations. In the 1980s and 1990s, more cities switched to such mixed systems than to pure districting in an effort to balance local and citywide perspectives.

Impact: Who Gets Elected

Just how much real difference these methods of representation make is disputed, but in general, at-large elections are more likely to produce moderately elitist councils of older, white, Republican businessmen.[2] These representatives focus on citywide issues, support growth, and worry more about efficiency and basic services than neighborhood and minority needs or little things that make a difference in people's daily lives, like a stop sign or a crosswalk. Council members act cooperatively and consensually (most votes are unanimous), and the government they oversee, from mayor or manager to the cop on the beat, shares the characteristics of the council members, who generally support their associates in the bureaucracy.

Supporters of the at-large system see all this as advantageous. They also argue that with at-large elections, the entire council is accountable to every voter, whereas with district elections, voters have only one representative. Critics, however, point out that one representative is better than none at all, which can happen when none of the at-large council members lives in a particular part of town or pays attention to it. At-large council members are often similar to one another (and the city's majority) and often live in the same parts of town—usually more elite neighborhoods. Leaders of minority groups and some neighborhoods are frustrated by the lack of representation for their constituencies and the lack of diversity on the council. This is not so much a problem in small or middle-sized cities with relatively homogeneous populations. In such places, at-large elections work well. But in large, diverse cities, the need for more direct representation leads to a preference for district elections. Cost of campaigns is also a factor. The citywide campaigns of at-large candidates can cost hundreds of thousands of dollars, while district campaigns cost only a portion of that amount. High-priced at-large campaigns enhance the influence of the city's majority population but also increase the already substantial clout of those who provide funds for expensive races—another reason at-large representatives tend to be more elitist, conservative, and pro-growth as well as less diverse.

District representatives, on the other hand, are usually more diverse, often tending to be minorities and less-affluent people. They tend to trust the bureaucracy less, to emphasize neighborhood and minority issues and services (including little things that matter a lot to some people), and to be a little more skeptical of growth because it might take services away from their neighborhoods. Council politics may be more conflictual, with more split votes and longer meetings, although this usually reflects city politics in general rather than district representation. Conflict may be muted, however, because council members tend to defer to one another on district issues (condemned as logrolling by critics), and community frustration may be mitigated by council members' insistence that the government agencies they oversee are more representative.

But the record is mixed. Based on an extensive study, political scientist Norman R. Luttberg found that "the use of district rather than at-large elections has no impact on representation of minorities." Increased minority representation, he reported, results more from growth in minority populations than from changes in government structure.[3] Political scientist Amy Bridges, on the other hand, found that "district elections have changed the face of local politics" in large southwestern cities that changed from at-large to district elections, producing councils that were "more racially diverse than the city councils of big-city reform."[4] Anecdotal evidence from many cities supports Bridges's findings, but this may reflect the initial impact of the change in method of selecting city council members. Bridges points out that in some cities, minorities weren't so successful at winning elections after the first few rounds and more traditional representation recurred. She also notes that the coalitions that produced the change to district elections failed to form "stable electoral and governing coalitions" after winning.[5] We should remember, however, that such change would not occur if the minority population had not grown to sufficient size and mobilized politically to bring it about.

In cities such as Dallas where council members are selected by a combination of at-large and district elections, council representation is mixed, with minorities and the majority clearly represented. In cities such as San Diego where council members are nominated by district and elected at-large, councils are also mixed, although minority communities are often frustrated that their preferred candidates don't win citywide elections. The system of having candidates nominated by districts and elected citywide was called the "black beater" in Cleveland, where militant candidates could win district nomination but not citywide elections. Amy Bridges found that the same thing happened to more assertive minority candidates in San Diego, who might have been the first choice in their districts but came in second citywide.[6]

Community activists are sometimes disappointed that local politics aren't changed more by district elections, but their expectations may be too high. After all, the same political forces are still active in a community after a change in representation. Although district campaigns are cheaper than at-large races, district candidates still need to cater to the traditional contributors and may remain captives of the growth machine, despite their neighborhood ties.

IN YOUR COMMUNITY

How are your city council members elected? What sorts of people are on your city council? Are they representative of your community? Check the records on council members for the past ten years or more at your city clerk's office. Check their backgrounds online, in newspaper archives, or at the library if these are not available at the clerk's office. Then compare these to census data on your community (available online or at the library). Has representation changed over time?

Impact: Styles of Policy Making

Political scientists have more modest expectations of these electoral structures. In theory, at-large council members are expected to act more as **trustees**, doing what they think is best for the community, while district representatives function as **delegates**, following the wishes of their constituents. But in reality, most council members, however they are elected, declare themselves to be trustees,[7] perhaps because they prefer to be seen as independent thinkers rather than as mere mouthpieces or because they have no idea how their constituents might want them to vote on most issues. In general, however, observers expect at-large council members to function more as trustees and to be more responsive to community elites, including business interests, while district representatives are expected to function more as delegates, speaking for their constituents and focusing on micro- rather than macroissues. Some council members, known as **politicos**, play their roles in both ways, acting as trustees on some issues and delegates on others depending on varying circumstances. When their constituents express themselves on an issue, a politico acts as a delegate, but when constituents are not interested or informed (which is most of the time), the politico function as trustees. According to James Svara, recent surveys report that however council members are elected and whether they operate in council-manager or mayor-council systems, they emphasize "representational functions" more and more—perhaps because their constituents are becoming more demanding.[8]

Research has not confirmed that differences in policy-making style are due to the method of selection of council members, however. Norman Luttberg found that the system of representation made no difference in the policies approved by council members.[9] Another study found that "the impact of political structure on policy views of council members appears to be quite small." Based on a survey of council members, the study concluded that while district representatives are more oriented to neighborhoods and basic services than their at-large counterparts, they are still (disappointingly for some) sensitive to citywide concerns. Yet, the same study found more conflict and pork-barrel politics (getting goodies for their own districts) as well as a greater "service orientation" on districted councils.[10]

Political scientists Peggy Heilig and Robert Mundt found that with district representation, routine city services were more equitably provided to different neighborhoods, some of which had previously been underserved.[11] Amy Bridges cites policy differences in the southwestern cities she studied, where district representation "introduced issues of equity into political debate." Neighborhood as well as minority representation played a major part in the movement for district representation in southwestern cities, as did efforts to control the sprawling growth of cities in that region. Where the movement succeeded, these issues came to the fore. "Unlike local politics in the era of big-city reform," Bridges writes, "in this political setting neighborhoods of every color, proponents of growth, environmentalists, and managed growth advocates alike must settle for representation, negotiation, and bargaining."[12]

Meanwhile, political scientist Susan MacManus found that where cities mix district and at-large elections, council representation of "different constituencies causes a wider range of policy issues to be discussed at council meetings . . . increases citizen participation—at council meetings and polls . . . [and] increase[s] the likelihood of responsiveness through council coalition building."[13]

While critics of at-large elections decry the lack of direct representation for minorities and some neighborhoods and an inattention to the mundane details of service provision, critics of district representation worry about conflict, parochialism, and a lack of attention to citywide issues. Conflict isn't necessarily a bad thing, however, if it reflects the genuine differences in perspective likely to exist in any large city. Parochialism and inattention to citywide issues are more serious concerns. Mayors and city managers, however, provide leadership on these issues and many district representatives rise above these limitations. Another concern is the tendency for all members of the council to defer to a district representative on land use or other decisions specific to his or her district—a form of logrolling—rather than to consider seriously the citywide repercussions of their decision. In San Jose, the local newspaper has labeled such council members "mini-mayors," ruling in their own fiefdoms by virtue of the deference of their colleagues—who want the same deference in return. Such deference isn't necessarily bad, since district council members clearly know the wishes and needs of their own districts best. But it is the responsibility of the rest of the council, the mayor, and administrators to see that decisions are not to the detriment of the city as a whole.

The difference in outcomes of these different systems of representation may seem marginal, yet anyone who attends a council meeting can tell from the behavior and comments of members whether they represent districts or not. Additionally, minority representation is greater under districting, at least when minority populations are concentrated (or segregated) into certain districts. In every city that has recently instituted district elections, the representation of minorities (and sometimes women as well) has increased. In cities with long-standing district representation, minorities (such as Latinos in Denver) have achieved "much greater . . . political representation, incorporation, and responsiveness" than in comparable cities using at-large elections, according to political scientist Rodney Hero.[14] Recently, however, minorities and women have also done better in at-large elections because of increasing tolerance, good organizing, and, in some cases, because minorities have become majorities. Meanwhile, whites who have recently become a minority in some cities now complain about at-large elections.

The struggle for representation continues, for even if these systems make little real difference in policies, as some researchers assert, people need to feel that they are part of the government of their community. Such reassurance encourages participation and may, eventually, change policies.

Council Dependence

Whether elected by district or at-large, councils are weak in relation to the executive branch. Although at-large council members represent the entire city, their precise constituency is vague and may be defined to suit a council member's own interests and ambitions. At-large members, for example, may pay attention only to some neighborhoods or interest groups or only to those that will help them advance to higher office. On the other hand, when a city has both an at-large council and an elected mayor, council members are not easily intimidated by the mayor since they are elected by the whole city, too.

District council members have more clearly defined constituencies to hold them accountable. This is a source of strength, but their narrow viewpoints and the fact that they represent only part of the city usually mean more power for the city executive. City managers can play district council members off one another, pleasing just enough of them to retain majority support. Mayors can do the same, with the added advantage of being the only citywide elected official, so they get more media attention and can claim to speak for all of the city, not just part.

Both at-large and district representatives, however, experience **council dependence** on executives and bureaucracies for information. In a council-manager system, the council is supposed to make policy and leave implementation to the manager and bureaucracy. In a mayor-council system, the council shares policy-making responsibilities with the mayor, who also oversees implementation. But the council needs information to make policy, and although citizens and interest groups provide some information, most comes from the city administration, whether headed by a mayor or a manager. This is a major source of power for the executive since information can be manipulated or even withheld. Study any council agenda or listen attentively at any meeting—executive control of information is obvious.

Asserting Legislative Authority

Many councils work comfortably with their executives and bureaucracies, especially in small or middle-sized, homogeneous cities with reform structures. But in other, usually larger, cities, councils often distrust the city administration and seek ways to depend on it less and to assert their own authority more. In some of these cities, counterreformers have sought ways to strengthen the council in relation to the executive.

The reformers expected council members to serve only part-time and paid them accordingly, which ensured dependence on the executive. Counterreformers, however, advocated full-time pay as a way to empower representatives. Better-paid council members can work full-time, helping their constituents more and providing a counterbalance to administrators. "It's ridiculous," said a Sacramento council member who was paid $20 per meeting, "to expect people with full-time jobs to also handle full-time council responsibilities."[15] Higher salaries also mean a wider variety of people can afford to hold public office—not just those with other means of support.

Full-time salaries are now common for council members in large cities, but **council pay** in most cities is still minimal—or nonexistent. In San Antonio, where council members are expected to work part-time, they are paid just over a thousand dollars a year; Bridgeport, Connecticut, pays $250; and Little Rock, Arkansas, pays its council members nothing at all. Full-time council salaries range from $37,500 in Dallas to $143,837 in Los Angeles. County commissioners or supervisors are more likely to be full-time and are usually better paid than their city counterparts. School board members are usually unpaid, although some receive small stipends for each meeting they attend.

Another way to lessen legislative dependence on the executive and the bureaucracy is to allow council members to hire their own support staff. Some **council staff**, such as an auditor or budget analyst, may work for the council as a group. Individual council members hire others to assist them with constituent services, research, and public relations. Whether hired by the whole council or by individual members, much of what these staffers do is to provide a critical perspective on the proposals and practices of administrators.

City councils also assert themselves through committees. Instead of always functioning as a full council, with each member a generalist needing to know about all the things a city does, they form smaller groups that can specialize on particular policy areas. Typical **council committees** include budget, public works, and planning or environment. In committees, council members are able to spend more time studying and considering proposals and may develop sufficient expertise (with their own staff assistance) to challenge the executive. They report to the full council, which usually follows its own committees' recommendations.

Pay, staff, and committees make city councils stronger and more professional, providing balance to the power of executives and bureaucracies and enabling council members to represent their constituents more effectively. According to political scientist Rodney Hero, having a relatively **professionalized council**, with pay, staff, and a formal committee structure is particularly helpful to minority representation. Hero cites the achievements of Denver's Latino minority compared to minorities in cities without such council support.[16]

Other devices help councils, too. In the pure reform structure of the middle-sized, suburban city of Sunnyvale, California, for example, the council asserts control over the direction of the city by an annual session to set priorities, review its general plan for growth, and project its budget ten years into the future. The council may still be dependent on the executive and bureaucracy, but these exercises provide both guidance and checks.

That's really about the best that can be hoped for by a city council. Even if they are professionalized, legislative bodies are always prey to disagreement, conflict, and disarray. They can never really compete with the authority that a single executive, whether mayor or manager, has over the city bureaucracy or the hundreds of experts at the executive's command, nor can they hope to supervise or even direct what city workers do in their offices and on the streets. Besides, some citizens are wary of professionalized councils, which they see as a waste of time and money. Council members in some (mostly large) cities have therefore been limited to two or three terms of office, ensuring constant new blood, but also guaranteeing councils full of amateurs at the mercy of the executive branch.[17] In most small and middle-sized cities, council members rarely serve more than two terms in office, so **term limits** aren't necessary—and amateurism can be a problem.

The Council Member's Job

Despite recent improvements in council representation, the vast majority of council members in the United States are middle class and middle aged and most are white males. As of 2001, 87.5 percent were white (down from 93.6 percent in 1986) and 77.8 percent were male (down from 84.5 percent in 1986).[18] As noted, most are paid little and must make professional and personal sacrifices to serve. Although in most communities the job is intended to be part-time, many council members, especially in larger cities, find themselves spending forty to seventy hours a week on city business. Besides their weekly council meetings, much time is taken up in committees and meetings with constituents and lobbyists. Preparing for these weekly council meetings often requires the assimilation of masses of reading material and reports with little assistance. The people they represent also expect council members to help with their problems, so much time is devoted to constituent service. Such efforts help with reelection (another demand on council members' time), so constituent service is usually taken on willingly and even eagerly. In addition to all this, effective council members need to "**work the halls**," talking to colleagues, administrators, and executives to pick up support for their pet issues. They must be careful about this, however, since city charters often forbid direct contact between council members and administrators other than the manager and mayor, and most states have **open meeting laws** that require public access to any gathering of a majority of council members except when they are discussing legal or personnel matters.

With so many demands on their time—plus the private jobs part-time council members must retain—many feel lucky just to keep up with the press of city business. For the most part, this means that they react to proposals and policies put forward by the executive, the bureaucracy, or businesses and interest groups, rather than initiating programs on their own. In other words, they tend to be followers rather than leaders.

Why do they do it? Surveys of council members report that the main motivation is community service and the spirit of volunteerism.[19] Most actually want to do good for their cities. Some are propelled by concerns about particular issues, such as growth or neighborhood or minority problems. Most get an ego boost out of being a local VIP and many enjoy the exercise of power—or at least the illusion thereof. Some may expect to further their personal careers, although not usually in politics. Except for big city mayors, most local politicians do not advance to higher office. They may, however, enhance their law practices or get better jobs through the connections they make as council members, perhaps as consultants or lobbyists or with developers. For the vast majority, however, being a council member brings little personal reward and remains primarily a way to serve their communities in the great American tradition of volunteerism.

Managers: Authority Without Accountability?

In contrast to council members, city managers are among the most powerful and least visible actors in local politics. Although the average manager may sit quietly, perhaps even wordlessly, through a city council meeting, virtually every item on the agenda will have been put there by the manager and his or her staff and virtually every decision will follow their recommendations. Sometimes a city manager takes a higher profile, lecturing the council and behaving more like a mayor than a manager, but although such publicly domineering managers were once rather common, they are now rare. Most modern managers work behind the scenes, prudently letting the council take the lead in public.

The Council-Manager System

That's more or less what the reformers who created the council-manager form of government intended. The council is to be the political element of local government, providing policy guidelines, representation, and accountability. (We've already seen that the reformers' part-time councils, elected at-large, have difficulty achieving these goals except in homogeneous cities, where representation and agreement on policy are easy.) The **city manager**, appointed by the council, is to be the objective, professional administrator, overseeing the city bureaucracy as it carries out council programs competently and efficiently. Most council-manager cities have a mayor, but unlike the executive mayor in the mayor-council form of government, the mayor in a council-manager system is basically a presiding officer who sits and votes with the council and has no separate powers.

In theory, the council-manager system concentrates power in the city council, with no checks and balances or separation of power. Although the manager is in charge of administration, the council provides policy guidance and, more importantly exercises the ultimate power to hire and fire the manager. Political scientist James Svara concludes that "the council ultimately wins all battles with the manager."[20] Battles, however, are not common in council-manager governments, where cooperation is the norm. Most issues are resolved before they ever reach the council, perhaps because its wishes are anticipated or because contemporary city managers are so skillful at building consensus. Then again, cooperation and consensus are common in the small and middle-sized communities that most frequently use the council-manager form of government. These communities tend to be homogeneous; even if they are not, reform electoral structures ensure a council that reflects the dominant majority, manufacturing consensus by suppressing disagreement and discord.

Professionalization

Having the right manager is crucial to making the system work. Reformers intended the position to be held by a neutral professional with expertise in administration who could oversee the technical details of delivering city services. Such professionals were rare when the council-manager system was initiated in 1912, and for a long time most managers were professionals only in the sense that they had skills and knowledge beyond those of politicians and were not themselves politically active. Some were professors, doctors, and merchants, but most were engineers: A 1934 study reported that 77 percent of managers with university degrees had studied engineering.[21] Most were locals, and few regarded city management as their life's work. Although reality fell short of the reform ideal, the first managers seem to have been satisfactory. More and more cities adopted the council-manager form of government and, unlike the commission system, most stuck with it. The engineer-managers who dominated the profession from 1912 until after World War II proved to be up to their jobs, partly because at that time cities concentrated on the provision of basic, physical services, such as streets, sewage, garbage collection and disposal, and public safety.

After World War II, local government and the **profession of city management** changed. Cities raised and spent more money and took on more responsibilities, including some social services. Federal programs and grants also expanded city activities. Growth, having been held back for nearly two decades by depression and war, went into high gear, adding the complexities of land-use planning to city operations and also adding many new local governments in the suburbs, most of which opted for the council-manager system. With the growing number of jobs and increased responsibilities, a true profession of city management emerged.

The International City/County Management Association, a professional organization for managers founded in 1914, provided support, information, and training, and universities developed courses and degrees in public administration. A national pool of career managers with administrative rather than only engineering expertise grew up, and by the 1950s and 1960s, city councils were selecting the sort of nonlocal, professional managers the reformers had originally intended. Although the number of such professionals has constantly risen, a 1989 survey reported that over half of all city managers were not employed in local government when they were hired.[22] However, more and more career managers work their way up through the ranks, starting in civil service positions or in manager-appointed jobs, eventually becoming a deputy manager or department head. The next step is to manage a small city, then

Table 7.1

Salaries of City Officials, 2005

City	Council	Mayor	City manager	Police chief	Population in 2000
Austin	$45,000	$53,000	$188,989	$136,011	681,804
Beverly Hills, CA	$7,858	$7,858	$240,000	$165,000	35,088
Boston	$75,000	$152,885	—	$160,000	569,165
Chicago	$85,000	$192,100	—	$104,208	2,862,244
Dallas	$37,500	$60,000	$263,027	$138,623	1,210,393
Honolulu	$43,350	$112,200	$107,100	$110,200	377,260
Los Angeles	$143,837	$186,989	—	$256,155	3,845,541
Miami	$58,200	$97,000	$239,144	$188,989	379,724
Oklahoma City	$12,000	$24,000	$133,500	$115,508	528,042
Philadelphia	$98,000	$144,009	—	$140,000	1,470,151
Raleigh, NC	$12,000	$15,000	$163,250	$128,494	326,653
San Diego	$75,386	$133,100	$223,527	$171,280	1,263,756

on to bigger cities with bigger budgets and higher salaries (see Table 7.1). As of 2004, the average pay for a city manager was $93,492, while county managers averaged $103,551.[23] Large cities and counties pay substantially more, however.

Professionalization of city managers has not brought diversity as yet. Like other professions and like the reformers who conceived the city-manager system, its practitioners are straight out of the traditional U.S. elite: As of 2001, 88 percent were male and 95 percent were white.[24] Minority and female administrators are moving up the career ladder, but few have reached the top as yet. Nearly all of today's managers are college educated; over 60 percent hold master's degrees in public administration or business or something equivalent. Most are middle aged. About equal numbers identify themselves as Democrats (25 percent), Republicans (27 percent), and Independents (26 percent).[25] County executives have similar characteristics.

Hiring the Manager

City councils in manager cities now hire mostly from among these professionals, announcing job vacancies and selecting from a pool of applicants, often supplemented by professional headhunters employed by councils to seek applicants. Current city employees hoping for promotion may also be included. The council reviews the resumes of the job seekers, interviews a few, and finally agrees on one. The choice is perhaps the most important decision a council makes and reflects its priorities. Councils that hire outsiders are usually pushing for administrative change, James Svara argues, while those that hire from within the city government hope to consolidate existing arrangements.[26]

Traditionally, the **hiring of managers** was open ended, subject to termination at the pleasure of the council. In the early days of the system, some managers stayed on for decades, but today, the average tenure is about seven years. Managers in cities with less than 10,000 people have the shortest tenure, but most move to advance their careers, not because they are fired or because the local politics in such places is too hot to handle. Only 3 percent report leaving their positions involuntarily.[27] Rather than being fired, most resign when troubles arise. Nowadays, many managers are employed under a contract with a fixed term of years. Some managers feel that a contract secures their rights and at least guarantees pay for a specified period, while some councils like contracts because they provide a fixed date to review the manager's performance and a way to get rid of an unwanted manager gracefully. Outright firing can look too political, getting the council in local political trouble and giving it a bad national reputation among professional managers.

Managers at Work

The basic job of the manager is to implement council policy and oversee the operations of the city. Most substantial among a **manager's powers** are hiring and firing department heads and developing and administering the budget. With these tools, a manager can shape city government and set its agenda. The manager is usually also responsible for putting together the agenda for council meetings, including staff recommendations on various items, and, of course, the manager and his or her staff are present at the meeting to advise the council and take its direction. According to the ideals of this form of government, the manager is strictly subservient to the council, providing information, carrying out its decisions, and remaining neutral on policy and politics, especially elections.

Most managers and council members, however, readily acknowledge that such subservience and neutrality are little more than fantasy. Studies of managers and council members show that most expect the manager to play a part in policy making. In one such survey, 37 percent of managers said they initiated policies and 75 percent reported participating in policy formulation.[28] This shouldn't come as a surprise since managers are experts who employ other experts. As such, they provide information to the council, and they usually accompany their information with a policy recommendation that the council almost always approves. Of course, shrewd managers consult council members before major decisions, and most know their councils well enough to anticipate reactions to recommendations without consultation. The reformers' idealized line between policy and administration is pretty fuzzy in practice.

Managers and Councils

When councils and managers disagree, the council usually wins due to its power to hire and fire the manager, although in rare cases managers have taken their cases to the voters and survived. But such direct confrontations are unusual in the cooperative culture of the council-manager system, with its clear council majorities reflecting clear community majorities. Managers usually have no trouble discerning what is expected and delivering it. In the process, however, they may exercise considerable influence, and, in subtle ways, their power may be greater than that of the council —or the voters.

According to the ideals of the council-manager system, policy and administration are supposed to be separate. Policy is the council's realm; administration is the manager's. But James Svara, the leading authority on local government in America, writes that "there is not [and cannot be] a complete separation of policy administration as the discredited but tenaciously surviving model has held."[29]

Managers have substantial formal authority. Their administrative command of the city bureaucracy is virtually unhindered by the council, which is usually prohibited from even talking to city staff except through the manager. Department heads can be hired and fired by the manager without council consent. Managers generally calculate the council's reaction, knowing that if the members don't like an appointment, they can fire the manager, but getting together a majority for such an action is difficult. Usually the council views few department heads as absolutely crucial, and they may also be afraid that voters will see their intervention as political meddling. The manager's budget power is a little more constrained, with formal council approval required; yet even there, councils are limited in time and expertise.

These, along with their professionalism, are the primary **political resources of city managers**. While the council is part-time and amateur, with only general knowledge, the manager and the bureaucracy he or she commands are full-time and impressively expert. Managers and their staffs are the primary source of information for council members. They can dazzle the council with information presented in such a way as to justify their recommendations. Many council members lack the time and expertise to read staff reports critically; most don't bother, putting their trust in the professionals. The public and interest groups are competing sources of information, but they are tainted by amateurism and bias, as compared to the purported professional objectivity of city staff. Besides, the manager and staff will have presented their reports and proposals to the council in advance of meetings and so have a head start on the public and often on lobbyists as well.

Council agendas are composed almost entirely of items from the city manager's office, including reports and recommendations. The council almost always unanimously approves whatever the staff recommends. The same process applies to the budget, the council's most important annual decision. The manager and a full-time staff work on it through the year, presenting a bulky document to the council about a month before the deadline for approval. The council pokes at the document, holds public hearings, shuffles a little money around, and then approves.

IN YOUR COMMUNITY

Check out the agenda for a city council meeting in your community, either online or in the city clerk's office. The source for each item on the agenda should be designated. Where do most items come from? The city manager? Department heads or staff? The mayor? Council members? The community?

There's nothing wrong with this if the manager's recommendations are objective and reflect the wishes of the council and the community, as they usually do. Managers who overtly thwart the will of the council and community don't last long. Yet managers exercise great power and do not necessarily do so neutrally. Every recommendation they make to the city council is a choice. The manager's own biases (and those of her or his chosen staff) influence these choices. After all, managers are human. Some are liberal, others conservative; some are racist, sexist, or punctiliously politically correct. These attitudes may show in their recommendations and actions. "Despite professional norms that deny such influences," one study concluded, "the political ideology of city managers plays a significant role in influencing council policy."[30] But other biases come from the profession of city management itself. Perhaps because of its roots in the reform movement and the early engineer-managers, the profession tends to see local government functions as limited and physical rather than social. It also apotheosizes expertise and quantifiable facts over intuition and sometimes-unquantifiable social values. Moving traffic, for example, may be given a higher priority than preserving the social fabric of neighborhoods. The former can easily be counted; the latter cannot. Managers and their minions sometimes show contempt for citizens and even council members who may instinctively know what is right but are unable to provide charts and data.

Nor do managers stay as scrupulously out of politics as the reformers expected. In one survey, managers said they spent 17 percent of their time on politics.[31] Most keep a low profile during elections (supporting losers is fatal), but may nevertheless provide incumbent council members with crucial information or defer controversial decisions until after the election. More commonly, managers meet with community groups, give speeches, and confer with newspaper editorial boards to sell their proposals. "If you view your job the way we used to do it, shuffling papers and having meetings, you miss the boat," said Camille Barnett, a former city manager of Austin, Texas. Barnett considered herself a negotiator and facilitator, bringing together diverse groups to reach consensus. Reformers would have assumed this was the city council's role, but Barnett's council, far from being upset, took credit for the change. "We [were] always telling the manager to bring all the interest groups together in a room and work something out," said one Austin council member.[32]

Other managers acknowledge their growing role as political brokers, balancing not only members of the council, but also community groups. The bottom line for managers, however, is keeping a majority of the city council happy. "I run for re-election every time the city council meets," managers often say. In a way, this is another source of power, for managers can play different council members against each other to prevent them from banding together to form a majority in favor of firing. If those who wish to get rid of the manager have different reasons, the manager can make concessions to one or two and stay in office. Community groups are trickier for managers to keep happy because managers are professional administrators, not politicians. Except for a few, most managers prefer to keep their heads down and confine their political maneuvering to the city council. This may exacerbate the frustration of community groups that feel the manager and city government are not responding to their demands. These groups may grow angrier when they learn they have no way to hold the manager accountable. Since the manager is not elected, she or he cannot be recalled. Only the council can remove the manager, and it is difficult, if not impossible, for community groups to persuade a majority of the council to do so. Those who seek to dismiss a manager are often seen as one-issue groups acting on their own narrow interests or they are written off as political fanatics, while the manager enjoys the protective cloak of his or her purportedly neutral professionalism.

Evolving Systems

Such conflicts rarely arise in the generally homogeneous cities that have council-manager governments, but when the populace diversifies and political conflict increases, the council-manager system comes under serious stress. Sometimes the solution is a more politically active manager, engaging in negotiation and brokerage among various interests. However, managers can get into trouble doing this. More often, other changes are introduced to adapt a city's government structures to changing needs and expectations.

We've already seen that some cities have empowered their councils and mayors with full-time pay, support staff, and committee systems. Professionalizing elected officials makes them more assertive on policy and "appears to influence city manager roles," according to one study: As the council and mayor become more involved in policy making, managers pay more attention to administration.[33] In some cities, the council-manager form of government is retained but the mayor's powers are enhanced. Increasingly, mayors are expected to provide leadership, with the managers reduced to the status of a chief administrative officer, managing the bureaucracy while the mayor directs policy. In such cities, the mayor is directly elected, presides over and votes with the council, and may set its agenda as well. A full-time salary and staff are likely. Some mayors also gain the power to propose the budget and a special role in appointing the manager and possibly department heads. A few mayors of council-manager systems even have veto power over council actions. Almost all large cities that still use the council-manager system (including Dallas, Phoenix, and San Antonio) have moved in this direction, with mayors growing more powerful and prominent and managers fading into the background—or leaving to be replaced by more subservient successors.

In their book *The Adapted City*, H. George Frederickson and his coauthors argue that today few cities function with pure, traditional council-manager or mayor-council forms of government. Most city governments, they assert, have "adapted" their government structures because "citizens now appear to want, simultaneously, both political responsiveness and administrative efficiency." They classify council-manager cities that have accommodated these wishes "adapted administrative cities" because they retain the basic council-manager structures but with enhanced mayoral powers. Over 60 percent of council-manager cities now directly elect a mayor, for example, and additional powers have followed for mayors in many of these cities.[34]

A few cities have taken more extreme action, abandoning the council-manager system and returning to the more politically accountable mayor-council form of government. Among the largest cities to make the change are Albuquerque, New Mexico; Flint, Michigan; Oakland and San Diego, California; Pocatello, Idaho; and Schenectady and Rochester, New York. In some cases, the switch was the result of increasing diversity and political conflict that city managers couldn't handle. When Albuquerque made its change in 1974, respondents to a public opinion poll said "under the council-manager structure they often did not know who could help with a problem or who was responsible for municipal affairs. Many also felt that Albuquerque had outgrown manager government and that a full-time, elected mayor was needed."[35] One researcher actually found that these changes were most common in smaller cities where city managers dabbled in politics too much and "crises in legitimacy" arose.[36] Spokane, Redmond, and Tacoma, Washington, changed from council-manager to mayor-council systems; subsequent initiatives have challenged the change—unsuccessfully, so far.

However, outright **abandonment of the council-manager form** of government remains rare. More cities have considered and rejected such a switch than have approved it, largely because of unrealistic but heartfelt fears of autocratic executives and resurrected bosses. Dallas voters rejected such a change from council-manager to strong mayor in 2005, while El Paso voters, in an unusual move, approved a change *back* to a council-manager system. Previously, voters in Topeka, Kansas, similarly swam against the tide when they approved a switch from mayor-council to council-manager in 2004. Adaptation is more common than abandonment of either form, however, and the most common adaptation is retention of the manager and increasing the power of the mayor. If any office has gained in recent city hall power struggles, it is that of the mayor.

Mayors: Leadership Without Authority?

Mayors are more difficult to generalize about than other city officials because the powers of the office vary so much from city to city and the personality and skills of particular officeholders count for so much. We can, however, distinguish between the sort of nonexecutive mayors found in the council-manager form of government and the weak and strong mayors found in the mayor-council systems.

Nonexecutive Mayors

Mayors in council-manager cities are members of the city council who preside over meetings and represent the city on ceremonial occasions. Although over half of all council-manager cities directly elect their mayors, in the remainder the mayor is chosen by the council from among its members, rotating the position every year or two. In a few cities, the mayor is the top vote winner on the council.

Mayors in council-manager cities lack executive authority to hire and fire or propose a budget, and only 11 percent may veto acts of the council.[37] The power of such **nonexecutive mayors** comes almost entirely from their title and from being the focus of attention. Beyond that, it's up to individuals to make the most of their positions. This is difficult but not impossible. The **title of mayor** really means some-

thing to most Americans, whatever the formal authority of the office. Out of ignorance or idealism, most people assume mayors are important. This assumption actually gives mayors power, even if it is only symbolic. The public respects and focuses
on the mayor. So do the media, which reinforces the public bias, although media
concentration on the mayor is probably less out of ignorance than convenience. After all, it is easier to interview one mayor than several council members and the
media don't have to explain the role of the mayor (as opposed to that of a city manager or council member).

Surprisingly, the symbolic power of the title of mayor carries over to council
colleagues who know better. Although in many cities council members are the mayor's
equal, council members often look to mayors for at least some leadership, giving
mayors the first opportunity to take the initiative on policies, and often expect the
mayor to help steer them through controversial issues. Just by **presiding over meetings**, for example, mayors have some control over the meeting's agenda, not so
much as to whether an issue is heard as to how and when it is considered and how it
is resolved. The mayor may recommend referral to administration or to a committee
or force a vote. As presiding officer, the mayor also calls on speakers and so can
choose those who will say what she or he wants said or make the motion the mayor
wants at the appropriate time.

Like council members and the public, administrators also look to mayors for at
least some leadership even though few answer to the mayor alone. Managers and
department heads work closely with mayors on the agendas of public meetings and
rely on mayors to move programs through the council, to communicate with the
public, and sometimes to mediate. In return, the mayors expect to see their priorities
reflected by the administration. **Partnerships between mayors and managers** are
not unusual, especially in the larger cities using the council-manager form of government. "This awkward arrangement can work remarkably well," writes Alan
Ehrenhalt, "in the presence of a charismatic mayor and a detail-minded, self-effac-
ing city manager, as was the case in San Antonio for most of the 1980s with Mayor
Henry Cisneros and manager Louis J. Fox."[38]

James Svara, an authority on local leadership, observes that nonexecutive mayors
assert influence by facilitating and coordinating the actions of others, including the
city administration, council, and community groups. "The council-manager mayor,"
Svara writes, "is not limited in his or her leadership but rather is different in the kinds
of leadership provided."[39] Instead of being the dominant power, this sort of mayor is
first among equals, a potential facilitator with a chance to guide programs and policies. "Although these mayors lack formal powers over other officials," Svara writes,
"they occupy a strategic location in the communication channels with the council,
the manager, and the public."[40] Playing such a role, however, takes more than a title.
Considerable skill is required, so the real power of a mayor in a council-manager
system is very much dependent on the personality of the mayor.

Nonexecutive mayors can easily lose when there are conflicts. Council members
can outvote them. City managers can go around them to the rest of the council or
even to the public; they can also slow down the process, manipulate information,
and delay implementation. When such conflicts arise, however, they are far more

apocalyptic than these tactics imply. If the mayor is no pushover, the result may be gridlock or the factions may take their fight to the public, sometimes to be resolved in elections. Public esteem for their title gives mayors an advantage in these confrontations, at least in comparison to the commonly held stereotypes of bickering council members and bureaucratic managers. But again, the personality and skills of the individual mayor are crucial for success.

Maximizing the Power of Nonexecutive Mayors

In pursuit of leadership, some council-manager cities have strengthened the office of mayor. Sometimes such change is sought by community organizations frustrated by unresponsive managers or by business interests that want a mayor who can sell the city to investors. More often, the instigators are frustrated mayors themselves. If they are sufficiently popular, greater power may be their reward, although the public, despite its expectations of mayors, is usually reluctant to increase executive authority.

In most council-manager cities, strengthening the mayor starts with **direct election** rather than selection by the city council. Election gives the mayor no added authority, but it makes public support clear and may indicate a mandate. It also ensures that the mayor is the center of media and public attention and raises expectations, since candidates universally promise to get things done rather than admitting that without executive authority the mayor is only a member of a team.

In accordance with the basic premises of the council-manager form of government, most nonexecutive mayors are expected to work only part-time and are paid accordingly. San Antonio, for example, pays its mayor $3,000 a year; the mayor of Raleigh, North Carolina, earns $15,000 per year, and the mayor of Oklahoma City gets $24,000 (see Table 7.1). Some council-manager cities, however, pay something closer to a full-time salary: Phoenix pays $62,800 per year, while Cincinnati pays $121,291, and the mayor of San Jose, California, gets $105,500. Overall, about 25 percent of cities pay their mayors less than $5,000 per year and about 25 percent pay over $48,000; salaries in the rest fall in between these figures.[41] As with council pay, more money means the mayor spends less time earning a living elsewhere and more time on public duties, which can translate into power.

The stature of some mayors has also been enhanced by authority to hire and fire their own personal aides rather than working with city staff through the manager. Nonexecutive mayors in small and middle-sized cities usually have no staff except a civil service secretary, but in larger cities, mayors employ one or more aides. The **mayor's staff** in these cities may include a press officer, budget analyst, and policy specialists.

In addition to presiding over meetings and controlling agendas, nonexecutive mayors have gained power as **leaders of the council**. In the 1970s and 1980s mayors of San Diego and San Jose, California, organized their city councils into committees to specialize on various subjects and took the power to appoint the committees and their chairs for themselves as mayor, thus gaining a modest set of rewards for council allies as well as a little more influence over policy. Mayoral powers in some cities have also been expanded to include appointment of advisory committees and commissions, again adding a little more patronage and a little more influence over policy. The shift to district council elections in some cities also enhanced the stature and leadership role of the mayor as the only citywide elected official.

Executive Mayors

In rare cases, council-manager mayors actually gain powers beyond these. San Jose's mayor, for example, is directly elected, earns a good salary, hires a large personal staff, presides over a districted city council, and appoints its committees. But the voters of San Jose also approved a charter amendment giving the mayor power to propose the budget and nominate the city manager. Perhaps San Jose's mayor is now more like the mayor in a weak mayor form of government rather than the traditional nonexecutive mayor in council-manager systems. San Jose's system of government is probably best described now as mayor-council-manager rather than council-manager or as an "adapted administrative city" to use the terminology of Frederickson, Johnson, and Wood.[42] Kansas City, Missouri, is another example of an adapted administrative city.

The powers of mayors vary by degree, however. In earlier chapters we distinguished between the weak and strong mayor forms of government, and in this chapter, we have considered nonexecutive mayors. While these distinctions are useful for grasping the differences among forms of government, mayoral powers vary so much that once the basic forms are understood, we almost need to look at particular cities. Figure 7.1 presents a **hierarchy of mayoral powers**, ranging from the purely titular to the substantial authority of the executive mayor, culminating with the powers of appointment, budget, and veto. Council-manager mayors have the first few powers listed, but beginning with salary and staff, mayors become more executive, gradually shading from weak to strong depending on how completely the different powers are held by the mayor. We should remember, however, that while executive mayors have greater official power, their personalities still count.

Like most of their nonexecutive counterparts, **executive mayors** gain prestige from the title of mayor and credibility from being elected. Unlike most council-manager mayors, however, they are expected to work full-time and are paid accordingly. As of 2005, the salaries of executive mayors in large cities ranged from $96,507 in Seattle to $192,100 in Chicago (see Table 7.1). These mayors also employ sizable personal staffs. But three other powers are essential for the making of an executive mayor: **appointment, budget, and veto**. A strong mayor has the authority to hire and fire department heads and often a chief administrative officer as well as to appoint members of boards and commissions. The mayor, supported by an extensive staff, proposes the budget, which must be approved by the council. The mayor may veto council action subject to override only by a two-thirds vote of the council, which may be hard to attain. Additionally, the mayor may issue executive orders, reorganize city departments, and make appointments to fill vacancies when elected offices fall vacant. Some mayors have special powers over agencies that are associated with the city but are somewhat independent, such as redevelopment, housing authorities, or even school boards in the case of Chicago and New York City.

Figure 7.1

Hierarchy of Mayoral Powers
Suggested by Susan Ronder, City College of San Francisco

Weak to strong	Specific powers
Strongest mayor (Executive mayor)	Veto
	Budget
	Appointment of department heads
	Appointment of commissions and boards
	Appointment of council committees
	Personal staff
	Full-time salary
	Direct election
	Control of council agenda
	Presiding at council meetings
Weakest mayor (Nonexecutive)	Title of mayor

Strong mayors, by definition, have all these powers, but they are diluted in a weak mayor form of government (remember this is distinct from nonexecutive mayors in council-manager systems). Weak mayors may appoint some city officials, but budget authority is shared with the council and other executives, and the veto is usually denied. However, the powers of a weak mayor are still greater than those of most council-manager mayors.

These powers make it clear that the executive mayor is an administrator, not just a political leader. Overseeing the day-to-day operations of city government, choosing department heads, putting together a budget, and proposing programs all require considerable management skills, yet most mayors get their jobs through their political rather than administrative ability. This suits a city's need for political leadership, but may fall short on the effective and efficient management of a large organization. A few cities, including Cincinnati and Oakland, have adopted strong mayor forms of government while retaining the office of city manager. In such cases the manager is appointed by the mayor and works under the mayor's direction.

More commonly, cities try to balance the need for both leadership and management skills through the use of a **chief administrative officer (CAO)** or by deputy mayors appointed by the mayor (sometimes with council approval) specifically for their management skills. An increasing number of cities seem to be moving in this direction, seeking to balance political leadership with professional management.[43] Like city managers, CAOs oversee the daily operations of local governments and often assemble budget proposals, but while managers answer to councils, CAOs answer to mayors. Unlike managers, they do not appoint department heads and they play a lesser role in policy making, deferring to mayoral leadership on both. Frederickson, Johnson, and Wood designate mayor-council cities that have retained a manager or added a CAO as "adapted political cities." Whereas council-manager (administrative) cities adapt by enhancing representation and leadership, mayor-council cities adapt by augmenting professional management. Other examples of adapted political (or mayor-council) cities include Atlanta, Buffalo, Houston, Los Angeles, Minneapolis, Salt Lake City, and Tampa. Today over half of all mayor-council cities function with a CAO, while only 24 percent had a CAO in 1972.[44]

Executive mayors are also distinguished from nonexecutives in their relations with the city council. Executive mayors are separate from city councils; they do not preside over and rarely even attend council meetings. Instead, the council chooses its own presiding officer, and the relationship between the two branches of local government is often more antagonistic. Mayors lose some control of agendas and meetings, although they still shape what happens by the proposals they pass along to the council, and any loss of influence is compensated for by budgetary and veto powers. The council, like legislative bodies elsewhere, spends most of its time reacting to executive proposals, while mayors, like city managers, benefit from their control over city staff and information. A singular executive—whether mayor or manager— always has the advantage of being one while multimember councils are inherently prone to disunity.

Whether executive or nonexecutive, mayors use their political skills and resources to win council approval of their programs. They lobby council members and give their allies electoral support, including endorsements and fundraising. Moreover, executive mayors even more than other sorts of mayors have the advantage of being in the media spotlight. An effective mayor uses that spotlight to further his or her program with the council.

Who the Mayors Are

Mayors, like council members and city managers, are mostly white and male. As of 2005, 17 percent of mayors of cities with populations over 30,000 were female.[45] Far fewer were Asian, Latino, or African American. In general, women candidates do better in smaller cities while **minority mayors** are more likely in large cities with substantial minority populations or in smaller suburban and rural communities where Asians, Latinos, or African Americans are in the majority.

Despite the preponderance of white businessmen among mayors, women and minority candidates have achieved striking successes since the 1960s. Women have done particularly well in the West and in suburban cities, and, in the past, several large cities have also elected women mayors, including Chicago, Houston, San Antonio, San Diego, San Francisco, San Jose, and Washington, DC. Currently the largest city presided over by a woman mayor is Dallas, where Laura Miller was elected in 2002. As of 2005, 13 of the largest 100 cities in the United States had women mayors (see Table 7.2). African Americans have also done well in mayoral contests, especially in large cities (see Table 7.3). Latino mayors have led many small southwestern towns as well as large cities such as San Antonio, San Jose, Miami, Denver, and, as of 2005, Los Angeles. Asians, a smaller minority, have elected fewer mayors, although a Japanese American won the office in San Jose in 1971. Otherwise,

Table 7.2

Largest Cities with Women Mayors, 2006

City	Mayor	Population in 2004	Next election
Lincoln, NE	Coleen Sang	236,146	2007
Plano, TX	Pat Evans	245,411	2006
Lexington, KY	Teresa Isaac	266,358	2006
Tampa, FL	Pam Lorio	321,772	2007
Atlanta, GA	Shirley Franklin	419,122	2009
Virginia Beach, VA	Meyera E. Oberndorf	440,098	2008
Kansas City, MO	Kay Barnes	444,387	2007
Sacramento, CA	Heather Fargo	454,330	2008
Long Beach, CA	Beverly O'Neill	476,564	2006
Dallas, TX	Laura Miller	1,210,393	2007

Sources: U.S. Census; U.S. Conference of Mayors, www.usmayors.org; Center for American Women and Politics, www.cawp.rutgers.edu.

Table 7.3

Largest Cities with Minority Mayors, 2006

City	Mayor	Race	Population in 2004	Percent same race as mayor race	Next election
Newark, NJ	Cory Booker	Af-Am	251,352	48.7	2010
Buffalo, NY	Bryan Brown	Af-Am	267,436	38.5	2009
Santa Ana, CA	Miguel Pulido	Latino	321,147	80.2	2008
Miami, FL	Manuel A. Diaz	Latino	324,508	69.5	2009
Wichita, KS	Carlos Mayans	Latino	345,810	12.0	2007
Atlanta, GA	Shirley Franklin	Af-Am	348,555	54.2	2009
Honolulu, HA	Mufi F. Hannemann	Pac. Islander	362,262	6.9	2008
Colorado Springs, CO	Lionel Rivera	Latino	374,343	14.3	2007
New Orleans, LA	C. Ray Nagin	Af-Am	444,515	67.9	2010
Sacramento, CA	Heather Fargo	Latina	458,342	24.4	2008
Albuquerque, NM	Martin J. Chavez	Latino	495,571	42.9	2006
Washington, DC	Anthony A. Williams	Af-Am	518,074	57.8	2006
Memphis, TN	Dr. Willie W. Herenton	Af-Am	627,802	62.3	2007
Columbus, OH	Michael B. Coleman	Af-Am	700,874	28.3	2007
Detroit, MI	Kwame M. Kilpatrick	Af-Am	840,006	84.6	2009
San Jose, CA	Ron Gonzales	Latino	873,882	31.7	2006
Philadelphia, PA	John F. Street	Af-Am	1,114,245	44.6	2007
Miami-Dade County, FL	Carlos Alvarez	Latino	2,363,600	57.3	2008
Los Angeles, CA	Antonio Villaraigosa	Latino	3,745,742	49.7	2009

Source: U.S. Census; U.S. Conference of Mayors (www.usmayors.org); National Association of Latino Elected Officials (www.naleo.org); Joint Center for Political and Economic Studies (www.jointcenter.org). All websites accessed January 2, 2006.

only a few small cities have elected Asians to the office of mayor, mainly in Hawaii and California. Asian Americans, however, are a relatively new and diverse immigrant group, only now emerging as a political force.

In office, women and minority mayors are usually expected to pay more attention to social welfare and neighborhood issues while their white male counterparts are expected to focus more on business and development. These expectations are often accurate, but women and minority candidates almost always have to reach out to white male voters, leaders, and campaign contributors. To gain such support, they often emphasize law and order, managerial competence, and/or economic development over programs that might more obviously benefit their own groups. Minority candidates de-emphasize racial issues and try to speak to a broader constituency (a phenomenon called "deracialization") while women candidates may de-emphasize women's issues. In doing so, women and minority mayors may alienate their basic constituencies and face bitter criticism as sellouts. Most minority voters nevertheless continue to support their own.

In recent contests, however, this has often not been enough to elect their candidates. Except in cities where a single minority has become the majority, as have Cuban Americans in Miami, Mexican Americans in San Antonio, and African Americans in Atlanta, Detroit, and Washington, DC, coalitions with other groups are essential for victory.[46] The election of several African American mayors in the 1970s and 1980s resulted from the solidarity of black voters as well as the support of Latinos and white liberals, especially Jews. But in the 1990s, these coalitions fell apart in some cities. Black and Latino mayors retired or were defeated and were succeeded by whites in New York, Los Angeles, Baltimore, Chicago, Denver, Oakland, and San Antonio, despite large minority populations in all those cities. In some cases, the coalition between African Americans and Latinos split, while the growing Asian population often did not identify or ally with these minorities. Elsewhere, African American candidates lost the support of Jewish voters, who had been crucial to their initial victories. In other places, white voters shifted their loyalties because of worries about the economy or the environmental impacts of growth, which minority coalitions usually supported because of the jobs growth brings. In minority-majority cities, white candidates won when white voters were united and minorities were divided. Although African American mayors have been elected with broad support in Seattle and Kansas City, where blacks are a minority, stable electoral coalitions are rare among large, diverse cities today and candidates must cobble together their support bases, drawing on their own groups and others, including business leaders.

Mayoral Style

Once elected, the formal powers of executive and nonexecutive mayors determine their behavior in office to a substantial degree. But anyone who has observed two or three different mayors of a single city knows how different they can be. Holders of a particular office all possess the same formal powers, but how they use these powers varies because they are different people.

Rudy Giuliani, a Republican mayor in Democratic New York City, managed to

Table 7.4

Time Magazine's Best and Worst Big City Mayors, 2005

The best	The worst
Richard Daley, Chicago	Kwame Kilpatrick, Detroit
Shirley Franklin, Atlanta	Dick Murphy, San Diego*
John Hickenlooper, Denver	John Street, Philadelphia
Martin O'Malley, Baltimore	
Michael Bloomberg, New York	

Source: Time, April 25, 2005.
Note: Mayors were ranked by a panel of urban experts.
*Resigned in 2005.

accomplish a fair amount through assertive leadership, but his confrontational style limited his popularity and his impact until the events of September 11, 2001, when he rose to the occasion to become the reassuring leader that New York City and the nation needed. If not for term limits, he would surely have been reelected and would have accomplished even more than he did in his two terms in office. His successor, Michael Bloomberg, another Republican, has functioned more as a technocrat, relying on his pragmatic skills as an administrator rather than the sort of charisma Giuliani had at the end of his term. Nevertheless, he's been rated one of America's best mayors. New York has a strong mayor form of government, so both Bloomberg and Giuliani had the same powers, but they used them very differently.

In Los Angeles, a weak mayor structure was changed in 1999 to give the mayor more authority, but the new powers did not enable Mayor James Hahn, elected in 2001, to be more effective in office than his predecessor, Richard Riordan, who led the city before the changes and was instrumental in their adoption. In 2005, Antonio Villaraigosa soundly defeated Hahn, and many believe Villaraigosa's dynamic personality will allow him to be a more influential force in city politics. Although supported by a broad-based coalition, Villaraigosa, too, will face challenges in governing the large and complex city of Los Angeles.

Race and gender, as noted earlier, affect how mayors do their job. So do previous experience, occupation, and education. More personal characteristics, such as knowledge, political instinct, ability to handle people (and the press), and star quality or charisma also play a part. Mayors may be lazy or dynamic, stupid or intelligent, foolish or shrewd. Some are willing to devote more of their own time and energy to their jobs than others. For some, being mayor is the pinnacle of a career, while for others it is the beginning, a stepping-stone to higher office. Those without such ambitions may focus more on strictly local issues; they may also be lackadaisical. Those hoping to move upward may be more aggressive about making their mark; they may also spend more time broadening their constituency, cultivating the media, and traveling to the state or national capital. Like other local officeholders, however, most mayors are homebodies. Only a few seek or win higher office.[47]

In addition to the formal powers of the office and personal characteristics, the local political culture also affects mayoral power. Some communities, for example, accept a high level of political conflict and rely on their mayors to provide leadership. Others emphasize professionalism and expect mayors merely to keep things moving while deferring to the experts on policy development and implementation. Still others value broad participation and resent domineering mayors. In some places, the mayor is a god; in others a joke (the attitude of the press has a lot to do with this). Public expectations, in other words, affect both a mayor's power and conduct in office.

These elements—formal powers, personal characteristics, political culture, and others—combine to shape the way mayors do their jobs. Political scientists have developed various categories of **mayoral styles**,[48] including:

The ribbon cutter: Concentrates on ceremonial aspects and makes no effort to influence policy.
The caretaker: Attempts to solve problems as they arise; has no personal program; seeks to survive and help the city get by.
The promoter: Spends time selling the city to investors and hustling state and federal aid, initiating only those policies that facilitate this.
The broker: A more aggressive version of the caretaker, seeks to put together coalitions to resolve issues, but still not an initiator of policy.
The individualist: Seeks solutions through personal leadership rather than broker-style coalition building; may initiate selective policies.
The executive: A city-manager-style mayor who emphasizes good administration and may initiate discrete projects but not broad change.
The oracle: Good at talking, at media manipulation, and at using the symbolic powers of the office, but weak at developing policies and at administration.
The entrepreneur or innovator: A strong leader with a clear, sometimes ambitious program and the ability to initiate it and carry it out.

Most mayors are easy to slot into one of these categories; some combine the traits of several. Nonexecutive mayors rarely manage to get beyond being ribbon cutters, caretakers, or promoters. By skillful use of their limited resources they can develop into most of the other types, but their powers are too limited to enable them to act as executives or entrepreneurs. Mayors with more extensive authority can fit any of the categories. Staffing of the mayor's office and clear command of the city's budget and bureaucracy are crucial, of course.

IN YOUR COMMUNITY

What sort of a mayor does your city have? Find out the mayor's formal powers by checking the city charter online, at the office of the city clerk or at the library. Observe the mayor at a meeting if possible. How would you describe your mayor's leadership style? Do some interviews or check your local newspaper's archives (usually available online).

City Characteristics and Mayoral Styles

As we learned in earlier chapters, when cities grow, they become more diverse and political conflict increases. Seeking leadership to resolve this conflict, larger cities tend to opt for the mayor-council form of government and to give their mayors executive powers. **Expectations of mayors** may be great in such cities, and disappointment is common. Mayors with limited budget and appointment powers may be unable to do much, but when stronger mayors take action, they may upset more people than they please. Whatever their powers, mayors may not be able to meet the high expectations of them (produced partly by their own campaign promises) because American cities have become increasingly difficult to govern. The very diversity that demands leadership may fracture a city into irreconcilable components. Conflicts such as the ethnic antagonisms that exploded into the 1992 Los Angeles riots may be beyond the ability of mayors to resolve. Concentrations of poverty produced by suburbanization also mean that urban problems and needs are greater while the resources are less. State and federal budget cutbacks have further limited local funds. Even skilled leaders with substantial official powers cannot solve problems without resources. As a consequence, many mayors are happy just to get by as caretakers.

Another option for mayors of cities with intractable problems is to spend their time promoting rather than governing the city. This means lobbying the state and federal governments for grants and trying to recruit business and industry. In the 1970s, some mayors built up formidable power through federally funded programs, but cutbacks since then have severely limited this option. Promoting economic development to bring in jobs and taxes, however, has become a primary mayoral activity, making some mayors seem like cheerleaders for the local growth machine. Although this offends environmentalists in some communities, most mayors find promoting their cities a politically safe activity—unlike proposing other ways to solve difficult urban problems.

Some mayors accept their reduction to caretakers and promoters while others, even in strong mayor cities such as San Francisco and Boston, have demanded greater power and authority to meet public expectations, cope with diversity, and solve increasing urban problems. As James Svara warns, however, "The elected executive leadership model is no panacea for resolving urban problems."[49] Even with the powers of the strong mayor, effective leaders must build a solid base of political support. This is particularly difficult in communities with nonpartisan electoral systems, but even in those with partisan elections, weakening parties mean mayors must rely more and more on their own personal organizations. Until the 1990s, some were able to use jobs provided by federal grants to build support, but these have been eliminated. Now ambitious mayors must spend their time hustling the media and stitching together alliances of interest groups and powerful individuals as a support base, but these alliances are unstable and putting them together diverts the mayors from dealing with the problems they were elected to solve. Increasingly, this is true for mayors in both mayor-council and council-manager systems. Politics plays a part, whatever the powers of the executive.

Converging Forms: Representation, Administration, and Leadership

The balance of representation, professional administration, and leadership is still being worked out in U.S. local governments. The trend is toward more professional and representative councils through full-time pay, staffing, and district elections, and greater leadership through empowered mayors, particularly in council-manager cities. But many mayor-council cities are concerned enough about professional administration to have introduced chief administrative officers or their equivalent. In the past ten years, 10 percent of cities report having votes on changing their structures of government. In 2001 alone, 180 cities considered changing their form of government. The most common change, however, was the addition of a chief administrative officer (CAO); the next most common change was shifting council elections from at-large to district representation.[50]

Are the council-manager and mayor-council forms of government converging? Each community works out its own balance. The pattern suggests **converging forms**, or what H. George Frederickson and his coauthors call "**the adapted city**." Their study indicates that mayor-council cities are gradually adopting aspects of the council-manager form to improve the way they function while council-manager cities are incrementally adopting elements of the mayor-council form to enhance representation, leadership, and accountability. "Most American cities are now best described as adapted," they write.[51] Demographic and political change produces these adaptations, which, in most places, are incremental. The voters almost always reject radical change, but they are more tolerant of small, gradual reforms that seem to be consistently in the direction of greater leadership in council-manager cities and more professional administration in mayor-council cities. However much they long for leadership, voters today are almost as skeptical about strong executives as were their revolutionary forebears. Instead, they've found a compromise: "City residents have essentially invented the adapted city."[52]

Essential Terms

city councils	political resources of city managers
district elections	abandonment of the council-manager form
logrolling	nonexecutive mayors
at-large elections	title of mayor
trustees	presiding over meetings
delegates	partnerships between mayors and managers
politicos	direct election
council dependence	mayor's staff
council pay	leaders of the council
council staff	hierarchy of mayoral powers

council committees
professionalized council
term limits
work the halls
open meeting laws
city manager
profession of city management
hiring of managers
manager's powers

executive mayors
appointment, budget, and veto
chief administrative officer (CAO)
minority mayors
mayoral styles
expectations of mayors
converging forms
the adapted city

On the Internet

- The National League of Cities (www.nlc.org) is a national organization for cities focusing on public policy and lobbying.
- The International City/County Management Association (ICMA) (www.icma.org) is a national organization for professional local government administrators.
- The U.S. Conference of Mayors (www.usmayors.org) is a national organization for public policy and lobbying for mayors of cities over 30,000 in population.
- Check individual city websites (including your own) for information about elected officials, government structures (charters), census data, and so on.
- The Center for American Women and Politics (www.cawp.rutgers.edu) has information on women elected officials.

Notes

1. *The Municipal Year Book* (Washington, DC: International City/County Management Association, 2003), p. 16.

2. Susan Welch and Timothy Bledsoe, *Urban Reform and Its Consequences: A Study in Representation* (Chicago: University of Chicago Press, 1988), p. 42.

3. Norman R. Luttberg, *The Grassroots of Democracy: A Comparative Study of Competition and Its Impact in American Cities in the 1990s* (Lanham, MD: Lexington, 1999), pp. 145–46. See also Peggy Heilig and Robert J. Mundt, *Your Voice at City Hall: The Politics, Procedures, and Policies of District Representation* (Albany: State University of New York Press, 1984).

4. Amy Bridges, *Morning Glories: Municipal Reform in the Southwest* (Princeton, NJ: Princeton University Press, 1997), pp. 201, 206.

5. Ibid., p. 201.

6. Ibid., p. 189. See Lee Sloan, "'Good Government' and the Politics of Race," *Social Problems* 17, no. 2 (Autumn 1969): 161–75 on the "black beater" system in Cleveland.

7. James H. Svara, *Official Leadership in the City: Patterns of Conflict and Cooperation* (New York: Oxford University Press, 1990), p. 126.

8. James H. Svara, "City Council Roles, Performance, and the Form of Government," in *The Future of Local Government Administration*, ed. H. George Frederickson and John Nalbandian (Washington, DC: International City/County Management Association, 2002), p. 225.

9. Luttberg, *The Grassroots of Democracy*, p. 124.

10. Welch and Bledsoe, *Urban Reform*, pp. 77–78, 102, 105.

11. See Heilig and Mundt, *Your Voice at City Hall*.

12. Bridges, *Morning Glories*, p. 206.

13. Susan A. MacManus, "Mixed Electoral Systems: The Newest Reform Structure," *National Civic Review* 74, no. 10 (November 1985): 490.

14. Rodney E. Hero, "Hispanics in Urban Government and Politics: Some Findings, Comparisons, and Implications," *Western Political Quarterly* 43, no. 2 (June 1990): 413.

15. Quoted in Ed Goldman, "Out of the Sandbox," *California Journal,* May 1993, p. 15.

16. Hero, "Hispanics in Urban Government," p. 411.

17. "Of the 60 largest U.S. cities, 32 percent had term limits by mid-1993, whereas only 8.3 percent reported limits a decade earlier," Chester A. Newland, "Managing from the Future in Council-Manager Government," in *Ideal and Practice in Council-Manager Government*, ed. H. George Frederickson, rev. ed. (Washington, DC: International City/County Management Association, 1995), p. 271.

18. Susan A. MacManus and Charles S. Bullock III, "The Form, Structure, and Composition of America's Municipalities in the New Millennium," *The Municipal Year Book* (Washington, DC: International City/County Management Association, 2003).

19. See, for example, Kenneth Prewitt, *The Recruitment of Political Leaders: A Study of Citizen-Politicians*, rev. ed. (Westport, CT: Greenwood, 1981).

20. Svara, *Official Leadership in the City*, p. 52.

21. Clarence E. Ridley and Orin F. Nolting, *The City Manager Profession* (Chicago: University of Chicago Press, 1934).

22. Tari Renner, "Appointed Local Government Managers: Stability and Change," *The Municipal Year Book* (Washington, DC: International City/County Management Association, 1990), p. 49.

23. Rollie O. Waters and Joyce C. Powell, "Salaries of Municipal Officials, 2004," and "Salaries of County Officials," *The Municipal Year Book* (Washington, DC: International City/County Management Association, 2005), p. 82 and 102, respectively.

24. Tari Renner, "The Local Government Management Profession at Century's End," *The Municipal Year Book* (Washington, DC: International City/County Management Association, 2001), p. 39.

25. Tari Renner, "Appointed Local Government Managers," p. 41.

26. Svara, *Official Leadership in the City*, p. 53.

27. Renner, "The Local Government," p. 39.

28. Ibid., p. 50.

29. James H. Svara, "Dichotomy and Duality: Reconceptualizing the Relationship between Policy and Administration in Council-Manager Cities," in *Ideal and Practice*, ed. Frederickson, p. 17.

30. Clifford J. Wirth and Michael L. Vasu, "Ideology and Decision Making for American City Managers," *Urban Affairs Quarterly* 22, no. 3 (March 1987): 468.

31. David N. Ammons and Charldean Newell, "'City Managers Don't Make Policy': A Lie; Let's Face It," *Public Management* 70, no. 12 (December 1988): 15.

32. Alan Ehrenhalt, "The New City Manager Is: (1) Invisible (2) Anonymous (3) Non-Political (4) None of the Above," *Governing,* September 1990, p. 43.

33. Charldean Newell, James J. Glass, and David N. Ammons, "City Manager Roles in a Changing Political Environment," in *Ideal and Practice*, ed. Frederickson, p. 66.

34. H. George Frederickson, Gary A. Johnson, and Curtis H. Wood, *The Adapted City: Institutional Dynamics and Structural Change* (Armonk, NY: M.E. Sharpe, 2004), pp. 13, 15, 70.

35. David R. Morgan, *Managing Urban America*, 3rd ed. (Pacific Grove, CA: Brooks/Cole, 1989), p. 53.

36. Greg J. Protasel, "Abandonments of the Council-Manager Plan: A New Institutionalist Perspective," *Public Administration Review* 48, no. 4 (July–August 1988): 809. See also Greg J. Protasel, "Abandonments of the Council-Manager Plan," in *Ideal and Practice*, ed. Frederickson, pp. 200–9.

37. Tari Renner and Victor S. DeSantis, "Municipal Form of Government: Issues and Trends," *The Municipal Year Book* (Washington, DC: International City/County Management Association, 1998), p. 39.

38. Ehrenhalt, "The New City Manager Is," p. 46.

39. Svara, *Official Leadership in the City*, p. 87.

40. James H. Svara, "Mayors in the Unity of Powers Context: Effective Leadership in Council-Manager Governments," in *The Future of Local Government Administration*, ed. Frederickson and Nalbandian, p. 47.

41. Evelina R. Moulder, "Salaries of Municipal Officials, 2003," *The Municipal Year Book* (Washington, DC: International City/County Management Association, 2003), p. 80.

42. Frederickson, Johnson, and Wood, *The Adapted City*. See p. 158 for their discussion of San Jose as an adapted administrative city.

43. Eric Anderson, "Two Major Forms of Government," *The Municipal Year Book* (Washington, DC: International City/County Management Association, 1989), p. 25.

44. Frederickson, Johnson, and Wood, *The Adapted City*, pp. 59, 66.

45. Center for American Women and Politics (CAWP), www.cawp.rutgers.edu (accessed January 2, 2006).

46. See Rufus P. Browning, Dale Rogers Marshall, and David H. Tabb, eds., *Racial Politics in American Cities* (New York: Longman, 1990).

47. According to Harold Wolman, Edward Page, and Martha Reavley only 25 percent of mayors of cities with populations over 100,000 found ran for or won higher office. See "Mayors and Mayoral Careers: A Research Note," *Urban Affairs Quarterly* 25, no. 3 (March 1990), p. 511.

48. See Svara, *Official Leadership in the City*; and John P. Kotter and Paul R. Lawrence, *Mayors in Action: Five Approaches to Urban Governance* (New York: Wiley, 1974).

49. Svara, *Official Leadership in the City*, p. 120.

50. MacManus and Bullock, "The Form, Structure, and Composition," pp. 6–7.

51. Frederickson, Johnson, and Wood, *The Adapted City*, p. 18.

52. Ibid., p. 169.

8 Bureaucracy
The Rest of the Iceberg

City councils, managers, and mayors are central to local government, not least because they are visible and accountable to the public. But they are often described as the tip of iceberg of local government since, like icebergs, only a tiny bit of government shows, while the bulk lurks beneath the surface. About 500,000 elected officials head U.S. cities, counties, and other local governments. Overall, local governments employ nearly thirty times that many people—over 13 million (see Figure 8.1) and growing. Over half of these work in education, while nearly 2 million are in public safety (police, firefighters, and corrections officers). Combined with state and federal employees, one out of every six jobs in the nonagricultural economy is in government. These public employees constitute the hidden, some say treacherous, part of the iceberg.

Workers in local government are variously referred to as administrators, civil servants, public employees, and bureaucrats. The term of choice often depends on the user's point of view. *Bureaucrat* is customarily a derogatory term for public workers applied by those outside of government, while *public employee* is usually the term such workers bestow on themselves. *Administrators* and *civil servants* are more neutral terms, but they are also more narrow. The former applies only to the top echelon of local government, not workers on the streets or at the desks, and the latter omits local government workers who are not covered by a civil service system. For lack of better terms, *bureaucrat* and *public employees* must suffice. We should try, however, to set aside their vernacular bias (bureaucrat = bad, public employee = good) and use them as neutrally as we did city council, mayor, and city manager. Neutral does not mean uncritical, however. As with the other institutions of local government, bureaucracy must be analyzed as well as described, for like these others, bureaucracy has its strengths, weaknesses, powers, and biases.

Perhaps the contempt most Americans feel for bureaucracy comes from the erroneous assumption that it should not have "strengths, weaknesses, powers, biases." Local bureaucrats are expected to be impartial public servants under the direction of elected officials. This is an ideal, however, and it is hard to achieve in practice. Some political activists and analysts believe bureaucracies have become the most important and most powerful single element of local governments, perhaps beyond the control of elected officials. How much power bureaucrats have is debatable, but few deny that it is substantial. The real issue is control, by both elected officials and the public. Making public bureaucracies accountable and responsive has long been a major concern in local politics and remains so today.

Figure 8.1   **Employees on Federal, State, and Local Government Payrolls, 1990–2004**

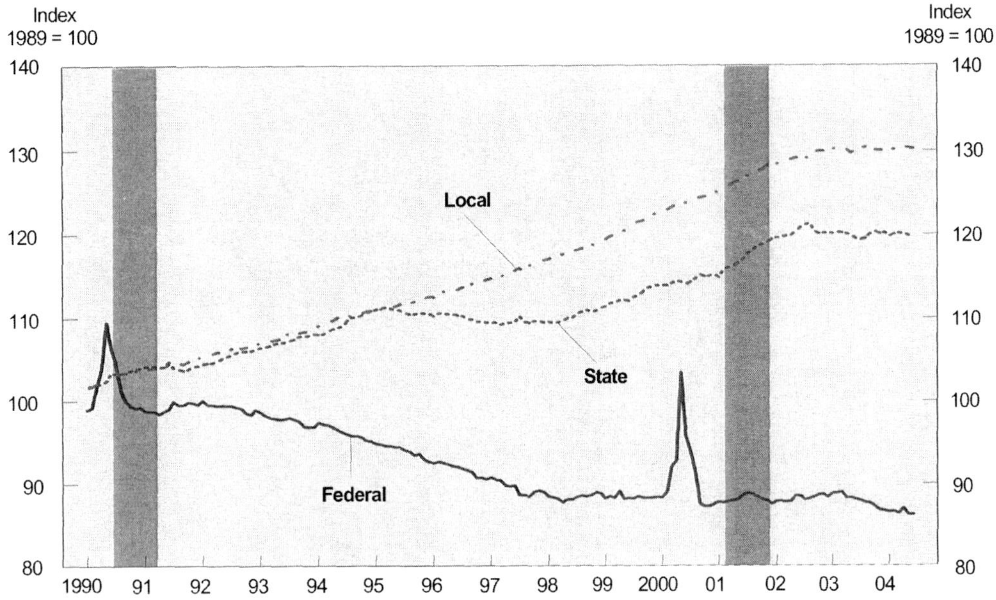

Source: Julie Hatch, "Employment in the public sector: two recessions' impact on jobs," *Monthly Labor Review* 127, no. 10 (October 2004): 39; available at www.bls.gov/opub/mlr/2004/10/art3full.pdf (accessed May 6, 2006).
Note: Shaded areas denote recessions.

Building the Iceberg: Patronage versus Civil Service

The bureaucracy of local government runs from the policy makers at the top, who are supposed to be in control, to the workers who put the policies into effect, providing services or regulating activities in their communities (see Figure 8.2). The chief policy makers are elected officials, mainly the city council and mayor, along with the highest-ranking appointed officials, including the city manager and department heads such as the police chief. The latter are also administrators who oversee operations along with their appointed assistants and deputies. Then come the bulk of the workers, the ones we deal with as citizens. Less visible is a vast army of support staff, including clerical workers.

IN YOUR COMMUNITY
Research the bureaucracy in your city or county. Go to a local government website and find an organizational chart to see how the hierarchy is arranged. Check out the budget or other appropriate documents to find out how many employees or positions are allocated to various functions, from managers to service workers.

These workers get their jobs through either a patronage or civil service system. Under **patronage**, election winners distributed the spoils of victory, including lots

Figure 8.2 **City Bureaucracy**

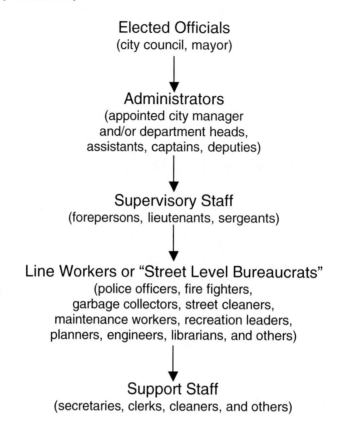

of jobs, to their supporters. If control of local government changed hands, all the old workers were out and the winners hired their own supporters. Government workers were responsive to their allies, but ignored or persecuted people who did not support the machine. The spoils system ensured political control of the bureaucracy, but the machine's interest in control was to accrue rewards for its supporters, not to provide good local government services.

Civil Service

The reformers were more worried about the fair and efficient provision of services than controlling bureaucracy. To them, machine control of local bureaucracies was at the heart of the problem. They therefore developed a system designed to increase not only the competence and fairness of government employees, but also their independence. Under the **civil service or merit system**, all city workers except department heads and their assistants are supposed to be hired, retained, and promoted on the basis of their ability to do the job, as measured by educational qualifications, written exams, interviews, and on-the-job evaluations. Employees who perform well gain job security, or **tenure**, and may be fired only for proven incompetence at their job, not because political control of local government changes hands.

Civil service systems operate to some extent in almost all local governments. In some cases, only a portion of the workers are covered, depending on rank or department. In others, the system is corrupted or abused in various ways. New York City's civil service system, for example, puts more emphasis on seniority than on merit in promoting workers. Elsewhere, qualifications or test scores may be manipulated to accommodate preferred applicants or discretion may be exercised when the final choice among those qualified is made (usually from the top three candidates). A variant of the affirmative action system may be used for buddies and political allies. Even if such favorites are not chosen, bureaucrats (like all humans in groups) tend to select people like themselves, people who will "fit in." This may produce bureaucracies that do not represent the communities they serve.

The variety of ways to subvert a merit system is illustrated by Chicago, home of one of the most famous and long-lasting political machines in the United States. Reformers managed to introduce civil service in Chicago in 1895, making it one of the first U.S. cities to adopt such a system, but the city's machine survived partly by its ability to accept reform when it had no alternative and then to find ways of getting around the reform or gaining advantage from it. For a long time, Chicago's civil service was little more than a front. At the peak of his power, the city's last great boss, Mayor Richard J. Daley (father of Chicago's current mayor), controlled 30,000 to 50,000 jobs, both inside and outside of government.[1] Chicago's civil service system did not extend to some departments, and even within the civil service system, machine supporters could get false qualifications recognized, cheat on examinations, or buy passing scores. Additionally, thousands of jobs were classified as temporary or seasonal, so workers could be hired and fired at will. Chicago's employees challenged the patronage system in the courts in the 1970s and 1980s and won reductions in its scope,[2] but its manipulation enabled that city's machine to outlast most others.

Chicago is an extreme case, but most cities and counties have evolved toward a civil service system rather than going through an instantaneous transformation. Reform was often nominal to begin with, taking hold only gradually. This evolution toward a merit system eased the pain and accommodated the residual power of machines. Besides, in the early days of civil service, the sorts of professionals the reformers hoped to recruit to local government were few. But gradually, as training and educational programs developed and local government jobs became more secure and professional, a pool of civil servants emerged.

Civil service systems are still not universal, however, and merely giving the title "civil service system" to a local government personnel program does not mean that it functions properly as such. The vast majority of local government employees are now covered by civil service, but the system is abused in some places, and particular departments or categories of employees may not be included. Civil service coverage is most thorough among local governments in the Sunbelt, where reform was most popular; those in the Frostbelt (like Chicago) tend to be more lax.

IN YOUR COMMUNITY

Investigate the civil service system in your city or county by examining job descriptions and application procedures online or at the personnel department. Try to assess how fair and unbiased the system is.

Pros and Cons of Civil Service

As the reformers hoped, civil service workers are by and large better trained and more skilled at their jobs than their amateurish machine predecessors. They also do their work with greater fairness and impartiality and much less corruption. Their professionalism is generally agreed to have increased the efficiency and effectiveness of local government, although this is sometimes disputed. Many urban analysts thought Chicago under its political machine was as well run as any other big city. Civil service systems don't necessarily save money, either. They may not waste it through corruption, like the machines, but they still find ways to spend it. Like other reforms, however, civil service has its own shortcomings, foremost among which are representativeness and accountability.

By imposing the not unreasonable requirements of educational or other appropriate qualifications for employment, the reformers immediately excluded many recent immigrants and their children. These groups had been well represented in machine bureaucracies because the only job qualification was support for the machine. (Some minorities, particularly African Americans, were excluded because of prejudice.) Civil service bureaucracies, particularly in their upper-echelon, white-collar jobs, tended to be dominated by the same white, middle-class males that had instigated the reform movement. By the 1960s, this lack of **representativeness** became a major grievance for minorities and women, who felt local bureaucracies did not adequately reflect or respond to the diversity of their communities. Making bureaucracies more representative and responsive thus became part of the counterreform effort.

Similarly, the control and accountability of civil service bureaucracies have become issues. In civil service systems, the job security public workers gain through tenure reduces control by elected officials and may make workers less responsive to the clients they serve. Under the spoils system of the machine, they could easily be fired, so the political bosses had great power over their workers, who cheerfully bent or broke rules to keep their clients happy in return for the support for the machine. Under civil service, however, political control and responsiveness to citizens is not so simple. To protect workers from political interference and the favoritism and corruption it may entail, civil service systems make firing them difficult. Incompetence on the job must be clearly proven, but this can be very hard to demonstrate except in extreme cases. Workers have gained further protections through their unions and through contractually agree-upon grievance procedures for complaints about unfair treatment. Supervisors may prefer to avoid the hassle and the confrontation of trying to fire a worker. Instead, unsatisfactory workers may be kept on or shunted to different positions. They call it "paving over" in New York, where "it is near impossible to fire a city employee for incompetence—or even criminality," according to journalist Joe Klein.[3]

Such practices are inefficient, costly, and infuriating for managers and coworkers as well as for the citizens who still have to deal with the unfit workers. Even competent employees sometimes offend their citizen clients because civil service protections make them so secure in their jobs that they do not respond as quickly or politely as they should. Yet, although we grumble to our friends about such treatment, how many of us make formal complaints about rudeness or incompetence? Like citizens, elected officials, city managers, and department heads may feel frustrated at their inability to control their own bureaucracies. Civil service systems contribute to this frustration, but the very nature of bureaucracy is also a factor.

The Nature and Inherent Powers of Bureaucracy

Beyond the practical workings of civil service systems, to which we will return, local government bureaucracies share the characteristics and powers of large-scale organizations—of bureaucracies—of all sorts. These universal characteristics and powers of bureaucracies are another element in the constant struggle for **control**, as those officially in charge seek to assert authority over their minions who, in turn, try to protect their autonomy. Although control is a primary goal in the organization of bureaucracies, their scale and other characteristics make it almost impossible. Even some mechanisms of control may be turned to the advantage of the bureaucracy.

The Characteristics of Bureaucracy

The classic conception of bureaucracy is a pyramidal **hierarchy or chain of command**,[4] as suggested in Figure 8.1. The goal of the hierarchy is for the democratically elected and accountable officials to control and direct, through a series of intermediary supervisors, a large number of workers.

The supervisors are there to make sure that the workers carry out policies and programs as intended. They can't watch all the workers all the time, though, so they usually devise elaborate **rules and regulations** to tell them how to do their work— how often streets should be swept, for example, or how long library books can be checked out. Parking and traffic regulations tell police officers when to issue tickets; construction codes tell building inspectors when to approve a building as safe. Without such rules, bureaucrats might do as they please, favoring their friends and discriminating against enemies or people who are different from themselves—as the political machines did.

As a further check, the actions of the workers may need approval by their superiors, which may be part of the infamous bureaucratic red tape most people hate so much. Approval can take time and it also usually requires lots of paperwork like application forms and reports. Even when approval by higher-ups isn't needed, a lot of paperwork can be involved because workers have to report what they've already done to their superiors who, in turn, use the reports to review and control their workers. All this paperwork and supervision is a pain, hated by both citizens and bureaucrats (most of whom would really rather just get on with their jobs), but its purpose is to allow those who are responsible (ultimately elected officials and the voters) to make sure that workers are serving citizens as the decision makers intend. In most cases that means fairly and impartially, so that all people or neighborhoods are treated alike. Streets in every neighborhood, rich or poor, should be swept regularly; police should treat all citizens the same way; anyone who is legally eligible should receive welfare benefits. In practice, the attainment of such **fairness and impartiality** may be rare, but the point is that, contrary to popular perceptions, regulations and red tape are usually intended to achieve these goals and to help rather than to annoy us; the aim is control of the bureaucracy.

Specialization is another sometimes exasperating characteristic of bureaucracies. As large organizations with lots of workers dealing with varied and complex problems (like governing cities), it makes sense for bureaucracies to divide up responsibilities and for some members of the organization to specialize in certain tasks, from policing to sanitation or library services. Specialization enables workers to develop expertise to a greater degree than if they performed a wide variety of tasks. Theoretically, that should mean the job is done better because an expert does it. Once the areas of specialization are defined, each specialist is assigned a jurisdiction and usually resists interference by others. For example, librarians don't issue traffic tickets and police officers don't select library books. This **division of labor** makes organizational sense, but it may also lead to frustration and anger when citizens are referred from worker to worker or even department to department and no one seems able or willing to deal with a problem. Better known as "passing the buck," this phenomenon is built into specialization, for all its good intentions. Condescending, know-it-all experts may also irritate citizens.

Yet another essential characteristic of bureaucracies is the development of their own systems of recruiting and promoting members. People are not born into bureaucracies, nor do they just walk in, volunteer, and start work. Neither is their advancement within the bureaucracy random. Some sort of system functions, both for recruitment and promotion. Usually this requires that workers have the qualifications and ability to do the job, that they retain their job and advance on the basis of the competence of their performance. In practice, however, this system may be subverted by favoritism and ill-defined or slack standards but, again, the intent is control and also fairness. Through their recruitment and promotion systems, bureaucracies develop their own cultures and traditions, which are sometimes narrow and exclusive.

These characteristics—a hierarchical chain of command; rules, regulations, written forms, and red tape; specialization; and a well-defined career structure—are inherent to bureaucracies, not only in local governments but in any large organization. Their essential purposes—including fairness, objectivity, and control by those who are supposed to be in charge—are good, but in practice these goals can be subverted and the system abused, for these essential characteristics are as much a source of power as a means of control. We should recognize, however, that bureaucracies are as inevitable as politics, and, like politics, are not necessarily good or bad.

The Practical Powers of Bureaucracy

In the day-to-day activities of local governments, the characteristics of bureaucracies translate into several formidable sources of power: discretion, expertise, legitimacy, and time. Each is rooted in the very nature of bureaucracy; each makes it more difficult for the officials who are supposed to be in charge to maintain control. To these must be added more overtly political sources of power, including interest group support and public employee unions.

Implementation and Discretion

The greatest power of bureaucracies is derived from their responsibility to implement or put into effect the policies and programs approved by the decision makers at the top of the bureaucratic pyramid. **Implementation** may be quick or slow, rigorous or lax. The same sorts of things happen in households when duties are assigned but not always carried out as promptly or thoroughly as intended. In bureaucracies, middle managers might fund or staff a program inadequately, or the employees who are supposed to do the work might ignore it or be kept busy doing other assigned tasks. If the decision makers at the top notice, recalcitrant bureaucrats may get in trouble, but excuses and promises of improvement are easy to offer. It takes very vigilant officials to push a bureaucracy to do things it really doesn't want to do.

The bureaucracy's power of implementation is made even greater through **delegation**. Councils, mayors, and managers cannot make every decision. Much as they might like to, there's too much to do and they're too busy. Some things must be left to subordinates. Decision makers thus often provide the outlines of a policy and leave their staff to fill in the details and make it work. Delegated responsibilities are usually carried out as the policy makers wish, but they nonetheless add to the powers of bureaucracy.

Bureaucrats enjoy another form of delegation that also enhances their powers: **discretion** on the job. A social worker or a land-use planner in an office, a teacher in a classroom, or a police officer on the beat all make choices as they carry out the duties prescribed for them by their superiors. Political scientist Michael Lipsky calls these workers "street-level bureaucrats."[5] They deliver direct services. They have a finite amount of time and many things to do: should they worry more about helping people or saving money? Preserving the environment or fostering economic development? Teaching facts or analytical skills? Arresting speeders or drug dealers? Should drivers going five miles per hour over the limit be ticketed or only those going ten, fifteen, or twenty miles per hour too fast? Should the social worker, planner, teacher, or police officer serve as many citizens as possible, or take the time to be courteous and thorough with each one? The policy makers at the top occasionally set priorities like these, but, generally, they leave the workers to get on with their jobs, trusting them to use their discretionary powers appropriately. Usually they do. If they don't and enough people complain, those in charge may try to do something, but although the whole bureaucratic hierarchy is created to supervise and control what the workers do, it is impossible for every worker to be watched all the time. A supervisor would be needed for every worker—and then a supervisor for every supervisor!

Expertise

Another practical source of bureaucratic power is **expertise** and the associated command of information. On the frontlines of bureaucracies, where services are delivered and policies enforced, workers specialize and develop expertise at their jobs. Higher in the bureaucracy, the expertise becomes a little more general in nature, so instead of adjusting stoplights, a higher-ranking traffic manager analyzes traffic flow and coordinates the lights. Still higher in the bureaucracy, the expertise may be in management and administration rather than particular policy areas. At the top of the hierarchy, however, specialization and expertise are rare. Here are the generalists—council members, mayors, and managers—who must deal with the whole range of local government programs. They need to know a little about a lot of subjects, although some may have special expertise developed from previous training or occupations and others develop impressive mastery of particular policy areas over time.

Mostly, however, the top decision makers remain generalists and are therefore dependent on the bureaucracy for advice and information on policies and programs. The politicians may (or may not) initiate discussion of an issue, but when they do, it is usually framed by information and recommendations from the experts on the city staff. Most items on the agendas of city council or county board meetings have been placed there by the bureaucracy through department heads or the city or county executive. Most are accompanied by reports from "staff" or "the administration"—the bureaucracy. At the meetings, the appropriate staff members will be called on to speak, perhaps orchestrated by their department heads or the city or county executive. Their presentations will be accompanied by masses of data and probably by charts and tables. They will usually recommend a course of action—or explain why what the council or community groups want to do is not feasible. The decision makers almost always follow their recommendations. Why shouldn't they? After all, these are the experts: civil servants, working for the public good. The decision makers know and trust them. And where else can they get information and advice? Citizens and interest groups may supply it at public hearings or when they lobby elected officials, but they are not experts—except perhaps in their own self-interest, which makes them suspect as informants. In contrast, the local government bureaucracy is supposed to be made up of objective professionals, with no axes to grind.

Bureaucratic Objectivity

Most of the time the information supplied by staff and bureaucrats is objective, but not always. Like the rest of us, bureaucrats have opinions and biases that may affect their recommendations, perhaps unconsciously through the narrow perspective that comes with bureaucratic specialization. Take, for example, the case of a neighborhood group that wants to have a pair of busy one-way streets turned back to quieter, two-way streets. The neighborhood advocates will object to the noise, pollution, and dangers of the one-way streets and talk about their social impact. Council members will nod in sympathy. Then the bureaucrats who are in charge of streets and traffic will present their computer projections of traffic flows with charts and slides. The council will almost invariably bow to the superior information of the experts they know and probably trust, despite their sympathy for the neighborhood. Part of the neighborhood's problem is that their concerns are unlikely to be the focus of a government agency (planning departments concentrate more on new development than on the quality of life in existing neighborhoods and rarely have the clout of their counterparts in traffic management). Another shortcoming for the neighborhood is that its concerns aren't as easy to count as cars, so their data can never be quite so hard and convincing as that of the traffic experts. The ultimate issue here isn't only information, of course. It's also specialization in terms of what components of community life are judged to merit bureaucratic staff—in this case, traffic, but probably not neighborhood quality of life.

This specialization and compartmentalization is typically bureaucratic; but in the case of local government, the values of the reform movement have had an additional influence. Foremost among these are the way the reform movement defined what local governments should do in terms of physical rather than social services (traffic management rather than neighborhood quality of life) and stressed the common good (traffic flow) over partial interests (neighborhoods). With some justification, bureaucrats can point out that what helps one neighborhood may hurt others.

It can be extremely difficult for the generalists on the council and the citizen novices to argue with the factual and often abstruse data of the experts. Those who do may be seen as irrational or uninformed. Consequently, the bureaucrats usually get their way. Besides their expertise, bureaucrats gain power from their image as objective professionals, which gives them a legitimacy that citizens, interest groups, and politicians lack. This is particularly true in reform cities, where professionalism is so highly valued and respected and where the staff of the local government is accordingly trusted and deferred to rather than seen as bureaucratic hacks.

Time

Bureaucrats also have the advantage of time—most are long-term employees. Job security was a goal of the reformers and remains one of the primary attractions of public employment. Local government workers devote whole careers of twenty to forty years to their specialties and their departments, developing estimable expertise, not only in their own specialization, but also in the structure and process of local government. Elected officials, in contrast, come and go, serving one or two but rarely more than three terms of office. By the time they master policies and process, they may well be on their way out. Professional city managers and department heads may face similar disadvantages. They move from city to city to advance their careers— the average tenure of a city manager is about seven years—and may have difficulty gaining command of well-entrenched, long-serving bureaucracies.

Time is on the side of bureaucracies in a more immediate way, too. Council members and executives have lots to do, both in terms of policies and politics. They can concentrate on particular issues and programs only for a little while and then are diverted by other issues, a crisis, an election, or a budget deadline. Citizens have their lives to lead and can devote little time to politics. Bureaucrats, however, are paid to focus on their responsibilities full-time. They know more and have more time to think of ways to do things or avoid doing them. One tactic of bureaucrats under pressure is to ask for a delay on an issue so they can try to find a satisfactory solution. They can then use that time to make their own case better or to allow citizen or council interest to dissipate.

Clientele Groups and Unions

Besides these inherent powers of bureaucracies, more traditional forms of political support are also available. **Clientele groups** (made up the people who are served by particular departments or agencies) sometimes organize to back up their bureaucracy in budget battles or when it is under attack. Police departments most commonly benefit from such support groups, but many communities have their "Friends of" the library or symphony, too. Recreation programs often enjoy the political support of their clients, with uniformed teams of softball or soccer players packing council chambers.

    Public employee unions also enhance bureaucratic power. Through their unions public workers can bargain with their employers (the city or county) over both wages and working conditions. The former affect local budgets and the latter infringe on policy making since they may include such issues as case loads for social workers, class sizes for teachers, weapons and training programs for police officers, and much more. Besides bargaining over contracts, public employee unions affect local government by supporting candidates for office to determine who their bosses will be.

Public Employee Unions and Bureaucratic Power

Public workers were denied union rights until the 1960s. Private-sector workers had begun to unionize in the nineteenth century although they struggled through the 1930s to see their rights firmly established in law. The predominance of political machines, which performed some of the functions of labor unions, probably diverted public workers from organizing and at the same time made lawmakers cautious about granting them union rights. But the prohibition on public employee unions outlasted the machines because opponents argued that public workers are distinct from private sector workers. They have greater job security and usually better benefits than private sector workers, which makes unions seem less necessary, but, more importantly, public workers are unique in their monopoly control of services that affect public health and safety. These services, the opponents of public sector unions argue, should not be bargained over or jeopardized by strikes.

The Right to Collective Bargaining

Public workers accepted the prohibition for a long time, perhaps appreciative of their job security in times of economic uncertainty. But they felt left out of the private-sector economic boom that followed World War II, and as government grew, the workers at the bottom—police officers, fire fighters, sanitation workers, and teachers —began to feel alienated and mistreated by the impersonal bureaucracy of which they were a part. Like their colleagues in the factories a century earlier, they began agitating for union rights.

Public workers started organizing, often supported by private sector unions. Gradually, governments in the United States began recognizing their workers' rights. The state of Wisconsin was first, passing a collective bargaining law for public employees in 1959. The federal government and other states soon followed. Although still a contentious issue in some places, forty states now recognize their public employees' right to collective bargaining (seven southern and three western states do not). **Collective bargaining** means that employees negotiate wages and working conditions with their employers as a group (or union) rather than as individuals. The group is supposed to be stronger than individuals, so everybody gets a better deal. Once public workers gained the right to collective bargaining, unionization proceeded rapidly. By 1983, 36.7 percent of all local government workers belonged to a union or professional association, while only about 15 percent of private-sector workers were unionized. In 2003, public employee union membership had grown only slightly to 37.2 percent, but private-sector membership had declined to 8.2 percent.[6] A combination of factors contributed to the slow growth in public-sector union membership, including recessions, globalization, reduced state and local budgets, and national administrations that were not union friendly. The most highly unionized sectors of public employment are education and public safety (teachers, police officers, and firefighters), but the largest single unions of public employees represent other local government workers. They are American Federation of State, County, and Municipal Employees (AFSCME) with over 1.3 million members and the Service Employees International Union (SEIU), currently the most rapidly growing union in the United States.

The Process of Collective Bargaining

Normally, a single union represents a particular group of workers in negotiations with management (local government). This union is selected by the workers in an election and is recognized as their bargaining agent by the local government. In most cases, workers are not required to belong to the union, although this is sometimes an issue because union members view nonmembers as free riders who get the benefits negotiated by the union without paying dues. Most local governments deal with several unions representing different groups of employees, such as police officers, fire fighters, middle management, or general workers. On average, cities negotiate with five such bargaining units, but larger cities (such as New York with over two hundred unions) face many more. Such fragmentation of the work force was once encouraged by local governments to weaken unions, but now it is seen as an inconvenience that makes collective bargaining more difficult and complicated.[7]

In the actual process of collective bargaining, representatives of unions and local government meet and negotiate an agreement on wages, benefits such as health insurance, working conditions, grievance procedures, and other matters. The unions are represented by their elected officers and professional staff, while the local government is represented by a team that may include the city manager, CAO, a full-time labor relations specialist, department heads, or an outside attorney or consultant who specializes in negotiations.[8] Mayors and council members usually stay out of the process, although they direct and confer with their designated negotiators and when an agreement is reached, it must be ratified by these officials on one side and by the union's members on the other. If both approve, the agreement becomes a contract and is binding for a specified time—usually one to five years. The public may have a say in a hearing at the time of ratification, but negotiations are conducted in private except in a few states.

Negotiators usually reach agreement, but what happens if they fail? In the private sector, the result may be a strike by workers or sometimes a lockout by management. Strikes occur in the public sector, but in most states they are illegal on the grounds that strikes by public workers hurt not only their employers but the citizens they are supposed to serve. Public safety workers such as police officers and fire fighters are prohibited from striking everywhere, although a few states permit strikes by some other sorts of government workers. Public employees are sometimes disgruntled enough to break no-strike laws and face the consequences, although sick-outs or epidemics of "blue flu" (police officers calling in sick) are more common. Public employee strikes and other such actions are rare, however, and most disagreements are resolved by a neutral third party accepted by both sides who mediates or arbitrates. In mediation, the third party tries to revive communications between the disputing parties and help them reach a settlement. In arbitration, the contending parties usually agree in advance to accept the recommendation of the third party (called **binding arbitration**).

Clout

But negotiating contracts is just one way organized public employees assert their clout. They are also a formidable electoral force. Many live in the city where they work and are reliable voters, making up a big electoral bloc. Besides voting, public employee unions also provide campaign contributions and volunteers. Police and fire fighters' unions are particularly active in local campaigns and candidates especially value their endorsement. The **electoral clout** of well-organized workers is greatest in nonpartisan elections, where few other groups are as interested or active, and in communities with low voter turnout in local elections. Most candidates find the promise of such bloc support irresistible, but, of course, the unions expect the support to be mutual. If their efforts are successful, they end up with friendly elected officials to whom they have ready access and from whom they can expect sympathy. Such activity backfires if the unions endorse losers, however, and since incumbent officials are often reelected with little opposition, endorsement options may be limited, leading some unions to back away from electoral activity.

Public employee unions also lobby decision makers and testify (often backed up by masses of members) at public hearings on issues that concern them between elections. Such issues might include complaints about police practices, new building or fire safety codes, banning library books, no smoking ordinances, or almost anything. Additionally, union representatives make sure that their hard-won contract is enforced and defend workers subject to discipline or firing.

The Impact of Unionization

Public employee unions have improved the lot of their members with higher wages, better fringe benefits, and even greater job security. Some studies suggest that unorganized workers don't do much worse,[9] but that may be because union contracts set the standard and the managers of unorganized workers cleverly avoid unionization by giving their workers almost as much. Beyond the direct benefits to workers, however, the unionization of public workers has increased the power of bureaucracies. Unions increase job security, which is already great enough in civil service bureaucracies to cause concern. The merit system may also be weakened by unions, which advocate promotion by seniority (time served rather than quality of work) and oppose merit pay (pay based on job performance). Top-level officials are limited by union agreements on issues like these and others. Their budgets may be predetermined by collective bargaining agreements, their workers are even harder to fire with contract-guaranteed grievance rights and union advocates, and their actions may be challenged by union representatives citing the contract. But while managers may not like unions much, they add balance to local government bureaucracies, protecting individual workers in large and impersonal organizations and vigilantly defending public services.

IN YOUR COMMUNITY
Research public employee unions in your city or county at the city clerk's office, online, or at the library. Try to interview a union representative (look under labor unions in the phone book) and someone in local government who deals with unions.

Managing Bureaucracies

Much as they benefit local government workers, public employee unions may also add to concerns about the inherent and practical powers of bureaucracies. Even before unionization, elected officials and political activists on both the left and right were searching for ways to make bureaucracies more responsive and accountable. Most of these efforts were part of the counterreformers' reaction to reform government.

Some counterreforms were aimed at increasing the power of elected representatives so they could assert their authority in the chain of command more effectively. Many mayors won higher salaries, expanded personal staffs, and greater budgetary and appointment powers, enabling them to dominate more bureaucratic city managers or even to replace them. Some local legislators were given full-time salaries and support staff of their own, so they could be less reliant on the bureaucracy. Some councils organized themselves into committees, so they could develop expertise to counter that of the bureaucrats. Legislators and executives also experimented with new budgeting systems designed to make bureaucracies justify their spending.

A few local governments went much further, attempting to reduce the range of city jobs covered by civil service and thereby to gain more control over the services and the workers themselves. In some places, this took the form of removing some jobs from the civil service system on grounds that greater flexibility in hiring was necessary. This ploy seldom succeeded, however, because the public reacted to it as a revival of machine-style patronage. Another tactic was the introduction of **sunset laws**, which set a fixed life span of a few years for new bureaucratic agencies on the theory that none should be permanent (as most bureaucracies tend to become). At the end of this period, the agency must defend its existence to win legislative approval to continue, usually for another fixed period. Sunset laws are a useful way to keep a rein on new agencies, but their application is limited since most of the functions of local government, such as police and fire protection, are sensibly carried out by on-going departments and new agencies are rarely created.

Empowering Communities

While elected officials have sought to control bureaucracies by increasing their own powers, community groups have attempted to gain influence by other means, sometimes with the support of local officials and the federal government. Bureaucracies in some cities, for example, have been decentralized to make them more responsive and accessible with "little city halls" in neighborhoods. Representatives of various departments are located in these neighborhood offices, so citizens are able to take care of problems there rather trekking to a big city hall and negotiating its mazes.

In some cities, residents have demanded more, including the power to make decisions themselves. In 1999, Los Angeles introduced **neighborhood councils** and **area planning commissions** in its last round of charter reform, partly to defuse secession movements in parts of the city that felt they were being ignored. Phoenix has "Village Planning Committees" to advise on local land-use decisions. This lessens the power of bureaucracy—in this case professional city planners—but may result in better-informed decisions. "Of course here at city hall we are just brilliant and we know everything," jokes Phoenix City Manager Frank Fairbanks, but he goes on to say "I can't tell you the number of times we've gone out and people on the Village Planning Committees have told us things we didn't know about their neighborhoods. They've kept the staff from making mistakes. They've kept the city from making mistakes."[10]

Mostly, such committees or councils are advisory only. Sometimes they are empowered to make final decisions on a limited range of issues that directly affect them—almost always neighborhood land use or neighborhood school issues. Some of these committees or councils are appointed by the city council or school board; others are elected. Birmingham, Dayton, Portland, St. Paul, and New York City, for example, all have elected neighborhood boards or councils. Due to the cost and the resistance of both bureaucracies and central decision makers, however, such devolution of decision making isn't very common. Still, many cities have small boards, committees, and commissions of appointed and sometimes elected citizens who advise the local government on selected issues. Such entities may bring pressure on bureaucracies and force them to confront their own clienteles, although citizen participants are also sometimes seduced or co-opted by the bureaucracies they deal with and end up being sympathetic supporters rather than critics.

Citizen Complaints

When citizens have complaints about bureaucracy, they usually take them to their city or county councilor. Local legislators spend a lot of their time dealing with constituent problems, providing advice, helping with red tape, or giving the bureaucracy a prod with a phone call or letter. This service has rightly been used to justify paying council members for full-time work and providing them with personal staff. Helping citizens with problems may seem mundane and even unnecessary (shouldn't the bureaucracy do it right in the first place?), but it gives citizens a useful means of appeal and also helps council members discern problems in the system.

Some communities provide more structured complaint systems, most often on police practices—a particularly controversial area in cities with large minority populations. Unless a busy council member takes up their cause, citizens are left to lodge their complaints with the bureaucracy that has offended them. Many citizens are suspicious of bureaucracies investigating complaints against their own members, not only because of the inherent impersonality of bureaucracy or the tendency of any group to protect one of its own, but because they think the bureaucracy is unrepresentative and unsympathetic. This is particularly true for minorities.

Some cities have therefore created **citizen review boards** to investigate complaints. Such boards usually deal with only one policy area, and as their name suggests, they are made up of citizens appointed by the council. Most common (but still rare) are police review boards. They hear and investigate grievances against the police, but usually have little real authority. San Francisco, New Orleans, Washington, DC, and Baltimore, however, are said to have relatively independent police boards. Arguments over citizen police review boards continue to arise in communities experiencing tension between racial minorities and police, as in Los Angeles. Independent police "auditors" are another way some cities have attempted to address citizen concerns about police practices. Such auditors are appointed by the city council or mayor and report to them on any complaints and their resolution. Police chiefs and unions vigorously resist citizen review boards, but they are somewhat more accepting of independent auditors.

Affirmative Action

Another response to community concerns has been to press for a more representative bureaucracy. Civil service bureaucracies have traditionally been dominated by white males. The sorts of professional skills required by merit systems were most accessible to white males, and, once employed, they were entrenched by job security. Like other social groups, they also tended to recruit in their own image. In many cities, as the population grew more diverse, the local bureaucracy did not. Minorities wanted access to jobs, but they also complained that unrepresentative bureaucracies were unresponsive to their needs. Police practices were often the central issue, but the same concerns applied to other departments. Minority groups therefore demanded special hiring programs to broaden the representation of the bureaucracy.

Women later made similar demands. The federal government added to the pressure with the 1972 Equal Employment Opportunities Act and requirements for **affirmative action** plans for all institutions accepting federal funds. Local governments responded with affirmative action programs designed to increase the employment of women and minorities. Bureaucracies had to learn to make a conscious effort *not* to discriminate. Most had to find new ways of recruiting to attract people who might not have known about the availability of jobs or who might have felt they would be unwelcome applicants. Testing and interviewing procedures were reviewed and revised to make sure they were not in themselves discriminatory, as they were often alleged to be. Middle-class verbal skills were said by minorities to be given too much significance, while women charged that physical standards were sometimes higher than the job required. Besides changes in recruitment practices, testing, and job standards, the composition of the panels that interview finalists was changed to better reflect the community rather than the bureaucracy. Even so, minority candidates often have a tough time competing, so to further facilitate affirmative action hiring, applicants who speak a language other than English may be given extra points or those hired might be chosen from the top ten instead of only the top three test scorers.

These reforms didn't happen without political pressure, however. In most places, real changes in hiring policy came with the political incorporation of minorities as their numbers and political mobilization increased. According to Browning, Marshall, and Tabb, "The necessity of the 1960s and 1970s was to overcome first the conservatives who controlled city councils and then an entrenched bureaucracy that was staffed by whites and thoroughly accustomed to the policies and routines of white business interests that controlled city government and to the assumption that people of color could be indefinitely excluded from city government employment and other city-controlled goods. Overcoming the bureaucracies took 10 years or more."[11] Big city mayors also often embraced affirmative action along with some federally funded programs as a way of building support in minority communities. Affirmative action programs have been most extensive and successful in communities where minorities have established themselves politically, as in Denver, where minorities have actually been overrepresented in city government in proportion to their share of the population since 1973.[12] Across the country, minority incorporation in city politics began to increase minority representation in city bureaucracies roughly in proportion to their share of city populations. In Atlanta, for example, as blacks gained political power, their share of city employees rose from 38 percent in 1970 to 80 percent in 2000.[13]

Women also did better, partly due to the nondiscrimination requirements of the Title VII of the 1972 Civil Rights Act and partly due to the women's movement and the political incorporation of women in city politics, with more and more women being elected to office. Women are now better represented in all categories of municipal employment, including police departments where 13 percent of police officers are women. Over 200 women have risen to be police chiefs in cities as large as Boston, Detroit, Milwaukee, Portland, and San Francisco—but that's only 1 percent of the total number of police chiefs.

Many local governments now have well-established affirmative action programs, and the employment of women and minorities has advanced greatly in many communities. But despite some successes the movement of women and minorities into the upper echelons of bureaucracy has been slow. Most affirmative action programs have been pretty mild, usually involving just a little more active recruitment of minorities and women and the setting of some hoped-for hiring goals rather than strict quotas with fixed numbers. Despite increasing controversy and even hysteria about affirmative action, only a minority of cities and counties set "numeric goals" for hiring. Such numeric goals are distinct from widely denounced quotas, according to *The Municipal Year Book*, in that they are "ideals to be strived for" rather than rigid "quotas to be attained" at the risk of penalties.[14] Very few local governments have gone so far as to set quotas. In a few extreme cases, however, local governments have been ordered by federal courts to hire only minorities until the composition of their workers is brought into reasonable balance. Such cases usually involve police and fire departments, which have been particularly resistant to affirmative action and which are often politically powerful. Even in liberal Los Angeles, for example, the fire department is said to have been "one of the most resistant" to minority employment, resulting in court supervision of hiring from 1974 to 2002.[15]

In most places, mild affirmative action programs have brought modest and much-needed improvements in the representativeness and sensitivity of bureaucracies. Concerns about reverse discrimination and the resistance of some entrenched bureaucracies have kept affirmative action programs controversial, however. In 1996, California voters passed Proposition 209 banning affirmative action in public employment and many communities elsewhere have phased out their programs. Budget cuts due to reduced federal funds and local revenues also capped such programs by stopping new hiring. In some cases, budget cuts worsened the employment balance because they required layoffs, which are usually done on a "last hired–first fired" basis, meaning that recently hired women and minorities were the first to go. Affirmative action programs continue in many communities, however, and in most they made local government work forces more diverse and representative. Minimally, they leveled the playing field for all applicants by reducing past discriminatory practices against women and minorities.

Contracting Out

Partly in response to general complaints about bureaucracy but largely because of reduced revenues due to recessions and voter-imposed limits on taxes, many local governments have turned to privatization or contracting out. Privatization involves turning over a local government service function to a privately owned business. Examples would be the sale of a city-owned utility company. Local government is no longer responsible for providing the service in question. Privatization is relatively rare, however, because local government still has to take responsibility for most of the services it provides. **Contracting out** is more common, Instead of providing services with their own employees, many local governments have begun contracting with private businesses to do the job. Trash collection is the service most commonly contracted out, but recreation programs, maintenance, cleaning, transit, and other services have been handed over to private companies in some places. Parking tickets were contracted out in Chicago, freeing police officers to perform more urgent tasks. Unlike privatization, with contracting out, local government still retains responsibility and ultimate control for these services—they're just provided by workers who are not its employees. Such services are paid for out of tax revenues or by directly billing users in the case of trash collection or parking tickets. Contracts for services as basic as police and fire can also be entered into with other governments.

Contracting out generally cuts costs, thus saving tax funds, and gives decision makers more options. The inflexibility and relatively permanent employment of the civil service system are circumvented and unions are often eliminated by private contractors. Some studies affirm that private contractors provide services more cheaply and efficiently than government,[16] but, overall, the evidence is mixed. Critics of contracting out assert that private companies often bid low to get contracts and then raise their prices later. They also insist that the system is used to pay lower wages, break unions, and get around affirmative action hiring.[17] Local governments and taxpayers may benefit from contracting out, but workers surely suffer. In over 100 cities, unions and their allies have fought to ensure a "living wage" for employees of companies contracting with the city by requiring pay higher than the federal minimum wage—enough to live on.[18] The goal of the living wage movement is to discourage contracting out by raising its costs but also to educate decision makers and the public about the extent to which money saved by contracting out comes from paying workers poorly.

After an initial surge in the late 1980s and early 1990s, contracting out slowed down significantly, but not only because of union resistance and living wage campaigns. Projected savings were not always realized and some services proved unsuitable for contracting out. Sometimes external service providers were not available. The costs of negotiating contracts and monitoring services also turned some cities against contracting out. By the mid-1990s, many local governments were contracting back in services that had been contracted out.[19] In some cases, responsibilities were simply returned to public employees. In others, public employee groups were empowered to bid against private companies for contracts. Such **contracting in** often resulted in cheaper, more efficient services as well as improved employee morale as workers gained self-determination and pride.

Reinventing Government

The 1990s also saw a significant change in management of local bureaucracies and services after the publication of the book *Reinventing Government* by David Osborne,

Table 8.1

Top-Ten City Websites

Denver
San Diego
New York City
Washington, DC
Los Angeles
Boston
Houston
Seattle
Albuquerque
Salt Lake City

Source: Governing magazine, "State and Local Source Book," 2005 supplement.

a journalist, and Ted Gaebler, a former city manager.[20] Osborne and Gaebler argued that the public sector could improve its services and efficiency by applying private-sector management techniques. Costs could be cut, services could be improved, and citizens could be engaged not by expanding bureaucracy but by making it more flexible, they argued. Some of their recommendations reflected trends we've already discussed, including greater involvement of citizens in their own communities (with neighborhood planning councils, for example) and contracting out. Local government was to be more entrepreneurial and competitive; clients were to be viewed as customers; authority was to be decentralized and the private and public sector were to be "catalyzed."[21] "Mission-driven" local governments were urged to develop quantifiable performance measures to set standards for service provision and shape budgets. The response time of police, fire fighters, or other service providers could be measured, for example, and these measurements could be used for budgeting—with increased funding for increased performance. This puts bureaucracies on their toes because they don't get money from year to year just because they're there—their performance determines their funding.

The **reinventing government** movement shook up local government in many cities, although it was more extensively discussed than adopted and relatively affluent cities with council-manager government systems were the most likely to implement its strategies.[22] Still, Osborne and Gaebler, who were actually reviving an earlier tradition of public management, put public bureaucracies in a different perspective and contributed to their improved performance.

E-Government

E-government, which provides access to government services and information online, is another critically important innovation. Over 90 percent of local governments now have a website,[23] although quality varies considerably. See Table 8.1 for the best city websites according to *Governing* magazine. Some provide minimal information; others make huge amounts of information available. Some are difficult to navigate; others are easy to use. Some allow direct contact with city workers and elected officials; others do not. Some provide online access to selected services ranging from building permits to bill payment, requests for services like pothole repair or tree trimming, business license applications, registration for recreational programs, and job applications.[24]

The main use of websites is for information, such as council agendas, memos and reports, maps, and crime or other statistics. Having such information available online has greatly increased citizen access to government and stimulated citizen participation. Probably the second-most common function of e-government is communications. Citizens can now contact elected and administrative officials more easily. As a consequence—sometimes to the irritation of public officials—government becomes far more interactive. But access to information and communication with public officials leaves the initiative to citizens and response may be minimal or pro forma. Writing for the *Municipal Year Book*, David Coursey observes that "services involving real-time processing and payments, such as online payments of utility bills and of fines and fees are among the least offered" online services, with only 7 to 9 percent of cities Coursey surveyed providing such services.[25]

Why aren't local governments doing more of their business online? Doesn't e-government offer significant opportunities to reinvent government? Maybe, but many local governments lack the resources to make e-government successful. Citizens may think online services require less staff time than in-person service, but that isn't always the case. Good, interactive websites require a substantial investment to create and continuing investment to maintain. Many local governments lack the in-house skills to do this or the funds to contract for the service—or both. Undoubtedly, however, some local bureaucracies resist e-government precisely because it makes it easier for citizens to contact them. They'd really rather be left alone.

In Your Community

How much e-government does your city or county do? Is the website informational only or is it interactive? If it's interactive, is it for communications only or can local government business be done online?

Public Administration and Politics

Are local government bureaucracies out of control? Some people think so, including elected officials who do not trust bureaucracies to carry out their will and grassroots activists who find local bureaucracies unresponsive to their concerns. As a consequence, both elected officials and community leaders have sought out ways to control bureaucracy, from reducing discretion to performance-based budgeting. This can also be seen as political interference in decisions that administrators think should be made objectively. Accusations of "micromanaging" are often directed at elected officials and others who want to give bureaucrats specific instructions rather than letting them get on with the job as they think best. "Political control in the form of interference with service delivery or hiring decisions," writes James Svara, "may diminish fairness and obstruct sound management," not to mention efficiency. "The tightly controlled and fully accountable agency," he continues, "may be the most rigid and clogged with red tape, since every action is done by the book."[26]

John Nalbandian, a political scientist who has also served as a city council member, points out that politicians and administrators approach issues from different perspectives based on the differences in their experience. Elected officials, he writes, are arbiters of values and community builders. They worry about power and influence; they must respond to their constituents and represent them. "Thus, their focus is often separated from the professional expertise that resides in city hall—which is rarely where elected officials do their most important work." Administration, Nalbandian continues, is "about problem solving" based on information, expertise, and knowledge. Politics is relatively subjective; administration is relatively objective. These are different worlds and different perspectives. Nalbandian argues that relations between elected officials and administrators "depend on the presence of a 'translator,' usually the chief administrative officer." But his larger point is that elected officials, bureaucracies, and citizens need to recognize one another's differing perspectives in order to work successfully together.[27]

Other analysts see the role of public bureaucracies less positively. Bureaucratic powers have grown so much, that some recent power researchers see bureaucracy as unconstrained by elected leaders and "relatively autonomous."[28] Political scientist Theodore Lowi calls local government bureaucracies **the new machines**." Their "functional fiefdoms" (departments or agencies with allied unions) recruit like-minded members, protect their self-interest rather than that of the public, and are beyond the control of elected officials whose selection they influence.[29] Lowi's new machines are most common in places like New York City, where public employee unions are particularly strong, but bureaucratic power in general is also great, if less blatant, in the middle-sized reform cities of the Sunbelt and suburbia. One study concluded that "nonpartisan, at-large city councilors . . . treat the interests of municipal workers with greater consideration than . . . ward or partisan councilors. They will provide greater job security through larger work forces and higher levels of compensation"[30] because bureaucracies are an important source of political support in a system where parties and other interests are limited.

The autonomy of bureaucracies can easily be overstated, however. Their discretion may be substantial, but in all but a few cases, it is constrained by broad boundaries set by elected officials and private power holders. Bureaucratic leaders, whether managers, department heads, or union officials, have a pretty good idea where these boundaries lie. They may test or push the limits, but those who go too far usually end up looking for employment elsewhere. Their experience sends a message to others.

Others view bureaucracy more positively. Amy Bridges studied southwestern cities with reform-style bureaucracies and reported not "a single instance of a runaway or rogue bureaucracy. . . . Public employees have not exercised the political influence in the Southwest that they have in machine-descendant cities."[31] Political scientist Peter Lupsha concurs, asserting that civil servants are "a voice of moderation, future orientation and professionalism" and "the key guardians of the public interest," filling "the vacuum and the role of public representation vacated by elected politicians."[32] Michael Lipsky, writing about "street-level" bureaucrats on the frontlines of local government, such as teachers, police officers, and social workers, recognizes that these workers often hide behind the impersonal structures of bureaucracy and treat those they serve coldly and even rudely, but he points out that they are under stress themselves, poorly supported by superiors, underfunded, understaffed, and often facing public antagonism.[33]

Implicit in the views of these writers are motivations for bureaucratic behavior other than pure self-interest. Although concerns about bureaucracies are valid, most bureaucrats see themselves as public servants and try to behave as such. Any of us who are personally acquainted with public workers know this is true and respect them. Most are dedicated to their jobs and try to do their best under adverse circumstances, including meddling politicians, a hostile public, inadequate funding and staffing, and unclear responsibilities and guidelines for doing their work. Besides the commitment of public workers to do their jobs professionally and properly, bureaucrats have individual and collective ethics that typically emphasize democratic accountability, honesty, equity, and professionalism. Inculcated by American society and by the bureaucratic professions themselves, these ethical standards may be imperfectly adhered to in practice, but their abuse is surely no worse than the abuse of ethical standards in other professions—and is probably less than in most. Of course, we may have a right to expect higher standards from public servants.

Why Be a Bureaucrat?

Given all these complications, why would anybody want a job in a local government bureaucracy? After all, nobody sets out to be a bureaucrat, even though most of us end up working in bureaucracies, whether governmental, corporate, nonprofit, or religious. Most public workers don't think of themselves as bureaucrats, but rather as public employees of various sorts, from cops to fire fighters, librarians, and clerks. Why do these jobs? For the most part, they're good jobs that pay reasonably well, often with less stress than private sector employment, and always with greater job security—it's hard (but not impossible) to fire a civil service employee. Until recently, public sector employees have also enjoyed good pensions, although pension funds in several cities are in deep trouble because of overcommitments and mismanagement.

Job security, decent pay, and good benefits attract people to public employment who could probably earn more money in the private sector, but there are other rewards, too. Fifty-six percent of local government employees report that they "like their jobs very much"—a higher percentage than workers at other levels of government or in the private sector.[34] These public employees—yes, bureaucrats—actually *like* their jobs. They also like serving the public.

Essential Terms

patronage
civil service or merit system
tenure
representativeness
control
hierarchy or chain of command
rules and regulations
fairness and impartiality
specialization
division of labor
implementation
delegation
discretion
expertise
clientele groups

public employee unions
collective bargaining
binding arbitration
electoral clout
sunset laws
neighborhood councils
area planning commissions
citizen review boards
affirmative action
contracting out
contracting in
reinventing government
e-government
"the new machines"

On the Internet

- The International City/County Management Association (ICMA) (www.icma.org) is a national organization for professional local government administrators; lots of information on civil service systems and employment, especially in their year-books.
- Research contracting out and living wage ordinances at www.livingwageresearch .org/.
- The American Federation of State, County, and Municipal Employees (AFSCME) (www.afscme.org) is the largest union of public employees and health care workers in the United States.

Notes

1. See Mike Royko, *Boss: Richard J. Daley of Chicago,* rev. ed. (New York: Plume, 1988) on the Chicago machine and Mayor Richard J. Daley in their prime. Daley died in 1976; despite defeats in subsequent mayoral elections, the formidable remains of his machine helped elect his son, Richard M. Daley, as mayor of Chicago in 1989.

2. Anne Freedman, "Doing Battle with the Patronage Army: Politics, Courts, and Personnel Administration in Chicago," *Public Administration Review* 48, no. 5 (September–October 1988): 847–59.

3. Joe Klein, "The Pinochle Club," *New York Magazine*, October 29, 1990, p. 19.

4. See *From Max Weber: Essays in Sociology*, trans. H. H. Gerth and C. Wright Mills (New York: Oxford University Press, 1946, reprinted 1980).

5. Michael Lipsky, *Street-Level Bureaucracy: Dilemmas of the Individual in Public Services* (New York: Russell Sage, 1980).

6. U.S. Census Bureau, *Statistical Abstract of the United States*, 2004–2005.

7. See David R. Morgan, *Managing Urban America*, 3rd ed. (Pacific Grove, CA: Brooks/Cole, 1989), p. 252.

8. Timothy David Chandler, "Labor-Management Relations in Local Government," *The Municipal Year Book* (Washington, DC: International City/County Management Association, 1989), pp. 89–90.

9. Morgan, *Managing Urban America*, p. 251.

10. *Dallas Morning News*, April 18, 2004, p. 14W.

11. Rufus P. Browning, Dale Rogers Marshall, and David H. Tabb, "Can People of Color Achieve Equality in City Government?" in *Racial Politics in American Cities*, ed. Rufus P. Browning, Dale Rogers Marshall, and David H. Tabb, 3rd ed. (New York: Longman, 2003), p. 25.

12. Rodney E. Hero, "Hispanics in Urban Government and Politics: Some Findings, Comparisons, and Implications," *Western Political Quarterly* 43, no. 2 (June 1990): 411.

13. Michael Leo Owens and Michael J. Rich, "Is Strong Incorporation Enough? Black Empowerment and the Fate of Atlanta's Low-Income Blacks," in *Racial Politics in American Cities*, ed. Browning, Marshall, and Tabb, p. 216.

14. Evelina R. Moulder, "Affirmative Action in Local Government," *The Municipal Year Book* (Washington, DC: International City/County Management Association, 1991), p. 51.

15. Raphael J. Sonenshein, "Post-Incorporation Politics in Los Angeles," in *Racial Politics in American Cities*, ed. Browning, Marshall, and Tabb, p. 68.

16. Lori M. Henderson, "Intergovernmental Service Arrangements and the Transfer of Functions," *The Municipal Year Book* (Washington, DC: International City/County Management Association, 1985), pp. 194–202.

17. See, for example, C. J. Hech, "Contracting Municipal Service: Does It Really Cost Less?" *National Civic Review* 72, no. 6 (June 1983): 321–26; Ronald C. Moe, "Exploring the Limits of Privatization," *Public Administration Review* 47, no. 6 (November–December 1987): 453–60; and Harold J. Sullivan, "Privatization of Public Services: A Growing Threat to Constitutional Rights," *Public Administration Review* 47, no. 6 (November–December 1987): 461–67.

18. www.livingwageresearch.org/factsheets/adopted.asp and www.epionline.org (accessed May 6, 2006).

19. See Mildred Warner, "Contracting Back In: When Privatization Fails," *The Municipal Year Book* (Washington, DC: International City/County Management Association, 2003), pp. 4–13; and Mildred Warner and Amir Hefetz, "Pragmatism over Politics: Alternative Service Delivery in Local Government, 1992–2002," *The Municipal Year Book* (Washington, DC: International City/County Management Association, 2004), pp. 4–16.

20. David Osborne and Ted Gaebler, *Reinventing Government: How the Entrepreneurial Spirit Is Transforming the Public Sector* (New York: Plume 1993).

21. See Barry M. Feldman, "Reinventing Local Government: Beyond Rhetoric to Action," *The Municipal Year Book* (Washington, DC: International City/County Management Association, 1999), p. 21.

22. See Anirudh V. S. Ruhil, Mark Schneider, Paul Teske, and Byung-Moon Ji, "Institutions and Reform: Reinventing Local Government," *Urban Affairs Review* 34, no. 3 (January 1999): 433–55.

23. David Coursey, "E-Government: Trends, Benefits, and Challenges," *The Municipal Year Book* (Washington, DC: International City/County Management Association, 2005), p. 15.

24. See Gregory D. Streib and Katherine G. Willoughby, "Local Governments Becoming E-Government: Getting the Sizzle, Avoiding the Fizzle," in *The Future of Local Government Administration*, ed. H. George Frederickson and John Nalbandian (Washington, DC: International City/County Management Association, 2002), pp. 199–208.

25. Coursey, "E-Government," p. 17.

26. James H. Svara, *Official Leadership in the City: Patterns of Conflict and Cooperation* (New York: Oxford University Press, 1990), p. 168.

27. John Nalbandian, "Reflections of a 'Pracademic' on the Logic of Politics and Administration," *Public Administration Review* 54, no. 6 (November–December 1994): 532–3.

28. Stephen L. Elkin, *City and Regime in the American Republic* (Chicago: University of Chicago Press, 1987), p. 60.

29. Theodore Lowi, "Machine Politics—Old and New," *Public Interest* 9 (Fall 1967), p. 86.

30. Jeffrey S. Zax, "Reform City Councils and Municipal Employees," *Public Choice* 64, no. 2 (February 1990): p. 169.

31. Amy Bridges, *Morning Glories: Municipal Reform in the Southwest* (Princeton, NJ: Princeton University Press, 1997), p. 214.

32. Peter Lupsha, "Structural Change and Innovation: Elites and Albuquerque Politics in the 1980s," in *The Politics of Urban Development*, ed. Clarence N. Stone and Heywood T. Sanders (Lawrence: University Press of Kansas, 1987), pp. 237, 242.

33. See Lipsky, *Street-Level Bureaucracy*.

34. Victor S. DeSantis and Samantha L. Durst, "Job Satisfaction Among Local Government Employees," *The Municipal Year Book* (Washington, DC: International City/County Management Association, 1997), pp. 10–15.

PART III

Outside City Hall: Elections, Influence, and Power

Thus far we've studied the socioeconomic and intergovernmental environment of local politics and the formal decision makers and institutions of local governments, noting the interplay among them. Now we turn to the elements of local politics that connect them. Many players outside city hall and the formal institutions of government influence or perhaps even control what goes on there. We've already seen their power in the shaping of the institutions of government themselves through the reform and counterreform movements and their changes in city charters.

We begin with the voters—those outside local government who have the most legitimate claim on influencing it. Their input is shaped by both community demographics and, more formally, by the electoral structures through which they express their will, a part of the political system shaped and reshaped by reform and counterreform. We will also examine the roles of campaigns and the media in local politics. In the following chapters we'll consider interest groups and the informal or extragovernmental power structures of communities, a subject that summarizes and reviews all that we've studied before.

211

9

Elections and Campaigns
The Voters (and the Media) Have Their Say

In a democracy, voters should be the most important influence on government, yet in local politics their interest and participation are often lamentably low. Some people blame such apathy on the voters themselves, but other factors also play a part, including community demographics, electoral structures, local campaigns, and the media.

Local elections were more radically altered by the Progressive reform movement than any other element of local government except perhaps the bureaucracy. The reformers introduced electoral structures that affect who votes, how they choose their representatives, and who those representatives are. Not resting at that, the reformers also instituted direct democracy, giving voters the power to make policy and to discharge officials through the processes of initiative, referendum, and recall. Not all communities adopted these systems and not all have been content with their results. But reform electoral structures operate in a majority of U.S. communities, and few have not used parts of the package or at least debated them, often more than once. Controversial even when they were first introduced, the reforms remain controversial in many places. The argument is not abstract. These electoral structures control who has influence in and over local governments. They allocate power. They determine winners and losers. They connect the public to its government, either loosely or closely.

Elections and the act of voting are also shaped by the way local candidates campaign for office. Reform structures caused a different sort of campaigning to evolve in local, as compared to state and national, politics, although professional campaign consultants and communications technology are again changing the nature of local campaigns. As at the higher levels, the media play a part in local politics, especially in election campaigns. Contrary to the national pattern, however, newspapers are much more powerful than the electronic media in most communities. Reform structures have something to do with their influence, too.

Who Votes

Anyone over eighteen years old is eligible to vote in local elections provided that they have resided in a community for a minimum time specified by law (thirty days

213

is common) and are not confined to prison or a mental institution. To exercise this right, citizens must **register to vote**, which involves filling out forms usually available at public places such as post offices and libraries or from the county registrar of voters. Some states once made registration difficult to discourage minority voters, but federal voting rights laws and state legislation have now simplified procedures.

Many people nevertheless decline to register, and many who do register don't vote. Some don't register because they think voting doesn't matter; others just haven't gotten around to it, can't be bothered, or don't know how. Although some are eager voters, many recent immigrants who are new to democracy don't participate now that the old political machines are no longer around to organize them. Some people don't vote because they're apathetic or unaware, especially about local as opposed to national elections. Some can't see how elections will affect them. Others think voting is a sham because the system is rigged or the candidates are all alike anyway.

More and more people seem to share these views, because voting in American elections at all levels has declined by about 25 percent since 1960.[1] Cities that once saw participation rates of 60 to 70 percent now report turnout at 30 to 40 percent. Even fewer voters participate in some communities.

The Voters

Most of us know which sorts of people are most likely to vote: white Anglo-Saxon Protestants (WASPs) head the list, although some other ethnic groups are also highly probable voters, including, for example, Jews, Cuban Americans, Japanese Americans, and middle-class African Americans. Among those registered to vote, actual participation is almost equal among whites, blacks, Asians, and Latinos. Whites, however, are more likely to be registered, while blacks are a little less likely to register. Only about one-third of eligible, adult, citizen Asians and Latinos are registered, however, so their ultimate participation is always lower.[2] In the old days, machines would have assured the quick political incorporation of these groups, but with the machines gone, assistance and encouragement for new immigrant voters are minimal in most cities. We should note, however, that Asians and Latinos are also disproportionately less eligible to vote because these populations are younger and many are not yet citizens. The end result in voting at all levels is a racially skewed electorate, although participation is rapidly rising among Latinos and Asians, especially in California and other states with high concentrations of these populations. A few communities, including Chicago and Cambridge, Massachusetts, encourage participation (and parental involvement) by allowing noncitizens to vote in school elections.

In all racial and ethnic groups, greater affluence or higher class status makes people more likely to vote, and the higher the class, the greater that probability. Education is associated with class and has an identical effect on voting. Older people are more likely to vote than the young. Republicans are more likely to vote than Democrats. Especially in local elections, stability is a factor in voting: the longer people have lived in a place, the more likely they are to take part in its elections, because they know and care more about the community and also are more likely to see how local politics affects them. Other, more temporary factors may also influence the propensity of individuals to vote. Belonging to an interest group, like a neighborhood association or labor union, could be a stimulant. In other cases, issues in a particular election may hit home and turn a nonvoter into a voter, as may a particular candidate, usually by drawing out members of their own ethnic group. Political campaigns can make a difference, too, by making a special effort to get certain people to vote.

Of course, these are generalizations, reflecting tendencies among different sorts of people. They vary from person to person and from community to community, but they generally hold true and they have proven highly accurate in predicting voter participation, or **turnout**, for state and national elections. Voting in local elections is a little more complicated, however. Some communities have higher turnout than others, but not necessarily because they have a large number of the sort of people who usually vote. Other characteristics of communities also influence participation.

Electoral Structures

We're already familiar with one set of these variables: structures and forms of government. In general, **reform structures** depress voter turnout. Nonpartisan elections, used by about three-fourths of all U.S. cities and over 90 percent of cities in the West,[3] pull fewer voters than partisan contests, where the party label provides cues for voters and motivation for people with party loyalty. The effect of at-large city council elections on turnout is less clear, although district representation may be a modest stimulant for voters because the candidates are more likely to be known personally and to be more like their constituents. In Buffalo, which uses a mixed system of district and at-large elections, a study found that "proximity rather than prestige encourages participant activity" and concluded that at-large elections "may reduce the incentive for participation."[4] Electing a mayor rather than having an appointed city manager as executive also stimulates voting. Even when the office of mayor holds little power, it has a certain glamour for most voters as well as for the media, which pay more attention to mayoral races.

But the single biggest structural influence on voting is whether local elections are **isolated or concurrent elections**. In many communities, reformers shifted local voting to a time separate from national elections because they thought the parties and candidates for office at the higher levels drew voters who otherwise wouldn't participate and probably weren't very knowledgeable about local politics. Of course, they also hoped to discourage the lower-class ethnic supporters of the political machines. They succeeded. Voter turnout is dramatically lower in isolated than in concurrent elections. San Jose, California, is an instructive example. The city used isolated elections from 1916 to 1974, when, to save on election costs, it shifted to concurrent elections. Voter turnout in San Jose's last isolated election in 1973 was just 16 percent; its first concurrent election in 1974, which also featured a hotly contested mayoral race, nearly quadrupled turnout to 60 percent.

More generally, turnout among registered voters in isolated local elections averages around 30 percent,[5] although some big cities, such as Jacksonville (50 percent), Philadelphia (49 percent), and San Francisco (39 percent) achieve higher rates. Chicago was just above average, with 34 percent voting in its 2003 mayoral election. The contentious 2005 mayor's race in Los Angeles drew only 31 percent of the voters, but that same year in San Diego a special election to replace a mayor who resigned in disgrace produced a turnout of 44 percent. That's pretty good compared to the turnout in Phoenix (21 percent), Memphis (17 percent), Dallas (10 percent), and San Antonio (6 percent). These figures are from recent mayoral elections; turnout with only city council elections on the ballot is lower. Just 13.7 percent voted in Los Angeles in 2003 with only council races on the ballot. Turnout in isolated elections in smaller cities rarely exceeds 20 percent, and turnout for school board elections is often much lower.

Overall, turnout is roughly double in cities without reform structures of government. With parties, elected mayors, district representatives, and the added stimulus of concurrent state and national elections, participation is much higher. Yet a majority of U.S. cities use some components of reform. Defenders of these structures argue that although voter turnout is lower, those who vote are better informed. Something else important also happens, however. The electorate is not only smaller, its composition is different and it elects different sorts of people. The factors associated with making some individuals more likely to vote than others (ethnicity, class, education, and so on) mean that the die-hard voters in reformed systems will be more white, more affluent, better educated, older—and more conservative and Republican.[6] Winning candidates, reflecting these characteristics, will be more upper class and Republican, too. The electorate and the elected will be less representative of the community as a whole, at least in terms of race and class. Moreover, incumbents and candidates with well-known names win more easily because challengers lack the legitimizing influence of the party label or the assistance of the party organization. The dominance of incumbents could be broken by challengers with sympathy from the media or the money to publicize their names in the campaign, but campaign contributors and the media usually support incumbents anyway, making the task of the challengers even more difficult.

Reform structures, in short, depress voter turnout and alter the composition of the electorate and the sorts of people who are elected. They stack the deck in favor of the sort of people who created the reform movement in the first place. A more conservative electorate elects more conservative representatives and enacts more conservative policies.

IN YOUR COMMUNITY

Does your community conform to this chapter's generalizations about voter turnout? Collect data on voting and the electoral system from your city or county clerk and census data online or at the library, and make an assessment.

Community Characteristics

Other **community characteristics**, especially size and diversity, also affect voter turnout, and sometimes these are strong enough to overcome the bias of reform.

Larger cities tend to be more diverse, which means many elements of the community compete for influence. The more they come into conflict, the more they stimulate voter turnout—and broaden representation. Communities with strong political parties (Chicago or San Francisco, for example) also tend to have higher voter turnout even with nominally nonpartisan elections because the parties are out there working and organizing, even if their labels aren't on the ballot. Stable communities also have higher turnout because when people stay put for a long time they are more likely to become informed and organized. Voting is much lower in mobile communities such as many suburbs and most edge cities.

Voter turnout in communities is a tricky subject, not only because we need to generalize so broadly, but also because of the contradiction between individual and community factors associated with voting. The characteristics of individual voters (ethnicity, class, education, and so on) suggest the likelihood of one person voting. But characteristics of their communities (electoral systems, size, diversity, and so forth) also stimulate or depress turnout.

Robert Putnam and other theorists of **social capital** (see chapter 2) suggest that communities with strong social networks exhibit greater civic engagement, including voting and group membership. Better-educated and more affluent individuals tend to have higher levels of social capital, as do communities of such individuals. "Social capital is inevitably easier to foster within homogeneous communities,"[7] Putnam observes, because people more readily trust and associate with others like themselves. Dora L. Costa and Matthew E. Kahn take this one step further, reporting that "civic engagement is lower in more-heterogeneous communities" and that "homogeneity increases civic engagement."[8] With higher social capital and greater civic engagement, it follows that voter participation would be greater in small and middle-sized, homogeneous communities—usually suburbs—rather than big, diverse central cities.

All things being equal, that's probably true—but all things are not equal. Larger, more diverse cities with many minority, lower-income, less well-educated voters often have higher voter turnout than those with predominantly affluent, well-educated voters. The latter cities are more likely to be smaller and more homogeneous. Since their citizens are pretty much like one another, they have less to disagree about and so have less encouragement to participate in local politics (they still vote in high numbers in state and national elections). Low participation may also indicate general satisfaction with the governance of their community—partly because those who do vote and those who are elected are pretty much like those who don't bother to vote. But the primary reason voter turnout in city elections is lower in small, homogeneous communities is their propensity to adopt reform structures of government—especially isolated elections—that consistently depress voter turnout.

Thus, we find a rough pattern among U.S. cities. Larger cities, particularly those in the Frostbelt, tend to reject reform structures and consequently attain higher voter turnout. Smaller cities and suburbs, as well as many large Sunbelt cities, operate with reform electoral systems that produce lower turnout. Increased size and diversity have led some Sunbelt cities to return to electoral structures that predated reform, such as elected mayors, district council elections, and concurrent elections.

Turnout in these cities has risen, as has voter satisfaction with representation, especially among minorities.

Direct Democracy

In addition to the reforms already discussed, the Progressives countered the power of political machines by introducing **direct democracy** to ensure that "the people" had a say in their governance through the processes of recall, referendum, and initiative. A majority of American cities now enjoy some form of direct democracy (see Table 9.1), but like other elements of the reform package, these devices are most common in Sunbelt communities rather than those of the Frostbelt.

The Recall

Local officials may be removed between scheduled elections through the **recall** process in twenty-nine states and no less than 60 percent of American cities (more than use initiatives and referenda).[9] Those who wish to recall an elected official circulate a petition with a statement of their reasons (which need not be substantial). They must collect a certain number of voter signatures within a specified time; both the number and time limits are fixed by law and vary from community to community and state to state. A number of signatures equal to anywhere from 10 to 30 percent of those who voted in the last election might have to be collected over periods of 40 to 160 days. If enough signatures are collected and verified by the city or county clerk, an election is held. The ballot reads something like: "Shall X be removed from the office of Y?" The official is recalled if a majority of voters vote yes, and the vacant office is filled by either an election or an appointment, as appropriate. About half of those facing recall are removed from office; if recalled, in most cases they cannot be candidates to replace themselves.

Recalls are most frequently used by angry parents against school boards, although council members and mayors are also challenged and voters have recalled mayors in Detroit, Los Angeles, and Seattle in the past. Neil Giuliano, a gay man who was mayor of Tempe, Arizona (population 158,880), from 1994 to 2004, faced a recall in 2001 when he and a colleague on the council demanded that the local United Way stop funding the Boy Scouts because they exclude gays. His critics forced a recall election, but Giuliano won with 68 percent of the vote and went on to win re-election in 2002. Mayor Laura Miller of Dallas nearly faced a recall election in 2005 when Clergy for Recall, a group of African American church leaders, gathered signatures alleging she had been insufficiently attentive to the needs of blacks in Dallas. In the end, the group chose not to submit the recall petitions, perhaps satisfied that they had already made their point. Voters in Spokane, Washington, however, recalled Mayor James E. West in 2005 following charges that he had used his office to solicit young men for sex. West had previously been an outspoken opponent of gay rights.

The Progressive reformers intended recall as a way to remove incompetent or corrupt officials, but clear standards are rarely specified in state law. As a consequence, recalls are now more often used to express disagreement about policies such

Table 9.1

Direct Democracy in U.S. Cities

Form of government	Initiative (%)	Legislative referendum (%)	Citizen referendum (%)	Recall (%)
Mayor-Council	45	65	40	55
Council-Manager	64	76	49	66

Source: The Municipal Year Book (Washington, DC: International City/County Management Association, 2003).
Note: Data are based on a survey of cities.

as gay rights, school curricula, or city growth plans, requiring costly ballots between regular elections. The frustrated (usually conservative) voters who instigated the tax revolt and campaigned for term limits have also sometimes played the recall card, with mixed success. Several states, including Idaho and Georgia, have tightened their laws on recall to curtail its misuse.[10] Overall, recalls are rare, but after the successful recall of the governor of California in 2003,[11] recalls have been threatened more often and actual attempts have increased.

The Referendum

Far more common on local ballots is the **referendum**. These measures or propositions are mostly placed on the ballot by the city council or county board in the form of a legislative referendum. Borrowing money (bond measures) and amending charters must almost always be referred to the voters. For example, the Los Angeles City Council responded to citizen discontent after the 1992 riots by placing two referendums on the ballot, one amending the charter to limit the term of office of the city's police chief and another increasing taxes to pay for more police officers. By state law, the council could take neither action without a referendum. The voters approved the charter amendment but rejected the tax increase. In most cases, a simple majority is needed to approve charter amendments, but in many states, taxing and borrowing measures must be approved by 60 to 67 percent of those voting. Such "super majorities" are difficult to attain, however, so local governments may not attempt to win elections on tax proposals—or they may look for ways around a referendum.

Another form of referendum allows voters to nullify acts of local government. When a local law they dislike is passed, advocates of a protest (or popular) referendum have a limited time (specified in law) to collect a number of voter signatures (also specified in law). If they meet the deadline and the quota, the measure is put before the voters, either at the next regular election or, occasionally, at a special election. A simple majority is required to overturn the legislation. Protest referenda are rare. In recent years, they have most often been used by fundamentalist religious groups attempting (often successfully) to overturn local gay rights ordinances.

The Initiative

Recalls and referenda are reactions to what local officials do, but the **initiative process** allows voters to take a direct policy-making role. They may do so by drafting a new law or a charter amendment and then putting it on the ballot by obtaining a specified number of voter signatures (usually 5 to 10 percent of those voting in the last election) in a specified time (usually around ninety days). The initiative is put to the voters at the next election and takes effect if it wins a majority.

The subjects of initiatives vary widely, from reform of city government to growth control to whether a city should be a nuclear-free zone, and they are sometimes the most controversial measures on the ballot. Besides referenda, antigay fundamentalists have also taken advantage of the initiative process to further their cause. In 1993, for example, opponents of a Cincinnati policy that included sexual orientation in a nondiscrimination law forced a vote on a charter amendment that deleted sexual orientation from the law and prohibited the city council from passing a gay rights law. In 2004, voters repealed that charter amendment to permit their council to enact legislation to protect lesbians and gays from discrimination. But initiatives are more commonly used by opponents or proponents of the growth policies of cities to push their own policy preferences.

The Politics of Direct Democracy

Most local ballot measures or propositions are pretty trivial and boring, however, merely tidying up the charter or dealing with minor, technical matters. Many voters don't bother with this part of their ballot resulting in a **drop-off in voting** of as much as 15 to 25 percent. Voters who complete their ballot, usually more affluent, better-educated voters, and more conservative, thus gain greater influence. Tax measures attract more interest and excitement, although voter antagonism has made local governments shy away from such proposals. Sometimes individual politicians seek to get their pet causes on the ballot, often to further their own careers. Interest groups also occasionally use the technique to further their causes. Endorsements by interest groups and newspapers are particularly important on ballot measures since voters lack many other sources of information.

Perhaps disappointingly, direct democracy has not lived up to the expectations of those who introduced it. More often than not, it is used by special interests, politicians, or governments to get what they want, rather than by citizens. The rising cost of campaigns only strengthens this tendency. Still, direct democracy offers hope to the relatively powerless by enabling them to take their case to the public over the opposition of elected officials. But whether instigated by citizens or special interests, direct democracy may not result in good law. With the drafting of the legislation often left to self-interested sponsors, and campaigns placed increasingly in the hands of professional political consultants, careful and rational deliberation is rare. Confused by the maze of contradictory language, bewildering issues, and intentionally deceptive campaigns, disgusted voters often, and probably sensibly, respond by simply voting no.[12]

Local Campaigns

Whether choosing leaders or voting on ballot measures, elections wouldn't be elections without campaigns, and electoral structures do not absolutely determine the election results. Campaigns are crucial intervening variables that attempt to inform and motivate voters. Like other factors, they, too, may stimulate or depress voter turnout. Although far smaller in scale, much of what goes on in a race for mayor, city council, or county board is similar to what goes on in campaigns for state or national office. Some things, however, are different, most notably the potential for grassroots or volunteer activity.

The Candidates

Candidates for office must go through a process defined by law to appear on the ballot. Usually this involves gathering a prescribed number of signatures of registered voters who live in the candidate's district or city and paying a small filing fee. Of course candidates are also required to live in the district or city they hope to represent. An additional optional fee may also be required to cover the costs of printing a statement by the candidate in the ballot booklet that all voters receive—an important expenditure because the booklet is the primary source of information for many local voters.

But beyond the formal filing process, where do political candidates come from? Some people would say "out of the woodwork," and they might be right. If you get a chance sometime, ask a candidate how he or she came to be running. Some seem to be self-generated while others are recruited.

Self-generated candidates are people who decide pretty much on their own that they should run, although sometimes they consult friends or political leaders. It's easy to run for local office in most places—only a small fee and/or a few signatures on a petition are required, so almost anybody can do it. (No wonder we get a lot of eccentric candidates in local politics!) But even the most serious candidates may also be virtually self-nominated. This sort of candidate is most common in homogeneous communities such as suburbs and in places with reformed political structures, weak parties, and weak interest groups. Self-generated candidates are thus more numerous in Sunbelt cities.

In cities with stronger parties and interest groups, greater diversity, and unreformed electoral systems—usually larger, Frostbelt cities—**recruited candidates** are more common. A party organization, interest group, or clique of community leaders puts them forward or encourages them to become candidates and campaigns for them. Where local parties remain strong, as in New York City, they are crucial for candidate recruitment. But even in nonpartisan systems, party-like organizations of community leaders such as San Antonio's Good Government League (now defunct) or Cincinnati's City Charter Committee select and support candidates, usually successfully. Business leaders as well as unions and other less elite groups may also be active recruiters. The candidates are usually members or at least sympathizers of the group that selects them.

Self-generated candidates reflect relatively open political systems, with opportunity for all, but they often campaign more on personality than policy, and when elected, their behavior can be unpredictable because they've managed to get there more or less on their own. They are directly accountable to no one except perhaps their own campaign organization, which probably disintegrates after the election and which, in any case, is personally loyal to the candidate. Recruited candidates, in contrast, are found in more closed and rigid political systems, where they need to work their way up through existing organizations. They will probably have some sort of record, having paid their dues by serving in lower-level offices or on commissions. They are more likely to be policy-oriented than self-recruited candidates because in order to get support they will have had to satisfy their backers, and, once they are elected, these backers will hold them accountable. The disadvantage of recruited candidates, however, is that they may be accountable only to a narrow constituency rather than to the people whom they are elected to represent. Categorizing candidates as self-generated or recruited is a little arbitrary, of course, and many are a little bit of both. Nevertheless, these types exist and whether one or the other predominates in a community reveals something about its politics.

Candidates vary in other ways as well, most notably by sex and race. Lately, women have done well as candidates in suburbs and other small communities and in large cities that elect their councils by districts. At least until they become majorities in particular communities, minorities have been less successful except in cities with district elections where minority populations are geographically concentrated. Prejudice has proven hard to overcome for African American, Latino, Asian, and other minority candidates, especially in reformed cities where, besides at-large councils, elections are isolated, so interest in the campaign and information are minimal and minority turnout is low. Nonpartisan elections also deny minority candidates the legitimizing blessing of a party label telling majority voters that the candidate is okay because he or she is a Democrat or Republican. Nevertheless, minority candidates such as San Jose's Norman Y. Mineta (Asian), Denver's Federico Pena (Latino), and Seattle's Norman Rice (African American) have won mayoral elections in cities where residents who share their ethnic background are a minority of the population. (See Tables 7.2 and 7.3 for a current listing of women and minority mayors of large cities.)

African American, Asian, and Latino candidates have played an important part in local politics in recent years. Just by being on the ballot, these candidates have increased voter participation among the groups they represent. When Harold Washington, an African American, ran for mayor of Chicago, black voters were mobilized, as were Latino voters when Ron Gonzales ran for mayor of San Jose. Such ethnic mobilization is important in itself, but it's sufficient to win elections only when a minority group becomes a majority, as blacks have in Detroit and Atlanta, for example. In other places, minority candidates must seek coalition support from other minority groups as well as white liberals if they hope to succeed. To build such coalitions, they must "deracialize" their presentational style and the issues they emphasize, focusing less on the concerns of their own minority group and reaching out to others with broader concerns. Deemphasizing ethnicity may alienate a candidate's base somewhat but the strategy is essential for victory.[13]

The People in the Campaign

Candidates are not the only people involved in the campaign, of course, and one of the first things a candidate needs to do is put together an organization. This is easier for recruited candidates because the people and groups that encouraged them to run form the nucleus of the campaign team. Self-generated candidates start with friends and associates, and as their campaigns gain credibility they add other community leaders, activists, and organizations.

In small communities, and even in many large ones, volunteers are the heart of the campaign. Candidates draw on family, friends, individual supporters, and members of groups whose endorsement they win. These **campaign volunteers** staff the headquarters, address mailings, canvas door to door, and staff phone banks. Some spend their time recruiting other volunteers, working from the candidate's Christmas card list or membership rosters of churches, neighborhood groups, labor unions, or other sympathetic groups.

Key staff must also be selected. The **campaign manager** is essential.[14] Managers must be planners and strategists, working intimately with the candidates, but leaving them free to spend time in the community winning votes rather than at headquarters overseeing the organization. The larger the campaign, the more the staff grows, often including an office manager, volunteer coordinator, fundraiser, scheduler, media specialist, and sometimes a press person, although the manager usually assumes this function.

Many of these jobs can be done by volunteers, but paid professionals are more and more common. Dependence on such professionals has become greater as campaigns have become more technically complex with opinion polls, direct mail, and television and radio advertising. **Campaign consultants** are now so specialized that candidates can contract for particular services, such as polling, mailing, signs, or TV ads, from different firms or hire just one firm to do it all (usually with subcontractors). Sometimes party organizations or interest groups provide these services.

Once one campaign in a community goes professional, others soon follow, and the days of amateur campaigning become history. Volunteer campaigns are still most common in small communities, but professional consultants predominate in larger cities and their influence has reached many small ones as well. Many would-be consultants serve their apprenticeship in smaller places as volunteers or with nominal pay. The availability of professional guns-for-hire who don't care who they work for makes it easier for self-generated candidates with money to succeed. Indeed, the professionals give an advantage to any well-funded candidate, whether self-generated or recruited. Their high prices have made money more crucial in local elections.

The Money

Campaigns in small cities or in districted council races used to cost just a few thousand dollars. That's still the case in some places, but in others they can cost anywhere from $10,000 to $300,000 and more, depending on how competitive the race is and how dependent local candidates have become on professional campaign techniques and consultants. At-large council races in big cities are the most expensive, but the money is spread thinly, so candidates for district offices may actually spend more per voter than their at-large counterparts.[15] Mayoral candidates in any of the fifty largest cities in the U.S. spend from $300,000 upward; $2 million is typical in large cities. Several times that amount is spent in some cities. In Los Angeles, the two finalists for mayor spent more than $10 million in the 2005 runoff election alone. But the all-time record is held by Michael Bloomberg, who spent $75 million of his own money to win the 2001 election for mayor of New York City.

Candidates can get by with less money if they can generate lots of volunteers to do what they might otherwise have to pay for, although campaigns don't really save a lot of money with volunteer public opinion polls of questionable accuracy or with hand-addressed mailings (even though recipients are more likely to read these). Candidates can spend less on other forms of advertising, however, if legions of volunteers work phone banks or canvas door-to-door. Unfortunately, such volunteers are becoming more and more rare as Americans lead busier lives.

Money is essential, then, and getting it is a major activity of most campaigns. Fundraising specialists may be hired, and the campaign manager and candidate may spend more of their time raising money than contacting voters. Family, friends, and associates of the candidate are early contributors. Banquets, picnics, wine-and-cheese receptions, and other events with ticket prices ranging from a few dollars to hundreds are held. **Group endorsements** are eagerly sought—so candidates can add their names to lists of supporters—but also because the groups supply volunteers, and their **political action committees (PACs)** are a major source of funds. Public employee unions are particularly active, providing both money and workers to the candidates they endorse.

But the bulk of **campaign contributions** come from individuals and businesses with a vested interest in local government: those who stand to benefit or lose from whoever is elected. Because so much of what local government does involves land and development, the growth machine—landowners, builders, construction trade unions, attorneys, architects, and related businesses—is prominent on lists of campaign contributors. Companies that contract with local governments to provide services such as garbage collection, street paving, or towing chip in, as do other beneficiaries of local policies and programs, ranging from hotels to big industry. Businesses licensed by local government, such as taxis, cable TV, or tow trucks, also pay up. Campaigns that cost big money get it from big money. Some businesses contribute to candidates who seem opposed to their interests (for example, builders giving to environmentalists) in hopes of making them more friendly should they win. A few even give to rival candidates to cover all bases.

Given these sources of campaign contributions, a candidate needs to be well connected to the local business community. White businessmen are more likely to have such connections and so do better at fundraising than working-class, women, and minority candidates. Because of this disadvantage, minority, gay and lesbian, and women's groups have worked to redress the balance with contributions of their own, with some success. Many of their candidates still operate at a financial disadvantage, however. Neighborhood groups are even less likely to give money, but they often compensate with volunteers.

IN YOUR COMMUNITY

Research campaign financing for selected offices in your community by going to the city or county clerk and checking the records. What are the major sources of campaign contributions? If available, what are the major ways candidates spent their money? What is the average cost of a city council campaign?

Worried about the influence of money, many state and local governments have introduced requirements for disclosure of all contributions and expenditures. Such **sunshine laws** help voters measure the rhetoric of candidates against the interests of their supporters. A few communities buy space in local newspapers to publish these reports, but in most the voters won't know what the reports contain unless the news media or opposing candidates publicize them, which they usually do. Some cities, including Los Angeles, Sacramento, and San Francisco, make campaign finance reports available online. Over half the states and many local governments go further than disclosure, limiting the dollar amount of contributions to, say, $250 for a council candidate and $500 for a mayoral candidate, or prohibiting contributions from specially formed PACs.

Twenty-seven states and over a dozen cities and counties, including New York and Los Angeles, have gone one step further, to **public financing of campaigns** (see Table 9.2). In New York City, for example, each dollar contributed by a city resident up to $250 is matched by $4 in public funds. Candidates must disclose the amount and source of their private contributions and accept a spending limit to qualify for funds. They can spend more if they refuse public funding, but then they look dependent on fat-cat contributors. If most candidates accept public financing and spending limits, the playing field will be more level for candidates without ready access to big money. Additionally, public finance increases the number and diversity of candidates, according to the Center for Governmental Studies.[16] Other cities have considered public financing of campaigns, but budget crises have made the public and some decision makers reluctant to spend taxpayer money on campaigns, and critics have pointed out that partial public funding did not stop lavish spending on campaigns in Los Angeles (although it may have slowed the increase in spending somewhat). Another problem with public financing, as we saw in the case of New York, is that wealthy individuals can circumvent public financing systems by dipping into their own deep pockets. Of course, many of those who benefit from the current system are happy to leave it as it is.

Table 9.2

Public Financing of Local Campaigns

Austin, TX
Boulder, CO
Cary, NC
Long Beach, CA
Los Angeles, CA
Miami-Dade County, FL
New York, NY
Oakland, CA
Petaluma, CA
Portland, OR
San Francisco, CA
Suffolk County, NY
Tucson, AZ

Source: Center for Governmental Studies,
www.cgs.org (accessed May 6, 2006).

The Campaign Strategy

Probably the least obvious but most important element of electioneering is the **campaign strategy**. Simply put, this is a framework for using the candidate, people, and money available to the best possible effect. Each of these is a limited resource. The candidate only has so much time, energy, and ability. The campaign only has so many people, all with limits on their time, energy, and ability. Money, too, is finite. The principal task of campaign consultants, and the major skill they provide, is to work out a way to maximize the use of these limited resources. Instinct plays a part in this, and most gifted campaign managers have excellent political instincts, giving them the ability to make snap judgments that are right.

But strategy comes from careful research, too. This is another area where volunteers can help—or where data can be bought from consultants. Such data include voting patterns in past elections in which the candidate, the opponent, or similar candidates and issues have been involved. Census data also are useful in constructing a profile of the city or district and its problems. With the increasing availability of data and easy-to-use mapping programs, campaign consultants can target their candidate's message in ways that maximize their resources. Opinion polls may be carried out, but usually only in larger cities and high-profile races, because most voters know too little about local politics to say more than "don't know." If either candidate has held office before, the records are checked for past votes and positions. Further research may be carried out on the opposition candidate in newspapers and other public records in hopes of finding something embarrassing if the campaign descends into mudslinging, as is increasingly common, especially with the increased involvement of political consultants.

As all the information comes together, the campaign manager, the candidate, and the advisors and top staff lay out a strategy for using their resources. This will include what areas or groups the candidate should concentrate on, where and how to allocate volunteers, and what messages to convey as well as how they are to be sent and to whom they are to be addressed. At the heart of the strategy is the judicious use of available media.

Campaign Media

Although the news media are important in elections, local campaigns rely heavily on other means to achieve their primary function—communicating with voters. These **campaign media** are essential to their success.

Because the scale of local races is so much smaller than that of state and national contests, the most basic local campaign medium is the candidate talking to voters in person. Candidates walk door-to-door, lurk in shopping malls, and attend neighborhood gatherings or house parties organized by their supporters. Many community groups also invite candidates to their meetings or organize debates or candidates' forums at schools or community centers. In small communities, campaigns may amount to little more than such candidate appearances, local news reports, and a few signs. In larger places, however, a wider variety of media come into play. A mix of media is necessary because experts on the marketing of any product—from corn flakes to candidates—report that sending the message once or twice is never enough. Repetition is essential to inform voters about the candidate and his or her positions and to seek their support. "Typically, to get a vote," writes an experienced candidate and campaign manager, "you must ask for it anywhere from three to eight times."[17]

Signs

Because local politics and candidates have such a low profile in most communities, campaigns must first let people know an election is coming and develop name familiarity for their candidate or issue. That's why we see so many tacky signs all over the place when an election is coming. Notice that statewide and national candidates don't use them as much because they benefit more from news coverage (especially TV) and are probably already well known. But particularly in nonpartisan local campaigns, signs along the road, on lawns, and in windows are a fundamental starting point. Lawn and window signs are thought to be most effective because they suggest the endorsement of the household where they are placed. Such signs may be produced and placed by professionals or volunteers. The former do a better job, of course, but they can also be expensive.

Brochures

The other ubiquitous media item in campaigns from little to large is some kind of pamphlet or brochure about the candidate or issue: a few photos (coat over shoulder, talking to cops, smiling with family), a little text (antidrugs, anticrime, antigrowth, pro-neighborhood), maybe a splash of color, depending on campaign finances. Some are glossy and elaborate, others are awkward and amateurish; either kind can work

or backfire, depending on the campaign and the community. If the campaign literature is too slick, voters may reject the candidate for appearing to have too much
money; if it's not slick enough, the candidate may not be taken seriously. In any case,
the brochure will be backup material for another essential campaign medium: candidate appearances, where the candidate or campaign staff will hand it out to whoever
will take it. The brochure will probably also be left by volunteers at voters' houses
just before the election.

Canvassing

Such door-to-door **canvassing** was once the primary campaign medium, and it still
is in small communities. In many places, however, it has been replaced by **phone
banks** staffed by volunteers or paid workers. Like canvassers, they hope to talk with
the voters and, if possible, find out how they'll vote. These calls may be followed up
with a mailing and, if the voter supports the candidate, another call or visit on election day to make sure she or he actually votes. These were effective techniques in the
past, and they're still effective in small communities with substantial social capital.
But because of the busy, often disconnected lives of residents of big cities and many
suburbs, campaigns are finding it more and more difficult to recruit volunteers, and
those going door-to-door often find no one at home while those telephoning are more
likely to talk to an answering machine than a human being these days.

The E-Campaign

The Internet and widespread access to computers have transformed American society, but the effect on local campaigns, while notable, has not yet been so significant.
Many candidates now build websites; in most large cities this is required for minimum credibility as a candidate. But a website is mostly passive. Although people can
sign up for e-mail news or contribute funds (an increasingly important function),
websites require the voters to come to the candidate—unlike other campaign media
which take the candidate's message directly to the voter. The challenge of an **e-
campaign** is to find ways to reach out to voters rather than waiting for them to come
to the website. Campaigns achieve this by encouraging supporters to communicate
with their friends and neighbors by email, perhaps following up with house parties or
neighborhood gatherings for the candidate. Such personal communication has been
well documented as among the most influential messages voters receive during campaigns, so the potential for e-campaigning is huge. As the e-campaign proceeds,
candidates build their own email lists and can communicate directly with voters who
have made some previous connection to the campaign, providing news of the campaign or soliciting contributions or volunteers. Some officeholders conscientiously
build their lists in between elections. The result is a valuable resource: a list of sup-
portive contacts with whom communication by email is instant—and free.[18] More
recently, lists of email addresses of voters have become available for purchase by
candidates and campaigns, but the efficacy of using such lists is not yet clear because
voters may view messages delivered by this means merely as annoying spam.

Direct Mail

Because it has become more and more difficult in today's world to make personal contact with people in their homes, local campaigns have turned increasingly to a medium that seems to ensure better access to voters. Targeted or **direct mail** involves sending a selected message to specific voters. Thanks to computers, campaigns can target mailings to members of just one political party or to independents; to men or women; to homeowners or renters; to residents of different neighborhoods; to members of different ethnic or religious groups; or to many other types of people, such as the elderly or same-sex couples. Volunteer campaigners can develop some of the lists (party affiliation and neighborhood are easy) and address envelopes, but professional direct mail consultants can target just about any special group and get a piece in the mail overnight telling them whatever the campaign wants them to be told. Campaign managers love direct mail because they can tell different groups different things. They don't necessarily take contradictory positions on issues (although some do), they just put the pro-growth stance in their union mailing and play up crime prevention in the neighborhood piece. Managers can also include endorsements from individuals and groups that they know will be effective with the targeted voters. Besides all these advantages, direct mail can be tailored very nicely to the amount of money a campaign can raise. A mail piece can always be added or deleted, while using TV and radio involves higher production costs and advance buying of time. No wonder direct mail has become the dominant medium in contemporary campaigns. It has, however, brought increasing dependence on professional campaign consultants and driven up campaign costs.

Advertising

Local campaigns advertise in newspapers and on radio and television, but, although patterns vary, these media are used less than the others discussed thus far. In big cities, political ads in newspapers are ignored by readers and are a waste of campaign funds. Most candidates don't bother. But in the daily or weekly newspapers of small communities or in weekly neighborhood newspapers in larger cities, such ads can be as helpful as street signs. Television and radio are another matter. In small to medium-sized cities and in district council races, the expense of TV is out of the question and radio, while cheaper, is of doubtful utility. The problem is that, in either case, candidates are paying to communicate with people who can't even vote for them, since TV and radio are broadcast media that reach well beyond most local constituencies. Most campaigns conclude that their money can be better spent on targeted mailing. Except for some isolated communities where the broadcast media reach mostly local voters, radio and especially TV are used mainly in mayoral races in big cities.

Media Coverage and Endorsements

Besides advertising, campaigns also seek free publicity in the local news media. Press conferences are a little pretentious for most local candidates and are usually ignored by the media, except in big-time races. Press releases and staged events are common, however, and many candidates and campaign managers work the media by cozying up to local reporters and sharing gossip with them. Most news coverage focuses on mayoral elections, with spotty reporting on council races. This applies especially to TV. Small-town newspapers, however, provide more thorough, if sometimes more biased, coverage. Beyond the news pages and especially in small cities, the campaign is waged in letters to the editor, a well-read part of every newspaper and a good place to get free publicity.

Candidates also eagerly seek the endorsements of local newspapers. In some cases this may mean more favorable news coverage, but increasingly, endorsements are confined to editorial pages. Publishers, editors, and/or an editorial board make the endorsements from their personal knowledge of the candidates in smaller cities or from questionnaires and interviews in larger cities. These endorsements are highly prized and considered quite influential because people usually know little about local races (unlike those for higher and/or partisan offices) and take their cues where they can. Researchers estimate that newspaper endorsements are worth 10 to 20 percent of the vote in nonpartisan, at-large races, and can be particularly helpful for women and minority candidates and for ballot measures.[19]

Getting Out the Vote

As election day approaches, campaigns begin to focus on turning out their supporters to vote, a special challenge in local races. **Get-out-the-vote (GOTV)** drives are an essential element of campaigns for minority, liberal, and Democratic candidates, whose supporters are less likely to vote than those of whites, conservatives, and Republicans, although the latter may also work to get out their voters. Nonpartisan organizations such as the League of Women Voters and more partisan groups such as labor unions and minority groups also work to get people to vote. To prepare for these efforts, campaigns and groups like these often do **voter registration drives** months before the election, hoping to recruit new voters who are likely supporters. To assure this, they target certain neighborhoods or shopping centers, or perhaps colleges and universities if they expect student support. Then, during the campaign, door-to-door and telephone canvassers identify probable supporters. On election day, volunteers again phone or visit these voters to make sure they've cast their ballots. Childcare and transportation to the polls are frequently offered. Despite such efforts, voter turnout continues to decline—which only makes both getting out the vote and the votes of those who do turn out more important.

IN YOUR COMMUNITY

Working in teams, select a few blocks in one area of the city. Organize a voter registration drive in anticipation of the next local election. Register voters outside public places or major markets or by going door-to-door. What patterns are discernible among those you register? What are the challenges to voter registration?

Campaigns in Perspective

These elements of campaigns are aimed at the basic goal of communicating with voters. The main task is to get the candidate known by building name familiarity. Campaigns can then move on to persuading people to support the candidate by creating a favorable image. Finally, they must motivate supporters to actually vote. Like all forms of advertising, this requires much repetition or cumulative reinforcement, especially in nonpartisan races where name identification and image are all-important.

Much of what goes on in local campaigns is similar to contests for state and national office, particularly in mayoral races in big cities and in partisan elections. But local campaigns differ from state and national campaigns in important ways. They rely on different media—more mail, less TV—and grassroots, volunteer campaigns are far more common. Newspapers and campaign contributors, however, are even more important because nonpartisan elections generally keep party organizations out of the game. (These elements also apply to campaigns for recall, referenda, and initiatives.) Campaigns, of course, vary considerably from community to community. In big cities with partisan elections—mostly in the Frostbelt—they are far more structured and more like statewide races. In most large Sunbelt cities with reformed electoral systems, they are a free-for-all where money and media count a great deal. In smaller communities, local elites sometimes dominate, but grassroots campaigns have considerable success, too. The professionalization of local campaigns and the higher costs it brings bodes ill for grassroots campaigns, however.[20] Professional consultants also aid and abet the propensity, especially in nonpartisan elections, to emphasize both the personalities of the candidates over the issues as well as increasingly negative campaigning. Higher costs and professionalization will not help women and minority candidates, either. Still, local elections are where grassroots campaigns by ordinary people have their best remaining chance. Volunteering for a local campaign is an excellent way of learning about this process while making a contribution to your community. Campaigns at this level matter more—and so will your participation—because most people know less about such races than they know about national campaigns—partly because of the news media.

The News Media in Local Politics: "Shrill and High the Newsboys Cry/The Worst of the City's Infamy"

In most communities, "news media in local politics" means newspapers because television and radio cover local news minimally and superficially.[21] Television and radio are **broadcast media** and usually have audiences well beyond the boundaries of any single city. Their news editors believe that these audiences are not interested in one community's issues or candidates, so they allocate more time to stories of broader interest (or very narrow human interest). Besides, local news is not very visual or glamorous. The programmers know we have our fingers on the remote control and think we'll switch channels when the local news comes on. Television and radio news teams are also usually understaffed and unable to designate a city hall reporter to specialize in local politics. As a consequence, when their reporters, by necessity generalists, are assigned to cover a local issue, they sometimes misinterpret it because they don't know very much. In some big cities where local politics is more dramatic and glitzy, the electronic media make more of an effort—New York and San Francisco are notable examples—but these are the exceptions to the rule, and greater effort doesn't necessarily mean good news coverage.

Newspapers

Although their influence has declined, newspapers are still the most important news medium in local politics. Studies of power in particular cities consistently find the publishers and editors of local newspapers in the top ranks of local power holders.[22] Before TV, newspapers were even more powerful because they were the only source of news. Now more and more of us choose to get our news from TV rather than newspapers. Television doesn't tell us much, but by converting readers into viewers it decreases the power of newspapers.

Most newspapers used to be locally owned and operated by powerful families. In the nineteenth century, some newspapers played a key role in maintaining political machines while others opposed them. Journalistic muckrakers were a crucial part of the Progressive reform movement. As the machine era ended, however, most newspapers settled in as part of the establishment of their community. Their news coverage was highly biased, usually conservative, and progrowth. Candidates who received their blessing won not only editorial praise, but also favorable news coverage. When communities had more than one newspaper in competition, this wasn't such a problem because alternative views could be expressed. But as competition faded and one-newspaper towns became common, the bias became alarming. Many communities —especially small ones—find themselves in this situation.

Corporate Journalism

In others, even where one newspaper predominates, the balance has improved. A majority of U.S. newspapers, including small-town and suburban newspapers, are now owned by national or regional corporations. Instead of being run by a local family, they are managed by professionals with fewer local axes to grind and ambitions to move on to bigger and better jobs. Reporters, too, are more professional, which means they generally try harder to be objective in their reporting. Alarmingly, however, a recent study of newspaper reporting on candidates found that "information on news pages is slanted in favor of the candidate endorsed by the newspaper's editorial pages."[23] Objectivity may be a bit of a myth, but it is a laudable goal that means better coverage of local politics than that produced by the shameless bias once so common.

Professional objectivity doesn't mean the power of newspapers has declined, however, only that it has changed. Newspapers still frame the issues by choosing what to report and what to ignore. Whether they play a story as serious or a bit of a joke (easy to do with lots of local issues) also matters, as does the timeliness of the coverage, which may merely report events as they happen or give enough advance notice to people who might be affected so they can organize and do something. Newspaper power is further enhanced by the laziness or understaffing of TV and radio newsrooms, which rely on newspapers for their coverage of local politics.

Endorsements

Newspaper endorsements of candidates and issues are another way the papers exercise clout. Many readers ignore these recommendations, and in some places people conscientiously vote against whomever the newspaper endorses, but others (10 to 20 percent of the voters according to one study)[24] are influenced by them, especially in nonpartisan, at-large races and on ballot measures. Moreover, newspaper endorsements give candidates credibility with campaign contributors, and as we have seen, they may lead to slanted news coverage. Candidates and officeholders also pay attention to editorial positions on community issues, knowing they will influence the public—and knowing they will want an editorial endorsement for themselves one day.

In fact, the power of newspapers is probably greatest on nonelectoral issues such as civic projects, proposed developments, or local policies on land use or contracting out. Few other voices are heard throughout the community on these issues and those that are must be filtered through the newspaper anyway. Merely by choosing to cover an issue, the newspaper makes it important, but the manner of coverage as well as editorial opposition or support also matters. Most newspapers are conservative in their endorsements of both candidates and issues, although many take the part of reformers or crusaders for good government. The reformist impulse is often compromised, however, by the newspapers' interest in promoting their cities, which may lead them to ignore or gloss over some issues, especially those concerning social problems or minorities. Most newspapers are big boosters of growth and an integral part of the local growth machine. Growth is in their business interest, of course, because it increases their circulation and advertising revenues. "Trees don't read newspapers," said one publisher whose newspaper supported housing development on orchard land.[25]

Clout

The most powerful newspapers are probably not major metropolitan dailies as one might expect, but those of smaller communities, where readership is more common and alternative news sources are few. Big city dailies face more competition as well as some of the same problems as the broadcast media: they want to reach a metropolitan audience larger than any single city, and their readers are not interested in any one city either. Most big newspapers have responded with zoned editions in which one section (often just its front page) is targeted to a particular area. Zoned editions have actually improved coverage of suburban politics.

Nevertheless, newspaper readership is in decline. Surveys report that only 44 percent of Americans rely on newspapers as a primary source of news whereas 74 percent rely on television—which means little local news. The Internet is an increasingly popular source of news (24 percent cite the Internet as a primary source of news),[26] but while the Internet provides access to a wide array of news sources, most of these focus on politics at higher levels. Local bloggers and listservs for community groups, however, provide people with information about politics in their cities that may be available nowhere else.

Newspapers retain their clout in local politics, however. We don't have ward heelers to advise us anymore, we have less time to talk to our neighbors, television news informs us poorly about local politics, and the Internet has yet to make a significant impact at this level. Newspapers are still the major source of information about local politics. They're also important because the politically active community elite reads the paper. To be a player in local politics, you have to read what everybody else is reading, even if you don't much like it. Equally importantly, those who read the local paper are the people who are most likely to vote. Newspaper endorsements of candidates and ballot measures carry great weight, especially in nonpartisan elections, but their greatest influence is in framing local issues on their news pages.

IN YOUR COMMUNITY

Does a single newspaper dominate news coverage of local politics in your community? Are there alternative media sources, like weekly community newspapers or television news? What are the dominant newspaper's editorial positions on issues and candidates? Would you describe the newspaper as conservative or liberal? Pro-growth or for controlled growth? Can you assess how influential these editorial positions are?

Voters and the News Media

Outside city hall, nothing is as important or as influential as the voice of the voters, despite the fact that it is only occasionally heard and is usually muffled because so few participate and because it is so hard to hold elected officials accountable in between elections. A vigilant press is essential both to encourage participation and ensure accountability. Unfortunately, neither the media nor the voters are always alert. Electoral systems that dissipate interest and discourage participation do not help.

Voting is not, however, the only way that citizens express their concerns in local politics. One alternative is to move to another city. This "**exit option**" is not so readily available in state and national politics, but in most urban areas in the United States (unlike other countries), different communities are near enough for people who can afford it to move fairly readily and still be near work and friends.[27] The phenomenon of white flight to the suburbs is a case in point. Alternatively, people can voice their concerns individually or through interest groups, although this can be costly and exhausting and most don't bother. Many do, however, and as we'll see in the next chapter, some are much more successful than others.

Essential Terms

register to vote
turnout
reform structures
isolated or concurrent elections
community characteristics
social capital
direct democracy
recall
referendum
initiative process
drop-off in voting
self-generated candidates
recruited candidates
campaign volunteers
campaign manager
campaign consultants

group endorsements
political action committees (PACs)
campaign contributions
sunshine laws
public financing of campaigns
campaign strategy
campaign media
canvassing
phone banks
e-campaign
direct mail
get-out-the-vote (GOTV)
voter registration drives
broadcast media
newspaper endorsements
exit option

On the Internet

- Check out the *Campaigns and Elections* (www.campaignline.org) website for leading trade magazine for political consultants.
- Check individual city websites (including your own) for information about candidates and campaign finance (data may be available online).
- Check individual candidate websites for information about their campaigns.
- Find commercial campaign software at www.epoliticalcampaign.com for information about various elements of political campaigns; software available for purchase.
- The website for the Center for Governmental Studies (www.cgs.org) has information about public finance of campaigns (CGS is an advocacy organization).
- The website for the Pew Research Center for the People and the Press (http://people-press.org/) has information about politics, public opinion, and the press.
- The website for the Center for Voting and Democracy, Fair Vote (www.fairvote.org), has news and ideas about election reforms, including proportional voting, instant runoffs, and so on.
- The website for Emily's List (www.emilyslist.org) focuses on the election of women to state and local office.
- The website for Project Vote-Smart (www.vote-smart.org) has information on candidates and ballot measures in your community and beyond.

Notes

1. Robert D. Putnam, *Bowling Alone: The Collapse and Revival of American Community* (New York: Simon and Schuster, 2000), p. 32.

2. U.S. Census Bureau, *Current Population Survey,* November 2004.

3. Tari Renner and Victor S. DeSantis, "Municipal Form of Government: Issues and Trends," *The Municipal Year Book* (Washington, DC: International City/County Management Association, 1998), p. 40.

4. Michael Haselswerdt, "Voter and Candidate Reaction to District and At-Large Elections: Buffalo, New York," *Urban Affairs Quarterly* 20 (September 1984): 42.

5. Paul E. Peterson, *City Limits* (Chicago: University of Chicago Press, 1981), p. 119.

6. Peterson, *City Limits*, p. 115; see also James Svara, *Official Leadership in the City: Patterns of Conflict and Cooperation* (New York: Oxford University Press, 1990), p. 137.

7. Putnam, *Bowling Alone*, p. 400. See also Sidney Verba, Kay Lehman Schlozman, and Henry E. Brady, *Voice and Equality: Civic Voluntarism in American Politics* (Cambridge, MA: Harvard University Press, 1995).

8. Dora L. Costa and Matthew E. Kahn, "Civic Engagement and Community Heterogeneity: An Economist's Perspective," *Perspectives on Politics* 1, no. 1 (March 2003): 108. See also Rodney E. Hero, "Social Capital and Racial Inequality in America," *Perspectives on Politics* 1, no. 1 (March 2003): 113–22.

9. National Civic League and 2001 ICMA Municipal Form of Government Survey, www.iandrinstitute.org/Recall.htm (accessed: May 6, 2006).

10. David R. Berman, "State Actions Affecting Local Governments," *The Municipal Year Book* (Washington, DC: International City/County Management Association, 1990), p. 56.

11. See Larry N. Gerston and Terry Christensen, *Recall! California's Political Earthquake* (Armonk, NY: M.E. Sharpe, 2004).

12. Eugene Lee, "The American Experience: 1778–1978," in *The Referendum Device*, ed. Austin Ranney, American Enterprise Institute Symposia (Washington, DC: American Enterprise Institute, 1981), p. 58.

13. Katherine Underwood, "Ethnicity Is Not Enough: Latino-Led Multiracial Coalitions in Los Angeles," *Urban Affairs Review* 33, no. 1 (September 1997): 3–27. See also Rufus P. Browning, Dale Rogers Marshall, and David H. Tabb, eds., *Racial Politics in American Cities*, 3rd ed. (New York: Longman, 2003).

14. See Catherine M. Shaw, *The Campaign Manager*, 3rd ed. (Boulder, CO: Westview Press, 2004) for a step-by-step description of local campaigns.

15. Haselswerdt, "Voter and Candidate Reaction," p. 40.

16. *Investing in Democracy* (Los Angeles: Center for Governmental Studies, 2003), p. 8; available at www.cgs.org (accessed May 6, 2006).

17. Shaw, *The Campaign Manager*, p. 170.

18. See Joe Trippi, *The Revolution Will Not Be Televised: Democracy, the Internet, and the Overthrow of Everything* (New York: ReganBooks, 2004).

19. Susan A. MacManus and Charles S. Bullock III, "Minorities and Women DO Win At Large!" *National Civic Review* 77, no. 3 (May–June 1988): 233.

20. See J. Cherie Strachan, *High-Tech Grass Roots: The Professionalization of Local Elections* (Lanham, MD: Rowman and Littlefield, 2003).

21. The "Newsboys" quote in the subtitle for this section is a nineteenth-century critique of newspaper coverage of local politics from William Vaughn Moody, "In New York," quoted in *The City: A Dictionary of Quotable Thought on Cities and Urban Life*, ed. James A. Clapp (New Brunswick, NJ: Center for Urban Policy Research, 1984), p. 169.

22. Philip J. Trounstine and Terry Christensen, *Movers and Shakers: The Study of Community Power* (New York: St. Martin's Press, 1982), pp. 131–38.

23. See Kim Fridkin Kahn and Patrick J. Kenney, "The Slant of the News: How Editorial Endorsements Influence Campaign Coverage and Citizens' Views of Candidates," *American Political Science Review* 96, no. 2 (June 2002): 381–94 on coverage of U.S. Senate races.

24. MacManus and Bullock, "Minorities and Women," p. 233.

25. Richard Reinhardt, "Joe Ridder's San Jose," *San Francisco Magazine*, November 1965, p. 66.

26. "Public More Critical of Press, But Goodwill Persists" (report by the Pew Research Center for the People and the Press, released June 26, 2005), http://people-press.org (accessed May 6, 2006).

27. See Albert O. Hirschman, *Exit, Voice, and Loyalty: Responses to Decline in Firms, Organizations, and States* (Cambridge, MA: Harvard University Press, 1970).

10 Interest Groups in Local Politics
Types, Tactics, and Targets

Individual citizens participate in the politics of their communities when they vote or actively campaign for favored candidates and causes. They are also involved in governing their communities between elections. Some write, phone, or meet with their representatives to talk about issues that concern them. Others attend meetings, give public testimony, or serve on committees and commissions, of which most local governments have many. But perhaps the most common and substantial way that citizens take part in community politics is through interest groups.

Interest groups result when individuals get together and organize themselves to attempt to influence the policies and programs of government by applying whatever political resources they have. Although most people correctly assume that interest groups are more active in state and national politics than in local politics, a variety of such groups take part in community politics, too. Sometimes they are a little harder to see because they are people we know rather than slick lobbyists in expensive suits. Often they are organizations we don't think of as interest groups, such as businesses and corporations or even churches. Although the primary purposes of these organizations are not political, they sometimes function as interest groups when their concerns are at stake. Businesses or churches, for example, may act like interest groups when a local land-use decision will affect their property, or on issues such as parking and traffic. More generally, businesses want low taxes, good services, and growth in their communities, and churches may seek to protect what they perceive as public morality on issues such as homelessness or gay rights. In fact, this is a common pattern in interest group activity in local politics: many groups organized for purposes other than politics sometimes operate as interest groups. Politics is the primary purpose of many others, however. In larger cities, such groups are increasingly common and some say even dominant in local politics.

Types of Interest Groups

To get an idea of what sorts of groups are active in a particular local jurisdiction, study the agendas of the meetings of its governing body. States divide the responsibilities for local governments among cities, counties, and sometimes other governments. The week-to-week decisions of city councils and other governing bodies revolve around these responsibilities, which are readily apparent in their agendas. When items of concern to particular groups are on the agenda, representatives of the groups generally show up at the meeting itself. So when you read the agenda for a meeting, its subject matter will pretty much predict who will be there. Better yet, attend a few meetings and you'll see the groups in action. Of course, every group will not be there every week. Groups—and individuals—show up when their own interests are at stake, take part in deliberations on the specific items that concern them, and leave the meeting immediately after their item has been heard. Nothing could better illustrate the narrowness of their interests. Go and watch.

IN YOUR COMMUNITY

Attend a series of city council or commission meetings (on your own or as part of a research team) to observe and inventory interest group activity. What sorts of groups are most active? Which are most successful?

The sorts of groups active in local decision making vary, not only according to the responsibilities assigned by the state to a particular unit of local government, but also by the social and economic composition of the community. Nevertheless, some types of groups are commonly involved in community politics all across the United States.

Business Groups

Business groups speaking for economic interests are probably the most common organizations active in local politics. Individual businesses may be active on a land-use decision that affects their company or on broader issues that concern them, such as taxes or regulations on signs or parking. In general, the more local the business is, the more active it is in community politics. Multinational corporations tend to focus on state and national politics, taking scant interest in particular communities. But businesses that are locally headquartered or exclusive to a single community tend to take what goes on there very seriously, indeed.

The most ubiquitous business organization in American communities is the local **chamber of commerce**, which is usually dominated by retail merchants, although many chambers try to represent the full spectrum of business interests. Associations of ethnic and small business owners are also active in most communities, and big businesses such as manufacturers often form organizations of their own in larger cities or regions. Sometimes, businesses with a common specialty, such as builders, manufacturers, or merchants, form groups to represent their interests.

Because a primary power of local government is land use, perhaps the most active of all business interests in city and county politics are those related to land and development—the growth machine. Landowners, builders, and their suppliers and associates (such as lawyers, architects, surveyors, realtors, and advertising agencies) are active and powerful in local politics in most communities, usually successfully promoting growth and thus furthering their own interests. Builders and realtors often form organizations of their own, but the growth machine as a whole operates more as an informal alliance rather than a structured interest group.

As with all categories of interest groups, it is important to remember that business interests are not homogeneous. Indeed, they vary considerably and may well come into conflict. Downtown merchants may oppose suburban shopping malls or hotels; manufacturing companies may express caution about growth when it brings traffic congestion that hurts their business; realtors may be less enthusiastic about new development because their business is to sell homes, not build them, and limiting the housing supply may raise prices and thus their commissions. In general, business is antitax, but small business groups are more vehement in their opposition (and generally more conservative) than big businesses, which may accept or even support tax increases when persuaded that such increases will improve services, especially infrastructure like housing and transportation. Like any other group, business will first protect its own well-being or self-interest, and the bottom line is profit. More than most other groups, however, business groups are likely to push for the broader goal of growth, which to them means economic expansion and more business for themselves. The more local the business is—as opposed to being part of a multinational corporation—the greater its enthusiasm for growth will be.

Labor Groups

Labor groups or unions are powerful interest groups in some large cities, mostly in the East and Midwest, although there are a few elsewhere, such as Los Angeles. In most of the Sunbelt and suburbia, however, membership in unions is low and their influence is limited. Private-sector unions such as autoworkers or retail clerks take part in city politics when issues that affect them arise, but such organizations usually focus on state and national rather than local politics because more of their concerns are dealt with at those levels. If they are active locally, it is usually in support of associated unions with more at stake.

The most commonly active local unions are the building trades and public employees. The construction trade unions—carpenters, electricians, plumbers, and others —have as big a stake in the politics of land use and growth as do their employers, the landowners and builders, and they are solid political allies of local growth machines. Union support for growth proposals gives them a legitimacy (jobs and housing) that wealthy landowners or corporate developers don't have and thus may win the support of liberal decision makers. Public-employee unions, which are the only growing sector of union membership, attempt to influence decision makers on wages and working conditions for their members, and in so doing, they often shape the delivery of public services, from police and fire protection to parks and libraries. The most active and influential public employee unions are usually police, fire fighters, and teachers (in school district politics).

In most counties, individual unions come together in an umbrella organization called a **labor council**, usually under the auspices of the national American Federation of Labor and Congress of Industrial Organizations (AFL/CIO). Through these councils, unions are connected to state and national labor organizations and support one another—or work out their differences. As with business Interests, unions do not always agree. In political endorsements, for example, public-employee unions tend to be liberal, while the construction trades tend to be conservative. And while the construction unions are unequivocally pro-growth, public-employee unions (and others as well) worry about growing so rapidly that the quality of public services and the environment decline. With private-sector union membership shrinking and public-employee unions growing, the balance of power within the labor movement is shifting. In 2005, a cluster of the largest and most liberal unions, including the Service Employees International Union (SEIU) representing many public workers, split from the AFL-CIO—a manifestation of political differences within the labor movement.

Neighborhood Groups

Almost as common as business interests in local politics are **neighborhood or homeowner groups**. These organizations are territorially based, speaking for a particular section of the community, which may range in size from a few square blocks to a few square miles. Membership in the groups may also range from a few activists to hundreds. Typical concerns are new developments of almost any sort, traffic, crime, and local amenities such as parks and libraries. These groups usually find themselves trying to prevent something from happening to their area that they perceive as a threat, either to their local quality of life or to property values. Neighborhood opposition to proposals coming from developers or from city hall is so common that these groups have earned the acronym **NIMBY** (not in my backyard). Often this involves objections to particular projects considered locally unacceptable land uses (**LULUs**), from dumps and factories to community care facilities and low-income housing. Politically, neighborhood or homeowner groups are often on the defensive, opposing changes in their areas, but their activities are not all negative. Many play a productive part in building community and even in providing some local services.

Some—often those that refer to themselves as homeowner rather than neighborhood groups—have extremely narrow interests, however. Urbanist Mike Davis reports that homeowner groups first formed in the 1920s in Los Angeles "as instruments of white mobilization against attempts by blacks to buy homes outside the ghetto," with "white homeowners band[ing] together as 'protective associations.'"[1] Others in California and elsewhere were formed for other reasons, all involving protection, although not always racist. Recently, California has led the way in the emergence of a new variation of these protective associations. **Common Interest Developments, or CIDs**, are the mandatory organizations that provide services in condominiums, gated communities, and some other housing developments. More than 250,000 such organizations now operate across the country. They collect fees (like taxes), provide services such as maintenance and security, and function not only as interest groups, but also as minigovernments.

Homeowner groups and CIDs are most common in white, middle-class areas, where they concentrate mainly on the property values and homogeneity of their communities, opposing developments they think might lead to decreasing home prices or to the arrival of different classes or ethnic groups (also perceived as lessening property values). Minority and working-class neighborhoods often behave in the same way when they sense similar threats. Although this NIMBY mentality is widely condemned, critics sometimes forget that the biggest investment most families make is in their home. Naturally, they want to protect their investment, even if that means being seen as class or race biased. Mixing cheaper homes or different class and racial groups in a neighborhood does not always lead to lower property values, however. The impact of such changes depends on the strength of the neighborhood, the specific projects, and the extent of commingling. Nevertheless, the fears of the NIMBYs aren't purely paranoid in a society in which most neighborhoods are not mixed and in which property values often supersede social values.

Opposition to Growth

On a broader level, neighborhood/homeowner/NIMBY politics often extend to antagonism to growth, pitting these interests against business and labor. But while neighborhood opposition to growth may align these groups with environmentalists, their opposition to growth has less to do with open space or clean air and water than with its impact on local services. Growth may generate economic activity in an area, but it doesn't necessarily pay for itself. Somebody has to foot the bill for new roads, fire stations, parks, libraries, and the like. Until the 1970s, when they started saying no, existing neighborhoods paid much of the cost of growth. Since then, however, local governments have shifted more of the bill to the new developments themselves (and thus to the consumers). But even if older neighborhoods don't have to pay for new infrastructure, existing services such as streets, police, and parks must be shared with new developments, so service levels in older areas decline. When that happens, neighborhoods may join environmentalists to forge a formidable antigrowth coalition.

Proactive Politics

Whether narrow NIMBYism or a broad antigrowth coalition, the politics of these groups is mostly negative and defensive. Some territorial groups go beyond this, however, to more positive and even proactive politics. Homeowner groups may evolve in this way, although proactive organizations tend to refer to themselves as neighborhood rather than homeowner groups, taking a broader, more generous, and inclusive view of their territory and expressing concerns about its various components. Some such groups, for example, form neighborhood watch programs to fight crime, helping each other and the police. Some organize neighborhood cleanups or tree plantings—again, helping both themselves and their local government. Many get involved in the operation of local schools, libraries, parks, and community centers, making them more responsive to their clients and better integrated with their service areas. Some neighborhood groups cooperate with their local governments in planning new developments to avoid NIMBY confrontations. Some, like The Woodlawn Organization (TWO) in a predominantly low-income, African American neighborhood of Chicago, work to improve or build housing and/or to encourage small businesses and create jobs. All these are examples of **coproduction**, or neighborhood efforts in cooperation with local government, that can improve services, cut government costs, and build community. Newsletters, festivals, and street parties are also part of their community building, addressing the need of urban dwellers to feel a sense of identity and belonging. All of these are things any of us can do and feel good about, and they make our neighborhoods better and more pleasant places to live.

Groups that take on these more positive functions tend to be long lasting (TWO is over forty years old) and may attain considerable clout.[2] This power is narrowly confined to issues specific to their territories, but such narrowness is true of most interest groups. Although neighborhood groups aren't always apparent as major players in community politics, many have confronted and faced down big powers such as developers—or at least given them a run for their money.

But while most neighborhood groups operate in middle- or upper-class areas and focus exclusively on their own territorial concerns, the Association of Community Organizations for Reform Now (ACORN) is an unusual exception. ACORN is neighborhood-based organization with over 175,000 member households organized into 850 neighborhood chapters in 80 cities throughout the United States. ACORN's local organizations have taken action on issues ranging from affordable housing and the rights of renters to schools and living wages for poorly paid workers.[3] ACORN is remarkable not only because it focuses on low-income areas, which are less likely than other neighborhoods to be organized, but also because it links these neighborhoods together to work on common causes. Most other neighborhood groups function in isolation, but in some cities umbrella organizations bring neighborhood leaders and organizations together to share concerns and information and sometimes to form coalitions. ACORN is unique, however, in its national scope.

Tenuous Organizations

Most neighborhood or homeowner groups, however, are tenuous organizations at best. They commonly emerge in response to a crisis—some threat to their territory—and fade away when the crisis is resolved. The chief disadvantage for these groups, then, is that they are reactive—and often their reaction comes too late. Only a few neighborhood groups manage to achieve the stability and on-going vigilance that are common to business and labor groups. More common, as Mike Davis asserts in his study of Los Angeles, are "individualistic" groups "dominated by cranky personalities, consorting in temporary coalitions and then, inevitably, remolecularizing around their own back yards."[4]

The stability of neighborhood groups is further challenged because their self-interest is not always as easy to define as the self-interest of businesses and unions. Although they tend to be homogeneous, most neighborhoods contain some diversity —Republicans and Democrats, liberals and conservatives, middle- and working-class households, members of racial minorities, and others—and may not readily reach consensus on issues not involving a direct threat. Dissent and even opposing groups within neighborhoods are common. In addition, the mobility of American life as we move from community to community and spend parts of our day in different areas makes the emergence and sustenance of such groups less likely.

Minority Groups

Another very common sort of group represents ethnic or racial minorities. Almost every wave of immigrants since the first English settlers of North America has, at one time or another, felt itself a minority and suffered discrimination. In cities, various newly arrived immigrants often formed protective associations that acted, partly, as interest groups. Depending on the city and the time, these have included the Irish, the Germans, the Italians, and many others. Some of these groups worked their way into mainstream U.S. politics through political machines. And because they were white, many individuals merely melted into the larger society.

Other groups—blacks, Asians, and Latinos in particular—have had a harder time. Nonwhites or people with cultures distinctly different from that of the community majority have had to struggle even harder for political recognition. Shunned by the political machines and denied the right to vote or even own property in some states, it was not until the middle of the last century that racial minorities began to win the right of political participation. A great surge of political organizing during the civil rights movement of the 1950s and 1960s, supplemented by federal support for community organizing during the War on Poverty and the Great Society programs of the 1960s, brought visibility and eventually clout, particularly for African American groups in big cities. Latinos and, a little later, Asians organized similarly and began to achieve success in the 1980s and 1990s.

People of almost every racial and ethnic group in America—Europeans, African and Asian Americans, Latinos and others—have formed associations that are active in local politics. Those most integrated socially and economically generally concentrate on sustaining their cultural heritage, with St. Patrick's Day parades, Octoberfests, or Italian festas. Those less well integrated and less well off still fight discrimination and struggle for basic rights, including housing, jobs, and political representation. When ethnic and racial groups are territorially concentrated, they overlap with neighborhood groups. This can be an added source of strength, making organizing easier since people live closer together and have more in common. But more often than not, the concentration of a particular group in a specific area is the result of discrimination, so the group has more to struggle against.

Massive immigration in recent decades (see chapter 3) has resulted in thousands of groups based on shared ancestry from another country. In a sense, these groups are doubly minority—as members of a particular nationality, race, or ethnicity and as immigrants. Most of these groups form initially to preserve the culture of the homeland (including language and religion) or to provide mutual assistance. Over time, some grow more assertive and work for the political incorporation of the immigrants, organizing citizenship classes and voter registration drives and eventually supporting candidates.

As with other types of groups, **minority groups** are far from unified or uniform. Their interests vary depending on how well they are integrated socially and economically with the larger society. They often compete with one another for community resources or representation. When their interests coincide, coalition makes sense, but racism and ethnocentrism often prevent such unity. Antagonism between groups is more likely, particularly when new groups arrive in neighborhoods and threaten to "take over." In the past, this meant blacks moving into white neighborhoods, but more recently in large cities it has meant Asians and Latinos moving into black neighborhoods. Even within some racial and ethnic groups, competition and conflict may occur. For example, the differences among Japanese, Chinese, Koreans, and Vietnamese, or among Mexicans, Cubans, and Puerto Ricans may be both substantial and politically debilitating.

Nor do minority groups always find easy allies among other sorts of groups. Minority leaders denounce businesses for discriminating and unions for denying them jobs. Even though they frequently represent neighborhoods themselves, and so might share a concern for basic services and community control, minority leaders often denounce other neighborhoods for housing discrimination and elitism. On growth issues, minority groups usually line up with business and unions on grounds that growth means jobs and housing.

Environmental Groups

On the other side of the growth issue are **environmental groups**. Mostly white and middle- or upper-class, well-educated professionals, their self-interest is not tied to growth like that of business, developers, unions, and minority groups pushing for jobs, although they are often sympathetic to these concerns. Besides fighting local growth machines, many environmental groups have also been active on such issues as airport expansion, highway siting, building heights, architectural design, public transit, footpaths, bike lanes, parks, and open space. They gained extra leverage when some states began requiring local governments to consider environmental impact reports (EIRs) on development projects. These EIRs may be challenged at public hearings or in court, opportunities many environmental groups eagerly seize.

Local politics can be difficult for environmental groups, however. The growth machine attitude on land use held by most local governments means environmentalists are fighting the mainstream. The rhetoric of jobs rather than owls is especially leveled against environmentalists at the local level. As we have seen, however, neighborhood groups concerned about the adequacy of city services may be allies in an antigrowth coalition. Another difficulty for environmental groups is that many of their concerns, such as air and water quality and open space, overlap local government boundaries and so are beyond the ability of individual communities to control. Environmental advocates must therefore take their case to a higher level of government —if an appropriate one exists. Despite growing public concern, these factors limit the influence of environmental organizations in local politics.

Other Groups

Although the groups discussed thus far are the most common ones in local politics, a variety of others take part in many communities. Perhaps most numerous are fraternal and **civic associations** such as Elks, Rotary Clubs, and Kiwanis. These are predominantly social and service organizations, but in many communities a particular club—often Rotary—becomes the meeting place for community leaders. While such clubs do not engage in politics directly, they provide a common venue for the informal exchange of information and gossip and facilitate consensus among leaders on issues or candidates.

The involvement of **women's groups** in local politics goes back to the social reform movements of the nineteenth century. They also played a prominent part—even before women could vote in most places—in the Progressive movement. Since the 1970s, women's groups like the National Organization for Women and the National Women's Political Caucus have worked to elect women to local offices, with great success.[5] These groups and many female elected officials helped to change hiring policies in most communities to further the recruitment, employment, and promotion of women and minorities. At their instigation, police, courts, and social service bureaucracies have changed their policies on the treatment of rape victims and on domestic violence. Women's groups have also impacted the education system and campaigned for childcare. Although the red-hot issue of abortion rights is mainly a matter of state and national policy, women's groups have been active on that issue with local health and social service agencies and in protecting access to abortion clinics.

In big cities and some small ones as well, gay and lesbian groups, like other minorities, campaign against discrimination and often complain about police practices. Activist groups have helped elect out-of-the-closet gays and lesbians to city councils in many communities and campaigned for domestic partner rights, civil unions, and same-sex marriage, most notably in San Francisco, New York City, and Los Angeles. Such actions produced a potent backlash in many other cities, however, as religious conservatives campaigned to overturn gay rights laws, often at the ballot box. In 2005, however, voters in Cincinnati chose to reinstate, rather than repeal, one such law.

Conservative religious congregations have become a potent force in group politics in many cities, in opposition not only to gay rights, but also to abortion and even teaching evolution in schools. As other organizations that link people in cities together have declined or died, these religious organizations have grown and become increasingly engaged in local, state, and national politics, even though their primary purpose is not politics. But these aren't the only religious organizations that are active in local politics. Black churches have engaged in political activism for over a century and were essential to the success of the civil rights movement. Liberal religious congregations have been active with AIDS projects, providing food and shelter for the homeless, and improving race relations. Church groups of all sorts also take an interest in local education policy since many operate schools themselves.

Age-related groups have also become active in community politics in recent years. Youth groups may be involved through recreational facilities, while senior citizens have become more vocal as the number and needs of the elderly have increased. Both types of age groups seek services and facilities such as community centers where they can gather and sometimes they clash over the limited resources of local government.

Reform groups have played a significant role in most cities at some point in their history, particularly in the movement against political machines. Their vestiges remain in many communities, continuing the fight for "good government." Those words are often in the group's name. The League of Women Voters is perhaps the most common reform group found in U.S. cities. Reform issues today include ethics, campaign funding, open meetings, access to information, controlling bureaucracies, and sometimes changes in government structures such as stronger mayors or district elections. Reformers in many metropolitan areas advocate the creation of a regional government to deal with issues that can't be solved by the current fragmented array of governments in cities and counties.

More conservative reform groups have campaigned to limit elected officials to two or three terms of office to increase turnover and hopefully responsiveness. This reform is particularly popular among **taxpayer associations**, which normally concentrate on fighting tax increases of any sort. Most common in suburbs and the Sunbelt, these groups are usually small and often eccentric—some seem to consist of just a couple of old guys who like to harangue elected officials at public meetings and are often dismissed as cranks. Yet by opposing taxes when more established groups will not, they often strike a chord with the voters, as the national tax revolt in the 1970s and 1980s proved.

Housing groups are active in some communities, although housing is a transient issue for most people. That is, once they have their own, most people quit worrying about it. Realtors and landlords (business groups, really) are organized in most communities, however, and in some, renters are also. Rent control (limits on how much landlords can charge) was a hot issue in many communities in the 1970s and 1980s. When housing prices rose in many parts of the country in the late 1990s, groups advocating the construction of "affordable" housing formed in many cities. ACORN has been a primary advocate of renters' rights and affordable housing in many communities. Builders and unions may advocate development, but rarely for those most in need of shelter. Groups campaigning for the homeless, however, emerged as that problem grew in U.S. cities in the 1990s.

Cultural and recreational groups supplement all these participants in local politics. Many communities fund activities ranging from opera to square dancing or from soccer to tennis. Often such allocation of funds is the result of group advocacy, and the continuation (or expansion) of funding is actively pursued by groups formed to do just that, giving important clientele support to the bureaucratic agencies that oversee or provide the service. The interests of these groups are, of course, quite narrow, yet they can marshal considerable resources when they feel threatened.

Many other sorts of groups operate in communities, although often only briefly. Sometimes other governments even act like interest groups, seeking to influence a local governing body through the use of group tactics such as lobbying. Urban areas in the United States are characterized by multiple governments and a high degree of fragmentation. Sometimes one government needs to petition another to coordinate policies. School districts, for example, often address city councils on proposed developments since they have to provide schools for the new growth. But while they may be acting like groups, the range of tactics available to these governmental petitioners is limited.

Interest Group Tactics

The groups we've just surveyed have varying political resources and apply them in varying ways with varying degrees of success. Groups with substantial and diverse resources, such as money, prestige, leadership, and organization, are able to use more of the **tactics** described in this section and are more likely to succeed, while those with tighter resources find themselves limited in the range of tactics available and, often, in their efficacy as well. But groups have to use what they've got and use enough of it to get what they want—or lose. They also need to make careful strategic decisions about which tactics to use, avoiding both overkill and overconfidence.

Group Maintenance

Before exercising any of the tactics discussed next, interest groups must see to their own maintenance in order to be effective. They need to build up their resources of people and money by recruiting members, generating and sustaining leaders, and raising money through dues or contributions. Organizations that do not do so end up depending on a handful of activists or even an individual leader. Ultimately they may not be groups at all but just one or two people purporting to speak for a group. Decision makers soon see through this false front and pay less attention.

Interest groups recruit and engage members by communicating with them through newsletters and email listservs as well as regular meetings. Email and the Internet have significantly democratized group participation in city politics because they cost almost nothing. Hundreds of neighborhood and other grassroots groups now communicate regularly in this way. Through their email lists, they can mobilize members to attend meetings or contact elected officials more quickly and on a larger scale than in the past. Nevertheless, phone trees, face-to-face communication, and organizational meetings remain important for most groups.

Some groups gain membership support by providing services. Labor unions and business organizations, like chambers of commerce, provide representation for their members, but they also provide a wide range of services such as training and providing information about public policy or discounts on purchases, insurance, and more.

The most effective groups also give members social benefits. Through events like annual banquets, festivals, or other celebrations, or simply through social hours before or after meetings, members gain a sense of belonging, identity, and community that most people value. We're all more willing to participate when we can socialize with others and have a little fun. Groups that neglect such social benefits engage their members less and are less sustainable.

Effective groups also need leadership and money. For grassroots groups like neighborhood or minority organizations, this is always a challenge. Leaders must be volunteers. Although they may be likeable and committed, many lack real leadership skills. Some learn these skills quickly while others falter and most eventually burn out, exhausted by the strain of combining their work and family commitments with their group leadership responsibilities. Fundraising is also tough for grassroots groups. Their members aren't rich, so they can't rely on big donations or expensive dues.

Events like annual banquets or bake sales raise money but rarely in substantial amounts. Fortunately, most grassroots groups don't need a lot of money for their operations, at least not if they can recruit and sustain good volunteer leaders.

Business groups, labor unions, and some other types of groups are more sustainable, however, because their economic base through membership dues is more substantial and reliable. Although many of their activists and leaders are volunteers, these groups usually have paid executive directors as leaders, supported by paid staff. With paid, full-time staff, these groups can be more effective than grassroots groups at recruiting, mobilizing, and nurturing their members as well as at fundraising and organizing events. These groups face challenges as well, however. Some take the financial contributions of their members for granted and gradually lose touch so that they are unable to mobilize members when they need to and ultimately lose credibility with decision makers.

In short, groups of all sorts face challenges in building and maintaining their resources of people and money, but **group maintenance** is crucial for their success with any or all of the tactics discussed in the next sections.

IN YOUR COMMUNITY

Attend a meeting of an interest group such as a neighborhood association. Which issues discussed are related to local politics or policies? Can you observe social activities that help maintain the group as well as political activities?

Public Hearings

The most common and visible group tactic is attendance and testimony at **public hearings** by the city council or other appropriate local governing body. This is also the group tactic that we can most readily observe and evaluate.

Effective groups systematically monitor council agendas to watch for items of interest to them. Contacts inside city hall (sympathetic elected officials or staff) let groups know that such items are coming up. Occasionally, groups manage to take the offensive and place items on a council agenda themselves, thus gaining the advantages of framing the issue and controlling timing. But, usually, groups learn that a subject that concerns them is coming up a week or two in advance and must quickly decide how to respond.

Well-established groups confident of victory may need to send only a representative or two to observe the meeting and perhaps speak on the issue. But no matter how confident they are, it is important that their representatives be present and visible. To fail to attend insults the decision makers, leading them to conclude that the issue is insignificant to the group and even that they might be able to make concessions to the opposition (if there is one).

Less confident groups need to send not only representatives but also "troops." **"Packing the chambers"** is a time-honored group technique to show both the strength of feeling within the group and its numerical (voting) strength. Once a group is well established, turning out the troops is not always necessary, but decision makers grow suspicious of advocates who pretend to speak for many when they represent only themselves, so shrewd group leaders will get their members to meetings now and then just to remind the decision makers that the group has "legs" (people willing to work). Packing the chambers is also a good way to keep up the morale of the group, especially when victory is assured.

At the meeting, groups balance factual argument with emotion and, sometimes, veiled political intimidation. The testimony of a really angry citizen can be just as persuasive as the most factual presentation because it shows intensity of feeling. Overt political threats, however, usually backfire. Able groups often choose a few speakers who represent the range of their membership (old/young, majority/minority, male/female, and so on), delegating each to emphasize a particular point and instructing them to be brief. Groups that go on at length and repeat points gain no advantage, but leaders cannot always control their followers when a forum is available. The presentation of petitions, circulated by group members in their neighborhoods or elsewhere, is often a feature of public hearings. Well-organized groups will also prime decision makers in advance with phone calls, postcards, or letters from supporters.

A public hearing is sometimes a real decision-making forum, but more often the meeting is a performance, with decision makers going through the motions of listening while citizens and interest groups go through the motions of giving testimony. This is because most issues have been kicked around long enough that the decision makers already have their minds made up. Effective interest groups will have talked to them and counted their votes in advance. That doesn't mean that the performance at the public meeting is irrelevant. It is an essential part of the decision-making process in most communities; groups that disdain it will lose.

On the other hand, citizens and groups that rely solely on what happens at the public meeting are likely to lose, too—unless they are totally unopposed. The public hearing is the end of the process. Leaving their participation to this point often means it comes too late. The sight of disgusted citizens shaking their heads as they leave a meeting is all too common. They are disappointed to have lost, but they may well have been naive (or idealistic), assuming that decisions really are made at meetings. To assure their influence, groups must find ways of taking part before the public hearing—or risk losing.

Lobbying

The expression *to lobby* comes from the activity of group representatives in the lobbies of legislatures, including those of the local government. You can see it happen in the corridors of city halls before meetings. But, more often, **lobbying** is done in private meetings between group representatives and decision makers. Designated group members meet with the decision makers in their offices and talk about issues that are coming up. Sometimes they invite a decision maker to come to a meeting of the group, a good way to show numerical strength as well as concern about the issue.

Such lobbying focuses on the merits of the issue, with groups presenting factual arguments. Political threats (withdrawing support in coming elections, for example) can easily backfire, so groups generally avoid making them explicit. Besides, politicians are shrewd enough to figure out when they risk alienating groups—taking into account both how strongly a group seems to feel about a particular issue and the alternatives available to the group. As with the public hearing tactic, able groups carefully choose their delegations to lobby decision makers. They also tailor their arguments to suit the person they are lobbying and often provide the decision maker with a succinct written summary of the group's arguments.

In most cases, interest group lobbying is done by the leader and group members, but in large cities lobbying is increasingly done by professionals who are hired to speak for a particular cause. These lobbyists are often former elected officials or city staffers who know the inner workings of their local government intimately and have ready access to decision makers. Some are campaign consultants who support themselves in between elections as lobbyists. Others are public relations experts or just individuals with skills in persuasion and contacts in city hall. Also known as "contract lobbyists" or even "guns-for-hire," these professionals are employed by clients to present their case. The clients are usually development or other business interests; few grassroots groups can afford their services. With the increase in professional representation, some cities have introduced requirements for registration and reporting of activities of such lobbyists.

Schmoozing

Groups also gain influence through social contacts between their leaders and decision makers. Such **schmoozing** happens before and after meetings, over coffee or drinks, and at community and political events such as fundraisers attended by both officials and group leaders. It also happens when paths cross, which they often do. Most communities have a bar or restaurant frequented by political insiders, including elected officials, administrators, and group representatives. These insiders also frequent community institutions such as the symphony or sports teams.

Group representatives knowingly exploit these opportunities, although they do not necessarily engage in explicit persuasion. Schmoozing mostly enables them to show knowledgeable sympathy with the decision makers and to keep relations friendly, even if they disagree on issues. Sometimes, schmoozing shortcuts the process of influence. A group representative might point out that an issue is coming up soon and ask if the decision maker has any problems with it or if they need to meet with the group. The decision maker will indicate agreement or difficulty, and the lobbyist can decide whether to shift into a higher gear (but probably not where the schmoozing is in progress).

Campaigns

Groups prime their contacts by supporting sympathetic candidates in **election campaigns**. Financial contributions are a key element of campaign support, but groups also endorse and provide volunteers for candidates. Endorsement is usually done by a committee, based on knowledge about the candidate or, often, on questionnaires and interviews. Group **endorsements** are much valued by candidates desperate for support from any quarter—especially in nonpartisan elections. Endorsements usually mean money and volunteers, but they also legitimize candidates and are often used in campaign literature. Volunteers help get the word out and cut the costs of campaigns, so groups such as labor unions[6] and minority or feminist organizations that can turn out their members may compensate for their lack of money (although all these groups also raise funds for their chosen candidates). Giving money nevertheless remains the major campaign tactic of interest groups and as the costs of local campaigns have risen, so has the influence of group contributors. In small communities, however, money doesn't count for quite so much.

Some groups—notably neighborhood and homeowner associations and reform groups such as the League of Women Voters—avoid campaign activity, remaining strictly impartial. Often, however, individual members of such groups will support candidates, thus assuring access while preserving the group's neutrality.

Direct Participation

Most local governments have numerous boards and **commissions** made up of citizens who advise them on various issues and sometimes even make final decisions. Some of these **citizen participation** mechanisms date back to the Progressive reform movement and more were established during the 1960s and 1970s to counteract the power of bureaucracies, often in response to group pressure. Some, such as planning, transportation, human rights, or senior citizens commissions, are relatively permanent; others, such as a committee to review a city's general plan or a task force on gangs, might be temporary working groups. Some cities, including Birmingham, Dayton, Los Angeles, New York, Portland, and Saint Paul, have district boards or councils to advise on neighborhood issues. Although a few of these are elected positions, most are appointed by city councils or county boards.

Naturally, interested groups lobby hard and compete vigorously with one another to get one of their members appointed to citizen participation bodies that deal with their concerns. Various neighborhoods, environmental groups, business interests, and labor unions might vie for a seat on the planning commission, for example, while groups representing homosexuals, women, business, or different neighborhoods and minorities might contend for a place on the police commission. The winners assume a more formal role in making decisions that affect them as well as increase their credibility and their access to other decision makers and to information.

A few groups get even more involved by contracting with local governments for the coproduction of particular services, such as running a community center or a homeless shelter. Chambers of commerce sometimes operate convention or tourist bureaus for cities in this way.

Public Relations, Direct Democracy, and Litigation

Besides all these sorts of insider tactics, groups sometimes resort to other means, including public relations, direct democracy, litigation, and protest politics. All of these, however, are riskier, more difficult, and costlier, in dollars or in public sympathy.

Public relations involves going over the heads of the decision makers and trying to win public support for the group's case. Ads in newspapers or on television, mailings, and public meetings might be used. Press releases and staged events can gain free news coverage. If all else fails, most newspapers assiduously publish letters to the editor. Groups also try to lobby the editorial boards of newspapers to win their endorsement. The public relations tactic is rarely used, however, because it is so difficult both to win public sympathy and motivate action (letter writing or attending public hearings). Besides, decision makers don't like it when groups by-pass them and go directly to the people.

In many states and communities, the Progressive reformers gave voters a direct say in their governance through the devices of the initiative, referendum, and recall. Actually, voters rarely take any of these actions spontaneously. Most of the time, the tools of **direct democracy** are used by interest groups with the organization, skills, and money to conduct sometimes-rigorous petition drives and the expensive election campaigns that follow. Growth is the issue that is most commonly dealt with through direct democracy, as environmental and neighborhood groups campaign for controls on growth that they cannot persuade elected officials to impose. In general, interest groups prefer the easier, insider techniques discussed earlier, but direct democracy offers them one more option that they have proven adept at using.

Similarly, groups litigate, or take issues to court, when they can and when they must. Failing to get their way by other means, groups may raise issues about the legality of a governmental action. Were all required procedures followed? Could state or federal law supersede a local decision? A court case could, at best, reverse the action. But astute groups know that legal action may usefully delay implementation of a policy. Even the threat of **litigation**—with all its delays and expenses—may be enough to win compromises useful to the group.

Protest

A less socially accepted, though still common, means of exercising group influence is through **protest** actions such as demonstrations, marches, rallies, sit-ins, and strikes. Such actions may be about anything from dangerous crosswalks and closure of popular public facilities to police practices, abortion, or civil rights. Protest sometimes escalates to civil disobedience, which entails the intentional violation of a law with the expectation of arrest. Such actions may be taken because the law itself is held to be bad (segregation, for example), to show intensity of feeling (parading without a permit), or to prevent an event (blockading abortion clinics). At its most extreme, protest may involve violence. Abortion clinics have been attacked, for example, and some community activists and political leaders emphasize the political significance of urban riots in the 1960s by describing them as uprisings. Most practitioners of protest politics condemn such violence, however.

As the distinction between a riot and an uprising suggests, protest is not always an effective group tactic because the message and its targets may be unclear even when the protests are peaceful and lawful. Also, protests often express general discontent rather than focusing on specific policy goals on which officials can take action. Decision makers may feel threatened by the protesters, who may be aiming more at public opinion anyway. Even then, their message may be unclear because the organizers can't control the way their message is filtered by the media, which may focus on the most bombastic speakers rather than the real leaders, or which may present the protest in a negative way to an already suspicious or hostile public.

Despite the role protest has played in U.S. history since before the Boston Tea Party, it has never been accepted in mainstream politics. Protest is an outsiders' tactic and often the last resort of groups that have no alternative. It may be ineffective because of its ambiguity and public hostility, but it can also be effective, at least over the long run. The civil rights movement is the best example of successful, long-term protest, but not the only one. Saul Alinsky, the renowned community organizer, was a flamboyant advocate of protest politics, not least because such events can be fun and can help build essential solidarity in a group, a result he thought as important as any policy outcome.[7] Despite its drawbacks, contemporary groups in many cities continue to rely on protest as a tactic. Advocates for the homeless, for example, have put up "tent cities" outside many city halls, successfully attracting the attention of both the media and local officials. And the local chapters of ACORN, the most prominent nationwide effort in community organizing today, often rely on what they call "direct action" (meaning protest politics), along with more traditional group tactics like lobbying, packing public meetings, and participating in campaigns.[8]

The Targets of Group Influence

Interest groups try to influence whoever makes decisions that affect them. The primary **targets of group influence** are formal decision makers such as mayors and city councils, but discerning groups are well aware of alternative and supplementary targets. In addition to elected officials, groups try to influence aides, administrators, and appropriate commissions and committees. Outside city hall, their targets may include other groups, the media, the public, and powerful individuals.

Inside City Hall: Staff, the Bureaucracy, Commissions, and Committees

In large cities, mayors and, increasingly, council members, hire their own personal staffs to assist them. Groups soon learn that these aides have an important influence over their bosses and court them assiduously. Bureaucrats are also prime targets, although they are often and wrongly thought to be beyond group influence. Some group tactics are not applicable to them, but appointed administrators such as city managers and department heads may be as much politicians as elected officials are. Civil servants, secure in their jobs, are even less susceptible but are still subject to influence. Bribery is possible, though increasingly rare. More often, groups try to win the sympathy of administrators by persuasion, playing on the expertise of the administrators with their own expertise. Many groups also manage to find sympathizers inside the bureaucracy who help them with both tactical and factual information.

Groups also target commissions and committees. Dozens of these citizen-participation bodies operate in most local governments, advising elected officials on a wide range of issues. Groups may pave the way to victory when the issue reaches these elected officials by winning the support of the commissions and committees (as well as appropriate administrators) early in the process. Tactics for influencing these bodies include public hearings, lobbying, and schmoozing. As previously noted, groups also try to get their members appointed to commissions that concern them (builders on the planning commission or public employee unions on the civil service commission, for example).

Some groups, especially those representing economic interests, also hire former elected officials, aides, administrators, and commissioners to represent them. The **revolving door** between city hall and interest groups has resulted in what political scientist Peter Lupsha calls a mediator/consultant class, providing access to developers and corporations and "linking" them to elected officials.[9] Fearing payoffs and conflicts of interest, some local governments have tried to inhibit this phenomenon by prohibiting, for a fixed period of time, ex-officials from working for groups whose interests they formerly decided on.

Outside City Hall: Other Groups, the Media, the Public, and Powerful Individuals

The broader the support for an issue, the more likely it is to win approval, so groups often court one another to win endorsements for causes or active participation. Sometimes one group (a labor union or the chamber of commerce) will have better access to particular decision makers than others, so alliance also increases lobbying and schmoozing opportunities. The most ubiquitous **coalitions** in local politics are the growth machine (landowners, developers, and related businesses) and the opposing antigrowth coalition (environmentalists and neighborhood groups). In big cities, minority groups have formed coalitions with one another and with liberals and sometimes with Jewish voters to elect African American and Latino mayors.[10] Multiracial coalitions composed of minority, feminist, neighborhood, and labor groups came together in many cities to support district elections for city council members, although once district elections were achieved the citywide coalitions dissolved—a common fate for coalitions that form around one shared interest.[11] More recently, ACORN and labor and faith-based organizations have joined to advocate a "living wage" for employees of companies contracting with cities by requiring pay higher than the federal minimum wage. Such coalitions have succeeded in winning living wage policies in over 100 cities as well as demonstrating what grassroots organizations can do when they join toether.[12] Where a coalition cannot be created, one group may lobby others to neutralize their opposition by making a proposal seem less threatening or even by tactful compromise.

The support of the local media, public opinion, and powerful individuals may also help. Reporters and editors can be schmoozed and lobbied, encouraging positive news coverage and sympathetic editorials. Visual events can be staged and timed for television. Sound bites can be called in to radio stations. Media coverage gives an issue urgency, makes the group and its cause more credible to decision makers, and may also win public support. Such support is usually a mushy source of group clout at best, but sometimes groups need public opinion behind them to push decision makers to act. Public relations or protest tactics may be used, or sympathetic media coverage may be sought. The problem, as previously noted, is that even a sympathetic public is hard to move to action. Lastly, groups try to win support from powerful individuals in their communities, outside as well as inside government, including business, religious, and social leaders. These individuals have direct access to decision makers and sometimes enough clout to resolve an issue with a phone call.

Allies, whether other groups, the media, the public, or powerful individuals, help interest groups achieve their short-term goals and integrate them with the larger community, making them players in its decisions and assuring their long-term interests. Mayors, council members, and other elected officials will always be the primary targets of interest groups, but we should be aware of these others as well—successful interest groups certainly are.

Patterns in Group Politics

All groups are not equal and all tactics are not equally effective. Nor is the activity of interest groups identical in all communities. Particular groups or tactics may succeed in some communities but not in others, and while some communities are fraught by group politics, others are almost free of group activity. Still, despite wide variation, some **patterns in group politics** can be discerned.

> **IN YOUR COMMUNITY**
> Interview leaders of interest groups such as the chamber of commerce, labor council, realtors association, or others. You can find them at council meetings or on the Internet. What local policies affect the groups? What are their resources and tactics? What sorts of groups do they say are most active and successful in your community?

Variation Among Communities

Better-off and better-educated people are more likely to belong to interest groups. They are more likely to know how local politics affects them because of their education and access to information and because they possess the resources to participate, including time and money for dues and baby-sitters. In any community, they are the most active participants and, in any community, those who are active are most likely to get what they want. Decision makers safely ignore the unorganized and inactive.

This notion applies to communities as well. Those with greater **social capital** (defined as "connections among individuals")[13] manifest greater civic engagement, from voter participation to activity in community organizations and interest groups. Better-educated and more affluent individuals tend to have higher levels of social capital, as do communities of such individuals. As previously discussed in chapter 9, Robert Putnam asserts that social capital is "easier to foster within homogeneous communities"[14] because people more readily trust and associate with others like themselves. Thus, according to Dora L. Costa and Matthew E. Kahn, "homogeneity increases civic engagement" while "civic engagement is lower in more-heterogeneous communities."[15] With higher social capital and greater civic engagement, it follows that citizen involvement with interest groups would be greater in small and middle-sized, homogeneous communities—usually suburbs—rather than big, diverse central cities.

Paul Peterson, on the other hand, argues that "local politics is groupless politics," with organized groups having only a "marginal impact," especially in "nonpartisan suburbia."[16] Although the better off and better educated are more likely group activists, this does not always predict the pattern of group activity among communities. Places populated predominantly by the affluent and well educated sometimes have low levels of group activity because of a lack of competition and a high degree of consensus. Communities with more varied class and ethnic interests—large, diverse cities—sometimes have considerably more vital group activity, for even though the poor and minorities are less likely to organize than the affluent and well educated, they sometimes do so, and faced with competition, those normally likely to organize assuredly do.

Like so much else in local politics, group activity in a community reflects its demographic, social, and economic makeup. More people may be involved to a greater degree in homogeneous communities but the range of activities is narrower and the groups themselves are less diverse. Larger, dense, diverse cities often have more group activity than smaller, less dense, homogeneous communities. Density—sheer proximity—makes organizing easier and may also create problems that precipitate organization, such as traffic congestion or poor sanitation. Diversity, which is closely related to population size, is an even greater factor in group formation, providing a variety of sources of organization ranging from class and occupation to race, ethnicity, sexual orientation, and life-style. What's more, when one interest in a diverse community organizes, others follow, either to protect their interests or to pursue their piece of the pie. Group organizing has a proliferating or snowball effect. Stable communities (those where people stay put for a long time) also have more group activity, simply because people have to live in a place for a while before they begin to perceive how local politics affects them and to make connections with others with shared interests. Since all these characteristics are strongest in Frostbelt cities, group activity there tends to be greater than in their Sunbelt counterparts.

That said, membership in interest groups—as in virtually all forms of civic participation—has been in decline all across America for some time. Robert Putnam's book *Bowling Alone* (referring to bowling as individuals with a few friends as opposed to bowling in organized leagues) chronicles this decline in organizational membership. Looking at surveys from the 1970s to the 1990s, Putnam wrote that "Year after year, fewer and fewer of us took part in the everyday deliberations that constitute grassroots democracy," from attending meetings to belonging to interest groups. "In effect," he continues, "more than a third of America's civic infrastructure simply evaporated between the mid-1970s and the mid-1990s."[17] The exception to this is faith-based organizations (such as churches) and mass-membership organizations that require little activity beyond paying dues once a year. Labor unions, parent-teacher organizations (PTAs), racial and ethnic organizations, reform groups like the League of Women Voters, and others have all seen consistent decline in both membership and participation over the past few decades. The causes of this decline are many, including greater population mobility (we move around more), television (we stay home more), and the pressures of time and money (we work harder).[18]

But while declining participation is the national trend, it doesn't apply to all communities, whether large or small. Civic activity in many American communities is still vibrant, with a proliferation of lively and engaged groups. Most veteran observers of local politics in your community and others will tell you that national studies notwithstanding, they see more groups at council meetings than they did thirty years ago. City politics still engages people and if, overall, fewer are involved, those who do put in the time and energy to participate are only further empowered.

Winners and Losers

Within these patterns of group politics in communities, some groups are consistently winners, confident and successful in obtaining their goals, while others feel frustrated and marginalized, consistently losing. **Political resources** and their skillful use determine a group's success. Such resources include leadership, organization, number of members, status (the esteem in which both individual members and the group itself are held in the community), contacts (in and out of local government), information, and, of course, money. The greater and more diverse the resources of the group, the more tactics they can apply. Such tactics as public relations, direct democracy, campaign contributions, or litigation are not available to most grassroots groups, for example.

Of all these group resources, money is the most important because it can buy the others and because it widens the range of tactics available. Money also gives a group staying power, the ability to persist over a long period of time. While some groups fade away as soon as their issue is resolved, persistent groups are able to protect their victories or outlast their opposition when they lose. For these reasons, economic groups, from chambers of commerce to small business associations and big corporations, are most successful. They have greater financial resources and social respectability than other groups, so they can build access and maintain it more easily. And because they are founded on the fundamental human motivation of greed (their primary goal is to make money), they are persistent. The membership of grassroots organizations, such as neighborhood, minority, or environmental groups, may outnumber that of economic groups, but the shared interests that glue these groups together are almost never as strong or as lasting as those of business. The fact that their interests overlap those of the local government gives business groups an added advantage. Local governments gain additional taxes from growth and business expansion, so all these interests have to do is show that their proposals add to the local economy and thus the tax base. No wonder the growth machine and other economic interests are so successful in local politics.

Groups, Communities, and Power

Interest group activity, like so much else we have considered in local politics, both reflects and influences communities. The pattern of group activity in a particular community reflects its very nature, while at the same time the activity of groups shapes the community, especially when they successfully promote growth. As we have seen, some groups are more powerful than others. In the next chapter, we will consider power in communities more generally.

Essential Terms

interest groups
business group
chamber of commerce
labor groups
labor council
neighborhood or homeowner groups
NIMBY
LULUs
Common Interest Developments (CIDs)
coproduction
minority groups
environmental groups
civic associations
women's groups
reform groups
taxpayer associations
tactics
group maintenance

public hearings
packing the chambers
lobbying
schmoozing
election campaigns
endorsements
commissions
citizen participation
public relations
direct democracy
litigation
protest
targets of group influence
revolving door
coalitions
patterns in group politics
social capital
political resources

On the Internet

- Google the names of interest groups in your own community. You'll find that lots of them have websites; one example is the ACORN website, at www.acorn.org.
- Try Googling Chamber of Commerce, a labor union, a minority group, or a neighborhood association. Many national organizations, such as the NAACP or League of Women Voters, have local chapters, usually with their own websites.

Notes

1. Mike Davis, *City of Quartz: Excavating the Future in Los Angeles* (New York: Vintage Books, 1992), p. 161.

2. See Matthew A. Crenson, *Neighborhood Politics* (Cambridge, MA: Harvard University Press, 1983); and Jeffrey M. Berry, Kent E. Portney, Ken Thomson, *The Rebirth of Urban Democracy* (Washington, DC: Brookings Institute, 1993).

3. www.acorn.org (accessed July 15, 2005).

4. Davis, *City of Quartz*, p. 210.

5. See Joyce Gelb and Marilyn Gittell, "Seeking Equality: The Role of Activist Women in Cities," in *The Egalitarian City: Issues of Rights, Distribution, Access, and Power*, ed. Janet K. Boles (New York: Praeger, 1986), pp. 93–109; and Janet A. Flammang, *Women's Political Voice: How Women Are Transforming the Practice and Study of Politics* (Philadelphia: Temple University Press, 1997).

6. See for example Barbara Byrd and Nari Rhee, "Building Power in the New Economy: The South Bay Labor Council," *Working USA* 8, no. 2 (Winter 2004): 131–53.

7. See Saul D. Alinsky, *Rules for Radicals: A Practical Primer for Realistic Radicals* (New York: Random House, 1972).

8. www.acorn.org (accessed July 15, 2005).

9. Peter Lupsha, "Structural Change and Innovation: Elites and Albuquerque Politics in the 1980s," in *The Politics of Urban Development*, ed. Clarence N. Stone and Heywood T. Sanders (Lawrence, KS: University Press of Kansas, 1987), p. 236.

10. See Rufus P. Browning, Dale Rogers Marshall, and David H. Tabb, eds., *Racial Politics in American Cities*, 3rd ed. (New York: Longman, 2003).

11. Ibid., p. 25.

12. Ibid., p. 384. See also www.livingwageresearch.org/factsheets/adopted.asp and www.epionline.org (accessed July 16, 2005).

13. Robert D. Putnam, *Bowling Alone: The Collapse and Revival of American Community* (New York: Simon and Schuster, 2000), p. 20. See also Sidney Verba, Kay Lehman Schlozman, and Henry E. Brady, *Voice and Equality: Civic Voluntarism in American Politics* (Cambridge, MA: Harvard University Press, 1995).

14. Putnam, *Bowling Alone*, p. 400.

15. Dora L. Costa and Matthew E. Kahn, "Civic Engagement and Community Heterogeneity: An Economist's Perspective," *Perspectives on Politics* 1, no. 1 (March 2003): p. 108. See also Rodney E. Hero, "Social Capital and Racial Inequality in America," *Perspectives on Politics* 1, no. 1 (March 2003): 113–22.

16. Paul E. Peterson, *City Limits* (Chicago: University of Chicago Press, 1981), pp. 116, 118.

17. Putnam, *Bowling Alone*, p. 43.

18. Ibid., p. 283.

11 Community Power Structures
Official and Unofficial Decision Makers

Who's really running your city? Ask around and you'll get different answers. Some will say the mayor and council or city manager—the obvious answer and the correct one if democracy is functioning well. Others will point to behind-the-scenes powers, perhaps major developers or landowners, or corporate leaders who they think pull the strings that control local government. The assumption behind the question of who's running the city is that it isn't necessarily the obvious officeholders who wield power—it could be others, inside or outside of government.

Power is the ability to make something happen—or to stop it from happening. Power is an element of politics that has come up in almost every chapter in this book, from the formation of local governments to their structures and the roles of voters and interest groups. As we have seen, many struggles within local politics are as much about who will exercise power as they are about what will be done with it. At this point, we need to pull back from studying particular elements of community politics to look briefly at their relative influence in terms of power.

The arrangement of power within a community is called a **power structure**. This differs from the structure of government in that all power is not held by the public officials. Interest groups, for example, play a part not only in decisions about policy but also, through their involvement in campaigns and elections, in choosing who makes those decisions. Even the formal structures of local government that allocate power have been fought over by those outside of government who are affected, from the municipal reformers to minority groups and pro-growth and antigrowth coalitions. These formal structures of government reflect informal local power structures, with unelected leaders or interest groups seeking to shape the official structures of power to their lasting advantage. The most powerful (and able) elements win, shoring up their informal power with formal, or official, power. Once a set of governmental structures is in place, it is frozen for years, even decades. But these structures are almost inevitably challenged when the informal balance of power within the community shifts. As new forces emerge, seek influence, and face frustration, they conclude that they must contest the formal structure of power, demanding changes that will enable them to advance their own causes. The battle over district and at-large elections, from reform to counterreform, is a case in point. But the forces of change could never succeed in altering the formal structures of government if they had not already taken their place in the informal power structure.

Power, then, operates both inside and outside government. Most of us know intuitively that some people and interests have more power than others. Which are most powerful in our own communities? Are there patterns among communities? Social scientists have addressed and argued over these questions for decades, and while their conclusions are far from final, they offer rich insights. Their theories and findings are not merely of esoteric, academic interest, however. Citizens also need to know who really rules their communities. We need to know not only in order to understand local politics, but also to participate, since knowing who holds power will shape our tactics and strategy. The study of community power gives us clues.

The Phenomenon of Power

Although defining power is easy enough, studying it is not, for power is complicated and multidimensional. Consider, for example, the varied sources of power. One might be physical strength, including muscle, guns, and armies. But official positions like those of monarchs and mayors are also a source of power, as are money, prestige, command of information, and personal charisma. A related but distinct dimension of power is the means by which it is exercised. Brute force—the power of a mugger— is the most obvious such means. **Authority** might be seen as institutionalized force. It is the ability of those in an official position of power (such as a parent, teacher, police officer, or city council) to order us to do something and penalize us if we refuse or if we do something they have prohibited.

A more subtle means of exercising power than force or authority is **influence**. It means you do what others want you to do not because they make you do it but because you respect or fear them enough to comply. Influence is partly the result of socialization, the process by which families, schools, and the media teach us the basic values and acceptable behaviors of our society. Among the ideas communicated are who has power and who should be respected and obeyed. Socialization is most effective when it teaches us to anticipate the responses of those in power so we act as they would wish without being asked or ordered. Related to the means of exercising power, and particularly to the accumulation of power, are two additional dimensions, scope and cost. Each of us has some power, although some have more than others. Those with the most power may influence a wide range of issues (scope) at little cost to themselves. Only a word, a gesture, a signature on a check may be necessary. Those with little power may influence a narrow range of issues, perhaps concerning their neighborhood or job, at greater sacrifice (in time, money, energy, and so on) to themselves.

With varying sources, means, scope, and cost, power is clearly a multidimensional phenomenon, and thus is hard to study. Although researchers agree that patterns in the exercise of power emerge, forming a power structure, no one has yet invented an infallible method to measure it. There is no machine, like those that take our blood pressure, that can be hooked up to an individual or institution to gauge their power. Social scientists have developed plenty of theories about power, explaining how it works and predicting patterns. But the next step is to develop methods to test these theories by scientifically collecting factual data. If the method is objective, it will prove or disprove the theory, but methods can be flawed. The wrong questions may be asked or the wrong sources used. The method may even be slanted or biased to prove the theory. Of course, if the method is imperfect, so are the findings. This is especially a problem with a subject as complex and multidimensional as power. No wonder social scientists have argued about it for so long. But we need not resolve the social science dispute about how to study power. For our purposes, reviewing the various approaches lends insight to the workings of power in communities in general as well as in specific communities.

One common element in the study of power has been the focus on individual communities, or case studies. Researchers initially tried to generalize from particular communities to the universe of communities but later came to see that power structures varied from community to community and even in one community over time. Thanks to hundreds of studies of single communities, we can now make some generalizations and even predictions about patterns of power in communities. But in addition to increasing our understanding of local politics and power in general, power studies help the residents of our communities understand their own local political systems by revealing who holds power, whether inside or outside government.

The Evolving Study of Community Power

For a long time, political scientists mainly studied the formal structures of government and tended to overlook the forces that shaped and influenced those structures. In terms of the multidimensional nature of power, traditional political scientists concentrated on authority rather than the other, more subtle manifestations of power. This focus began shifting when Marxist and other theorists on the left asserted that power was found in the class structure and that government was only a tool of the dominant classes. Then, when some political machines survived or adapted to reform, social scientists (many of whom were active reformers) learned that changing the structure of government does not necessarily change the distribution of power in a community. Later, systems theory gave social scientists the impetus to examine power in a broader sense. **Systems theory** is based on the idea of a political system as an organism with interdependent parts interacting within a larger environment. Governmental structure is only one part of the system, acted upon and in turn acting upon the society in which it functions. By opening the door for the inclusion of virtually anything that affected political decisions, systems theory took political scientists considerably beyond government structure. At about the same time, behavioralism—the study of how and why people behave as they do—also encouraged social scientists to examine politics outside of government.

Elitism

The first studies of community power were done by sociologists applying what came to be called **stratification theory**, the idea that societies are stratified into layers or classes and that these strata are distinguished by such characteristics as wealth, prestige, and power. Since these resources are not distributed equally, some have more than others. Early researchers, most notably Robert and Helen Lynd, who did pioneering studies of Muncie, Indiana, in the 1920s and 1930s,[1] found that stratification did reflect the power structures of their subject communities. The upper class had a virtual monopoly on prestige and money and, with these, ruled the community. Those with economic power controlled political officeholders, and the public was passive. The elite, the Lynds wrote, maintained its power through "the persuasiveness of the long fingers of capitalist ownership" and "the thick blubber of custom that envelop[ed] the city's life."[2] Other sociologists soon did similar studies and came up with similar findings.

Then, in 1953, Floyd Hunter's *Community Power Structure*,[3] a study of Atlanta, Georgia, was published. While power and politics had been only one component of the broad studies of community life done by the Lynds and other earlier researchers, Hunter chose to focus exclusively on power. He also tried to develop a rigorous method for researching power—one that could readily be used by others—to replace the subjective interviews and observations of earlier researchers. What came to be called the **reputational method** basically consists of the researcher asking a carefully selected series of local leaders who they think has power, why they have it, and how they use it.[4] Connections are then mapped to reveal the community's power structure.

Based on the power structure he unveiled, Hunter developed a theory that has been labeled **elitism**. Shaped like a pyramid, Atlanta's power structure was topped by a small group of businessmen, an elite upper class. Dominating the city's economy through a web of interlocking directorships, they lived in the same neighborhoods and belonged to the same exclusive clubs. According to the study, only four of Atlanta's forty most powerful people were public officials; the rest were bankers, manufacturers, and other business leaders. The members of the elite rarely held office and were not visible to the general public. Their power operated informally, with elected officials carrying out their bidding. Hunter and the sociologists who preceded him were pointing to a layer of power that had been ignored by other academics, particularly political scientists.

Pluralism

Political scientists soon came up with an alternative approach and theory. Alarmed that the subjects of their study—politicians and elected officials—were relegated to a secondary role by the sociological studies of power, political scientists criticized both Hunter's elite theory of power and his research method. Hunter's elite theory, his critics asserted, became a self-fulfilling prophecy when he asked respondents to name the most powerful people in their communities. They labeled Hunter's method "reputational" because in their view he relied too much on reputations for power rather than proof of its actual exercise.[5] But while these charges have some merit, they oversimplify Hunter's method and overlook the fact that reputation is itself a political resource and may be the best indicator of the more subtle manifestations of power.

Not content with denouncing Hunter, the critics went on to develop an alternative method and theory. Robert Dahl and a group of fellow political scientists at Yale argued that nothing could be assumed about the distribution of power and that it should be studied by examining specific decisions on specific issues. Their **decisional method** of research relied on interviews, observation, and documentary evidence to discern who influenced decisions on selected controversial or key issues. If an elite ruled, the Yale researchers insisted, their preferences would consistently prevail.

Robert Dahl reported their 1958 research on New Haven, Connecticut, in his book *Who Governs*,[6] concluding that no power elite ruled New Haven. Rather, Dahl reported, power was widely distributed. Economic leaders were only one active group among many, and they were not particularly active at that. Dahl also found that the holders of power varied over time and from issue to issue. No single group dominated in all issue areas. In fact, different groups and individuals were active in different issue areas. The only common figures were the mayor and the appropriate bureaucracy for each issue, not the elite. Dahl recognized that some individuals and groups had more power than others and that business leaders had great potential power, but he argued that much of that power was unused. His theory came to be called **pluralism**, reflecting the idea of multiple points of power specialized by policy area.

Thus, political scientists produced a theory about power, a method for studying it, and a set of findings that differed substantially from those of sociologists. Where elitists saw power as centralized, pluralists saw it as diffused. Where elitists believed power was based on class structure, pluralists believed it was centered on the formal political structure. Where elitists studied power through opinion, pluralists studied it through behavior.

Naturally, the elitists defended themselves and attacked the pluralists and their methods. The pluralists selected the wrong decisions, their antagonists argued, choosing controversial issues that are the exception to the rule rather than decisions that are taken without public notice. The elite is most powerful, they insisted, not all powerful. The elite has more power than others in a community, but others have some, too. Sometimes, therefore, elites are challenged and they may even lose— usually on precisely the sorts of controversial issues that the pluralists chose to study. Furthermore, the elitists argued, focusing on observable events and behavior provided only a simplistic and superficial view of the complicated exercise of power. The influence of the elite is not always readily observable because it operates behind the scenes or through anticipated reactions (when others do what they think the elite might want without being told). Furthermore, the decisional method did not take into account what elitists call **nondecisions**, whereby issues are kept off the public agenda entirely because of the anticipated reaction of elites (or sometimes voters). Particularly in communities with a single dominant industry or group of industries, local decision makers may anticipate the reactions of these interests and so avoid decisions that would offend them.[7] Matthew Crenson's study of Gary, Indiana, for example, illustrates how local officials failed to confront the problem of air pollution out of fear of that city's main employer, the steel industry.[8]

The pluralists defended themselves against these charges, saying the elitists' views were based on self-deception and ideological bias. Dahl felt his critics were saying that if the overt rulers were not members of the economic elite, then researchers had to dig deeper to find the covert economic rulers, the true elite. But how, Dahl asked, could researchers study things that could not be studied—unconscious actions, anticipated reactions, and nondecisions?[9] Proponents of elite theory scoffed at the naive superficiality of the pluralists' studies; pluralists dismissed elitism as something akin to conspiracy theory and even paranoia. Researchers on both sides presented empirical proof of their theories but the reputational or decisional methods they used were criticized and rejected by their opponents.

Synthesis

Eventually, the two schools of thought appeared to be in stalemate, even as they both broadened our understanding of power. The elitists alerted us to the less visible holders of power and its subtle exercise through informal consultation, anticipation, and socialization. The pluralists shifted the focus to overt behaviors, insisting on the need to study specific actions. This insistence stimulated both adherents and antagonists of elite theory to be more explicit about how actual decisions were made. The pluralists also alerted us to the possibility of power varying over time and from issue to issue. Their discussion of **inertia**, or unused resources (power held but not applied), helped explain why the upper class was sometimes not visibly active as well as why the general public often loses in a system that is ostensibly democratic.

But an irreconcilable gap remained between the two theories and the research methods associated with them. Hundreds of communities have been studied by elitists or pluralists or both, with their findings varying according to the approach they chose. Increasingly, researchers tried to combine the reputational and decisional methods, reaching toward synthesis, concluding that each method unveiled a slightly different set of influentials.[10] The reputational technique discovered the concealed leaders, while the decisional method identified the nominal decision makers, although there was substantial overlap in the names on the lists.

IN YOUR COMMUNITY
Do an informal power study by asking people at a city council or other public meeting who the most powerful individuals or organizations in your community are. (Bear in mind that where you ask the questions, as well as who you ask, may bias your survey.)

The achievement of synthesis, however, was limited by another aspect of community power studies: for practical reasons, most focused on just one community. Such case studies are instructive, but are they applicable to more than the community in question? Can researchers generalize and develop theories that pertain to a wide range of communities? The best way would be for a single research project to study many communities, but this has never been feasible, even if agreement could be reached on methodology.

Instead, scholars of community power have reached a sort of compromise by accepting that all communities may not have identical power structures and that power may vary from community to community. Perhaps Hunter's Atlanta really was elit-

Figure 11.1 **A Continuum of Power**

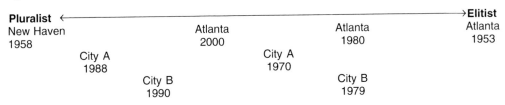

ist, and Dahl's New Haven really was pluralist (both studies are, after all, convincing). Other cities—as other studies have told us—might be more or less elitist or pluralist or somewhere in between. One might conceive of a **continuum of power**, then, at one end of which is a typical pluralist power structure and at the other a typical elitist power structure (see Figure 11.1). Communities might be placed at any point on the continuum (at either end, in the middle, or slightly closer to one end than the other), depending on the shape of each one's particular power structure. They might also move across the continuum over time, perhaps becoming more pluralist (as some people think Atlanta has since Hunter's original study). Various social scientists have generated such continua, sometimes with four or five different types or categories of power structures.[11]

The concept of a continuum is useful because it enables us to generalize broadly about power and communities and to include many theories and findings. We should bear in mind, however, that such generalizations may be simplistic, and that those who subscribe to traditional elite theory would be skeptical because the continuum tends to accept pluralist assertions that power varies in structure, over time, and between communities. Elitists insist that the only thing that varies is the composition of the upper class.

Explaining Variation in Community Power Structures

If we accept the idea of **variation in power structures** from community to community and/or over time, we are still left with the questions of why one community may be relatively pluralistic while another tends to be elitist or why a community grows more or less pluralistic over time. Past studies of communities and a measure of common sense provide some answers. Various researchers have developed the generalizations that follow,[12] but we should remember that they point out tendencies that are not necessarily universal truths.

Size and Diversity

Size seems to be a major determinant of a city's power structure. Larger cities are more likely to have pluralistic power structures, not so much due to size per se but because largeness is associated with an increased potential for competition and conflict among varied groups. Smaller cities are less diverse and more easily dominated by a single major economic force. As cities grow, they diversify. The class structure grows more complex, the ethnic composition of the city becomes more elaborate, and special interest groups emerge. Some cannot be controlled by the dominant elite and may even challenge it, so competition and pluralism increase.

Economic Development

In general, as economic development increases, so does diversity and pluralism. If the community is dominated by a single industry, its power structure reflects this domination, tending to elitism, while economically diversified communities tend to pluralism. As economies develop beyond locally based commerce to include service and industrial sectors, new interests are introduced, bringing competition and greater pluralism. As communities industrialize, workers organize, and unionization may add another challenge to the ruling elite. Communities with strong unions tend toward pluralism, although it should be noted that unions, in general, have grown weaker rather than stronger in recent years.

Another element of the economic structure of communities pertinent to their power structures is **absentee ownership** or management of local industries. Whereas most businesses were once owned and operated by people who live in the communities where the businesses were located, most modern businesses are part of national or international corporations. Their owners are not locals or even individuals, but stockholders who may number in the dozens or millions. These national corporations employ managers and executives to run their branch operations in various communities. Although the top executives of the corporations may be active in local politics in the city that hosts the corporate headquarters, their branch managers are less active in community politics than locally resident owners of local operations. The lives and careers of the executives of absentee-owned corporations are connected not to the community but to the corporation. They will advance by moving on, not staying in the community. Their political involvement will mostly be confined to issues of direct and specific concern to their corporation, such as getting necessary zoning approvals or gleaning goodwill. These executives tend to stay out of many local issues or to confine their political activity to support for the chamber of commerce or other locally based organizations. Home-owned industries, on the other hand, are led by locals. They have stakes in their community that go well beyond zonings and goodwill. They are part of the community and they won't be transferred to Houston or Tokyo next year, so their involvement in local politics is broader and more intense.

Corporate executives have great power when they choose to use it—especially if they threaten to move their operation elsewhere (a threat that lacks credibility coming from a locally owned business)—but because their interests are mainly outside the community, they exercise their power less. This leaves more room in the power structure for other interests, so communities with a high degree of absentee-owned, corporate industries tend to be more pluralistic. Those with predominantly locally owned industries whose owners and executives are more politically active tend to be more elitist.

The Structure of the Local Government

Another set of characteristics that influences a city's location on the continuum of community power is the structure of its government. Cities with a reformed, council-manager form of government and nonpartisan, isolated, at-large elections tend to elitism, while those with an unreformed, mayor-council form of government with partisan, concurrent, district elections tend to pluralism. This may seem counter-intuitive, because reform systems should be more open and democratic and unreformed cities usually had political machines that could be seen as a form of elitism. But reform structures often insulate government from the public. The chief executive is appointed rather than elected, and voter turnout is usually low. Traditional elites easily dominate or control such structures. A pluralistic power structure is more likely where the old-style structures bring higher voter participation and more accountable and diverse elected officials. Strong political parties help, too.

It is important to remember, however, that governmental structures do not appear out of thin air. At some time, somebody decides whether a city should be governed by a city manager or a mayor and how the city council should be elected. When those decisions are made, choices about power, access, and accountability are also made. Government structure thus reflects the community power structure.

The Political Culture

The shared values, traditions, myths, and accepted behaviors of a community consti-tute its **political culture**. These are maintained and passed on by socialization or the inculcation of ideas that affect our behavior. Included among these are such notions as "You can't fight city hall," or "The X family (or corporation) runs this town," or "What's good for business is good for the city." The values of the community affect which people are acceptable as leaders and who the leaders listen to and care about, as well as whether the public is active or passive in community decision making. In most U.S. communities, the people with the most prestige, and so the most power, are successful in business. Politicians and the public react to them with respect and thus give them power.

In pluralistic political cultures, a high value is placed on public participation, while elitist cultures may actively discourage participation. Pluralistic political cultures also accept and even welcome conflict and competition, while more elitist commu-nities suppress them.

> **IN YOUR COMMUNITY**
> Apply the community characteristics (size, diversity, economic development, struc-ture of government, political culture) associated with power structures to your community by doing library research or asking appropriate people. What sort of power structure would the characteristics of your community predict?

Patterns of Power

Every city is unique and every city changes over time. The characteristics of a community shape its power structure and are in turn shaped by that structure. Knowing the characteristics of a community—size, diversity, economic structure—allows us to make some good guesses about its power structure. But these variables also suggest **patterns of power** among cities across the country. This was the next step in the study of community power structures.

Larger cities tend to be more pluralistic, due to diversity and competition. Smaller communities incline to elitism, although this doesn't necessarily mean they are dictatorial or undemocratic. Often, such communities are homogeneous and have a high degree of consensus—agreeing on their leaders and supporting what they do. Dissidence, however, is not welcome.

Sunbelt and Frostbelt

Besides size, a pattern is discernible in the power structures of central cities in the Sunbelt and Frostbelt. Dozens of formal and informal community power studies suggest that power in older Frostbelt cities is more likely to be held by elites, while the newer Sunbelt cities are more pluralistic.[13] In the 1970s and 1980s, for example, elite leaders in the Frostbelt city of Indianapolis, Indiana, rammed through a transit system, a sports stadium, and a consolidated city-county government with no public vote and little consultation. Meanwhile in Sunbelt San Jose, an antigrowth coalition challenged the ruling elite, voters repeatedly rejected proposals for a stadium, and plans for regional government never got beyond the talking stage. This contrast is typical of Frostbelt and Sunbelt cities, but it is not simply a product of geography. It is related to the timing of the maturation of communities, their economic development, and the unique features of Sunbelt cities.

The key element is change: power structures are less entrenched in the Sunbelt because they are still new and in flux. Sunbelt central cities are young. Most were small and dependent on agriculture or oil, with few manufacturing or service industries, just forty years ago. They grew explosively from the 1950s onward, not only because they had a good climate and room to grow, but more significantly because of the expansion of sectors of the economy such as energy, electronics, aerospace, and defense. Federal spending, Sunbelt boosterism, cheap land and energy, low taxes, and nonunion workers helped, too. Frostbelt cities, with higher costs on every count, lost out.

In the 1940s and 1950s—and well into the 1960s—most Sunbelt cities had well-established elitist power structures.[14] These were the boosters who brought growth and, ultimately, their own demise, because growth brought change—new interests and, eventually, new elites. Neighborhood, minority, and environmental groups challenged the old elite, often demanding changes in the (reformed) structures of government or control of growth. But while new grassroots interests gained influence and old elites faded away, new elites also emerged. Many were associated with the new energy, aerospace, electronics, and defense industries—national corporations heavily dependent on federal contracts and lacking local ties. Other new economic leaders emerged as national companies bought out department stores, banks, newspapers, television stations, and industries. These changes meant that much of the decision-making power of these communities, at least in terms of economics, was elsewhere. Old elites declined and grassroots groups gained. The communities became more pluralistic. The new economic interests settled in, however, and began to assert their power. A new, corporate-based elite emerged, but although their potential power was great, they used it less because so many of their interests were beyond the community. The net result was a somewhat more pluralistic distribution of power. Frostbelt central cities, with more locally based economic interests, remained more elitist, although national corporations played their part in these communities as well.

San Jose is a case in point. The local newspaper did power studies in 1979, 1990, and 2000 using an adapted form of the reputational method.[15] The first study reported power shifting away from an old guard elite of local business leaders and developers and toward elected officials and the "new" San Jose. A decade later, as San Jose came to be known as part of Silicon Valley, new corporate leaders were emerging, but elected officials still held nearly half the positions in the city's "top 40." The third study shifted the focus from the city to the region (Silicon Valley). Perhaps predictably, eight of the top ten leaders in that study were associated with high-tech businesses—perhaps a new regime or at least a more elitist power structure. Few names reported as powerful in the first study recurred in subsequent studies, a reflection of rapid population growth and economic change. Older, Frostbelt cities manifested much more consistency in individuals and families in power studies taken over similar periods of time. But as San Jose grew from 625,763 in 1980 to 894,923 in 2000, power shifted from a land- and development-based elite to more diverse leadership, including the CEOs of multinational corporations. The latter, however, took little interest in most issues in local politics. Only when their economic interests were affected did they intervene, leaving most strictly local decisions to elected officials and their constituents. As regime theory (discussed later) points out, however, elected officials remained connected to these business interests out of concern for the economic well-being of the city.

The Movement toward Pluralism

As this Sunbelt/Frostbelt contrast and the San Jose case study suggest, the cumulative effect of the characteristics associated with the shaping of community power structure—especially size, diversity, and economic development, which all increase together—seems to indicate movement in the direction of pluralism, or at least power structures in transition from relative elitism to relative pluralism. Virtually every change in these characteristics broadens participation; and nearly every one is related to growth, which may be the single strongest summarizing factor in altering a city's power structure. The irony is that although it is usually old guard elites that force growth on a community, they sow the seeds of their own destruction by facilitating the development of competing interests. Cities that are shrinking and decaying, however, may also grow more pluralistic because of the departure of economic elites. On the other hand, almost anything the remaining or new businesses want is eagerly granted.

As the foregoing suggests, most changes bring a decline in the power of the elite and most are brought about by forces outside the community. New industries, new immigrants, new organizers—which may precipitate the reactive organizing of previously passive interests—all may challenge elites and, in so doing, push the power structure toward pluralism. Local elites have also been weakened by the federal government and its courts, which have extended the rights and electoral prospects of minorities, while states have regulated and limited the fiscal and land-use power of cities. The increasing autonomy of bureaucracies has eroded elite control, and the organization of minority and neighborhood groups has challenged elite policies on growth, government structure, and other issues.

But how pluralistic have power structures become when so many decisions are out of the control of individual communities? In a global corporate economy, industry locates where it pleases, with little commitment to particular communities. Federal, state, and regional authorities—all of which assert more and more control over local governments—are surely more susceptible to the influence of corporate economic interests than they are to that of communities. Such pluralism as U.S. communities enjoy may be merely the dregs of power.

Regime Theory

Clarence Stone—another political scientist—took the analysis of community power to the next level when he introduced regime theory in his 1989 book on Atlanta, the same city Hunter had studied earlier, and put it in a new perspective.[16] By this time Atlanta's power structure had clearly changed, as African American voters became a majority in the city and elected African American mayors beginning with Maynard Jackson in 1973. Clearly something had changed from the white, upper-class elitist power structure described by Floyd Hunter in 1953.

Stone's **regime theory** combines elements of elitism and pluralism—or economics and politics—suggesting that by the 1980s (and perhaps before), few cities were purely elitist or pluralist. Rather, most were ruled by an informally organized network of elected officials, developers, business interests, community groups, and professional administrators. Stone termed these alliances "regimes." Regime theory recognizes these interactions. The balance of these forces varies from city to city and in any given city over time. In many cities, the **governing regime**'s emphasis will be on growth and economic development. Stone calls these "corporate" or development regimes. Economic interests profit from growth while government gains tax revenues (the growth machine). In contrast, "caretaker" regimes emphasize maintenance of the status quo and even the prevention of change. Still others, termed "progressive" regimes by Stone, may address the concerns of particular minority groups (often as they attain majority status) or of neighborhoods or class groups, perhaps stressing public transit and social services. The middle-class variant of a progressive regime expresses concerns of homeowners and environmentalists and challenges growth.

But in every regime, elected officials and bureaucrats play a part, and business interests play a part as the basis of the community's economic well-being and as a source of support for political leaders. In some, an **electoral coalition** of minority and allied interests or homeowners and environmentalists may win elections, but for success, they will need to come to terms with economic interests and the governing regime. But governing regimes may also be transient; a true governing regime is one that survives from election to election, even as electoral coalitions come and go.

Political scientist John Mollenkopf reminds us that the two "primary interactions" between local officeholders and others in their communities are "first, between the leaders of city government and their political/electoral base; and second, between the leaders of city government and their economic environment."[17] While the relationship between elected officials and their electoral supporters is public, their relationship with economic leaders often is not. Regimes—or at least their economic elements—are "partly hidden," other political scientists have observed. "They thrive on secrecy about the extent of their power and their ability to produce governmental actions that enhance their power and profits."[18]

Regime theory thus has elements of both pluralism (politics, elected officials, and community groups) and elitism (economic interests). Many social scientists see regime theory as the most viable synthesis of past studies and theories. All of the factors previously seen as shaping the relatively pluralist or elitist power structures of communities—size and diversity, economic development, the structures of local government, and political culture—can also help us understand the shaping and reshaping of a community's regime

Perennial Powers in Communities

Critics of community power studies denounce their tendency to **focus on personalities** (naming individuals) rather than on the economic, social, and political institutions and structures that are the source of the individual's power. It's fun to name the names of the powerful, but as students and analysts it's important for us to remember that individuals who hold power usually derive it from their positions in institutions or organizations. The people who are mayor or publisher or CEO or city manager at a given point in time are unlikely to wield so much power when they're no longer in their positions. Bearing that in mind, we can consider a few of the key positions or institutions that consistently rank as powerful in city politics—as demonstrated in hundreds of community power studies.

Perhaps first and foremost are the local "land-based" elites of the growth machine, as described by Harvey Molotch, who "profit through the increasing intensification of land use of the area in which [their] members hold a common interest."[19] They compete for growth and investment with elites in other communities and use government to facilitate growth, usually supported by local businesses and newspapers. Molotch differs from elite theory in his suggestion that the main economic interest of community power holders will be land development. Other economic interests pursue benefits elsewhere, in state or federal tax, trade, or employment policies, for example. But land-based interests must act through local government because decision making about land is delegated to local governments by the states. Hence various economic interests are most active at that level of government that can benefit them most. "Some groups, more than others," observes Clarence Stone, "have strong and immediate incentives to play an active and on-going part in" local politics, and, equally significantly, "some groups, more than others, are valuable to city officials in meeting their governing responsibilities."[20]

IN YOUR COMMUNITY

Listen to the language spoken at a city council or other community meeting. Do you hear echoes of the growth machine? Or the countercoalition? To what extent does economics enter into discussions of local politics in your community?

That said, businesses and industries with no direct interest in land use and growth continue to play a powerful, if more circumscribed, role in local politics. Leaders of chambers of commerce often figure prominently in power studies. The retail and other local businesses they represent have a strong interest in local services and taxes and they also benefit from growth. Major industries and multinational corporations have narrower interests in local politics and are often less active, but the jobs and tax base they provide give them great clout when they choose to exercise it. Usually they intervene only when directly affected, perhaps by zoning or regulatory requirements. But in some urban areas, big business has taken an interest in regional problems such as transportation and the balance between jobs and housing—or growth.

Another common component of any governing regime or community power structure is the media, especially the major local newspaper. Publishers and editors commonly appear on lists of top leaders. Their institutions are also usually part of the growth machine, functioning as boosters and cheerleaders for expansion and big projects like airports, arenas, and stadiums.

Local officials are also a perennial part of community power structures and usually figure prominently in power studies. Mayors almost always rank at the top of the power structure, although this may reflect expectations and potential rather than substantive leadership. Communities in which elected officials dominate a list of the powerful are more pluralistic, but that doesn't mean these leaders aren't responsive to economic interests. Most are sympathetic to growth advocates because economic development is in their interest, too. As Paul Peterson points out, "economic prosperity is necessary for protecting the fiscal [tax] base of local government."[21] This diverts local governments from social programs such as job training or building low-cost housing, although many justify growth on the grounds that it will broaden the tax base and provide potential funding for just such programs. But as with land-use powers, the state structures the fiscal base of local governments, strictly limiting the sort of taxes they can collect. Primary among these is the land-based property tax. No wonder local officials become part of the growth machine. Not only is land use their major power, it is the major way that they can increase their tax base.

The propensity to go for growth is given further impetus by competition from other cities pursuing the same developments. Cities across the country compete with one another for major industrial or governmental projects. Even cities that try to plan growth carefully often make exceptions to their own rules when a local industry threatens to move to a more cooperative venue or when nearby communities recruit developments that might well cause them traffic or other problems without benefiting their tax base. State laws on incorporation and annexation generally encourage such competition. But the competition extends beyond metropolitan areas, states, or even the nation. The globalization of the economy now means that multinational corporations seek cheap labor, low capital costs, and access to larger markets all over the world—putting individual cities at an even greater disadvantage.

Sometimes top-ranking administrators—city managers, CAOs, and others—join the ranks of the most powerful. Indeed, some political scientists believe that the power of the bureaucracy has grown so great that it constitutes a third alternative to the elitist and pluralist theories. With civil service job protection, public employee unions, technical expertise, and the exclusive power of day-to-day implementation of policy, bureaucracies may have attained power independent from both economic leaders and elected officials.[22] Observing Albuquerque, political scientist Peter Lupsha noted that professional public administrators and bureaucrats "seek to provide a voice of moderation, future orientation, and professionalism" opposed to the short-term profit-seeking of the growth machine.[23]

But not all local officials buy into the growth machine. In many communities an antigrowth "**countercoalition**"[24] of neighborhood groups, environmentalists, and sometimes minority organizations emerges to resist growth to bring about what Stone called a progressive regime. Such countercoalitions have had some success in the Sunbelt cities of San Francisco, New Orleans, Denver, and San Diego.[25] Countercoalitions don't always win, however, because the forces aligned against them and the way states structure the conflict are so overwhelming, but sometimes, if only briefly, they prevail or win a compromise. Such coalitions do best in rich, small communities (usually suburbs and often university towns such as Palo Alto and Austin) that can afford to let growth happen elsewhere. Most large cities cannot afford such a luxury.

Minority groups have also increased their influence in local politics. "Exclusion is a thing of the past," according to Browning, Marshall, and Tabb. "Minorities are no longer completely excluded from governance in any city."[26] Their book, *Racial Politics in American Cities*, describes the success of minority candidates and coalitions in many cities, observing a significant shift in power. Regime change in Denver, for example, came about as "new configurations of interests—including African Americans and Latinos—displaced the dominant governing coalition. [Mayor Federico] Pena's 1983 upset election signaled the end of the Old Guard political elite dominating city politics since the 1950s and 1960s and the movement towards a political order more reflective of the city's changing demographic and economic character."[27] But while minority leaders may have joined the ranks of the powerful in many cities, Browning and his co-authors emphasize that to succeed they must find ways to work with the economic leaders of their communities—perhaps still the ultimate power.

Moreover, few minority leaders attain the ranks of the recognized powerful other than through winning elections. That's also true of other non-economic community and grassroots groups. Some power studies include a labor union leader or two and perhaps some socially prominent cultural or religious leaders or even the head of a well-known nonprofit group. But leaders of neighborhood and other grassroots organizations are rarely part of the dominant regime or power structure. That doesn't mean they are powerless. It just reflects the relatively narrow scope of their power. They may have considerable sway over what goes on in their own spheres of influence ("**niche power**"), but analyses of regimes and community power structures reflect community-wide power.

Power in Perspective

The theorists we've discussed sometimes make it sound as if local politics is predetermined by larger forces, but none of them writes off the role of real people in communities. The early theorists focused on elites, while their latter-day counterparts concentrate more on how the economy and the state-imposed structures of local government affect community politics. But all acknowledge that these forces are not omnipotent; what elected officials and ordinary people do makes a difference, too.

In fact, many observers and analysts of local politics believe power is more broadly distributed now than it was just a few years ago. "Not so long ago," *The Dallas Morning News* reports, "a city leader would have emerged from a Dallas business establishment that was all-male, all-white, and all-business. It had only one agenda—'What's good for business is good for Dallas'—and only a handful of people to push it. But that was then and this is now."[28] Political scientist Terrell Blodgett extends that generalization from Dallas to other cities: "The old titans, the small bunch of senior white males that met in exclusive clubs to make decisions that swayed cities' whole futures, are a virtually extinct species. Power in American communities seems to have been atomized by the rise of fresh power groups: upstart industries and businesses, powerful developers; ethnic alliances, organized blacks and Hispanics and Asians, environmental and women's and social service groups and many more."[29] Rufus Browning and his co-authors seem to concur. "Far more than even a decade ago," they write, "American political life is now dominated by competing agendas. . . . In the place of an Establishment that could be appealed to, we have instead a political market place."[30]

An example of these changes can be seen in the battles in many communities over "living wage" ordinances requiring hourly pay higher than the federal minimum for workers who provide services under contract with cities. We might expect employers in communities to vigorously oppose such policies. Some did, but mostly they were chambers of commerce and smaller, local employers who were likely to be affected by the ordinance (and higher pay for service workers)—not big industry. Such policies are beneath the radar of global corporations. They already pay their workers better wages and they don't contract with cities anyway. The disinterest of these powerful economic interests gave labor unions and their allies in the faith and minority communities an opening. They succeeded in winning approval of living wage ordinances in over a hundred American cities, surely partly as a consequence of changes in community power structures as major economic interests disengage somewhat and create openings for others to gain influence.

We've seen in earlier chapters that various elements play a part in local politics and power: the city council, the mayor and/or city manager, administrators and the bureaucracy, the voters, the media, and interest groups, from businesses and unions to neighborhoods and minority groups. Community power studies add to these by turning our attention to the informal, nongovernmental aspects of politics and power, and by putting all these in perspective, suggesting their relative influence. We gain not only a better understanding of politics in our own communities, but also of what we're up against if we want to achieve change.

Essential Terms

power

power structure

authority

influence

systems theory

stratification theory

reputational method

elitism

decisional method

pluralism

nondecisions

inertia

continuum of power

variation in power structures

absentee ownership

political culture

patterns of power

regime theory

governing regime

electoral coalition

focus on personalities

countercoalition

niche power

On the Internet

- Google the names of some prominent individuals who are not elected officials in your community. Check the same names in your local newspaper's archives to see if they're active in local politics.
- See if the records on campaign contributions are on your city's website. What sorts of individuals and organizations fund local campaigns?

Notes

1. Robert S. Lynd and Helen Merrell Lynd, *Middletown: A Study in American Culture* (New York: Harcourt and Brace, 1959); and Robert S. Lynd and Helen Merrell Lynd, *Middletown in Transition* (New York: Harcourt and Jovanovich, 1959, reprint 1982).

2. Lynd and Lynd, *Middletown in Transition*, p. 490.

3. Floyd Hunter, *Community Power Structure* (Chapel Hill: University of North Carolina Press, 1953).

4. See Hunter, *Community Power Structure*, and chapter 2 of Philip J. Trounstine and Terry Christensen, *Movers and Shakers: The Study of Community Power* (New York: St. Martin's Press, 1982).

5. See Robert Dahl, "A Critique of the Ruling Elite Model," in *The Search for Community Power*, ed. Willis D. Hawley and Frederick M. Wirt, 2nd ed. (Englewood Cliffs, NJ: Prentice-Hall, 1974); and chapter 2 of Trounstine and Christensen, *Movers and Shakers*.

6. Robert A. Dahl, *Who Governs? Democracy and Power in an American City* (New Haven, CT: Yale University Press, 1961).

7. See Peter Bachrach and Morton S. Baratz, *Power and Poverty: Theory and Practice* (New York: Oxford University Press, 1970).

8. Matthew A. Crenson, *The Un-Politics of Air Pollution: A Study of Non-Decisionmaking in the Cities* (Baltimore: Johns Hopkins University Press, 1971).

9. See Dahl, "A Critique of the Ruling Elite Model."

10. See Robert Vance Presthus, *Men At the Top: A Study in Community Power* (New York: Oxford University Press, 1964); and Delbert C. Miller, *International Community Power Structures: Comparative Studies of Four World Cities* (Bloomington: Indiana University Press, 1970).

11. See, for example, Frederick M. Wirt, *Power in the City: Decision Making in San Francisco* (Berkeley: Institute of Governmental Studies/University of California Press, 1974).

12. Robert L. Lineberry and Ira Sharkansky, *Urban Politics and Public Policy*, 3rd ed. (New York: Harper and Row, 1978), pp. 182–86; and Terry Clark, *Community Structure and Decision-Making: Comparative Analyses* (San Francisco: Chandler, 1968).

13. See Trounstine and Christensen, *Movers and Shakers*, chapter 6.

14. Ibid., chapters 4 and 6.

15. See Trounstine and Christensen, *Movers and Shakers*, for the 1979 study, and Philip J. Trounstine, "San Jose's Top Ten Changing Face of Local Leadership" and "Which City Institutions Really Wield Influence," *San Jose Mercury News*, April 1, 1990; and Becky Bartindale and Mary Anne Ostrom, "Power in Silicon Valley: Who Has It, How They Got It, What They Do With It, and How They Made This Year's List of Leaders," and "These Thirty People Round Out the List of the Most Powerful People in Silicon Valley," *San Jose Mercury News*, July 30, 2000, for the later studies.

16. Clarence N. Stone, *Regime Politics: Governing Atlanta, 1946–1988* (Lawrence, KS: University of Kansas Press, 1989).

17. John H. Mollenkopf, *A Phoenix in the Ashes: The Rise and Fall of the Koch Coalition in New York City Politics* (Princeton, NJ: Princeton University Press, 1992), p. 38.

18. Rufus P. Browning, Dale Rogers Marshall, and David H. Tabb, eds., *Racial Politics in American Cities*, 3rd ed. (New York: Longman, 2003), p. 14.

19. Harvey Molotch, "The City as a Growth Machine: Toward a Political Economy of Place," *American Journal of Sociology* 82, no. 2 (September 1976): 309.

20. Clarence Stone, "The Study of the Politics of Urban Development," in *The Politics of Urban Development*, ed. Clarence N. Stone and Heywood T. Sanders (Lawrence, KS: University Press of Kansas, 1987), p. 284.

21. Paul E. Peterson, *City Limits* (Chicago: University of Chicago Press, 1981), p. 29.

22. Lineberry and Sharkansky, *Urban Politics and Public Policy*, p. 179, propose a "triangular a model of community power" with economic elites at one point, political leaders at another, and bureaucratic administrators at a third point.

23. Peter Lupsha, "Structural Change and Innovation: Elites and Albuquerque Politics in the 1980s," in Stone and Sanders, ed., *The Politics of Urban Development*, p. 237.

24. See Molotch, "The City as a Growth Machine," p. 328.

25. See Richard Edward DeLeon, *Left Coast City: Progressive Politics in San Francisco, 1975–1991* (Lawrence, KS: University of Kansas Press, 1992); and Susan S. Fainstein, Norman I. Fainstein, Richard Child Hill, Dennis Judd, and Michael Peter Smith, eds., rev. ed. *Restructuring the City: The Political Economy of Urban Redevelopment* (New York: Longman, 1986).

26. See Browning, Marshall, and Tabb, eds., *Racial Politics in American Cities*, p. 38.

27. Rodney E. Hero and Susan E. Clarke, "Latinos, Blacks, and Multiethnic Politics in Denver: Realigning Power and Influence in the Struggle for Equality," in *Racial Politics in American Cities*, ed. Browning, Marshall, and Tabb, p. 317.

28. Victoria Loe Hicks, "Dallas at the Tipping Point: A Road Map for Renewal," *Dallas Morning News*, April 28, 2004, p. 14W.

29. Terrell Blodgett, "Beware the Lure of the 'Strong' Mayor," *Public Management* 76, no. 1 (January 1994): 11.

30. Browning, Marshall, and Tabb, eds., *Racial Politics in American Cities*, p. 353.

Part IV

Budget Politics, Public Policy, and Regional Government

The community power studies discussed in the previous chapter give us a new lens through which to understand local politics. The discussion views local politics, in essence, in terms of which groups exercise and maintain political power. In chapter 12, we will continue the theme by "following the money." No single document better illustrates who has power than the budget, which lays out a local government's spending priorities. Keep in mind that politics (at any level) is largely about the allocation of scarce resources, and the budget is the ultimate arbiter of how those resources will be spent. Although the budget is a part of the formal political process, environmental factors, including local, national, and international economic conditions, and the actions of other governments shape—and more often constrain—local spending options. And, of course, the spending priorities set forth in local budgets comprise a set of political choices that affect not only life in the community, but future budgets as well, as groups seek to protect their hard-fought gains.

Then we'll move on to a discussion of specific policy areas in chapter 13—education, welfare, crime, growth, and finally transportation. Again, we will see how the environment of local politics influences and constrains political outcomes. In chapter 14 we conclude the text with a look at what is for some the Holy Grail of local politics: metropolitan government. We will examine the arguments of those who believe that regional government is the best overall solution to the problems of metropolitan areas, which we have outlined throughout the book, as well as those who defend the current system. Regional government is appropriate to conclude with, not only because it sums up so much of what we have considered thus far, but because in one form or another, it very well may be the future of local politics.

12 Budget Politics
The Getting and Spending of Money

No single document tells more about a local government than its budget. Simply put, a budget is the ultimate expression of political power and policy priorities in a city. A careful or even cursory examination of the annual budget of a city or county reveals its sources of funds and the way the money is spent. We can see what they do and to some extent how they do it. We can extrapolate aspects of local politics, including how a community's political energies are exerted in acquiring revenues and which programs have political support. Much about relations with other governments is also revealed. In general, "following the money" is a good way to get an overview of government and politics at any level.

But as crucial as they are, neither budgets nor budget politics are transparent or instantly comprehensible. They tell us where the money comes from and where it goes and give clues about the politics involved in both. But it is not always clear how the money is acquired and how well it is spent, even to those directly involved. Often obscure and highly technical, budget politics are an insiders' game, best played by bureaucrats, experienced elected officials, and lobbyists. The public, community groups, and even the media tend to take little interest in the details of budget making. When they do take part in the public hearings at the very end of the process, it is usually to object to cuts in their favored programs, and it is generally too late.

But while the public rarely plays a major part in the budget-making process itself, it has had a significant impact on budgets through the tax revolt that swept the country over during the last two decades of the twentieth century and into the early twenty-first, rejecting new taxes, capping old ones, and electing antitax crusaders such as Ronald Reagan, George W. Bush, or Arnold Schwarzenegger to state and national office. As we discussed earlier, local revenues from taxes and intergovernmental aid also shrank as a result of voter action to limit property tax revenue, but other fiscal pressures also hit. During the 1980s and early 1990s, and again in the early 2000s, the roller-coaster effects of inflation and recession in the national economy, which were beyond the control of local governments, cut into their tax bases and expanded their payroll costs even as demands for social and other services were rising. During the mid- to late 1990s, local governments saw a greater share of the economic pie as a result of an expanding economy. But when the good times ended with the dot-com bust and the 9/11 terrorist attacks in 2001, local governments were once again forced to figure out how to do more with less. Soaring health care and pension costs also added to local government fiscal problems. In addition, partly in response to their

283

own fiscal problems, the state and national governments passed on or mandated programs without providing adequate funding, even while the tax base for many local governments contracted, as entire industries shifted to the suburbs, Sunbelt states, or other countries. But the economic challenges came in several varieties. As we saw in chapter 3, some cities and counties, especially in the Frostbelt, faced rising costs and declining revenues because of deindustrialization and economic decay; others, mostly in the Sunbelt, found themselves unable to pay for programs—from transportation, to education, to public safety and social welfare—associated with rapid population growth.

By 2005, talk in local government circles across most of the country was: "how to govern in a fiscal crisis?" Like other elements of local politics, the extent to which these pressures were felt varied greatly from place to place, as did the local responses. This is partly because the tax resources of communities vary so much, both in their tax bases and the types of revenue state governments make available to them. Service demands vary, too, depending on the responsibilities allocated to different types of local government (see chapter 4) and the characteristics of the communities themselves. As we know from studying the separation of needs resources between central cities and suburbs, service needs and tax resources are not always congruent.

To further complicate matters, local governments often work with more than one budget, dividing their money into separate pots according to its sources and what it can be spent for. Primary among these, and our focus here, is the **operating budget**, which covers salaries, maintenance, and on-going expenses, usually for a given fiscal year. Most local governments also have a **capital budget**, which allocates funds for major infrastructure projects such as roads, bridges, and buildings. Capital budgets pay for long-term expenditures and often have a five-to ten-year horizon. Sometimes special programs such as redevelopment have separate budgets and funding sources as well. We'll explain these terms in more detail, but whatever the budget's designation, the same officials usually decide how to spend it—and it all comes from the taxpayers.

IN YOUR COMMUNITY

Go to your city or county website and examine the government's operating budget. Where does the money come from? List the sources of revenue in terms of the property tax, sales tax charges and fees, income tax, and so on. How does your city or county compare with the patterns described in this chapter?

Where the Money Comes From

Local governments get money for their operating budgets from three basic sources: taxes, charges and fees, and intergovernmental aid (see Figures 12.1, 12.2, and 12.3). They also obtain money by borrowing, although this is almost always restricted to capital expenditures on infrastructure and must be paid back from one of the three basic revenue sources. Each of these basic sources includes its own variations.

Figure 12.1 **General Revenues of All U.S. Local Governments, 2002–2003**

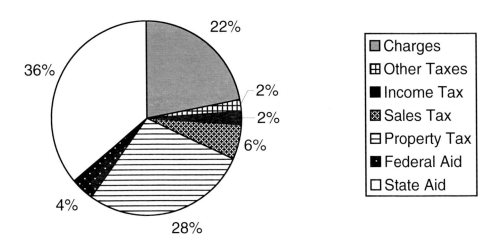

Source: U.S. Census Bureau, www.census.gov/govs/estimate/03s100us.html.

The Property Tax

Historically, the biggest single source of local revenues was the real estate or property tax, which accounted for more than half of all local income and sometimes much more. Taxing property made sense to local governments because it was a stable source of revenue that did not tend to fluctuate much from year to year. Today it contributes considerably less, due to increased intergovernmental aid and to the tax revolt, which made the property tax its primary target. Nevertheless, the property tax accounted for 28 percent of all local revenues in 2002. Its significance varied considerably, however, as Tables 12.1 and 12.2 reveal. School districts and counties, which are allowed little fiscal flexibility by states, depended on it as the primary source of local revenues. Townships also rely heavily on the property tax. Cities, however, relied on it somewhat less. Nevertheless, the property tax remains a crucial source of local tax revenue. It is also controversial and unpopular.

Although in some places the **property tax** once extended to household goods (and even pets!), today it is generally limited to buildings and land. It works through state-regulated formulas that combine the estimated or assessed value of real estate with a tax rate. Valuations are usually done by a county tax assessor, who is often elected, which tells us something about how politicized the office can be. The **assessed value (AV)** of property may reflect its approximate market value or only a percentage of it, depending on the jurisdiction and state laws and how they are applied. The **tax rate** is then applied to the assessed value, usually on the basis of a certain amount per $100 of assessed value imposed by states. The tax collected on a property is apportioned according to a formula among the various local governments with jurisdiction over it—usually a city, county, special district, and school district.

Figure 12.2 **General Revenues of U.S. Counties, 2002–2003**

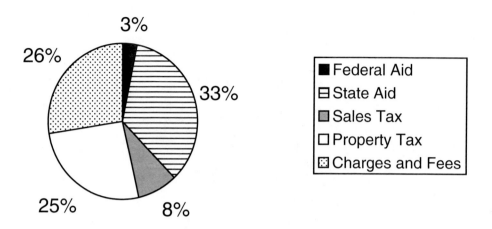

Source: U.S. Census Bureau, www.census.gov/govs/estimate/03gp00us.html.

Table 12.1

Property Taxes as Percent of General Revenue by Level of Government, 1962–2002

Year	All	Counties	Municipalities	Townships	School districts	Special districts
1962	48	46	44	65	51	25
1972	40	37	31	65	47	17
1982	28	27	21	52	36	10
1990	26	27	17	51	37	8
2002	28	24	25*	—	34	11

Source: U.S. Census Bureau, available at www.census.gov/govs/estimate/03gp00us.html.
*Percent is combined for municipalities and townships.

Table 12.2

Property Taxes as Percent of Taxes by Level of Government, 1962–2002

Year	All	Counties	Municipalities	Townships	School districts	Special districts
1962	88	94	94	93	99	100
1972	84	86	64	94	98	95
1982	76	77	53	94	97	80
1990	75	73	51	92	98	70
2002	73	69	56*	—	96	72

Source: U.S. Census Bureau, available at www.census.gov/govs/estimate/03gp00us.html.
*Percent is combined for municipalities and townships.

Figure 12.3   **General Revenues of U.S. Cities, 2002–2003**

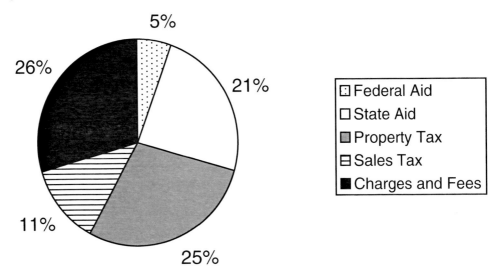

U.S. Census Bureau, www.census.gov/govs/estmiate/03gp00us.html.

Problems with the Property Tax

The most obvious problem that arises with this complex system is the **fairness of assessments**. This was a major issue in the past, when assessors affiliated with political machines used their evaluations to reward friends and punish enemies. Such worries have been resolved in most states by regulation and appeals procedures introduced by the Progressive reformers, more frequent turnover of property, and computerization of real estate transactions. In others, such as Indiana, infrequent and amateur assessments are still a problem. Complaints still arise elsewhere, too, especially about the accuracy of assessments of industrial or other large landholdings that change hands less frequently than houses. If such properties are underassessed, the burden of the property tax falls more heavily on homeowners. Their burden is also increased by the exemption of some properties, such as churches, educational institutions, government offices, and other nonprofit organizations, from paying property taxes even though they rely upon local government services. This is usually a minor problem, but it can be serious in capitol cities with many such institutions, such as Boston and Washington, DC, where over half of all property is exempt. Tax delinquency is also a problem in inner cities and some poor suburbs where landlords sometimes abandon slum properties. Nonpayment averages 3 to 4 percent among large cities, rising to as much as 9 percent in some cities.[1] Legally, cities may take over and resell these properties, but they often have difficulty disposing of them.

Another concern with the property tax is that it is a **regressive tax**—the less affluent pay a higher proportion of their incomes in property tax than do the rich. A

progressive tax, in contrast, falls more heavily on the rich; the income tax is intended to be such a tax. Of course, the less affluent pay smaller property tax bills in absolute terms because their homes are not as valuable as those of the rich. The regressivity results from the fact that the poor devote a bigger proportion of their income to housing—and therefore to the property tax—than do the rich. Fifty percent or more of the incomes of poor, working, and many middle-class people go to mortgages or rents. Higher-income people may allocate 25 percent or less of their income to housing. People who rent, as most low-income people do, may not even know they are paying the tax, since their landlords, who are responsible for it, merely calculate it into the rent. More middle- and high-income people are homeowners who are very conscious of their tax bill, even though it hurts them less. Many people think its regressivity makes the property tax unfair even when the homes of the rich and poor are fairly assessed. Others argue that its regressivity is balanced by the greater reliance of lower-income residents on city services. More affluent people, however, are usually better organized and more able to achieve the services or tax structure they prefer.

Critics of using the property tax as a primary source of local revenue object to the way governmental fragmentation of metropolitan areas reinforces the **separation of needs and resources**, with more affluent taxpayers and higher-value property in newer independent suburban enclaves and less affluent, more service-dependent populations in older central cities or inner suburbs. Each local government taxes the property within its boundaries, so a new suburb with expensive homes but low service needs can tax lightly and still cover its expenses. Older communities with lower-value properties and higher service needs must tax more heavily, raising their rates to generate enough revenue. But as we have learned, higher tax rates may drive out affluent homeowners, often necessitating even heavier taxes. As the surrounding affluent suburbs attract more wealthy residents, businesses tend to follow, simultaneously depriving inner cities and suburbs of revenue from property and sales tax and of jobs, while improving the tax and job base of newer subgroups. It's a cycle that creates a pattern of "have" and "have-not" cities so characteristic of urban America.

The Tax Revolt

According to public opinion polls, the property tax has long been the most hated of all taxes, making it the main target of the **tax revolt.** A combination of factors led to this targeting and ultimately to reduced property tax revenues for local governments.

In the 1970s, real estate speculation encouraged by federal tax laws combined with inflation was driving up home prices by 20 percent or more each year in some places, particularly in the Sunbelt. Modern assessment practices meant that these increases in home values could be almost instantly included in tax calculations, so property tax revenue also rose with inflation in home prices, which was well above the overall inflation rate. Local governments could have avoided or softened the tax increases by lowering their tax rates to keep their own budgets in line with overall inflation, but not so much as to anger taxpayers. Many local governments did lower their rates a little, but rarely in proportion to the rising tax revenues generated by the inflation in home prices. By announcing their slightly lowered rates with great fanfare, they may have increased taxpayer anger when big tax bills arrived. Most local governments, however, cheerfully increased their spending in accordance with their increased income.

Rapidly rising property tax bills both hurt and annoyed people. Low-income and elderly people on fixed incomes from welfare, Social Security, or pensions were hit hardest. Property tax bills could rise by hundreds or even thousands of dollars a year, but their incomes did not. Elderly people hoping to live out their lives in family homes long since paid for were put under great stress. But people who could afford to pay the property tax were also angered by the precipitous rises, and the way property taxes are usually collected intensified their anger. We pay sales tax a bit at a time, hardly noticing. Income tax is deducted from our monthly or weekly paychecks and many of us don't even notice our pretax wages; we may be surprised at the total we've paid when we file our income tax forms on April 15, but even then the system dupes us into celebrating a refund of a few dollars. We are eased into paying these taxes, but in many places the property tax slaps us in the face with a single big bill that comes in the mail. In the late 1970s, with the nasty surprises of bigger bills every year, many got mad enough to say they weren't going to take it anymore.

Some of their frustration was with the overall burden of combined local, state, and federal taxes, but the property tax was singled out as the most hated and least predictable of all. It was also relatively vulnerable because it could be attacked locally through a referendum, a means that could not be used against federal or, in some cases, state taxes. By the early 1970s, voters were regularly saying no to bonds and increases in property tax rates in referenda. State and local governments, conscious of both the problems and the unpopularity of the property tax, introduced reforms, including improved assessment practices, rebates, exemptions, and deferrals for the elderly and the poor, and even alternative taxes in some places.

These reforms were too little too late, however, and the tax revolt exploded, particularly in Sunbelt states where inflated house prices were driving up property taxes most rapidly. In June of 1978, the voters of California led the way with the passage of **Proposition 13**. This measure fixes the property tax rate at 1 percent of market value, based on the most recent sale of the property or its 1975 value if it has not been sold, with assessments rising by only 2 percent a year. When property is sold, however, it is again assessed at 1 percent of its new market value (usually a steep rise), subject to the 2 percent annual increase. By cutting the rate and rolling back assessed values, Proposition 13 immediately reduced property tax bills by more than 50 percent. Moreover, the burden on the taxpayer was made predictable through an additional 2 percent limit on increased assessments. Proposition 13 remains so popular as to be sacrosanct in California—it still referred to as "the third rail of California politics." During his 2003 campaign for governor, Arnold Schwarzenegger castigated legendary Wall Street investor Warren Buffett, his adviser on financial matters, for suggesting that California property taxes were too low and that Proposition 13 needed to be reformed. An observer in Colorado—which has its own version of Proposition 13—recently lamented the fact that Colorado now has budgeting that operates "without deliberation, without priorities and without consideration of the relationships among expenditure items or between revenues and expenditures."[2]

The measures saved property owners lots of money and forced local governments, which had been getting a little sloppy and self-indulgent, to trim fat and shape up. But the measure's impact on local governments in California has been devastating. State aid and belt-tightening helped local governments get over the initial shock of losing 57 percent of their primary source of revenue, but eventually services declined, and, in the long term, counties and school districts became less independent because of their reliance on state assistance, which always has strings attached. Cities with more varied revenue sources did a little better. As Clarence Lo found in his study of the impact of Proposition 13, since property is reassessed only when it is sold, the main beneficiaries were big businesses and large landowners, whose larger land holdings changed hands less frequently.[3] Homeowners who stayed put also benefited, but to a far lesser extent. Property taxes are thus higher on houses purchased more recently. Someone who has stayed in a $30,000 home bought in 1975 might be paying a small fraction of the property tax of the next-door neighbor living in an identical house purchased for $500,000 in 2006 and getting exactly the same services. The courts have thus far judged Proposition 13 constitutional, although in 1989 the U.S. Supreme Court struck down a similar "welcome neighbor" tax in Webster County, West Virginia, on the grounds that it violated the equal protection clause of the Fourteenth Amendment.[4]

Besides its unfairness, this reassessment procedure reduced the mobility of Californians, who now move a little less frequently because they fear bigger tax bills. On the other hand, because Proposition 13 assessments can be passed on to children and grandchildren, the measure has resulted in a higher level of community stability and continuity. Even so, California homes, on average, change hands every four or five years. Big business, however, stays put longer, thus reaping a greater percentage of the tax savings. Before Proposition 13, business carried more than half of the state's total property tax burden; within two years of its enactment, homeowners carried more than half, a proportion that has grown since then. In addition, Proposition 13 and similar measures that passed in subsequent years required a two-thirds vote of the state legislature to raise income taxes, further constraining the ability of government to respond to service needs.

Other states soon followed California's lead and the tax revolt swept the nation. In 1980, voters in Massachusetts passed Proposition 2½, limiting the property tax to 2.5 percent of a community's total assessed value and annual increases in assessment to 2.5 percent. As in California, the state's local governments were forced to slash their budgets and cut staff. All around the country, state and local governments backed away from tax increases and tightened their budgets as the message of the tax revolt sunk in. As of 1989, all but seven states had enacted some sort of limits on property tax rates or assessment increases, although many of these predated the tax revolt.[5]

Although modest tax increases were back on the agendas of governments at all levels by the 1990s, the tax revolt was not over. In 1990, Oregon voters passed Measure Number 5, which severely limited local governments' ability to raise property taxes. In 1992, Colorado voters passed a law requiring voter approval of new taxes or increases in existing taxes other than those justified by inflation and population growth. And in March 1993, the schools in Kalkaska, Michigan, were closed for the year when local voters rejected a tax increase for the third time. One recent exception to the antitax trend occurred in November 2004 when Maine voters rejected a California-style Proposition 13 measure. And in California, voters have grown more willing to approve taxes for schools.[6]

But while the tax revolt may have assuaged the public, dissipated antagonism to the property tax, and decreased what some viewed as overdependence on the property tax as a source of local revenue, serious problems remain. Its regressivity, its impact on the separation of needs and resources, and the impetus for the **fiscalization of land use** (making land-use decisions based upon their revenue potential) are all serious problems. Moreover, tax revolts have meant increasing reliance upon state governments and other less reliable sources of revenue. Finally, underscoring the "law of unintended consequences," in some places where tax revolts occurred, local governments were no longer competitive for state and federal grants that required locals to raise matching funds.[7]

Other Taxes

Nationally, no other tax equals the property tax as a source of local revenue, although since the 1970s, other taxes have become increasingly important and now raise more money in some localities than the property tax.

Fifteen states allow their local governments to levy a **local income tax**, but its use is extensive only in Kentucky, Ohio, and Pennsylvania, with more limited use in Michigan and Indiana. Many jurisdictions are afraid that local income taxes will drive away business and residence. Large cities levying an income tax include New York, Yonkers, Detroit, Baltimore, Indianapolis, Columbus, Toledo, Cincinnati, Washington, DC, and Kansas City, Missouri. The tax is usually set at a flat rate (such as 1 percent of wages), although the rates of New York and Washington, DC, are progressive, with higher rates for those with higher incomes.

Cities levy income taxes on their own residents, but a few central cities charge a **payroll tax** on everyone who works in the city, thus taxing suburbanites who use their services and partially redressing the needs/resources imbalance. Philadelphia even applies its payroll tax to visiting athletes. Altogether, however, income or payroll taxes generate less than 3 percent of local revenues. Cities might prefer a local income tax because it would be more fair, but it is not politically feasible. Taxpayers now hate the income tax almost as much as the property tax and will not hear of a further increase, even if it saves them elsewhere; nor are jealous states, themselves turning increasingly to the income tax, prepared to share it with local governments. Meanwhile, critics believe that cities with income or payroll taxes are driving jobs and middle-class people away and losing their economic competition with the suburbs.

Local **sales taxes**, found in thirty-three states, are a slightly more common means of raising local funds, generating 6 percent of all local revenues in 2002. Local sales taxes increased by 150 percent between 1978 and 1987 (the glory years of the tax revolt).[8] In some cases, such as in California, a percentage of the state sales tax is shared with cities, counties, or special districts, which may also add local sales taxes for special purposes such as transportation. The sales tax is a primary source of revenue for only a few cities, however, including Denver, where it generates nearly half of local revenues, and Oklahoma City, where it supplies almost 60 percent of revenues.[9] Most cities resist such reliance because, like a local income tax, the benefits of a sales tax are limited by the fear of driving businesses to adjacent jurisdictions and causing a political uproar. The increasing volume of commerce done over the Internet has caused some cities to lobby for legislation that would allow states and localities to tax Internet sales, although no agreement has been reached. One advantage of the sales tax is that it allows officials to shift part of the tax burden onto nonresidents. However, critics point to the sales tax's regressivity and its tendency to encourage the fiscalization of land use or "zoning for dollars."[10]

Although schools rely almost exclusively on money from the property tax and counties have few additional local taxes, states generally allow cities more flexibility. Besides the sales tax, many collect an assortment of minor taxes on hotels, rental cars, gambling, cigarettes, liquor, admissions, entertainment, and utilities. Most of these produce little revenue, but cities welcome whatever they can get and particularly like some of these because they come from tourists and commuters. The exception is the utility tax, which hits local residents and businesses and which generates more than 10 percent of local revenues in some places. Many states are also starting to legalize gambling to help balance budgets. Forty states now have lotteries with some of the revenues going to local governments, especially schools.[11]

Charges and Fees

Following the tax revolt, local governments turned not only to these other taxes, but to **charges and fees**, now the most rapidly growing source of local funds. As of 2002, cities and counties raised 26 percent of their general revenues from charges and fees. Unlike taxes, which everybody pays whether or not they use a service, charges and fees are paid only by users. "You should make services pay for themselves," says an Oklahoma City council member. "You know what the cost of water is; people who use water ought to pay for it."[12] Besides water, local governments charge for garbage collection, sewers, transit, airports, parking, and admissions to public facilities such as parks, zoos, golf courses, and swimming pools. Cities that own their own utilities do particularly well. Austin, Texas, for example, gets 46 percent of its revenues from its electric utility company, relying on property taxes for just 10 percent (as compared with 59 percent in Fort Worth).[13] Additionally, local governments make money on fees for business licenses, building permits, and franchises for private companies to provide city services. Finally, twenty-two states now authorize localities to levy impact fees on developers, in part to pay for new infrastructure. In theory, charges and fees should pay for the cost of providing a service and no more, but critics assert that cities desperate for funds may set prices too high and actually make money on their charges, in which case they are taxes.

IN YOUR COMMUNITY

Compare the operating budgets of several cities in your area. How do they differ in terms of funding sources and spending?

Intergovernmental Aid: The States

Taxes and charges are the two major means by which local governments generate their own revenue, but they are also heavily dependent on aid from the state and federal governments—or **intergovernmental aid**. States now contribute roughly 36 percent of local government budgets. As with other funding sources, this is not evenly spread among different types of local governments. School districts and counties are most heavily dependent on intergovernmental aid, while many cities receive very little.

This is because state funds concentrate on education, which, in many places, is not a city function. States also contribute to welfare and health care, which are the major services receiving federal funds. These are county functions in many states so, again, cities are not direct beneficiaries. In some states, however, particularly in the Northeast, cities perform one or more of these functions and so are the recipients of considerable intergovernmental aid. New York City, which handles education, welfare, and health, gets a third of its budget from the state and federal governments. Counties and school districts, however, rely on intergovernmental aid even more.

Although states provide much more aid than the federal government, the amount varies greatly among the states. In 2002, California, for example, gave its local governments more than three times more money per resident than did South Dakota.[14] In all, about one-third of state funds are passed on to local governments, where they comprise about one-third of all local revenues and over half of general revenues for school districts. Some of the money is allocated on a formula basis and designated for the provision of specific services, mainly education, welfare, and health. Some are **shared revenues**, usually a fixed percentage of state sales, gasoline, or other taxes that may be **earmarked**, meaning it must be spent for a designated purpose. This is almost always the case with gas taxes, for example, which usually must be used for roads or sometimes other forms of transportation. States are stingy about giving funds with no strings attached—only a small percent of state aid to local governments is "unrestricted"—and such money is usually eaten up by state-mandated programs anyway. Local governments complain that such **mandates** require them to do certain things; so for all practical purposes the states are allocating local revenues.

Local governments nevertheless welcome state aid, although they might also welcome fewer restrictions on how they spend it. Central cities and poor school districts and counties particularly appreciate the equalizing or leveling effect of state aid. With a broad and inclusive tax base, the states have the capacity to at least partially resolve the needs/resources dichotomy, although to date efforts in this regard have mainly been confined to education. But state funds are not unlimited and local governments have recently been reminded that what the state gives it can take away. In 1975, the City of New York was forced to turn over its fiscal autonomy to a governor-appointed state agency, following a series of economic events that led to the city's near bankruptcy. In California, for example, a 1993 budget crisis prompted the state government to shift more than $2 billion in property taxes from cities and counties to schools in order to reduce the state's own spending on education. In 2004, California voters approved proposition 1A, a measure to prevent future state mandates and appropriations of local revenue. Yet, the history of such legislation suggests that efforts to protect local fiscal integrity are likely to fail.[15]

Like state aid, federal funds have traditionally had an equalizing effect and have recently been cut. Categorical **grants-in-aid** for specific projects have been disproportionately awarded to big cities, but have been significantly downsized under the Bush administration. Funds for social programs, including welfare and Medicaid, also go disproportionately to big cities, where most of the needy are concentrated. Like state aid, most federal funds have at least some strings attached.

Overall, the federal government contributes about 4 percent of all local funds (compared to state aid at 36 percent). The bulk of this is for social programs—mostly health and welfare programs—and entitlements, both of which are distributed on a formula basis according to need. Federal funds are often supplemented by the states and passed along to local governments, where they are further supplemented by local money and actually administered. As noted, this is usually a county function, although cities carry it out in some parts of the country. In either case, little local discretion is allowed, so the local government is essentially an administrative agency of the state and federal governments.

Unlike grants for social services, local governments must apply for categorical grants-in-aid, and they are awarded selectively. More than four hundred different sorts of grants are available, funding projects ranging from airports to transit, housing, sewers, and parks. Local governments are happy to receive the money, although they complain about red tape, inadequate funding, and categories that may not include their top-priority projects. The federal government responded to these criticisms by loosening restrictions on some funds through block grants and (briefly) revenue sharing.

As we saw in chapter 4, federal aid to local governments rose dramatically through the 1970s, but the declining power of big cities, the rise of suburbia, and a succession of conservative presidents have shifted funding away from urban social programs. Whereas federal payments to state and local governments rose by 45 percent between 1975 and 1980, they increased by only 10 percent between 1981 and 1985 and by less thereafter.[16] Although the dollar amount increased, the total portion of the federal budget allocated to local governments shrank steadily from 29 percent in

1978 to 11 percent in 2002.[17] Such increases in local aid as occurred usually went for welfare and health programs, although conservative lawmakers attempted to trim these wherever possible. The biggest cuts, however, came in categorical grants-in-aid. Dozens of programs were eliminated and funding for others was greatly reduced. The budget of the Department of Housing and Urban Development was halved, and grants to cities were slashed by one-third, even without allowing for inflation. "Over the 1980s," *The Municipal Year Book* reports, "the percent of the average local government budget provided by federal funds was sliced in half—from around 16 percent to 8 percent," while "federal dollars for priority municipal programs—including housing, public transit, and job training—are now less than half of what they were a few years ago."[18] Large cities lost the most. The U.S. Conference of Mayors reports that federal contributions to the budgets of the fifty largest cities fell from 17.7 percent in 1980 to 6.4 percent in 1990, to about 4 percent in 2002.[19] Suburban and Sunbelt cities, however, were not as hard hit because most had not relied so heavily on federal largesse.

The Clinton administration, which placed two former mayors in charge of key urban agencies, was able to increase federal aid to cities only slightly. The current federal budget deficit, however, is almost certain to preclude a major turnaround in federal aid programs. Federal aid to local governments may yet rise (as it did in the postwar era) in the form of increased defense spending in the Sunbelt, but the ongoing problem of the deficit makes it unlikely that aid directed toward the needy will attain its past levels anytime soon.

Borrowing

While all the sources of funds discussed thus far may be used to pay for the operating budgets of local governments, covering ongoing costs such as salaries and maintenance, **borrowing** is usually allowed only for long-term infrastructure projects.

Local governments are required by law to balance their operating budgets, and in general, they must get by on revenues from the sources discussed earlier and may not borrow for ongoing expenses. But because revenues arrive in lump sums at different times of the year when particular taxes are collected or state and federal funds are distributed, and operating expenses are ongoing, income and spending may be out of synch. Some states therefore allow local governments to engage in short-term borrowing by issuing **tax or revenue anticipation notes (TANs or RANs),** which investors purchase and which the local governments repay with interest in 30 to 120 days. Cities can get in trouble by abusing this system, as New York City did in the 1970s. Philadelphia was so hard up in 1993 that lenders refused to loan the city money on the grounds that projected revenues were inadequate to cover its expenses and repay its debts.

Most—97 percent—of local borrowing is long term rather than short term, however, and goes into capital budgets rather than operating budgets. Larger amounts are involved and they are repaid over a period of years rather than months, rather like a home mortgage. Such borrowing is justified on the grounds that capital projects such as roads, bridges, and buildings will last for a long time and so may be paid for over a long period, at the end of which local governments have something to show for it. In contrast, borrowing for operating costs such as salaries, which are recurring and must be paid every month, could lead to an endless cycle of debt.

Long-term borrowing is done by issuing bonds, or IOUs, which are purchased by investors and repaid at a fixed rate of interest over a specified period of years. Traditionally, this was done in the form of **general obligation (GO) bonds**, which, under state law, are guaranteed by the local government borrower. If a local government goes broke and defaults on its loans, the state takes it over, slashes local services, and pays off the bondholders. Actually, several cities went bust in the 1930s, and a few local governments go bankrupt every year. Cleveland went into default in 1978, and only state intervention saved New York City from the brink in the 1970s. Orange County, California, one of the largest concentrations of wealth on the planet, went bankrupt in 1994, the result of risky investments, recession, and voter unwillingness to raise taxes.[20] Such desperate straits are rare, however, and the local government guarantees for GO bonds give them a security that makes them an attractive investment. Interest on these bonds is also exempt from federal taxes, which adds to their allure as an investment and helps out local governments by enabling them to offer better interest rates.

Guaranteed GO bonds are regulated by the states, many of which set borrowing limits. Most also require voter approval, often two-thirds of those voting. In the 1970s, some cities hit their borrowing limits, and in others, voters rejected the bonds, which are generally paid for by raising the unpopular property tax. Thus, local governments turned increasingly to nonguaranteed bonds, which are subject to fewer state regulations and generally do not need voter approval. These are usually **revenue bonds**, paid for by income from the facilities they provide, such as airports, stadiums, or toll bridges. Revenue bonds are easier to issue, but because they are nonguaranteed, investors are more cautious and expect higher interest rates.

Despite state restrictions and voter rejections, borrowing by local governments has continued to rise, in large part spurred on by historically low interest rates in the late 1990s and early 2000s. Cuts in federal grants for capital projects gave impetus to local indebtedness and nonguaranteed revenue bonds have provided means. In 1980, local borrowing was about equally split between guaranteed and nonguaranteed bonds; by 1990, two-thirds was nonguaranteed, a pattern that continues to date.[21] Not all voters have rejected bonds, however. Even at the height of the tax revolt, more bond measures passed than failed, and in better economic times voter approval becomes even more likely. Undoubtedly, local governments became more judicious about balloting on bond measures and some learned to conduct more effective campaigns in favor of their proposals, but where they could be persuaded of need, voters were willing to authorize borrowing and taxes.

The Bottom Line

Bond elections are not the only way voters have their say about local revenues. Some states also require **voter approval** of some other tax measures, what some call "ballot box budgeting." The tax revolt movement exploited these opportunities and used the initiative process as well. Such democracy is praiseworthy, yet it is also unfair in that local governments are singled out for referenda on taxes while the states are less restricted and the federal government is exempt. Discontented taxpayers may vent their anger with taxes in general on local governments in particular, simply because they are allowed to do so. If we could vote on taxes at all levels, local governments, which provide visible and necessary services, might come off best. Perhaps the voters have perceived this. The image of local governments seems to have improved, perhaps due to post–tax revolt belt-tightening or because the revolt supplied the public with a needed catharsis. Public opinion surveys usually report that more people have confidence in local government than in the state or federal governments.

Nevertheless, local governments have born the brunt of the tax revolt, a movement that shows no signs of subsiding. Twenty-four states voted on various tax limitation and spending measures in 2005, and even former proponents, such as Colorado Governor Bill Owens, sought to persuade voters to loosen voter-imposed restrictions on spending. When dissatisfaction reached higher levels of government, politicians responded by cutting local aid, especially to cities. The results over the last two decades have sent local governments scrambling for revenues. How have local governments responded? According to a local government official quoted in *The Municipal Year Book*, "It's not rocket science. . . . It's pretty much raise taxes or cut services. That's what it boils down to."[22] Schools have had to cut back on services, close altogether, or grow more dependent on the states. The experience has been similar for counties, which have also increasingly looked to raise charges and fees while hoping for intergovernmental aid to pay for social programs. Cities have also raised charges, imposed new taxes, and increased indebtedness. As *The Municipal Year Book* puts it, the "money chase continues unabated, and apparently uninhibited."[23]

How the Money Is Spent

Patterns of spending among local governments vary as much as their revenue sources. This is partly because of the way states allocate responsibilities to different sorts of local governments. Education, for example, is usually the responsibility of independent school districts, and counties often provide social services, while cities concentrate on public safety and a mix of other tasks. Spending also reflects community characteristics, such as those discussed in chapters 2 and 3. Central cities, with dense, needy populations generally spend more, while suburbs, although richer, spend less, and Frostbelt cities tend to spend more than Sunbelt cities, both because of greater need and because their states assign them more responsibilities. Richer communities may, however, spend more for amenities such as parks, libraries, and lighted tennis courts simply because they can afford to without taxing themselves heavily to do so. Spending patterns are thus determined by both state-imposed obligations and by community characteristics. But local budgets also reflect community priorities and history. Some communities take a more communal approach, providing extensive

Figure 12.4 **Spending by All U.S. Local Governments, 2002–2003**

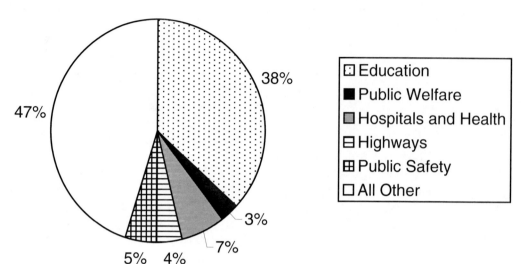

Source: U.S. Census Bureau, www.census.gov/govs/estimate/03gp00us.html.

social services, while others are more laissez-faire, minimizing government. The former are more likely to be central cities in the Frostbelt; the latter are usually suburban or Sunbelt cities, which incidentally are better off and so can afford to do less. Here again, community characteristics and the demands they generate come into play.

In turn, expenditures have important impacts on communities, their politics, and their environments. Local spending makes urban places, with all their problems, more livable—and spending usually rises as these problems increase. Spending also has an impact on the local economy. Businesses may encourage local spending as an economic stimulus, and local governments often see spending as a form of investment. If such spending works, it increases revenues, which makes further spending and further stimulation possible. If increased spending necessitates higher taxes, however, it can have the opposite effect, depressing the economy and driving business away. The balance is tricky, and local governments spend a lot of energy trying to get it right, although most seem to have a propensity to tax and spend as much as they can, hoping to satisfy their constituents while stimulating the local economy.

Spending Patterns

Education is the single largest local expenditure, followed by social services, public safety, and transportation (see Figure 12.4). Separating school districts, counties, and cities, however, reveals a more complex specialization of **spending patterns** (see Figure 12.5). Health and welfare rank high in county budgets, while public safety, sewers, and sanitation are the big spending categories for cities. Education

Figure 12.5 **U.S. County Spending, 2002–2003**

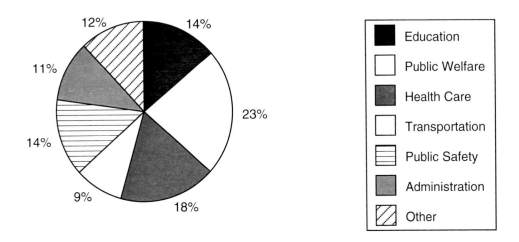

still ranks second in both cases because some large cities and counties have that responsibility; most, however, do not.

Spending also varies wildly among cities, again influenced by state-assigned responsibilities and community characteristics. Among the nation's thirty-five largest cities, total annual spending per capita in 2001 ranged from $936 in El Paso, Texas, to $10,209 per person in Washington, DC. Other cities, such as New York, spent $7,863 per person, whereas Las Vegas spent only $1,049. The big spenders, however, are mostly consolidated city-counties or large urban areas, and most are responsible for education, welfare, and sometimes health care; the low spenders—mostly in the Sunbelt—generally are not.

IN YOUR COMMUNITY
Compare the operating budgets of your city, county, and school district. How do their funding sources and spending differ?

The Budget Process

Each year local governments go through a long and complex process to put together a budget for the next year, what is sometimes called the **budget cycle**. Although this process arguably involves the most important decisions local governments make about public policy, it takes place mostly out of the public view, with its own special set of political actors, most of whom are bureaucrats rather than elected officials. Yet even though much energy is expended on the budget, each year's budget is much like that of the preceding year except for tinkering at the margins.

Figure 12.6   **U.S. City Spending, 2000**

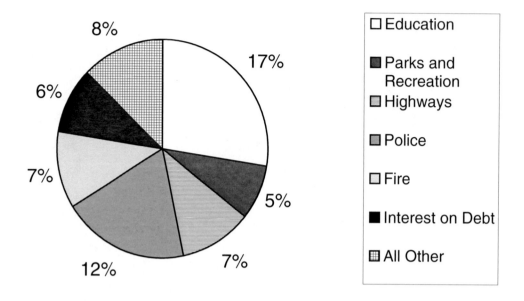

A local government's chief executive officer (CEO), whether mayor, city manager, county executive, or superintendent of schools, is usually in charge of the process, although in some local governments independent fiscal officers such as controllers or treasurers play a part. The budget process begins with the CEO's budget staff or agency developing a projection of revenues for the coming year, so the budget makers will know how much they will have to spend. This is easier said than done given the complex and varied sources of local revenues discussed earlier. Budget projections must predict not only what other governments will do, since local governments are so dependent on intergovernmental aid, but also how boom or recession in the national and local economies will affect local taxes: Will retail sales increase or decrease sales tax revenues? Will property values generate more or less income from property taxes? Will users pay more in charges and fees, or cut back on their use of services? In volatile economic circumstances, such predictions are difficult and risky. They are a particular challenge for small communities with limited staff resources, but even large ones with sophisticated computer projections have difficulty.

Revenue projections are next analyzed by the CEO and his or her executive staff, who develop overall guidelines for spending and sometimes for increases or decreases in particular programs. Normally, this is accomplished with only informal consultation with city councils or county commissioners. Although the CEO will want their support eventually, he or she will try to keep them from interfering in the early stages. Recognizing the significance of the budget and seeking to break into the process, some councils and commissions insist on formal consultation at this point and even issue their own budget guidelines. These are usually less effective than those of the CEO, however, because multimember legislative bodies rarely agree on a single, clear set of priorities.

Budget directives from on high next proceed to departments and agencies, whose heads, along with their own budget aides, put together proposals for their fiefdoms. These may or may not follow the directives. Some department heads, counting council votes and public support, may ask for considerably more than the CEO's guidelines would suggest. Police departments seem particularly able to do this. Most departments ask for a little more than their allocation for the previous year and even a little more than they really need, so that they can absorb expected cuts. Few departments trim their budgets as much as they might because they are competing with other departments that will not and because they know that further reductions are ahead. Most department budgets are therefore padded, at least a little.

The department budgets go back to the CEO and the executive budget staff, where they are reconciled and combined into a complete budget to be recommended to the city council or county commission. It is at this point that the CEO exercises maximum power, balancing various programs, rewarding or punishing departments and their heads, expanding or contracting her or his preferred services and possibly even introducing new ones.

Once this is done, the mayor or manager's draft budget is published, at which point the process becomes public, although few citizens show much interest. Most budget documents are hundreds of pages long, highly detailed, and, perhaps intentionally, incomprehensible. Within a few weeks of publication, the budget will be subject to one or more public hearings and a final vote by the council or commission. During this time, the legislators, few of whom have expertise in budgeting, grapple with this complex document, mostly individually, although sometimes in committees. Some have their own budget analysts or personal staffs to help, but most do not. Lobbyists, however, will offer help. Among these will be the executive, department heads, other bureaucrats, and public-employee union representatives, all trying to persuade legislators to favor their programs and interests. In addition to all this in-house lobbying, a few community groups may also assert pressure. These generally include the clienteles of particular bureaucracies hoping to retain services and chambers of commerce and other business organizations worried about taxes and fees as well as the maintenance of services they view as good for business. Other community groups may become active if they perceive a clear threat or opportunity in the budget. The local newspaper will run a story or two and an editorial on the budget; TV news will mention it only if dramatic (and visual) cuts or tax increases are projected.

This largely behind-the-scenes activity culminates in public hearings at which most of these players give formal public testimony and the council or commission makes a final decision. Besides a few lobbyists, public attendance at the hearings is almost nonexistent except for city hall regulars, a few members of local antitax groups, and clients of particular bureaucracies who may be present when their department's budget is discussed, after which point they leave. Council members and commissioners continue their struggle to assert themselves, but have difficulty changing so authoritative a document presented by an often-domineering CEO and his or her experts who have been working on it for most of a year and when an increase in funds for one program involves cuts in others. The legislators may fiddle with the details, possibly affecting 1 or 2 percent of the total budget, but in the end, with a fixed deadline impending and other business pressing, they will almost always of approve the CEO's budget more or less intact. Their vote and the public hearing that precedes it often amount to little more than a rubber stamp.

The Budget Process in Perspective

The budget process is a little like a runaway train in a tunnel, out of control, unstoppable, and in the dark. It is hidden from most voters, offering few opportunities for public input—and then usually after key decisions have already been made. Decision makers try to reassert their mastery of the process but usually just get run over by it. Some local governments have improved their budget controls, but most are still controlled by the process. Several problems, some of which are not strictly local, are built in.

Local budgeting, probably like our personal budgeting, is revenue driven, incremental, fragmented, insulated, and frequently uncontrollable.[24] The process is almost by necessity **revenue driven** because local governments must begin with an estimate, based on a number of economic assumptions, of how much money will be coming in before they can identify spending priorities. In a perfect world, budgets would be need driven, where policy makers would identify a set of spending needs and then allocate sufficient funds to cover those needs. In the real world, however, most local governments do not have sufficient control over their own revenues or even their spending to budget in any other way (who does?).

Local governments usually start by assuming that revenues will be a little more or a little less than in the previous year. Accordingly, they increase or decrease spending for their programs, adjusting as necessary. When revenue streams were constantly rising, particularly during the 1960s, local governments used this technique (and still do), which scholars call **incremental budgeting**. In recent years, however, decreasing revenue has made **decremental budgeting** more common. In either case, the point is that no major change occurs: the process is conservative. Almost no programs are eliminated entirely, and new ones are rarely introduced. The government and its budget go on more or less as before, often without very serious scrutiny, which may lead to waste and inefficiency. But this is the easiest and least controversial way to make a budget, and the budget process itself makes it inevitable. As we have learned, the process is fragmented, with multiple participants, most of whom are insiders and bureaucrats protecting their own interests. The mayor, manager, and council members could introduce concerns about the more general good and they sometimes do, but the insulated nature of the process usually keeps their attention focused on the trees (specific programs) rather than the forest.

Local officeholders are well aware of these criticisms; many have learned of the problems through firsthand frustration. Elected officials and top managers have tried various means of gaining better control of budgets and the budgetary process. Traditional **line-item budgets** (which allocate funds department by department and then by personnel, operating expenses, equipment, and other specific costs) are, budget expert David Morgan writes, "good for accounting but not so good for measuring the effect of spending on service delivery or quality."[25] Budget reformers in recent years have therefore attempted to impose more analytical and evaluative systems. **Cost/benefit analysis**, for example, requires each department to justify its budgets in terms of services rendered, with the benefits expected to outweigh or at least equal the costs. A related approach, **zero-based budgeting (ZBB)**, requires department managers to rank their programs in order of their priority. The thinking is that by forcing every program to be constructed from scratch and justified with each budget cycle, unnecessary spending can be decreased or eliminated. Essentially the opposite of incrementalism, ZBB sounds good in theory but it's hard to implement in practice.

In the 1990s, the era of "reinventing government" (see chapter 8), **performance-based budgeting (PBB)** caught on in local government. Modeled on similar techniques in the private sector, performance evaluation seeks to set and measure goals for performance of individuals and their departments. "Mission-driven" local governments were urged to develop quantifiable performance measures to set standards for service provision and shape budgets. The response time of police officers, fire fighters, or other service providers could be measured, for example, and these measurements could be used for budgeting—with increased funding for increased performance. Phoenix, for example, does elaborate internal performance evaluations and even sends questionnaires to people outside the government. Portland and San Jose audit departments, require a formal department response, make the reports public, and review improvements annually. Seattle "looks at what the city wants to accomplish across department lines" and opens the budget process "to citizen involvement."[26] However the system is devised, the main point is to connect expenditures with their impact on service delivery. Proponents say that this approach does a better job of ensuring accountability to the public. Although it may put bureaucrats on the defensive, forcing them to justifying their time and performance, performance evaluation makes the process a little more "customer friendly."

A *Municipal Year Book* survey reported cities using over a dozen different and innovative budgeting tools,[27] all in an effort to get past the limitations of traditional incremental or decremental line-item budgeting. Unfortunately, such reforms usually sound better than they work. Budget items do not easily crunch into new categories, and bureaucrats—the main budget players—still find ways of protecting their interests. In the end, whatever local governments do, much of the budget process is beyond their control. Revenues are subject to state regulation as well as the political tolerance of the taxpayers and voters. Spending can be almost as inflexible, as we have seen. In addition, many programs are virtually locked in by entrenched bureaucracies, labor contracts, and public expectations. Some, particularly police and fire departments, are popular and politicians tamper with them only at their peril. Others are mandated—but often unfunded—by state or federal law. Some of these are paid for by intergovernmental aid, in which case the mandates are even more rigid and may require the expenditure of local matching funds. Counties, which mainly deliver mandated programs and rely heavily on intergovernmental aid, have the least budgetary freedom. New York State's counties have local control over only 40 percent of their budgets,[28] and California's typically have discretion over less than 20 percent of theirs. Cities, which receive less intergovernmental aid, have slightly more freedom but often complain about a lack of intergovernmental aid or that programs are mandated without funding ("unfunded mandates"). State and federal officials respond by saying that local governments can't have their cake and eat it too.

Fiscal Stress

"On-going economic struggles, combined with soaring health care and pension costs, marked declines in state aid to local government, and other factors continue to cause serious fiscal problems for municipalities across the country," reported the National League of Cities in 2004.[29] The reality is that since the late 1970s, communities of all sizes have suffered severe **fiscal stress**, and most have had to find ways of cutting spending or increasing revenues, neither of which is easy. State and federal mandates and budget cuts are only part of the problem. Other fixed or rising costs, including labor contracts, and pension and health care costs have greatly impacted local budgets. Economic recession and tax revolts, largely beyond local control, have depressed revenues and increased expenses. Major demographic and economic trends have drained resources from central cities and the Frostbelt and concentrated them in the suburbs and the Sunbelt, isolating needs from resources. In the 1990s, migrating industry and recession brought these same economic conditions even to the relatively affluent central cities of the Sunbelt. Meanwhile, strict state limits on local taxation were made even stronger by the tax revolt movement, which shows no signs of abating. Local revenues were legally or politically capped, even as all the other factors cited above put them into decline.

To further exacerbate matters, the public, worried about crime, schools, traffic, and the environment, demanded increased services from local governments. Big cities found themselves in a particular bind, with businesses and middle-class taxpayers leaving as a social underclass grew, new waves of immigrants arrived, and racial tension increased. Suburbs were better off, but older, inner suburbs faced problems not unlike those of the central cities, and newer ones were often overwhelmed by rapid growth they could not control. Finally, many local governments exacerbated these external and structural problems by their own behavior. Decades of easy income had caused some to become lax in their budgeting even as the budget process, itself political, fragmented, and conservative, resisting tough decisions and innovation. Sometimes, outright mismanagement made matters worse.

Despite all these sources of fiscal stress, local revenues have not generally declined in absolute terms. Most local governments get more money every year. The increases, however, have not kept pace with increased costs and demands for services. Many cities and counties thus face **deficits** almost annually. Their deficits, however, are not like that of the federal government, because they cannot simply borrow to get what they need. Every state requires its local governments to balance their budgets every year, so they must cut expenditures, raise taxes, or at least attempt to increase revenue. One strategy has been to redouble efforts to develop local economies.

Coping: Approaches to Economic Development

Despite numerous obstacles, many local governments have responded to chronic fiscal stress with imagination and innovation. While some merely cut spending department by department in proportion to the overall loss of revenues, others introduced the new methods of budgeting discussed previously, attempting to evaluate what they do and to maximize what they get for their money. Some have found new ways of paying for services and others have found new sources of funds; some have even won voter approval of tax increases.

In some cases, responsibilities for funding of particular services have been shuffled around, usually with state governments taking on greater burdens. Several states, for example, have begun assuming the costs of operating the courts, previously a city or county obligation. The state role in funding education has expanded even further. At the local level, some counties now bill cities for services. For example, counties usually run the jails used by city police to incarcerate those they arrest; now some counties expect to be paid for providing these facilities.

Perhaps the most common solution has been **privatization of services** or **contracting out**. This strategy is another aspect of the reform movement known as "reinventing government." The authors of the book that gave the name to that movement argue that local governments must become more efficient, effective, innovative, and accountable to their "customers."[30] As Richard Kearney notes, decentralization of bureaucracies, employee empowerment, and market-based principles such as privatization of services are among Osborne and Gaebler's principal recommendations.[31]

Here's how contracting works: instead of providing some services with their own employees, local governments contract with private businesses to do the job, usually by a process of competitive bidding. Services are still paid for by tax funds or user fees and charges, but local governments can usually get more for their money. They also avoid adding to their bureaucracies, and when budget time rolls around, they can deal with private contractors much more firmly than with their own in-house departments. Among the services now commonly contracted out are trash collection and disposal, vehicle towing and storage, maintenance of buildings and grounds, data processing, recreation programs and facilities, and snow removal. Towing and disposing of abandoned cars once cost Chicago $25 per vehicle even after deducting the sale of the car for scrap metal; after privatizing, Chicago gained $25 for each vehicle, generating an annual income of $2 million.[32] Although major local services such as police and fire protection are generally not thought suitable for privatization, Scottsdale, Arizona, privatized fire protection during the 1990s and reported an annual savings of 47 percent.[33]

But while privatization as a way to deal with budget shortfalls is increasingly popular, especially in large cities, the evidence of its benefits is mixed. Critics point out that it does not always save money. Unions charge that it leads to lower wages and loss of jobs as private firms hire workers for lower wages and few, if any, benefits. Elected officials worry about loss of control and public accountability for services provided by private companies. Strict oversight is necessary to manage these problems and to prevent privatization from turning into another form of machine-like patronage.[34]

Another increasingly common response to budget problems is to allow alternative institutions to take responsibility for functions that were once city or county services. Special assessment districts have long enabled neighborhoods or business districts to impose small taxes for local improvements the city cannot provide, such as sidewalks or sewers. This mechanism was enhanced in the 1980s by the creation of **business improvement districts (BIDs)**. More than 1,000 BIDs operate around the country, collecting their own taxes to enhance or supplement city services in a particular area. In New York City, the Grand Central Partnership BID provides security, landscaping, street cleaning, and even a shelter for the homeless. Altogether, New York's fifty-one BIDs spend millions of dollars a year in supplemental services. BIDs and assessment districts are also common in St. Louis, where *The Economist* magazine reported years ago that "many streets have gone private."[35] **Common interest developments (CIDs)** (see chapter 4) similarly provide services for fees, but while BIDs are created with the approval of those who pay them taxes, membership in CIDs is a condition of residence. BIDs and CIDs relieve local governments of some service costs but often at the expense of public accountability and the fragmentation of communities into bits with different levels of service according to their ability to pay.

As noted earlier, many local governments have generated additional income by introducing or increasing charges and fees and minor taxes. According to the National League of Cities, the most common action taken by cities in 2004 to increase revenue was "to raise or institute new fees and charges for services."[36] Imposing impact or development fees and, surprisingly, increasing property taxes were also common, particularly in large cities. Voters in various parts of the country have passed bond measures and approved tax increases. The key to winning such approvals seems to be in the packaging of the taxes, which must be clearly linked to voter-perceived needs, such as for transportation or police. In 1989, for example, Oklahoma City voters rejected a tax increase, half of which was not earmarked. But later, voters gave 80 percent approval to a similar increase earmarked for public safety.[37] In San Jose, California, voters approved $400 million in bonds for parks, libraries, and public safety facilities in 2000 and 2002. "**Special-purpose taxes**," writes journalist William Schneider, "are the suburban ideal—not just private government but private taxes."[38] What has long been true for tax-sensitive suburban voters may now apply more broadly.

Generally, local governments have turned to "tried and true" strategies of economic development. According to a study in the 2002 *Municipal Yearbook*, expanding and retaining existing business, attracting new business, redeveloping downtown, diversifying the economic base, and developing small business were the most often cited economic development goals. In order to reach those goals, city officials cited investment in infrastructure, improved or expanded public services, beautifying downtown streetscapes, and marketing strategies such as advertising, special events, festivals, ans so forth, as the most common economic development policies.[39]

Some local governments are becoming even more entrepreneurial. Chicago, New York, and San Diego, for example, have "city stores" that sell old signs, fire helmets, and even bricks from Comiskey Park, once home to the Chicago White Sox. Elsewhere, cities recycle lawn waste to sell as mulch or convert sewage for marketing as fertilizer. Riverview, Michigan, sells methane gas recovered from a landfill it owns to the local utility company. The City of Fullerton, in Orange County, California, has even experimented with providing wireless Internet service in its downtown area in the hopes of enhancing the city's image as a magnet for high-tech firms and workers.[40]

But while many local governments have tried one or more of these methods of coping with fiscal stress, the almost universal response has been to gear up the local growth machine. No fewer than 15,000 local governments host economic development agencies, each hustling projects that will add to their community's tax base, thus increasing revenues without, they hope, costing too much in services. The governmental and tax structures of local governments in most states already impel them to act as growth machines. The fiscal stress of the last several decades has only added to this imperative. But even if it works, economic development is no panacea. Sometimes communities give away more in benefits than they gain in taxes, as many cities have found out. And even if they are net winners, economic development is often a "zero-sum game"—one city's win may be another's loss.

Running Cities on the Cheap

"Much of the urban problem in the United States is the result of trying to run cities on the cheap," economist John Kenneth Galbraith wrote years ago. "The one thing we have never understood was how expensive the . . . city is."[41] But we are not just stingy with money—from the perspective of some cities we are also becoming stingy with power. Because of their dependent status, local governments are prevented from raising the funds that they need and that many of their citizens might like them to spend. Some of this stinginess comes directly from local voters, which is democratic and appropriate, although as noted earlier, discontented taxpayers may be venting their general anger about taxes on local governments in particular because they are the most readily available target. But local voters are only one factor in the fiscal limitations on local governments, and perhaps not a crucial one at that. The deindustrialization of America's workforce as a result of global economic restructuring has begun to whittle away at the nation's middle class, leaving behind cities increasingly divided among rich and poor.[42]

Combined with the fact that "control of city finances," as political economist Mark Gottdiener writes, "has passed over into the hands of state, federal, and private interests and out of the grasp of local residents,"[43] it's understandable why observers of local politics sometimes sound a little gloomy.

Essential Terms

operating budget
capital budget
property tax
assessed value (AV)
tax rate
fairness of assessments
regressive tax
progressive tax
separation of needs and resources
tax revolt
Proposition 13
fiscalization of land use
local income tax
payroll tax
sales tax
charges and fees
intergovernmental aid
shared revenues
earmarked
mandates
grants-in-aid

borrowing
tax or revenue anticipation notes
　(TANs or RANs)
general obligation (GO) bonds
revenue bonds
voter approval
spending patterns
budget cycle
revenue driven
incremental budgeting
decremental budgeting
line-item budgets
cost/benefit analysis
zero-based budgeting (ZBB)
performance-based budgeting (PBB)
fiscal stress
deficits
privatization of services or contracting out
business improvement districts (BIDs)
common interest developments (CIDs)
special-purpose taxes

On the Internet

- Current and previous editions of the *Statistical Abstract of the United States* can be found at www.census.gov/statab/www/.
- The *County and City Data Book*, which contains Census 2000 information for cities and counties, can be found at www.census.gov/statab/www/ccdb.html.
- The *State and Metropolitan Area Data Book* collects statistics on social and economic conditions in the United States at the state and metropolitan area levels. It can be found at www.census.gov/statab/www/smadb.html.

Notes

1. Katherine Barrett and Richard Greene, "American Cities," *Financial World*, February 19, 1991, p. 36.

2. David R. Berman, "State Local Relations: Partnerships, Conflict, and Autonomy," *The Municipal Year Book* (Washington, DC: International City/County Management Association, 2004), pp. 43–59.

3. Clarence Y.H. Lo, *Small Property Versus Big Government: Social Origins of the Property Tax Revolt* (Berkeley: University of California Press, 1990).

4. *Allegheny Pittsburgh Coal Company v. County Commission of Webster County, West Virginia*, 485 U.S. 976 (1989).

5. See Steven D. Gold and Martha A. Fabricius, *How States Limit City and County Property Taxes and Spending* (Denver: National Conference of State Legislatures, 1989), p. 9. See also Advisory Commission on Intergovernmental Relations, *Significant Features of Fiscal Federalism* (Washington, DC: U.S. Government Printing Office, 1992), p. 18.

6. Berman, "State Local Relations."

7. Ibid.

8. Frederick D. Stocker, ed., *A Look at State and Local Tax Policies: Past Trends and Future Prospects* (Cambridge, MA: Lincoln Institute of Land Policy, 1991), p. 17.

9. Barrett and Greene, "American Cities," p. 29.

10. David R. Berman, "State Actions Affecting Local Government," *The Municipal Year Book* (Washington, DC: International City/County Management Association, 1992), p. 51.

11. Berman, "State Local Relations."

12. Barrett and Greene, "American Cities," p. 29.

13. Ibid., p. 32.

14. U.S. Department of Commerce, *Statistical Abstract of the United States, 2004–2005* (Washington, DC: U.S. Government Printing Office, 2004), p. 296.

15. Berman, "State Local Relations"; and U.S. Department of Commerce, *Statistical Abstract of the United States, 1992* (Washington, DC: U.S. Government Printing Office, 1992), p. 296.

16. Advisory Commission on Intergovernmental Relations, *Significant Features of Fiscal Federalism, 1989*, vol. 2 (Washington, DC: US Government Printing Office, 1989), p. 18.

17. Berman, "State Local Relations."

18. Berman, "State Actions," p. 51.

19. Eugene T. Lowe, *A Status Report on Hunger and Homelessness in America's Cities, 2002* (United States Conference of Mayors, 2002).

20. Matthew Alan Cahn, H. Eric Schockman, and David M. Shafie, *Rethinking California: Politics and Policy in the Golden State* (Upper Saddle River, NJ: Prentice Hall, 2001).

21. Advisory Commission on Intergovernmental Relations, *Significant Features of Fiscal Federalism*, vol. 2 (Washington, DC: U.S. Government Printing Office, 1990), p. 253.

22. Quoted in Berman, "State Local Relations," p. 55.

23. Roy Green and Randall Crane, "Debt Financing at the Municipal Level: Decision Making During the 1980s," *The Municipal Year Book* (Washington, DC: International City/County Management Association, 1989), p. 106.

24. See Robert L. Lineberry and Ira Sharkansky, *Urban Politics and Public Policy*, 3rd ed. (New York: Harper and Row, 1978), pp. 243–44.

25. David R. Morgan, *Managing Urban America*, 3rd ed. (Pacific Grove, CA: Brooks/Cole, 1989), p. 275.

26. Barrett and Greene, "American Cities," p. 24; other examples are also from Barrett and Greene.

27. *The Municipal Yearbook* (Washington, DC: International City/County Management Association, 1989), p. 47.

28. *New York Times*, March 31, 1991.

29. Michael A. Pagano and Christopher Hoene, *Research Report on America's Cities: City Fiscal Conditions in 2004* (Washington, DC: National League of Cities, 2004), p. iii.

30. David Osborne and Ted Gaebler, *Reinventing Government: How the Entrepreneurial Spirit Is Transforming the Public Sector*, repr. (New York: Plume 1993).

31. Richard C. Kearney, "Reinventing Government and Battling Budget Crises: Manager and Municipal Government Actions in 2003," *The Municipal Year Book* (Washington, DC: International City/County Management Association, 2004), pp. 28–33.

32. Barrett and Greene, "American Cities," p. 22.

33. Morgan, *Managing Urban America*, p. 191.

34. See for example, C. J. Hech, "Contracting Municipal Service: Does It Really Cost Less?" *National Civic Review* (June 1983): 321–26; and Harold Sullivan, "Privatization of Public Services: A Growing Threat to Constitutional Rights," *Public Administration Review* 47, no. 6 (November–December 1987): 461–67.

35. *The Economist*, July 25, 1992, p. 46.

36. Pagano and Hoene, *Research Report on America's Cities*, p. iii.

37. Barrett and Greene, "American Cities," p. 29.

38. William Schneider, "The Suburban Century Begins," *Atlantic Monthly* 270, no. 1 (July 1992): 39.

39. Laura A. Reese, Raymond A. Rosenfeld, and David Fasenfest, "The State of Local Economic Development Policy," *The Municipal Year Book* (Washington, DC: International City/County Management Association, 2002), pp. 12–14.

40. Rong-Gong Lin II, "More Cities Seeing WiFi Zones As Destinations," *Los Angeles Times*, April 4, 2005.

41. Quoted in the *Los Angeles Times*, October 4, 1970.

42. Sassen, *The Global City*.

43. Mark Gottdiener, *The Decline of Urban Politics: Political Theory and the Crisis of the Local State* (Newbury Park, CA: Sage, 1987), p. 15.

13 Politics and Public Policy
Some Local Issues and Battles

All of the elements of local politics discussed thus far, from its environment to its formal institutions and informal influences, come together to shape the programs and policies of local governments. After all, local governments exist to provide certain services and make certain kinds of decisions. We have referred to these throughout this book, but mostly in terms of which types of governments do what rather than how or why they do it at all. Yet political battles in local politics are usually over the latter and only occasionally over whether something should be done at all.

In this chapter, we will consider in greater detail several major policy areas that local governments deal with and some of the issues they confront in doing so, as well as the political forces involved. As we go through each policy area, be thinking about the factors that we have studied so far. Ask yourself how variables such as geography, demographics, and institutional and non-institutional players impact each issue, and how each of these factors interrelates with the others. Also, think in terms of political power: who has it, why, and how is it being used?

Focusing on policy helps us understand the real and human impacts of what local governments do. It also puts the elements of local political systems into a more concrete perspective, suggesting which factors are significant and which are marginal. Again, as we explore each policy area, be sure to employ the analytical tools for understanding politics that we have already introduced. Now that we've mastered the basics of local politics, we can use those tools to better understand politics and policy.

A Public Policy Sampler: Education, Welfare, Crime, and Transportation

What is "public policy"? In short, it is pretty much any action that governments take or fail to take to address a given problem. The major tools of public policy are "sticks" and "carrots." You can think of sticks as **disincentives**, ranging from a thirty-year prison sentence for armed robbery to a $10 ticket for jaywalking. Both of these examples are attempts to deter crime, perhaps with the ultimate goal being social stability. But you can also think of a government's ability to raise, say, gas taxes as a disincentive to driving, with the ultimate policy goal being an increase in public transit ridership. But governments can also use "carrots," or **incentives**, to address public policy problems. The home mortgage interest deduction is a classic example of a government incentive, in this case, to increase property ownership, perhaps with the goal of creating social stability.

311

Of course, not all problems require a government solution, and for almost all public policy issues, advocates of free markets argue for the need to take a laissez-faire approach. For example, many conservatives argued for decades that government welfare programs were a disincentive to work. Free-market enthusiasts believe that government should only play a minimal role in addressing issues such as poverty. In the area of public education, to take another example, free-market enthusiasts support the idea of vouchers, which uses market logic to improve public education. In each of the public policy areas that follow, be thinking about the ways that governments can use either sticks or carrots (or the free market) to solve problems.

As we have seen, local governments provide a wide variety of services, each of which makes up its own policy area. We can't consider all of them here, but we will briefly examine the four that eat up the most money: education, welfare, crime, and transportation. Then, we will study in greater detail what is perhaps the most important policy area over which local governments wield authority: land-use policy.

Education Policy

Although education is by far the largest single spending category for all local governments combined, it is ultimately a state responsibility that is locally provided. State governments supply the largest share of education funds and also regulate much of what goes on in schools, including testing, curricula, textbooks, employment of teachers and administrators, and more. Although a few states delegate the actual operation of the schools to cities or counties, most assign this responsibility to independent **school districts**. The districts supplement state funding through local taxes, particularly the property tax, but state regulations often mean that the districts have little discretion about either the taxes or the sort of education provided. Despite promises of national leaders to improve education, the federal government has historically provided less than 10 percent of the total money spent on public schools. It is critical to remember that education has long been almost exclusively a state and local issue. That is why a passage of the No Child Left Behind Act in 2001 represented such an unprecedented expansion of federal authority over education.

The nation's school districts are divided into "independent" school districts, which are counted as separate units of government, and "dependent" school districts, which are classified as agencies of some other governments, such as state-, county-, or municipal-run districts. Of the nation's 15,029 school districts, 13,522 are independent, and the remaining 1,507 are classified as part of some other government. Generally, most are governed by small elected **school boards**. Most board members are concerned parents rather than education experts. They serve only part-time and generally leave the management of the schools to the professional educators they appoint. Because they do much of the day-to-day governing, the selection of school superintendents is often hotly contested and sometimes politicized. Superintendents run school district bureaucracies that may be quite small, or, as in the case of New York City's Department of Education, they may oversee a huge bureaucracy and a $13 billion budget. Other important education issues include curriculum, testing, teacher hiring and evaluation, truancy and dropout rates, drug use, and even the hot button issues of sex education and, more recently, teaching the theory of evolution. Keep in mind that although local school boards make many of these decisions, state regulations often limit the options available to school boards.

The main participants in local education politics and policy are usually parents, administrators, and teachers and their unions. Business leaders also have a direct interest in education, particularly in ensuring a properly skilled workforce. For example, Microsoft founder Bill Gates and his wife, through the Bill and Melinda Gates Foundation, have already spent more than $2 billion on education policy and reform issues. The Gates Foundation views adequate educational preparation as essential for ensuring American competitiveness in the twenty-first-century global economy. But this level of commitment is rare among business leaders. Individuals or groups not directly impacted by education typically show little interest, which becomes problematic when school districts take tax proposals to the voters (as they must). Schools have particular difficulties passing referenda on taxes because although almost everyone pays, only a few benefit directly. Single people, childless couples, empty-nesters whose children have left home, and those with children in private schools may be reluctant to pay higher taxes for the benefit of others, particularly where community cohesiveness has grown weak. Of course, the quality of local schools often directly impacts property values, providing at least some direct incentive for community support. Yet if support declines, the burden on schools (as well as the larger community) only increases because such social problems as crime, violence, drugs, and cultural conflict all relate in one way or another to educational opportunity. All of these, along with the issues of segregation and funding, touch most of the school districts in the United States.

Segregation

Racial segregation of schools was common and legal in the United States until the 1954 U.S. Supreme Court decision in *Brown v. Board of Education of Topeka,* which ruled that de jure or intentional segregation by law was unconstitutional.[1] Many school districts were ordered to find ways of integrating their schools. After dragging their feet, sometimes for years, some districts reluctantly expanded their boundaries to include more minorities, but in other communities the problem went beyond the schools themselves. Many districts were segregated not because of formal school board policies or state law, but because neighborhoods in their communities were themselves segregated. Such de facto segregation—by practice rather than by law— was common not only in the South, but all across the United States. Recognizing that intentional segregation by race was harming the educational opportunities of minority students, particularly black students, lower federal courts eventually ordered reluctant school districts to integrate. The primary—if controversial—means to implement the goal of racial integration was busing.

Busing proved highly controversial and resulted in hundreds of court cases, referenda, and electoral defeats for school board members and other officials, as well as protests, violence, and even riots. Violence took place not only in southern cities, but even in supposedly liberal northern ones such as Boston, where working-class Irish and Italian families deeply resented the forced busing of their children to schools in black neighborhoods during the 1970s.[2] But although racism was a main reason for local resistance to busing, opponents legitimately pointed to the fact that busing would upset long-standing traditions of neighborhood schools and local control. The federal courts, they asserted, had placed the constitutional rights of individual students above the rights of communities to decide how to run their schools. Busing was also disruptive for schools and students, especially where it was ordered by federal courts. Perhaps in recognition of these problems, as well as public backlash, the courts eventually softened their approach somewhat, allowing school districts to develop voluntary busing schemes often centered around magnet schools with specialties designed to attract a mixture of students. Although these actions improved integration in some school districts, neighborhood segregation, especially in the North and in the suburbs, made meaningful integration impossible without crossing district lines. But the U.S. Supreme Court overruled cross-district busing or other integration plans unless it could be demonstrated that district lines were drawn with the intention of segregation—an extremely high legal threshold. Because intentional segregation is difficult to prove, the vast majority of integration plans stop at district boundaries.

Has desegregation worked? The evidence is mixed. Certainly the policy had a number of unintended consequences. First, court-ordered busing may have served to *increase* school segregation by accelerating white flight from central cities to suburban school districts. Moreover, many middle-class and affluent parents simply removed their kids from public schools and enrolled them in more expensive private schools. As a result of high rates of private school attendance, particularly among children of the wealthy, many communities today lack broad-based support for their public schools.

After decades of attempted desegregation, a 1993 Harvard study reported that 66 percent of African American and 73 percent of Hispanic students were attending schools that were over half black or Latino, or both, and that these figures were slowly rising, not falling. According to the study, this was due not to white flight but to immigration and higher birth rates among minorities along with the isolation of minorities in certain school districts.[3] In a 1999 report entitled *The Resegregation of America's Schools*, Harvard researchers again documented the increasing segregation of Latino and black students across America. The authors noted that, increasingly, "whites are remaining in overwhelmingly white schools even in regions with very large non-white enrollments."[4] Indeed, even the federal courts have begun to back away from the notion of integration.

The year 2004 marked the fifty-year anniversary of the *Brown* decision overturning the doctrine of "separate but equal." Reflecting upon on the legacy of the *Brown* decision, many civil rights advocates now question having focused their legal fight on racial integration, which has had only limited success. Many civil rights leaders believe that primary emphasis should have been placed on ensuring **funding adequacy** for minority school districts. Yet as we will see, politically, ensuring adequate funding has been at least as difficult as ensuring integration.

Funding

The issue of school funding is closely related to the issue of segregation. The fragmentation of urban areas into multiple local jurisdictions produces segregation not only by race but also by class, resulting in the familiar needs/resources dichotomy, with the poor and minorities concentrated in some districts and the more affluent in others that are richer in tax resources. Since the property tax is the primary local source of funds and since the tax base is not evenly distributed, some districts are richer than others and can spend more on education. Studies show wide variation in per pupil expenditures for education. States such as Vermont, New Jersey, and New York have traditionally been the most generous, spending an average of $11,000 per student per year. Other states, such as Mississippi, Utah, and Oklahoma, spent roughly half that amount per student. Moreover, because many school districts are primarily funded by local property taxes, there can also be wide disparities among districts in the same state. In 1973, the U.S. Supreme Court ruled in *San Antonio v. Rodriguez* that such funding disparities were not unconstitutional.[5] However, the supreme courts of several states have declared that unequal education spending does violate their state constitutions. Texas and other states are currently grappling with this issue while some states, such as California and Hawaii, have attempted to equalize funding between districts, with only limited success and many unintended consequences.

And yet, some education researchers downplay the impact of funding disparities. Underscoring the lack of consensus in education policy circles, some studies have found that per pupil spending is less important than other factors such as income and community and family support in predicting student achievement. Students in Utah, for example, which is near the bottom in per pupil spending, consistently perform above the national average on standardized tests. Most studies, however, reveal that money does matter, at least to some extent, and particularly in poor communities. But it is also clear that other factors such as income and family and community support also matter.[6]

But the problems in public education are related not just to unequal funding. Besides having less money, central city school districts have more expensive problems and often less discretion over how to spend their limited funds. Inner-city schools often must cope with maintenance expenses of older buildings, for example, while newer suburban districts need not. Inner-city schools also enroll more than their fair share of children with learning disabilities and disadvantaged kids who require expensive, and often state-mandated, compensatory education. Moreover, increased immigration in the 1980s and 1990s, mostly to metropolitan areas, brought many pupils who speak little or no English. More than a third of the students in big-city schools in California, New York, and Texas, for example, are not native English speakers. The courts have ruled that minority-language students are entitled to special assistance, and although the federal government provides some aid, most of this expensive burden, as with desegregation and teaching the disadvantaged, falls on already underfunded central city schools. Meanwhile richer suburban districts, with fewer problems and mandates and more money, can provide educational enrichment. Finally, even where state governments mandate equal spending per districts, such as California, wealthier communities have turned to a new source of revenue—**educational foundations**—nonprofit, community-sponsored entities that raise revenue from parents and other private sources to supplement state spending. Because this money does not need to be shared with other districts, some criticize educational foundations for furthering funding disparities.

Funding remains a critical issue in education, but with states in charge, courts intervening, and local voters reluctant to raise taxes, school districts can do little about it except spend what they get as best they can. Unlike cities and counties, they cannot expand their tax base by ramping up development. More often, they may be victims of that development, obliged to educate growing populations without much tax benefit. These issues again suggest the ways that local governments are limited. Although 90 percent of the nation's school districts are formally independent, their local discretion is severely constrained by the actions of the state, federal, and other local governments, as well as by the voters and by individuals making decisions about where to live and where to send their kids to schools.

IN YOUR COMMUNITY

Discuss the pros and cons of policies intended to equalize school district spending. Have there been any attempts to equalize spending in your state or community?

Recent Policy Reforms

In recent years, education reform has become an increasingly hot topic in policy circles. However, numerous initiatives to address an "education crisis" have come and gone since at least the early 1980s when the report *A Nation at Risk* identified serious inadequacies in the American K–12 public education system, and warned of dire consequences for America's economic competitiveness if reforms were not made.[7] However, there has since been little agreement among researchers as to how to even define what the problems are, perhaps the most important step in addressing any policy issue. Education policy experts generally divide into two camps. Some focus on "student-centered" explanations and view underperformance as a result of class deprivation, family upbringing, and other cultural factors that fail to instill educational skills and values in students. Others research "school-centered" explanations and view poor performance as resulting from problems with the education system, in particular teacher preparation and pay, curriculum, and school organization and management. These widely divergent explanations as to how to define the problems has led to uncertainty on the part of policy makers as to which reforms will work.

An important recent reform spearheaded by the administration of George W. Bush is known as the **No Child Left Behind Act (2001)**. The law mandates annual standardized testing for students in grades three through eight and greater accountability for teachers, among other reforms. The law represents a radical departure from the federal government's historically "hands-off" role in public education. Prior to 2001, education had been almost exclusively a state and local issue, with the exception of a handful of federal nutrition and disability programs that make up most of the roughly 10 percent that federal sources contribute to school district budgets.

Many states and school districts have criticized the No Child Left Behind Act as an expensive, unnecessary, and in some ways counterproductive intrusion into local affairs. First, critics say that most states already had their own testing procedures in place to assess student performance. Second, opponents object to the fact that if a school fails to perform to standards, federal money may be taken away from that school, compounding rather than fixing the problem. Moreover, many classroom teachers cite increased pressure to "teach to the test," which they say may increase test scores through rote memorization, but does so at the expense of developing more important skills such as critical thinking. Some education professionals also say that a "one-size-fits-all" test cannot possibly measure the diversity of individual learning experiences. Perhaps above all, states and local school districts view the Act as another federal "unfunded mandate," which they say requires significantly more money to implement than the federal government currently provides. Although the jury is still out on its effectiveness, the No Child Left Behind Act represents one of the most significant education policy reforms in decades.

Voucher programs are another popular reform alternative, particularly with free-market advocates. The theory behind vouchers is to use the power of school choice to motivate educational improvement. Under a voucher system parents who are dissatisfied with their current public school can use government money—usually several thousand dollars per year—to enroll in a better performing private school. The market-based logic behind vouchers is that the threat of exit will motivate public schools to come up with a better product for their customers. However, critics of voucher programs, particularly teacher unions, cite a number of objections, including the fear that vouchers will eventually undermine the nation's commitment to public education. Although voucher programs have been tried in a number of places—most prominently in Milwaukee and Cleveland—the evidence for their utility still remains unclear.[8]

Another frequently mentioned educational reform in recent years has been **charter schools**. The idea behind charter schools is that state- and school district–level management of schools does not allow sufficient flexibility to administrators and teachers. Thus, charter schools typically free schools from most state controls, allowing administrators and teachers greater freedom in their educational roles. At least thirty-nine states have enacted legislation to enable charter schools, but, as with vouchers, the evidence of their effectiveness is still unclear. According to a 2003 study by the nonpartisan National Association for Education Progress (NAEP) found that "in mathematics, fourth-grade charter school students as a whole did not perform as well as their public school counterparts." The study also reported "no measurable difference" in the performance of charter school and comparable public school students on reading exams.[9] Again, the fact that there is little agreement as to whether education will improve with greater federal oversight or with more flexibility for administrators and teachers at the individual school level should tell you something about the lack of consensus on how to properly reform America's public schools.

IN YOUR COMMUNITY
Have there been attempts to institute charter schools or voucher programs in your community? Discuss the pros and cons of these policies.

Welfare Policy

Welfare policy covers a broad spectrum of programs in the United States. If health spending for the uninsured poor is included, welfare ranks second only to education in local government spending. Counties are usually the major players in administering welfare and health services, although in some states, mainly in the Northeast, these are city duties. In either case, the funding is chiefly by the state and federal governments with local ones sometimes adding matching funds and delivering the services under guidelines from the higher levels.

Until 1996, the biggest welfare program was **Aid to Families with Dependent Children (AFDC)**. First created during the Great Depression, the program was funded by federal grants to the states, which both state and local governments could supplement. States had some discretion as to who qualified for benefits and how much they would receive. In its final year, roughly 14 million people received AFDC, costing taxpayers roughly $14 billion.[10] In 1992, monthly AFDC payments combined with food stamp benefits (a separate federal welfare program) for a family of three ranged from $412 in Mississippi to $1,184 in Alaska, although in most states the figure was closer to $600, leaving the vast majority of families well under the federal poverty level.

During the 1980s and early 1990s, momentum built up for reform of the nation's welfare laws. Among other reasons, reformers argued that the existing system was creating a "culture of dependency" among many of the nation's poor. Momentum for reform was such that Democrat Bill Clinton, who was facing reelection, announced his intention to "end welfare as we know it." In 1996 Clinton signed the Personal Responsibility and Work Opportunity Reconciliation Act. The Act replaced AFDC with a new program, **Temporary Assistance for Needy Families**, or **TANF**. States were given TANF block grants and had to force welfare recipients to work in exchange for their benefits. More importantly, the new law limited welfare benefits to a lifetime total of five years. So far, most observers believe the law has been generally successful. By 2000, many states, such as Idaho, Oklahoma, and Wyoming reported huge (around 90 percent) reductions in welfare caseloads.[11] The caveat, however, is that although more people were working, at least part of the reason was due to an improved economic climate in the late 1990s. Following the recession of 2001–2, many feared higher welfare caseloads might return. An even bigger unknown that many are concerned about is what will happen when large numbers of welfare recipients use up their five-year program benefits.

Medicaid is another important federal welfare program. Not to be confused with Medicare, a separate federal health insurance program for the elderly and disabled, Medicaid is intended to provide medical care for the poor, and those eligible for TANF are usually also eligible for Medicaid. Created in 1965, Medicaid is funded by federal grants to states, and, like welfare, is administered by states, counties, and, in some cases, cities. State and local governments set eligibility standards under federal guidelines and may supplement funding. Local governments (usually counties) also operate hospitals providing emergency and general services as well as special facilities for the mentally ill. In recent years, one of the major issues that impacts local governments has to do with the exploding cost of healthcare. As costs have risen, funding for programs such as Medicaid have not kept pace, and local governments have been forced to make draconian cuts in service, particularly in areas with large numbers of uninsured poor people. Together with Medicare, federal spending on health care accounted for 21 percent of all federal spending in fiscal year 2006. Many believe that such spending is unsustainable, making health care reform a policy area of particular importance to local governments.

Other forms of welfare include Supplemental Security Income (SSI), a direct federal program for the aged, blind, and disabled; food stamps, a program run by the Department of Agriculture; and general assistance (GA) or general relief (GR), primarily state-run programs for which people without children may qualify.

Local governments administer all of these programs, but funding and guidelines from above leave them with only narrow choices. Local officials complain that they lack discretion not only over funds provided by the state and federal governments, but also over increasing portions of their own locally raised revenues due to mandates for matching funds and administration costs for programs that they are legally obliged to provide. The big battles in welfare and health care are fought in state and national, not local, politics. Local governments remain at the margins of these debates, although their mayors speak out and they participate through their state and federal legislative representatives and their lobbyists. They push for more funding by the higher levels of government, but most find welfare eating up more and more of their own discretionary funds, and some mostly rural counties allege that mandated welfare spending is pushing them into bankruptcy. Cities and counties also debate special programs for the homeless or others in need, but budget constraints often prevent action. Battles over these issues are mostly bureaucratic, fought within local governments by elected officials, administrators, welfare workers, unions, and private-sector service providers. Because they are almost always poor, welfare recipients have little representation or say, although some advocacy groups speak on their behalf. The general public, while worried about abuses of the welfare system, shows little interest.

Welfare programs emerged during the Great Depression and expanded during the "war on poverty" of the 1960s. Although not exclusive to urban areas, poverty, and the problems that go with it, are often concentrated in and around urban areas. If poverty in urban areas seems bad now, imagine what it would be like without public assistance. Both the economic problems that cause poverty and the welfare programs intended to deal with it are beyond the control of local governments—again underscoring the ways that local politics is limited. Many local governments do, however, attempt to indirectly address the problem through economic development programs intended to increase local revenues and provide jobs. Unfortunately, many of the new jobs being created in cities are in the low-skilled service sector and don't offer much promise for stability and upward mobility. "Living wage" policies introduced in many cities are another, albeit limited, attempt to address this concern (see chapter 8).

In Your Community
Discuss the merits of welfare programs such as Social Security, Medicaid, and Medicare.

Crime Policy

"I hate to say it," San Francisco Mayor George Moscone once declared, "but crime is an overhead you have to pay if you want to live in the city."[12] Still, one of the big stories during the 1990s was the dramatic drop in crime rates, with violent crime falling by nearly 31 percent between 1994 and 1999, while property crime rates fell even more dramatically.[13] Although researchers cite a number of reasons for falling crime rates, including demographic and economic factors, crime can never be too low. As we learned in chapter 2, urbanization breaks down families and communities, the informal agents of social control. Urbanization increases the propensity for crime through proximity brought about by higher density, the social conflict that comes with diversity, and the social psychology of isolation and alienation. One of the main reasons local governments exist in the first place is to provide public safety. And if you think about it, police forces are the only government agencies that are sanctioned to use coercive force—sometimes lethal force—against the community itself. Ultimately, that power is in the hands of individual officers, who must make split-second decisions about how to use their authority. It's a pretty awesome responsibility, and one that makes the governance of police agencies particularly important.

Like the other government functions discussed thus far, public safety is a responsibility of all levels of government: federal, state, and local. The FBI and ATF are examples of federal law enforcement agencies, while the Highway Patrol and State Capitol police are examples of state law enforcement agencies. But in general, public safety is a responsibility of cities, except in unincorporated areas, where it is a county function usually through the county sheriff's department. Most funding for police is raised locally, all of which underscores the extremely fragmented nature of policing in the United States. Except for minor infractions, however, the laws enforced by city police or county sheriffs are made by the states. States also organize the courts, which are usually administered by counties with some funding from states. Prisons, where those convicted of serious crimes are incarcerated, are normally provided by the states, while counties (or cities in some places) run jails for people awaiting trial and those unable to make bail or for those serving short sentences for minor crimes.

The Police

Policing is the job of cities and is often their biggest single expenditure. Police spending is also usually the most controversial annual budget issue, with almost perpetual community and police pressure on decision makers to spend more and hire more police officers, even at the expense of other programs. Some cities attempt to save money by contracting their police services to county agencies. Crime is usually a top item on the list of public concerns, and thus public officials often make the promise to hire more cops a centerpiece of their campaigns. Interestingly, there is no consensus in the literature on policing about the link between the number of police officers and crime rates. Some scholars believe that crime rates are affected far more by factors such as the economy than the number of officers in a given area.

Besides funding, a whole array of policy issues revolves around **police-community relations**. The videotaped police beating of Rodney King in Los Angeles and the 1992 riots following the acquittal of the police officers involved put this issue in the national spotlight. But most civil rights activists will testify that police abuse is a familiar problem in many minority communities. Police departments have been slow to accommodate demographic change in their communities, with many remaining predominantly white and male, with little emphasis on training that deals with increasing cultural diversity.

One of the reasons for this has to do with a reform movement during the early twentieth century which sought to professionalize police departments. Prior to the 1900s, many police agencies were essentially arms of immigrant-run political machines (see chapter 5). Police jobs became patronage positions, tied to support for the machine. In many cases hiring was based on one's ethnicity rather than preparation or training (think of the old stereotype of the Irish cop). In response, Progressive Era reformers, mostly middle-class white Protestants, attempted to undermine immigrant political power by creating professional police agencies. In deploying the new "science" of police administration, police agencies began to take on a quasi-militaristic culture and hierarchical structures of organization. Standardized tests also became a requirement for admission to police academies, favoring the native-born Protestants, and police agencies began issuing standard service revolvers and requiring officers to wear military-style uniforms. Even today, many police officers are military veterans, sometimes contributing to an "us versus them" mentality within police departments. The notion of a "war on crime" also emerged during this time.

In addition, new policing technologies such as the use of radios and automobiles came into widespread use. While improving the efficiency of some aspects of policing, many officers were no longer "walking the beat," further distancing them from regular contact with communities. And all of these changes coincided with increasing ethnic diversity in many American cities during the twentieth century. Some police seemed set on exacerbating these tensions by behaving like occupying armies, cruising through neighborhoods in armored cars and treating residents like criminals. In some places, the combination became volatile as minority communities rioted in protest of deteriorating economic conditions and police abuse, especially during the 1960s. Many scholars believe the current atmosphere of mistrust and alienation in some cities such as Cincinnati—which experienced anti-police rioting in 2001—are a direct legacy of this history.

Since the 1960s, a new approach known as **community-based policing** emerged as a response to some of the failures of the professional model of policing. Although hard to define, the approach emphasizes decreasing the social distance between officers and the community, enlisting the support of neighborhood watch and other citizen groups in police decisions, and improving civilian oversight and accountability over police departments. In some communities, **civilian review boards** composed of a diverse range of community members have been appointed to adjudicate complaints about police. The idea is that an outside group of nonprofessionals is necessary because the police cannot objectively deal with complaints against themselves—so-called "internal affairs." Led by police chiefs and unions, the police vigorously resist outside review, usually until the next incident forces more pressure for reform. But by raising the issue, community groups have improved the internal police investigation of complaints, and in some places they have succeeded in establishing independent review boards, police auditors, and **inspectors general** to investigate allegations of police abuse.

For the most part, where it has been tried, community-based policing has improved police-community relations, and reforms have not been as disruptive as police departments feared. But the approach's effectiveness varies considerably depending on how much authority, independence, and financing community oversight boards and investigators are given. In addition, successful implementation requires the support of both command staff as well as street officers. Police departments have also tried to better community relations by training officers in how to deal with cultural diversity, and by hiring more minorities, women, and, in some cases, gays so that they better reflect the communities they serve. Critics, however, respond that meaningful change will result only from a fundamental shift in police culture. Moreover, they say that community policing does not adequately address the underlying social causes of criminal activity.

In the 1990s, two additional policing strategies were implemented with considerable success in many communities, perhaps most prominently in New York City under Mayor Rudy Giuliani and Police Commissioner William Bratton. One strategy involved a crackdown on minor or nuisance crimes, from vandalism to panhandling, jaywalking, and the "squeegee men" who washed the windshields of motorists at stoplights and expected payment whether the motorist wanted the service or not. This "zero tolerance" strategy implemented the "broken windows" theory of political scientist James Q. Wilson,[14] which argued that the run-down appearances of some neighborhoods actually encourage crime. City governments applied Wilson's theory by sprucing up neighborhoods, at least superficially. But the New York City Police Department also implemented "strategic policing," which concentrates police resources in particular areas based on real-time collection and computer analysis of crime statistics ("CompStat"). Crime rates dropped dramatically in New York City and the mayor and police commissioner credited their innovative strategies for the improvement. No doubt these strategies were a factor, but crime also decreased dramatically in cities where they were not applied. Most experts view economic and demographic trends as more powerful influences on crime rates than any particular policing strategy.

IN YOUR COMMUNITY

How would you characterize community-police relations in your area? Does your local police department practice "community-based policing" or a more traditional style of policing?

Guns and Gun Control

Widespread possession of guns makes the United States one of the most violent societies in the world. Some experts believe that the availability of guns gives police justification for overreacting when threatened. In 2000, the FBI reported that 65 percent of murders nationwide were committed with firearms, most of them handguns.[15] Some police leaders and many big city mayors have campaigned for **gun control**, and a few cities have banned or required permits for the carrying of handguns, but constitutional issues and the vigilance of powerful interest groups such as the National Rifle Association make it difficult for local governments to act. Besides, given the multiplicity of governments in most metropolitan areas, banning guns in only one might make little difference—criminals could simply buy their guns in the next town over. Although local law enforcement agencies may want to experiment with various gun-control policies, the issue of gun control is larger than any one locality.

Recognizing this, some states have passed modest gun controls such as bans on assault weapons or waiting periods for the purchase of handguns. California's 1989 Assault Weapons Control Act, which passed following a schoolyard shooting in Stockton, California, in which five children were killed and thirty wounded, appeared to give momentum to gun-control advocates. However, difficulty with enforcement blunted the measure's effectiveness. It also galvanized opposition to gun control at the state level during the 1990s. In 1997, legislation to improve the safety of cheap "Saturday night specials" was vetoed by California Governor Pete Wilson. Six weeks later, a measure in Washington state that proposed to require locks for handguns and safety licenses for their owners garnered only 29 percent of the vote. Gun-control proponents attributed the losses to a last-minute lobbying and advertising blitz largely funded by the NRA.[16]

At the federal level, gun-control advocates have also met with limited success. As the country mourned a series of political assassinations in the 1960s, Congress passed the Gun Control Act of 1968, which attempted to limit the sale and production of handguns and prohibited private ownership of such devices as submachine guns and bazookas. In 1993, the U.S. Congress passed the Brady Bill (named for the press aide who was wounded in the attempted assassination of President Ronald Reagan in 1981), which imposed a national five-day waiting period to buy handguns and also required background checks on gun buyers. These controls may help cities in the long run, but most advocates of gun control, including many police agencies, feel they are too limited to have much impact. Opponents of gun control believe that such measures are actually counterproductive, citing studies that purport to show a reduction in personal crime in states with "right to carry" laws.[17] Such contrary findings again underscore the way that politics can insert itself in gun-control policy debates. Realistic advocates of gun control believe the nation's history of individual gun ownership makes sweeping reform of the nation's gun laws highly unlikely.

Drugs

Drugs, another national problem that hits cities hard and gives cops an impossible task, was designated the number one issue by city officials in 1989[18] and still ranks at the top of public safety concerns. Experts believe that drug addiction is partly a social and medical problem, but police deal with drug use only as a crime. During the 1980s and 1990s, the arrival of crack cocaine, crystal meth, and other cheap forms of drugs set off a frenzied response among Americans and government officials. What became known as the "war on drugs" signaled a major crackdown on drug use and distribution. But some began to question the disproportionate focus on urban minority communities, even as the majority of drug users were white and suburban. For example, the Comprehensive Crime Control Act of 1984 imposed mandatory minimum sentences for drug offenses. However, many critics questioned the vastly differential sentencing between laws against powder cocaine, a favorite among more affluent users, and crack cocaine, common in low-income minority communities.

By the end of the 1990s, the focus on drug crimes was in part responsible for the nation's exploding prison population, which, at nearly 2 million people, was the largest in the world. But while local police struggle to cope with the law enforcement end of the drug problem, experts agree that enforcement alone will not stop drugs. Focus needs to be placed on the demand side in terms of greater funding for education and treatment programs. Advocates of the **decriminalization of drugs** such as former Baltimore Mayor Kurt Schmoke argue for repealing laws that make the use or possession of "soft" drugs such as marijuana a criminal offense. They argue that, like the prohibition of alcohol, the current policy has only exacerbated the situation and has made drugs big business for organized crime, particularly urban street gangs. Decriminalization, they assert, would shift the focus to education and treatment and let police concentrate on more traditional crime. Obviously, opponents disagree and feel that decriminalization would increase the use of such "gateway" drugs, leading to widespread use of more harmful drugs such as cocaine and heroin. Cities do not make drug laws, however, so again cities are limited in their response. In any case, the decriminalization approach is unlikely to be widely adopted anytime soon, although in 2000, California voters passed Proposition 36, which decriminalized possession of small amounts of some drugs, requiring drug treatment instead of prison time. Even though the impacts are felt most profoundly in cities and suburbs, like guns and the problems of education and poverty, the scope of the problems that result from drugs are frequently beyond the capacity of local communities to deal with.

Youth Gangs

Gangs are another contemporary urban problem. Like drugs, they are a social phenomenon and, in part, a response to the alienation of urban life. Gangs give young people an identity and a sense of community, however misplaced these may be. Most gangs are based on territory or turf and on race. In Los Angeles County, for example, gangs identify by telephone area codes and sometimes postal zip codes, in addition to traditional neighborhood affiliations. As of 2005, experts estimate there are over 21,500 gangs in the United States, with a total of 731,500 gang members,[19] making it one of the largest armed forces in the world. Fortunately, gangs are highly decentralized and most of their violence is directed at one another. In addition to their social function, gangs also operate economic networks, involved in drug dealing, protection rackets, and other criminal activity. Heavy-handed policing strategies such as **gang injunctions**—which place limits on the ability of gang members to associate with one another—may contain but do not solve the problem. Community policing may help, but most experts view gang membership as a manifestation of wider social problems that are beyond the capacity of police or cities to solve.

One of the bizarre ironies of American immigration policy during the 1990s and 2000s is that stepped-up efforts to deport immigrants who are gang members and who have committed crimes may have had the unintended consequence of spreading gang influence around the world. Experts estimate the gang population in Central America and Mexico alone at nearly 100,000, where gangs have participated in brazen political assassinations, bombings, and other criminal behavior. Central American gangs such as the infamous MS-13 have combined American-style gang organization with extremely violent elements of Central American society emerging from those countries' brutal civil wars during the 1980s to pose a unique and growing threat to American law enforcement agencies. In addition to drug and immigrant smuggling rings, there is evidence that gangs such as MS-13 may be involved with groups such as al-Qaeda in smuggling terrorists into the United States.[20]

Crime and Local Politics

Even as issues such as drugs and gangs have become transnational, they are ultimately fought out on the battleground of local politics. Police-community relations, guns, drugs, and gangs are mostly big-city issues, although many suburbs confront them as well. Crime is a universal worry, however, and most communities fight about the funding of police. In big cities, the main political activists on law and order issues are mayors, council members, administrators, minority leaders, social service agencies, and some community groups. Voters typically favor elected officials who project a "tough on crime" image. The chief of police, usually the most powerful executive officer after the mayor or manager, and police unions are major players and usually winners, thanks to public support. In smaller suburban communities, participants are fewer—council members, the manager, the chief, and the police union (if any)—but the politics are usually the same. In budget battles, police do not always get what they want, but they usually do better than other departments, with at least small annual increases. No amount ever seems to be enough to solve the problem, though, because police concentrate on enforcement and containment, which is their job, rather than on the underlying roots of crime, which is certainly beyond the capacity of any local government agency to address. And despite public support and relatively high levels of funding, even police enforcement activities seem inadequate or at least unable to keep up with rising crime. As a consequence, many individuals, businesses, and communities have turned to **private security** companies, whose forces now considerably outnumber police, a trend that only increases division and social inequality (in this case, in police protection).

On these issues and others, cities and counties find themselves on the frontline, facing social problems they did not create and that they cannot solve single-handedly. Most attempt to contain the problems, but fiscal and political constraints limit even these activities.

Transportation—Policy or Nonpolicy?

Along with education, crime, and growth, the issue that comes up most frequently in opinion polls in both suburbs and central cities is transportation, usually expressed as complaints about traffic. Of course, the issues of growth and transportation are closely connected, since the way communities grow depends on available transportation, and growth, in turn, affects transportation. As with most other policy areas, transportation policy is a complex hodgepodge of federal, state, and local initiatives. In 2001 alone, federal funding for transportation projects amounted to roughly $55.2 billion, while the fifty states added another $91.1 billion.[21] As we will see, American transportation policy has been impacted by many of the factors discussed in chapter 2, including geography and demographics. But over the last hundred years or so, our approach to getting people from point A to point B has been largely determined by one particular technological advancement: the car. But as our highways approach capacity, and as gasoline prices continue to skyrocket, it may be that we are finally nearing an end of the automobile age and quickly approaching a time when we need to more seriously consider transportation alternatives.

Auto Transit

More than any other country in the world, the United States has opted for the automobile as its primary transportation mode, so however communities deal with the issue of transportation, the car is at its heart. Most people do not think of cars as "public transportation," like buses or subways, but the truth is that most of us wouldn't get very far without a vast network of publicly funded roads, bridges, and highways—*a public transportation system*. Most people don't think of the full range of **costs of auto transit**, either—cars seem to be a cheap way to get around for just the price of a little gas. But as a transportation system, cars are actually very expensive for individuals, governments, and society.

Although gas has been relatively cheap in the United States, many of its costs have been subsidized by governments. The Automobile Association of America

(AAA) estimates the total operating costs for a car driven for an average of 12,000 miles at around $8,400 per year. Of course, it depends on the car and the driver, but besides gas, the bill includes a share of the initial purchase price of the car, insurance, maintenance, parking, taxes, and more. Residents of urban areas with good public transit systems, in contrast, might spend as little as $2,000 to $4,000 per year, including the occasional taxis and auto rentals for weekends away. But these direct costs are only a small portion of the total price of our reliance on automobiles. And that figure does not include environmental and other less direct costs. Vast amounts of land are required for auto transportation systems, too, not only for roads and parking, but also for driveways, garages, gas stations, and sales lots. As much as a third of the land in a typical Sunbelt city may be devoted to automobiles, but even their denser Frostbelt counterparts reserve a fifth of their territory for cars.

Look around you. Surely this land, which generates no taxes itself, could be put to more productive uses. Instead, it is paved over, which is not only expensive in itself but which requires further spending for storm drains and flood control, since water runs off the pavement. Some cities are even sinking (or subsiding) because the run-off does not replenish their underground water tables. To all these must be added the social costs of the automobile transportation system. As much as 20 percent of all U.S. households and 33 percent of those in central cities have no car. Children, the elderly, the disabled, and the poor are denied access to the system. Freeways have built walls through cities, isolating poor and minority neighborhoods. Some of those trapped in poverty can't get out simply because they don't have a car to get to the suburbs, where entry-level jobs are increasingly located. Finally, the segregation and isolation wrought by extensive suburbanization would not be possible without the automobile. In short, our nearly exclusive reliance on the automobile has many environmental, health, and social costs, most of which are unseen (don't forget stress!). Total annual public subsidies for cars, including government subsidies, have been estimated at anywhere between $559 billion to $1.6 trillion.[22]

If cars are so costly, why do we continue to rely on them so exclusively for urban transportation? The simple answer is that we love them. Americans are not the only ones; people elsewhere, most recently evidenced by a car-buying frenzy in China, eagerly acquire cars when they can afford to. Yet our love affair with the car is more passionate. In the United States, getting a car is as much a part of coming of age as sex. We give our cars names, put all sorts of bumper stickers and slogans on them, and see them as an expression of our personalities. Of course, some of this passion is the result of massive advertising by automakers, who sell us cars not just as a means of transportation, but as a lifestyle, a way to make ourselves feel more glamorous. We also love cars for the independence and privacy they give us. We can jump in and go where we want when we want, and not have to rely on some transit system that runs on its own schedule rather than ours and that doesn't stop at our doorsteps. In our cars, we can enjoy our own sound systems, talk on the phone, feel secure, and not have to deal with strangers. For many of us, they are a way of coping with urban diversity by avoidance.

But on a more practical level, we need cars to get around. Lots of people say they'd use public transit if they could, but viable alternatives are rarely available because our cities have been built around automobile transportation, with low densities and suburban sprawl, especially in the Sunbelt. Our metropolitan areas are highly decentralized, with downtowns, edge cities, and industrial areas scattered, so they have many centers rather than one, and complex rather than simple, singular commute patterns. But to make public transit systems work, as they mostly do in European cities, high densities and regular commuter corridors are necessary, with enough people going to the same places and living near fixed-rail or bus routes with easy access. Except for our oldest and most geographically compact cities, these conditions are rare in the United States. We urbanized—or suburbanized to put it more accurately—mainly in the twentieth century, the century of the automobile, and our cities were planned accordingly.

Public Transportation Policy

Our **auto-dependence**, however, was not merely an accident of technology and the popular appeal of cars. Powerful economic and political forces were also at work. In the 1920s, most U.S. cities, including those in the Sunbelt, had transit systems, usually electric trolleys running on rails. "Who needs a car in L.A.?" asks a character in the movie *Who Framed Roger Rabbit?*, "We've got the best public transportation in the world." This is taken as a joke now, but Los Angeles's Red Car trolleys once provided a good service. Then, in the 1930s, automakers, oil companies, and tire manufacturers conspired to purchase and eliminate these systems and replace them with buses and private autos. By the time the companies were taken to court and convicted of criminal conspiracy, a hundred trolley systems in forty-nine cities had been eliminated; by the 1950s, most trolleys in the United States were history. The same corporate interests, along with construction companies, also lobbied the state and federal governments to earmark funds raised by gas taxes exclusively for highway building. Many historians qualify this interpretation by noting that it did not take a conspiracy to get Americans into cars. Rather, many were drawn—as Americans inevitably seem to be—to the status, privacy, ease, and convenience of a new technology. In addition to the highway lobby, local growth machines eagerly supported road building to provide access to their land and make development possible. So did the public. Governments in the twentieth century responded, concentrating transportation spending almost exclusively on roads and highways, a policy that stimulated suburbanization that, in turn, may have made alternative modes of transportation impossible.

Changing Priorities

Initially, for the vast majority of Americans, the system worked well. By the 1970s, however, with the costs of using a car rising and traffic congestion and air pollution increasing, governments and the public began to consider alternatives. A modest anti-auto, protransit movement emerged. Environmentalists concerned about sprawling growth and air pollution took the lead, and the antigrowth movement often opposed road building to limit growth. Central city neighborhoods fought threatening freeway projects and won in Boston, New York, San Francisco, and elsewhere, in some cases bringing highway construction to a halt. In the 1960s, leaders in the City of Portland, Oregon, successfully removed a freeway near downtown, diverting it around the city, and opening the door to a more pedestrian-oriented street culture and parks. By the 1980s, the tax revolt hindered road building, but only slightly since highway money comes from gas taxes and is usually earmarked for highways only. In many communities, groups organized to lobby for transit. In a few, groups such as Walk Boston, Auto-Free New York, and the Pedestrian Council of Philadelphia even advocated both the radical transportation alternative of walking and better planning to facilitate it.

Federal, state, and local governments have responded by changing policies. The federal government and most states continue to spend most of their transportation funds on roads and highways, but allocations for transit have increased from virtually nothing to more notable sums. By 1989, for example, the states were spending $57.9 billion on highways and $8.7 billion on public transit projects, while the federal government allocated $15 and $2 billion, respectively. In 1992, President Clinton even proposed $8.4 billion for transit in his first budget. Still, the vast majority of government expenditures have been steered toward road construction rather than public transit.

In the 1970s, many cities and counties took over failing private bus services, sometimes with state or federal aid or with voter-approved tax increases. Sunbelt cities, facing the expense of building new **mass transit systems** to serve their sprawling communities, began to envy older cities with transit systems in place or under construction as in Washington, DC (1975), Baltimore (1983), and Buffalo (1985). San Francisco (1973), Atlanta (1979), and Miami (1983) built expensive but fast heavy-rail systems, while San Diego (1981), Portland (1986), Sacramento (1987), San Jose (1990), and Dallas (1995) opted for cheaper light-rail or trolley networks. In the 1980s and 1990s, Los Angeles built both; however, the vastness of the Los Angeles region makes it unlikely that public transit will ever become the dominant mode of transit. Other communities improved bus services, sometimes dedicating special traffic lanes for buses only. Often, cars with more than one passenger are also allowed to use such **high occupancy vehicle (HOV) lanes**. In 2005, Congress even passed enabling legislation to allow single drivers of hybrid vehicles the ability to use HOV lanes. Some cities built networks of bike lanes or footpaths for walkers.

In recent years, public transit advocates have pointed to statistics showing that Americans are beginning to climb on the public transit bandwagon. For instance, during the late 1990s, public transit ridership was increasing at a higher rate than automobile ridership.[23] However, from an environmental standpoint, despite increased use of public transit, use of the automobile has continued to increase as well. Nationwide, the number of vehicle miles traveled (VMT) doubled between 1970 and 1990, and kept on increasing during the 1990s. The trend has been evident even in cities like Seattle, where governments have sought to create public transit alternatives. Between 1992 and 2004 vehicle miles in the Puget Sound region increased by 23 percent, higher than the rate of population increase.[24] It seems that even good public transit systems are unlikely to woo Americans out of their automobiles.

Alternative Systems

These disappointing statistics fueled the debate about solutions. Big, heavy-rail systems like San Francisco's Bay Area Rapid Transit (BART) and Washington, DC's Metro, are fast and attractive, but expensive, partly because to attain their speed their tracks must be completely separated from roadways. Critics say they serve mainly white-collar suburbanites commuting to central city business districts, while helping intrasuburban commuters and central city residents little. Trolleys, which can be built along existing streets and use well-tested technology, are cheaper, but much slower, and so are less attractive to long-distance commuters. Those that have been built also tend to serve white-collar, suburban commuters best. Buses are the most flexible form of transit because they are not tied to a track, so routes can be changed easily and a wider clientele can be served. For the working poor in many cities, buses are their primary link to workplaces and recreation. But middle-class commuters seem to have an aversion to buses and personnel costs for buses are higher than for trolleys and trains. HOV lanes and, staggered work hours ease traffic congestion, but mostly by spreading it out. Bikeways and footpaths, although attractive, are a realistic solution for few people as yet. "Telecommuting," enabled by computers and high-speed Internet connections, offers some the ability to work from home one or more days a week, cutting down on traffic.

Some transit advocates insist that the best way to get people out of their cars and into public transit is to make driving more expensive and unpleasant. They push for higher gas taxes and parking fees (public policy "sticks") and a halt to road building to allow traffic to grow more and more congested. Some have suggested higher tolls or fees on roadways, possibly electronically charged. Such a punitive approach might well get us out of our cars, but most likely it would be to storm the offices of the bureaucratic agency that imposed it.

Land Use and Transportation. Other transit advocates argue that transit planning needs to be better integrated with local land-use planning if any of these systems are to work. Instead of taking use of the automobile and suburban sprawl for granted and planning accordingly, cities need to plan in such a way as to make public transit more feasible by concentrating people and jobs near transportation corridors, whether that means freeways or trolleys. Generally, this means higher densities. One study found that "doubling residential density reduces the annual auto mileage per capita by 25 to 30 percent."[25] Some transit systems, however, require higher densities than others. The Sierra Club estimates that rail systems need densities of forty-three homes per acre within one-eighth of a mile of stations, but a University of Indiana study found eight units per acre sufficed for buses.[26] Central cities in the Frostbelt have been concentrating densities along transportation corridors for decades, but some Sunbelt and suburban cities, especially where the growth-control movement is strong, have only recently begun to do so; many also require a transportation study for any new development.

IN YOUR COMMUNITY

Are there public transit alternatives in your community? Do you use them? If not, why not?

An alternative to higher densities is planning for a better balance of housing, jobs, and shopping so people need to travel shorter distances. Edge cities are an example of such developments. Instead of dense, centralized urban regions, we could plan for decentralized or multinucleated metropolitan areas with many centers rather than just one. To some extent this is already happening. As early as 1980, twice as many workers commuted to jobs within the suburbs as commuted from suburb to central city. This shift in commuting patterns helps, but it doesn't always solve transportation problems and may merely complicate the building of viable transit systems because commuters take a variety of routes rather than a single one. As transit systems reach capacity, intersuburban commuting may also take as long or longer than commuting between suburb and central city. The goal of better land-use planning—discussed in more detail in chapter 14—is not merely to redistribute the commute but to reduce it by bringing jobs, housing, and other facilities closer together.

The Issues—Which Systems, Who Rides, Who Pays, Who Decides?

Which alternative is best? The answer is that no single system suffices. Big cities not wholly dependent on the automobile rely on a complex network of trains, subways, trolleys, buses, roads, bikeways, footpaths, and even ferries. People have diverse transportation needs and differing tolerances for the various modes, so each system will attract and serve different clienteles. Many people need to use two or three modes to reach their destinations, perhaps walking or driving to a station, taking a train or heavy-rail system to another, then a bus and a short walk. The problem is that few will find that a subway, trolley, or even bus takes them door-to-door, like their cars can (or could). Until an extensive and elaborate system is in place, with easy and convenient changes from one mode to another, it will be difficult to get people out of their cars. Yet building such a network takes time and tremendous financial support and despite the great hopes for systems such as San Francisco's BART or all the trolley lines that have been built in recent years, each is only a piece in the puzzle— with the solution years away. As systems come on line and the cost of driving rises in money, time, and air quality, more and more people will get on board. Or so transit planners hope. Changes in land-use planning, including higher densities and mixed uses, will also help, but only in the long term.

Who Rides and Who Pays?

The issue, however, is not only which system or combination is best. Other questions arise about who should be served and who should pay. Minority, civil rights, and central city leaders usually push for transit for those most in need—low-income people without cars—arguing that lack of transportation is part of the poverty trap. Environmentalists and most transit planners, however, argue that the primary goal should be getting people out of cars, so their ideas mostly target riders who are less needy, middle-class, mostly suburban commuters. Deciding who the riders should be affects the mode of transportation chosen, since the neediest will primarily use buses, while experts say a "sexier" form of transit, like sleek heavy rail or trolleys, is required to get middle-class commuters out of their cars. Of course, low-income, inner-city dwellers can use systems designed for middle-class suburbanites, but they usually need to go to places not served by these systems. A related issue is who should pay—the riders or the taxpayers? Although taxpayers are reluctant, some of the new systems, such as those in California, have been funded by taxes approved by state or local voters. None would have been built without substantial federal subsidies, however. Once built, transit systems continue to require subsidies for operating costs. Fares paid by riders are never enough, and raising fares to cover costs would only mean fewer riders. Continuing subsidies will be necessary, but while who pays for public transit remains an issue, we need to bear in mind that automobile transportation is heavily subsidized, too.

Who Decides?

The ultimate issue in transportation, however, is **who decides**. And the answer is no one. Rather, many decide. We each make decisions when we choose where to live in relation to our work—and more people are making this decision consciously and carefully. Transportation is also affected by the land-use decisions of individual cities and counties. Taken together, these decisions structure the transportation needs of a region, yet they are not necessarily made with that in mind. The state and federal governments, which supply much of the funding for transportation, set their own priorities as to which cities and counties must adapt their decisions about road building and public transit. As always, another major problem is political fragmentation. Some transit or bus systems are operated by individual cities, but most cross city boundaries. Many are managed by counties or special districts that encompass several cities. This is more appropriate because transportation is a regional issue—few cities are self-contained and few of us confine our lives to just one city. Recognizing this, most metropolitan areas also have regional transportation planning agencies whose primary goal is to try to coordinate all the transit systems in their areas, including land-use planning. As we will see in the next chapter, these regional governments often operate with little or no formal authority. The answer to *who decides*, then, is individuals, cities, counties, separate transit systems and agencies, regional authorities, and the state and federal governments. True coordination occurs only by occasional miracles of cooperation and luck.

The absence of a coordinated transit policy makes democratic accountability difficult because no one is in charge. Having no central decision maker also means that the system is biased in favor of the status quo—the automobile—which suits the powerful forces of the growth machine and the highway and oil lobby very well. The nonpolicy is, in fact, their policy. Perhaps it is ours, too. Americans love their cars and although opinion polls report majorities in favor of public transit, most of us mean we support transit for other people—so we can drive in less traffic. Ultimately, solving the transportation problem will require regional planning and regional authority, not only for transit systems, but also for land use, which takes us to the issue of controlled growth and on to the subject of our next chapter, metropolitan regional government.

Land-Use Policy: The Politics of Growth

We chose to end this chapter on public policy with a focus on an area we think deserves particular attention. Regulating land use and development is probably the greatest discretionary power allocated to cities and counties by states as well as the main way they attempt to affect their own fate and well-being. As such, the politics of land use and growth policy have cropped up throughout our study of local politics and they often dominate local decision making, particularly for cities.

Zoning and General Plans

Cities have land-use authority within their borders, which they may expand by **annexation**. Counties have fixed boundaries within which they generally regulate land use only in areas that are not part of any city ("unincorporated areas"). In either case, the basic mechanisms for land-use control are zoning and general planning. Development was once freely allowed in communities, but problems arose when adjacent projects didn't fit together, like a factory or a slaughterhouse next to homes or a park. **Zoning** was conceived to avoid such problems by setting out districts exclusively for certain kinds of development, ranging from single-family, suburban-style homes to high-rise apartments, commercial and retail, and industrial areas. In recent years, mixed-use zoning, when, for example, housing units are built above shops in a commercial zone, has become an increasingly important alternative.

At first, zoning was controversial because it limited the rights of property owners to do what they want with their land, but the U.S. Supreme Court ruled it a constitutional use of local power in 1926,[27] and its use spread rapidly. Property owners nevertheless still bring court cases on alleged unfairness. The courts have ruled zoning restrictions based on race, religion, or national origin unconstitutional, but zoning is generally allowed to segregate by class (which often equals race) through the concentration of homes of a similar value in a particular area so that only people of a certain income level can afford to move there. Such **exclusionary zoning** has been challenged in the courts, but unless an explicit intent to discriminate by race can be proven, it is allowed to stand.

General or master plans, another twentieth-century innovation, aim to rationalize all of a community's zones and to project a coherent vision of future development. Sewers, street plans, parks, and other public facilities are also included. The idea of a **general plan** is to project development into the future, although many reflect only what already exists. General plans typically look ten to twenty years ahead, but as conditions change plans must change. Minor alterations usually are made at annual hearings with reconsideration of the entire plan every five years or so.

Once a community's general plan is in place, developments that conform need only formal approval by the city council or county board. Landowners or developers who want to do something different need to apply to the city or county for a **zoning variance**, or exception to the general plan. The city or county's professional planners study the requested change and make a recommendation, which is often considered by an advisory planning commission before it goes before a public hearing and a vote by the city council or county board. Much of the meeting time of local bodies like these is taken up by such land-use decisions, especially in growing communities. Zoning variances are often highly controversial, because they often favor developers or business owners over local residents.

Capital improvement projects such as roads, sewers, storm drains, and other infrastructure facilities are also included in general plans, as local governments attempt to make sure that growth and infrastructure remained in balance. Traditionally, capital improvements were paid for by borrowing, which required voter approval, but when the tax revolt and antigrowth movement challenged such borrowing, private developers sometimes began footing the bill, passing the costs onto new residents.

Local land-use decisions involve one or more of the mechanisms of annexation, zoning, general plans, and capital improvements and sometimes all four. Tax structures also play an important part. Participants in land-use decisions include elected officials, bureaucrats (both planners and service providers), interest groups, powerful individuals and organizations, and sometimes the states, which set the framework for decisions and seem to intervene increasingly frequently.

The Growth Machine

Although we have used the term "**growth machine**" frequently throughout the book, we have not yet discussed the term's theoretical foundation. The idea of cities as growth machines emerged from a 1976 article by sociologist Harvey Molotch who argued that localities are properly conceived as "growth machines," operated for the most part by a "mosaic of competing land interests capable of strategic coalition and action."[28] According to growth machine theory, land is the basic commodity in a city, and as such, alliances of business elites and government officials—growth machines—have a compelling interest in maximizing a city's productive land use. Later, in 1987, Molotch teamed up with John Logan to write *Urban Fortunes: The Political Economy of Place* in order to more fully articulate the growth machine thesis. Essentially Logan and Molotch argue that land-based elites such as developers, real estate interests, unions, and the local media join forces with local government officials to intensify the use of land.

Logan and Molotch distinguish between the motives of developers who pursue "exchange value" from antigrowth activists desiring "use values." They argue that for business interests—again frequently allied with government officials—land is viewed as a commodity to be exchanged, intensified, and developed in order to create profits. Conversely, use values are defined as the more qualitative benefits that residents derive from the free flow of traffic, open spaces, and uncrowded schools. Because exchange and use values are in direct opposition, Molotch and Logan view urban politics as primarily a battlefield for control over land.[29] Local officials become boosters of growth and use their land-use tools to facilitate growth, often in competition with other communities. But local governments are not only responding to powerful interests within their communities. They are also pursuing their own interests.

Some local leaders may see growth as a way of furthering their personal ambitions, but a more fundamental force is also at work. "Economic prosperity is necessary for protecting the fiscal base of local government," notes Paul Peterson. "As policy alternatives are proposed, each is evaluated according to how well it will help to achieve this objective."[30] Because local governments depend so heavily on property and sales taxes, they, too, have a vested interest in growth which results in fiscal zoning. The pro-growth attitude of local governments is thus not only a response to the political power of the growth coalition, which is formidable, but also to their structural dependence on growth. "Those promoting a policy must show how the plan is consistent with the economic interests of the city as a whole," Peterson asserts. "If a particular policy can be shown to be of long-range economic benefit to the city, its chances for adoption are increased."[31] Among these benefits are increased taxes, profits, investment, and jobs, all of which help sell growth not only to local decision makers, but also to the public.

Growth coalitions dominated land-use politics in most U.S. cities from the 1940s through the 1970s and beyond, although their power was most blatant in the booming central cities of the Sunbelt and in some expanding suburbs. Growth was not only an unchallenged good, but a major industry itself in many of these communities as they annexed aggressively, won voter approval of bond measures to subsidize capital improvements, and zoned for the convenience of developers. General plans were minimal or nonexistent in most Sunbelt and suburban cities until the 1970s. New industries were eagerly and expensively recruited, with readymade zonings and capital improvements often lavishly subsidized. Such self-promotion seems superfluous since growth was flowing to the Sunbelt and suburbia anyway, but keep in mind that communities were competing with one another within regions and all over the country.

Many suburbs, however, eschewed growth at any cost. Peterson points out that "in some smaller communities the emphasis is more on status than economic interests." These communities "externalize the negative effects of commerce and industry by zoning these productive activities outside their own jurisdiction."[32] They want them close, but not too close, preferring to remain affluent residential enclaves, which still gives them a rich tax base they can spend on schools and amenities. Combined with exclusionary zoning to keep out low-income residents, this increases land and property values and still brings economic development, albeit of a different sort.

Such an option was not available to the central cities of the Frostbelt, nor were they as aggressively pro-growth as their Sunbelt counterparts during this time. Already bounded by independent incorporated suburbs, they had nowhere to annex. Already taxing heavily, bond measures were tough to pass, even though their aging infrastructures needed rebuilding. People and industry were leaving rather than arriving, and developers made few proposals. The growth machine was not dead in these communities; however, it had fallen on hard times. Land-based interests and developers still exercised great power over land-use issues, particularly those connected to downtown commercial centers in cities such as Philadelphia, Pittsburgh, Boston, New York, San Francisco, and Chicago. To fight decay and decline, these cities instituted urban renewal or redevelopment programs for their downtowns. They established economic development offices to retain and recruit industry. And they launched promotional campaigns like "I (heart) New York." In fact, the desperation of these communities for taxes and jobs may have given economic interests even greater power. If anything, cities in decline could not afford to be choosy about the developments they accepted. Nevertheless, the growth machine was not so dominant as in the Sunbelt and suburbia. Other interests, including well-established businesses and community groups, played a part in local power structures, and other matters, such as social issues, were on the local agenda.

The Anti-Growth Movement

By the 1970s the **costs of growth** were beginning to become apparent in many suburban and Sunbelt communities. What Logan and Molotch referred to as "use values" declined as the open space of the countryside that had attracted residents and even industries to the peripheries of these cities was disappearing with continued development. Where growth was rapid, infrastructures such as roads and schools had often not kept up, leading to traffic congestion, air pollution, and crowded classrooms. Middle-class workers found their commute time lengthening and their children in schools with double sessions in temporary buildings and class sizes larger than in older areas. Other services, including police, fire protection, parks, libraries, and sewage treatment were stretched to the limit and often judged inadequate. The low taxes that had once been an attraction rose steadily but seemed to pay for continuing growth rather than improving these services. Soon the pro-growth paradigm of endless cycles of economic expansion, unfettered boosterism, and public support for growth that had existed prior to the 1970s was being challenged by new players on the scene: homeowners and environmentalists.

In a way, the growth machine sowed the seeds for a challenge to its dominance, not only by the problems it caused but also by the kinds of people it brought to communities. Middle-class professional homeowners, who had themselves benefited from upward economic mobility resulting from the growth machine economy, begin to organize politically an effort to challenge the "growth is good" mentality.

These middle-class professionals were conscious of the environment and high taxes, and they were outraged at the deteriorating quality of life. They began to rally against poor services, traffic congestion, and air and water pollution. By the mid-1970s, they were running controlled-growth candidates for local office and putting growth limits on local ballots by initiative—and winning. In San Diego, their organization was called PLAN! (Prevent Los Angelization Now!), while the slogan in Seattle was "Have a Nice Day—Somewhere Else." They joined the tax revolt, which decreased subsidies for growth and somewhat reduced its justification as a generator of property taxes, although ultimately it forced local governments to increase commercial construction through fiscal zoning (see chapter 3). The **antigrowth movement** continued through the 1980s and beyond, with most successful candidates in the suburbs and Sunbelt cities using the rhetoric of growth control, even if they failed to practice what they preached once in office.

Meanwhile, back in the central cities where decay was more common than was growth, a similar backlash to growth was underway. Urban redevelopment programs had begun extending downtowns into lower- and working-class residential areas, which, to the amazement of many local politicians, organized resistance to growth machines. The civil rights movement of the 1950s and 1960s had boosted the confidence of minorities and expanded their voting power, as had their continued migration to central cities. Federal antipoverty programs stimulated and even subsidized community organization. Middle-class central city neighborhoods also organized, often to fight threatening projects such as freeways and stadiums. In Sunbelt central cities, they sometimes joined the antigrowth coalition, although minority groups that were worried about jobs generally did not. In short, the end of the growth consensus came not only to middle-class suburban areas, but also to poor, inner-city communities fed up with their lack of power over development. Growth was no longer an unqualified social good. Rather, communities across the nation were clamoring for the right to have more say over the pace and character of growth.

Controls on Growth

Zoning and general planning, the basic tools of growth control, were already in the hands of local governments—the question was could homeowners, environmentalists, and minority groups wrest power away from local growth machines? Suburban communities had long used zoning keep out low-cost housing, apartments, and industrial projects. By adding quality-of-life concerns to their arsenal, the growth-control movement found a new sort of legitimacy—protecting the environment and community services. But these powers remained in the hands of elected officials, whose campaigns were often funded by the growth machine. Even candidates elected on a growth-control platform were sometimes co-opted by these interests.

Frustrated by the failure of traditional zoning and general planning to limit development, antigrowth and environmental organizations proposed a variety of more rigorous **growth controls**, for example:

- Limits on the number of homes built
- Greenbelt or urban development lines
- Limits on population
- Limits on commercial or industrial square footage
- Limits on commercial or industrial height
- Downzoning
- Voter or council supermajority approval for upzoning
- Infrastructure requirements
- Growth management as an element in general plans
- State or regional growth management plans[33]

In the early 1970s, communities in New York and California set limits on the number of housing units that could be built each year. Builders challenged both cases in court and, in precedent-setting decisions, both were upheld as reasonable uses of planning powers.[34] The legal case of Petaluma (just north of San Francisco) was helped by provisions for low-cost housing within annual quotas. Instead of limiting housing construction, some communities, such as Boulder, Colorado, sought to control growth by setting population caps. Others attempted to concentrate growth close to existing services by setting boundaries for development or by designating or in some cases even purchasing land around their city limits for greenbelts in which construction was prohibited or deferred.

Some communities, particularly larger ones, restricted commercial, office, or industrial development rather than housing. Neighborhoods in these cities blamed such developments for declining services and rising taxes and, in some cases, felt directly threatened by commercial expansion. Height limits were one response, as were restrictions on the amount of square footage that could be developed. In San Francisco, for example, a 1986 ballot measure limited new office construction to 950,000 square feet a year (about three 20-story buildings).[35] Elsewhere, both central cities and suburbs attempted to manage growth by **downzoning** areas to less intense uses. Commercial or industrial zones were changed to residential uses and areas zoned for high-density housing were redesignated for lower density, single-family homes. Even in booming Los Angeles, voters gave a 70 percent yes vote to a 1986 initiative that set out a ten-point growth management plan and slashed future commercial development density in half. Some communities instituted requirements for approval of zoning or general plan changes that increase densities (upzoning) by voters or a "supermajority" (such as a two-thirds majority) of the city council. During the 1990s in Ventura County, California, north of Los Angeles, voters in a number of cities approved initiatives placing strict limitations on growth. Often lumped together as Save Our Agricultural Resources, or SOAR, initiatives, most Ventura County cities have their own separate limit on future development. Also known as "**ballot box zoning**," requiring citizen approval for development represents a powerful tool for communities in battling growth machines.

Where frustration was greatest, communities set moratoriums halting growth either for a fixed period, as in Cape Cod, Massachusetts, or until infrastructures or other services could be supplied, as in Boulder, which drew a "blue line" around the city and would not supply water to housing built beyond it. By the mid-1980s, infrastructures had become a key factor, and many cities began requiring that development be deferred until specified facilities such as roads, transit, sewage treatment, or schools could be supplied. This sometimes resulted in moratoriums on growth since tax revenues, especially after the tax revolt, were insufficient to fund such facilities. With taxpayers no longer willing to subsidize development, many cities turned to **impact fees** or charges on developers to pay for infrastructure improvements. This relieved local taxpayers, but since developers passed the cost on to consumers, it raised the price of housing by as much as 18 to 34 percent according to one study,[36] and so controlled growth in a different way.

To cap these controls, many communities strengthened their general plans to include comprehensive growth plans, although in some cases this was a way of avoiding more stringent limits. Growth-control advocates and environmentalists also pushed for better regional planning, seeing that the problems of growth were larger than any one community. At the same time they were enacting their moratorium on new development, Cape Cod voters approved a regional land-use management agency or special district by an even greater majority, taking a more "proactive and longer-term" approach to growth according to political scientist Scott A. Bollens.[37] That same year on the West Coast, voters in San Diego County rejected stringent growth controls but approved the creation of an advisory committee to recommend policies for regional growth management. Other metropolitan areas moved in the same direction, and a few, including Atlanta, Minneapolis–St. Paul, Portland, and Seattle, established new multipurpose regional authorities.

Local growth issues soon moved to state capitols. States are the source of local land-use powers, so losers in local contests, whether pro- or antigrowth, sometimes take their cases to the higher level—a strategy political scientist E. E. Schattschneider termed "expanding the scope of conflict."[38] State involvement is also justified by the fact that growth issues overlap local jurisdictions, thus becoming issues of "state-wide concern." As a consequence, some states reviewed and revised their laws on annexation, consolidation, and interjurisdictional agreements to facilitate regional coordination, and many increased their requirements for regional planning on transportation, air quality control, and other environmental issues. A few, including Florida, Georgia, Hawaii, Maine, New Jersey, Oregon, Rhode Island, Vermont, and Washington, developed statewide plans. Florida, Washington, and some others imposed **concurrency requirements** limiting development to areas with infrastructure facilities in place or where they could be built concurrently to accommodate development. New Jersey's State Planning Commission, established in 1988, channels growth to existing cities and suburbs by seeing that state funds for roads and sewers are spent there and by added incentives for new developments within existing cities. Eighteen states have enacted **consistency laws** requiring that zoning policies conform with general plans. A California state court ordered downzoning in parts of Los Angeles as a result of that state's consistency law, although activists complain about a lack of enforcement.

State intervention has not, however, always been on the side of controlled growth. In Virginia, for example, the state legislature overturned a 1987 downzoning by a suburban, antigrowth county outside Washington, DC. Oregon and Massachusetts can override local zoning that excludes low- and moderate-cost housing. Both state and federal courts have also been active on growth issues. Although generally accepting growth controls, some state courts have warned local governments that they must "take account of the 'extra local consequences' of their decisions,"[39] and both state and federal courts have proven wary of exclusionary zoning. State courts, for example, have overturned local minimum floor area requirements (causing large, expensive homes to be built). The New Jersey Supreme Court has ruled exclusionary zoning contrary to the state constitution and ordered communities to allow the construction of affordable housing. Federal courts in some areas of the country have banned the zoning of apartments to only certain areas as discriminatory, whether intentional or not.

The Politics of Growth

As this review of the various mechanisms of growth control suggests, the movement has been both widespread and varied. In California, for example, a comprehensive study by the Lincoln Institute of Land Policy reported that about 80 percent of all cities and counties enacted some form of growth control in the 1970s and 1980s. Half established at least two of the mechanisms discussed earlier and a fifth imposed four or more. Los Angeles legislated eight growth-control measures and San Francisco approved seven, but the smaller city of San Luis Obispo topped them with no fewer than nine. Among the array of measures, infrastructure and zoning controls were the most commonly adopted.[40] State and regional bodies also introduced planning requirements.

Although journalistic and academic analyses of the growth-control movement often focus on its use of the initiative process, one California study reports that 85.6 percent of local growth measures were enacted through the normal city or county lawmaking process rather than by the voters.[41] Several factors were at work to produce this result. From the early 1970s onward, growth-control candidates were winning elections in cities where growth was an issue. In some communities, the electoral structure was changed to facilitate their victories. At-large election of council members became a target of the neighborhood and growth-control movements, usually in alliance with minority groups. The high cost of these citywide races enhanced the power of developers, who made major campaign contributions and helped elect council members who were more concerned about citywide issues than about neighborhood services. Counterreformers therefore advocated a return to district council elections, which cost less (thus decreasing dependence on campaign contributors) and resulted in a more neighborhood- and service-oriented city council. Whether by winning at-large or district elections, as council majorities committed to controlling growth took hold, initiatives became less necessary because policies could be changed by legislative action.

The growth machine also played its part in this shift by adapting to changing circumstances. After losing several initiative contests, corporate developers hired sophisticated political consultants to conduct their pro-growth campaigns. They denounced antigrowth crusaders as "elitists" who were denying young families housing, driving jobs away, and threatening the economic well-being of their communities. In alliance with labor unions, local business, and sometimes minority groups, they presented themselves as "friends of the people"[42] and succeeded in defeating slow-growth measures in many booming areas, including Orange County and San Diego (both in California). Recessions in the early 1980s and 1990s strengthened the developers' economic arguments, which may explain why voters in the environmentally conscious state of Washington rejected a statewide growth-control initiative that included supporting funds in 1990. Developers have also tried to blunt environmentalist arguments by labeling their developments environmentally friendly or as "smart growth"—a topic which we'll explore in the next chapter.

Developers also adapted by compromise and lobbying. Accepting mild measures like a comprehensive growth element of a general plan could often fend off more radical controls. Impact fees or charges for building permits could be tolerated since the alternative of voter-approved bond measures to fund infrastructures was unrealistic, and besides, costs could be passed on to home purchasers. Developers also found that even antigrowth candidates needed campaign funds. Controlling growth was politically popular and resulted in bursts of activity but stable groups failed to materialize in most communities, so candidates and elected officials, lacking party or organizational support, often turned to those with a long-term interest in local politics and the money to back it up—the growth machine. Developers also applied their lobbying skills to the new officials. In some cases, they cut deals with minority council members, promising jobs or that work would be subcontracted to minorities. As a consequence, growth measures were often moderated, and neighborhood advocates and environmentalists were disappointed in candidates who, in their view, "sold out."

The Impact of Growth Controls

As the foregoing suggests, in most communities the battle over growth resulted in compromise. Although some opponents of growth were so fanatic that they were labeled BANANAS (Build Absolutely Nothing Anywhere Near Anybody), most did not argue that all development should be halted. Rather than no growth, they wanted controlled growth that would not cost them money or harm their quality of life, local services, or property values. If projects could be shown to be of net benefit, they continued to win approval. In short, many believe that developers merely worked harder to make their case.

Some analysts argue that the battle over growth control is more symbolic than practical. John Logan and Min Zhou assert that growth is so heavily influenced by external factors, such as national and regional economies and corporate decisions about where to locate, that local governments can't control it anyway. Even when they adopt measures to do so, these are often ignored or abused—making exceptions for a major industry, for example. Growth control, they suggest, has more to do with "elitism" and "stability" than with environmental issues.[43] Their argument is supported by evidence that communities that adopt growth control measures are not necessarily experiencing rapid growth themselves. The Lincoln Institute reported that cities with larger populations were more likely to adopt growth controls than smaller ones, but there "was no simple relationship" between the growth rate of individual communities and control measures. They found that growth measures were often a response to regional or statewide, rather than strictly local, growth.[44]

Developers, advocates of low-income housing, and many academic analysts have concluded that growth control amounts to a contemporary manifestation of traditional suburban patterns of exclusionary zoning. Virtually all of the measures discussed previously drive up the cost of houses, either by limiting the supply, adding impact fees, or increasing size and land area. Some communities (usually larger ones) try to include mixed-price housing, but lower-cost homes are rarely built because they don't offer enough profit to private developers and public funds are limited.

Such exclusivity is not limited to the suburbs. In central cities, growth controls often take the form of downzoning to protect housing in old neighborhoods that have been zoned but not yet developed for high-density residential, commercial, or industrial uses. Such neighborhoods, which may once have been upper class, have usually declined as their original population moved to the suburbs and lower-income and minority people moved in, often splitting big homes into flats or boarding houses. Beginning in the 1970s and continuing to date, fashion, environmental consciousness, and increasing numbers of couples without children brought some middle-class people back to such inner-city neighborhoods. They bought the grand old houses and fixed them up, formed residents' groups, and sought city assistance, including downzoning to protect their reemerging neighborhoods. Cities usually welcome such requests, happy to see middle-class taxpayers returning rather than fleeing. But the process has been labeled **gentrification** because middle-class homeowners (or "gentry") replace poor and minority people, who cannot afford the rising prices in these downzoned and rehabilitated areas. Nor do the new residents always make their predecessors feel welcome, demanding that police move street people on and that community facilities such as alcoholic drop-in centers or homeless shelters be relocated.

Traditionally, neighborhoods of homeowners, whether in suburbs or central cities, resist nonconforming incursions on their territories. On a small scale, this not-in-my-backyard, or **NIMBY**, phenomenon revolves around objections to particular projects that are considered locally unacceptable land uses or LULUs, from dumps and factories to community care facilities and low-income housing. As a result, the so-called LULUs are located only where they run into little or no resistance, which means they tend to be concentrated in the least well-off parts of central cities rather than distributed evenly throughout metropolitan areas. Many scholars have called this phenomenon "environmental racism" or "environmental justice," although activists' efforts to prove intentional discrimination in the courts have not been very successful thus far. No regional authority exists to address the unequal distribution of undesirable land uses. But growth controls, with their propensity to exclusion, take the potential for NIMBYism to a larger scale.

Yet it would be unfair and short-sighted to dismiss the growth-control movement as merely an extension of narrow-minded NIMBYism, bigotry, or elitism. These motives play a part in many communities, but so do the issues of rising taxes, declining services, and quality-of-life issues such as traffic congestion, disappearing open space, and air and water pollution. These are real and serious issues of great concern to many residents and not just a smokescreen for elitism. Nor are all communities that seek to control growth wealthy and white. This could hardly be the case in ethnically diverse California, where 80 percent of cities and counties have adopted growth controls. The Lincoln Institute study of these communities found that those without growth measures had only slightly lower per capita incomes and education levels than those that instituted controls and found no difference in ethnic composition.[45]

The End of the Growth Machine?

With growth controls and resistance to development so extensive and by all evidence still expanding, it might seem that the death knell of the growth machine has been sounded. But while the politics of growth have changed, the imperative remains.

Growth was so widely accepted and supported for so long that resistance came as a shock, not only to development interests but to local officials who had ruled their communities unchallenged. In the beginning, growth machine interests lost many battles, not necessarily because their arguments lacked merit but because their power had declined as their communities changed. In some new suburbs there was no established power structure, so when residents got around to organizing they could dictate to the developers who had created their communities. In central cities in the Sunbelt, new residents felt no allegiance to the old elites. Newly organized minority communities and neighborhood groups also challenged faltering growth machines in Frostbelt central cities. In many places, locally owned businesses were replaced by multinational corporations whose managers and employees shared few interests with the old guard growth machine.

But although the growth machine was challenged, it was not defeated. Growth controls often merely resulted in the redistribution of growth from communities that could afford to reject it to those that couldn't or to those that ardently welcomed it. This redistribution of growth facilitated the development of the edge cities that sprouted at freeway interchanges, often in areas that lacked single, traditional local governments and were unincorporated county areas with private governments in the form of the owners of office, commercial, or residential complexes. But except for the most affluent and elite suburbs, development also continued in communities with traditional municipal authorities even when constituents worried about growth instigated control measures. The growth was usually different—better planned and paying for itself rather than imposing greater tax burdens on existing residents—but it was still growth.

Cities and counties are, above all, growth machines not just because of the power of development interests, but also because of the fundamental design of local governments. State-dictated dependence on property and sales taxes makes cities and counties seek growth to expand their revenues. Increased revenues might not be necessary, except that the cost of maintaining existing services has risen while their constituents demand more due to rising crime rates or other problems. The tax revolt denied many local governments the alternative of raising property taxes on existing development even as declining federal and state aid reduced their income. Because property taxes on housing don't generate nearly enough revenue to fund even basic services, more local governments are now zoning for commercial and retail property —increasing traffic and congestion and contributing to shortages of affordable housing. For decades, growth seemed a painless way to generate revenue without raising taxes. The growth-control movement altered this perception by demanding greater scrutiny of whether the benefits of each new project outweigh or at least equal its costs in services.

Additionally, state laws of incorporation have fragmented metropolitan areas into many independent governments in competition with one another for tax resources. Each wishes to strengthen its tax base, seeking the most lucrative developments while rejecting those that might cost more in services than they would generate in taxes. Resistance to low- and moderate-cost housing is not only NIMBY bigotry, it is economic realism for local governments given the current tax structure. In fact, many cities resist any sort of housing at all, preferring tax-rich industrial and commercial developments. This preference creates regional problems associated with growth, since jobs are concentrated in communities that have managed to attract lots of industry and housing is elsewhere, necessitating heavy commuting and causing traffic congestion and air pollution. Local governments also find themselves presented with offers they can't refuse when a developer wants to build a major project such as a shopping center, hotel, or industry on their territory and credibly threatens to go elsewhere if rejected. In the nightmares of local decision makers, they stand firm on growth control, the development is built in an adjacent community, they lose the taxes, their own businesses suffer, and they still bear some of the problems the development generates, such as traffic. No wonder communities compromise on growth control—the whole system seems set up to perpetuate economic development.

Public Policy Meets the City Limits

In this chapter, we've briefly considered several policy areas that local governments deal with: education, welfare, crime, transportation, and finally, land use. Hopefully, in your reading and class discussions you have used some of the tools we learned in earlier chapters to understand and analyze each policy area. Several themes run through all the policies considered in this chapter. Race and class, although not discussed separately, are central factors in each policy area. If politics is about the allocation of scarce resources, then the poor and some minorities are often least equipped to gain access to those resources. The power of bureaucracies is also more apparent than it may have been in previous chapters. Again, bureaucracies are the chief implementer of policies that are made by local government officials. Without follow-through on the part of "street-level bureaucrats" to implement policies, the goals of those policies are unlikely to be met. Also evident has been the power of growth machines, particularly in the section on land use. If land is the chief commodity in urban politics, then growth machines must concentrate an inordinate amount of their energies on intensifying land use through economic development. Perhaps most evident, however, are the limits local governments face in dealing with these pressing issues. These limits, as noted throughout the book, include legal, fiscal, and structural constraints imposed by state and federal governments as well as political limits set by the voters and local power structures. What local governments do still matters, but their choices have narrowed, particularly as local sovereignty is undermined by larger economic forces. No wonder they so often function as growth machines. Land-use policy is one of the last remaining primarily local powers, and a tool to which local governments can turn in the face of all their other difficulties. This may change, however, because of the larger problems of fragmentation of metropolitan areas and the separation of needs and resources, two more themes that interact with all of the policies discussed in this chapter. In the next chapter, we will discuss one of the most often proposed, yet infrequently implemented, solutions to the problems of metropolitan fragmentation and social inequality: regional government.

Essential Terms

disincentives
incentives
school districts
school boards
racial segregation
busing
funding adequacy
educational foundations
No Child Left Behind Act (2001)
voucher programs
charter schools
Aid to Families with Dependent
   Children (AFDC)
Temporary Assistance for Needy
   Families (TANF)
Medicaid
police-community relations
community-based policing
civilian review boards
inspectors general
gun control
decriminalization of drugs
gangs
gang injunctions

private security
costs of auto transit
auto-dependence
mass transit systems
high occupancy vehicle (HOV) lanes
who decides (about transit)
annexation
zoning
exclusionary zoning
general plan
zoning variance
capital improvement projects
growth machine
costs of growth
antigrowth movement
growth controls
downzoning
ballot box zoning
impact fees
concurrency requirements
consistency laws
gentrification
NIMBY

On the Internet

Education-related Websites:

- The U.S. Department of Education (www.ed.gov) is the major federal government agency involved with a formulation and implementation of education policy.
- The National Center for Education Statistics website is www.nces.ed.org.
- The Policy Analysis For California Education website is http://pace.berkeley.edu.
- The Edsource-California Online website is www.edsource.org.
- The Education Commission of the States website is www.ecs.org.
- The Council of Great City Schools website is www.cgcs.org.
- The WestEd website is www.wested.org.
- Useful information can also be found from your state, city, or local school district's website.

Crime- and Policing-related Websites:

- The American Civil Liberties Union (www.aclu.org) is an organization that has acted in civil rights, use of force, and other crime and policing issues.
- The Bureau of Justice Statistics Clearing house (www.ncjrs.org) is an arm of the Justice Department that compiles reports on crime rates.
- The Federal Bureau of Investigation (www.fbi.gov) compiles statistics on crime rates for the nation and other political jurisdictions.
- The Community Policing Consortium (www.communitypolicing.org) is a federally funded project aimed at promoting the practice of community-based policing.
- The International Association of Chiefs of Police (www.theiacp.org) is a professional organization for police administrators.
- The Police Foundation (www.policefoundation.org) is a research organization that examines police practices.

Welfare- and Poverty-related Websites:

- The Finance Project (www.financeproject.org) is a nonprofit organization that provides useful statistics and links to poverty-related issues.
- The Office of Family Assistance (www.acf.dhhs.gov/programs/ofa/) is an arm of the U.S. Department of Health and Human Services that oversees the federal program Temporary Aid to Needy Families.
- The Center for Medicaid and Medicare Services (www.cms.hhs.gov/) is a division of the U.S. Department of Health and Human Services.

Transportation-related Websites:

- The American Highway Users Alliance (www.tripnet.org) lobbies for increased funding on road construction and maintenance.
- The Federal Highway Administration (www.fhwa.dot.gov/) is administered by the U.S. Department of Transportation.
- The Surface Transportation Policy Project (www.transact.org/) is an advocacy group for alternative modes of transportation.
- The Sierra Club (www.sierraclub.org/) is an environmental organization that promotes alternatives to the automobile and urban sprawl.

The following websites offer resources on a wide variety of public policy issues:

- The Public Policy Institute of California website is www.ppic.org.
- The Brookings Institute website is www.brook.edu.
- The California Public Interest Research Group website is www.calpirg.org.
- The Cato Institute website is www.cato.org.
- The Reason Foundation website is www.reason.org.
- The Urban Policy Institute website is www.urban.org.

- The Pacific Research Institute website is www.pacificresearch.org.
- The Tomas Rivera Policy Institute website is www.trpi.org.

Notes

1. *Brown v. Board of Education of Topeka*, 347 U.S. 483 (1954).

2. See J. Anthony Lukas, *Common Ground: A Turbulent Decade in the Lives of Three American Families* (New York: Knopf, 1985).

3. *New York Times*, December 14, 1993.

4. Gary Orfield and John T. Yun, *Resegregation in American Schools* (Cambridge, MA: The Civil Rights Project, Harvard University, 1999).

5. *San Antonio v. Rodriguez*, 411 U.S. 1 (1973).

6. Bruce J. Biddle and David C. Berliner, *What Research Says about Unequal Funding for Schools in America*, Policy Perspectives (San Francisco: WestEd, 2003).

7. "A Nation at Risk: The Imperative for Educational Reform: A Report to the Nation and the Secretary of Education, United States Department of Education" (Washington, DC: The National Commission on Excellence in Education, 1983).

8. Dennis L. Dresang and James J. Gosling, *Politics and Policy in American States and Communities*, 5th ed. (New York: Pearson Longman, 2006).

9. National Assessment of Educational Progress, U.S. Department of Education, Institute of Education Sciences, *America's Charter Schools: Results From the NAEP 2003 Pilot Study*, NCES 2005–456 (Washington, DC: National Center for Education Statistics, 2004).

10. Michael E. Kraft and Scott R. Furlong, *Public Policy: Politics, Analysis, and Alternatives* (Washington, DC: CQ Press, 2004).

11. Dianne Rahm, *United States Public Policy: A Budgetary Approach* (Toronto, Canada: Thomson/Wadsworth, 2003).

12. *Newsweek*, December 20, 1976.

13. Rahm, *United States Public Policy*.

14. James Q. Wilson, "Broken Windows," *Atlantic Monthly*, March 1982, pp. 29–38. See also George L. Kelling and Catherine M. Coles, *Fixing Broken Windows: Restoring Order and Reducing Crime in Our Communities* (New York: Martin Kessler Books, 1996); and Hope Corman and Naci Mocan, *Carrots, Sticks and Broken Windows* (Cambridge, MA: National Bureau of Economic Research, 2002).

15. "Crime in the United States, 2000" (Federal Bureau of Investigation, 2000). Available at: www.fbi.gov/ucr/00cius.htm (accessed July 20, 2005).

16. Kenneth Jost, "Gun Control," in *Issues for Debate in American Public Policy*, 2nd ed. (Washington, DC; CQ Press, 2000), pp. 191–208.

17. Ibid.

18. Randy Arndt, "Drugs and Housing Plague Cities, Towns," *Nation's Cities Weekly*, January 18, 1989, p. 1.

19. Andrew Popachristos, "Gang World," *Foreign Policy*, March–April 2005, available at: www.foreignpolicy.com/cms.php?story_id=2798&page=1.

20. Ibid.

21. Rahm, *United States Public Policy*.

22. *The Real Price of Gasoline: An Analysis of the Hidden External Costs That Consumers Pay To Fuel Their Automobiles*, no. 3 (Washington, DC: International Center for Technology Assessment, 1998). Available at: www.icta.org/doc/Real%20Price%20of%20Gasoline.pdf (accessed: August 12, 2005).

23. Lindsay Layton, "Going Forward: Mass Transit Popularity Surges in the U.S.," *Washington Post*, April 30, 2000. Available at: www.commondreams.org/headlines/043000–01.htm (accessed: August 1, 2005).

24. Puget Sound Regional Council, "Puget Sound Trends: Growth in Traffic and Vehicle Miles Traveled," Seattle, Washington, August 2005. Available at: www.psrc.org/datapubs/pubs/trends/t2aug05.pdf (accessed: August 22, 2005).

25. A study by John Holtzclaw for the Natural Resources Defense Council, cited in the *San Jose Mercury News*, April 6, 1991.

26. Ibid.

27. *Village of Euclid v. Ambler Realty*, 272 U.S. 364 (1926).

28. Harvey Molotch, "The City as a Growth Machine: Toward a Political Economy of Place," *American Journal of Sociology* 82, no. 2 (September 1976): 130.

29. John R. Logan and Harvey Molotch, *Urban Fortunes: The Political Economy of Place* (Berkeley: University of California Press, 1987).

30. Paul E. Peterson, *City Limits* (Chicago: University of Chicago Press, 1981), p. 29.

31. Ibid., p. 129.

32. Ibid., p. 31.

33. Madelyn Glickfeld and Nick Levine, *Regional Growth—Local Reaction: The Enactment and Effects of Local Growth Control and Management Measures in California* (Cambridge, MA: Lincoln Institute of Land Policy, 1992), pp. 13–15. See also Irving Schiffman, *Alternative Techniques for Managing Growth*, 2nd ed. (Berkeley: Institute of Governmental Studies Press, University of California at Berkeley, 1999).

34. *Golden v. Ramapo*, 285 N.E. 2d 291 (NY 1972) and *Petaluma v. Construction Industry Association*, 552 F.2d 897 (CA 1975).

35. See Richard Edward DeLeon, *Left Coast City: Progressive Politics in San Francisco, 1975–1991* (Lawrence, KS: University of Kansas Press, 1992), chapter 4.

36. David E. Dowall, *The Suburban Squeeze: Land Conversion and Regulation in the San Francisco Bay Area* (Berkeley: University of California Press, 1984), pp. 133–34.

37. Scott A. Bollens, "Constituencies for Limitation and Regionalism: Approaches to Growth Management," *Urban Affairs Quarterly* 26, no. 1 (September 1990): 47.

38. E. E. Schattschneider, *The Semisovereign People: A Realist's View of Democracy in America*, repr. with an introduction by David Adamany (Fort Worth, TX: Harcourt, Brace, Jovanovich, 1988).

39. David R. Berman, "State Actions Affecting Local Governments," *The Municipal Year Book* (Washington, DC: International City/County Management Association, 1989), p. 129.

40. Glickfeld and Levine, *Regional Growth*, pp. 21–22, 43.

41. Ibid., p. 33.

42. Mike Davis, *City of Quartz: Excavating the Future in Los Angeles* (London: Verso, 1990), p. 211.

43. John R. Logan and Min Zhou, "Do Suburban Growth Controls Control Growth?" *American Sociological Review* 54, no. 3 (June 1989): 461–71; and John R. Logan and Min Zhou, "The Adoption of Growth Controls in Suburban Communities," *Social Science Quarterly* 71, no. 1 (March 1990): 118–29.

44. Glickfeld and Levine, *Regional Growth*, pp. 34 and 58.

45. Ibid., p. 26.

14 Metropolitan Politics
The Future of Local Government

In previous chapters, we have considered politics and government in individual communities. But as we learned in chapter 3, many large metropolitan areas are made up of dozens or more cities, a governance system that many critics have derided as a "crazy quilt."

But the fragmentation of metropolitan areas into many municipalities is only the beginning. City boundaries overlap with counties, towns, or townships, special districts, and school districts. "Even the professionals can't keep track of who does what," says Ann Siracusa, a Los Angeles city planner.[1] Responsibility for the governing of most neighborhoods is divided among a city, a county (or town or township), a school district, and several special districts. Some metropolitan areas, like the one centering on New York City, spill across state lines, and a few, such as San Diego and El Paso, even cross international borders. In this chapter, we will examine what many urban scholars and planners believe is one answer to the problems of governing the "crazy quilt": **metropolitan government**.

In chapter 3, we examined what the Census Bureau refers to as **Metropolitan Statistical Areas (MSAs)** and **Combined Metropolitan Statistical Areas (CMSAs)**. We looked at the demographics of these areas and studied the way that political boundaries—and in particular the use of exclusionary zoning—have been used to segregate metropolitan areas by class and ethnicity, resulting in what we have called the needs/resources dichotomy. Although not everyone may agree, we know that to a large extent, cities and suburbs are economically and socially interdependent, with none able to stand fully on its own.

But this arrangement is not inevitable. In most other countries, urban regions have a single government or perhaps a two-tiered system a little like our national government, with a large-scale regional "federal" government with powers over certain things, and smaller units performing other responsibilities. But in the United States, state laws of incorporation (see chapter 4), much influenced by the politics of suburbanization, facilitate the formation of multiple local governments in metropolitan areas. Ironically—or predictably?—most metropolitan areas have responded to the problems of multiple governments by adding yet more layers of government, which rarely achieve solutions. The future promises worsening problems, a continuing search for answers, and challenges to local government as we know it. Yet, unlike many European nations, no metropolitan area (broadly defined) in the United States has a single government, although some have consolidated their city and county governments, while others have experimented with regional governments with limited powers.

Proponents of metropolitan government in United States believe that the benefits of having a single, unified government structure for urban areas can best ameliorate social inequality, while providing leadership and a unified vision for tackling regional problems such as transportation, education, housing, the environment, and so on. Opponents of metropolitan government say that the current system is more democratic, efficient, and best tailored to the range of service desires of metropolitan populations. But this isn't an academic debate. Just as the current structure of local government is the result of political choices, proponents of metropolitan government believe that, under the right circumstances, Americans can be convinced of the merits of alternative ways of governing urban areas.

The Case for Metropolitan Fragmentation: Public Choice

The most influential defense of metropolitan fragmentation comes from a school of thought known as **public choice**, which is heavily influenced by free-market theory. Essentially, public choice scholars see metropolitan areas much in the way that they might view a typical marketplace. Take, for example, the restaurant industry. In a competitive marketplace, consumers will have a tremendous amount of choice about where to shop, the kinds of food to shop for, and the quality of the food that they will eat. Competition ensures that restaurants will provide the best quality and service at the best price. If service at a restaurant is slow or the food is bad, consumers will simply take their business elsewhere.

Well, public choice theorists view metropolitan fragmentation in much the same way. Like in a restaurant, local governments present their products—in this analogy taxes and services instead of food—competing with one another to attract "customers"—residents and businesses. Citizens who prefer low taxes and minimal services will opt for one municipality, while those who are prepared to pay for a better range of services will choose to live in another. Those who are discontented with the taxes and services in their communities may try to alter them through participation in the political process, exercising what public choice theorists call "voice"—showing up to complain at a public meeting or voting their representatives out of office. Alternatively, they may "exit," voting with their feet to another more suitable community.[2] Above all, public choice theorists believe that monopolies are bad; the more local governments, the greater the choice, and the better things will be for consumers.[3] How would you like it if there were only one or two restaurants to choose from?

In Your Community

In your area, how many different cities are there that you could potentially live in? What decisions did you or your family take into consideration when choosing the city where you live? Does public choice theory's claim that individual actors are "rational" makes sense to you?

With one or more big cities and a plethora of highly diverse suburbs, most metropolitan areas offer plenty of choices. In recent years, these have been supplemented by thousands of Common Interest Developments (CIDs) and Business Improvement Districts (BIDs) in self-contained housing developments and business districts. In a sense, these private, minigovernments are an enhancement of public choice, covering areas that are smaller and more internally homogeneous than most suburbs, and providing services that public agencies otherwise might not.

Public choice theory explains, accepts, and even justifies metropolitan fragmentation, but critics believe the theory has some serious shortcomings. Many residents and businesses make careful choices about where they locate, especially with regard to taxes, schools, housing, and homogeneity. Some do not, however, and even for those who wish to, information may be incomplete or inaccessible. Many citizens do not use or even know about all the services available. Moreover, some factors in our decisions about where to live are not under the control of the communities we choose, such as the amount of time it takes us to get to work or the distance to amenities such as shopping centers or sports or theater facilities in other cities.

The most serious shortcoming of public choice theory, however, is its glossing over or acceptance of many formal and informal limits on individual choices. Racial discrimination, although now illegal and weaker, has long limited the choices available to minorities, while the cost of housing in the carefully zoned suburbs prevents all but the richest from exercising complete choice. In terms of where they want to live, what kind of choices do poor and working-class people have? They usually end up in the central city, often paying the highest taxes and receiving poor services. Public choice theorists would point out that in return for their high taxes, they get a bigger package of services, such as housing or health care subsidies, which they need, and that they couldn't get by on the minimal services of rich, low-taxing communities. This is true, but many residents of the rich, low-taxing communities take advantage of facilities paid for by poorer central city residents, and disparities in spending on some services, such as education, may mean that the neediest are denied what they need most. Indeed, conditions are such in many central cities and inner suburbs that the only realistic choice available to the poor may be more of a trap, containing them and condemning them to perpetual poverty.

Critics of public choice theory also rightly point out that most people and businesses, especially small ones, do not calculate locational benefits as consciously as the theory implies. Moreover, critics are correct in arguing that even if locational advantages were obvious, many working-class people are simply priced out of most neighborhoods in metropolitan areas. Yet the market-based logic of public choice theory has its merits. Along with other factors, many people and businesses do include tax and service packages (particularly schools) in their deliberations about where to settle, at least to some degree. Meanwhile, local governments clearly compete with one another to present the most attractive package and entice the most advantageous residents and businesses. Although critics dismiss public choice theory as an acceptance of the fragmented and inequitable metropolitan status quo, it nevertheless helps explain the actions of citizens, businesses, and local governments and the political popularity of fragmentation.

Fragmentation and Local Democracy

In addition to arguments about choice, proponents say the fragmentation of big urban regions into many local governments has the advantages of enhancing the sense of community and local democracy.

As we saw in chapter 3, many Americans identify with small towns much more than with big cities or their neighborhoods. Self-governing suburbs give them some of the feel of a small town, a sense of identity, and community. Often, this feeling is illusory because people don't put down roots in a suburb the way they do in a small town. They usually commute to work and move on to other suburbs after a few years. Yet because people nevertheless long for a **sense of community**, even the illusion offered by most suburbs takes on meaning. Besides, the sense of community comes not only from the fantasy of small-town life but also from the hard reality of segregation. As we know, most suburbs are homogeneous due to choice, discrimination, and zoning. Being surrounded by people like themselves gives suburbanites the illusion of a close-knit community even if residents rarely interact.

Defenders of fragmentation also assert its benefits for local democracy, at least theoretically. The governments of small communities are more accessible and easier for citizens to influence than big ones. Instead of competing with lots of other people and groups for access to decision makers, you're likely to run into your representative at the local hardware store where you can voice your concerns. Moreover, if you're inclined, you have a shot at becoming a decision maker yourself because running for office costs hundreds of dollars rather than hundreds of thousands. In short, a multiplicity of local governments is a fairly good approximation of Jeffersonian democracy in which the voices of individual citizens can be heard. Yet, the evidence shows that residents of suburban communities overall participate in local politics *less* than those of big cities. Homogeneity and the uniformity of values may mean that residents believe that others like themselves are making decisions, so they get what they want without much participation. Although passive, this is still a sort of democracy by consensus, and although relatively few actually participate, the potential for easy access and influence is still greater than in larger cities.

The Efficiency Argument

A final argument proposed by public choice advocates in the defense of urban fragmentation is that, because of competition, fragmented metropolitan areas provide better and more efficient local services. Again, the argument hinges on the logic of a free market. The **efficiency** argument begins with the proposition that under urban fragmentation, local governments are forced to compete with one another for residents and business. Thus, they are likely to produce better services at a lower cost. For example, if one city is providing a poor level of, say, library services, residents who object will move to a city that is providing a level of service more in line with their preference. Public choice advocates say that if metropolitan areas were governed by a single, overarching government, that government would, in effect, have a monopoly on local services. From there, public choice proponents extrapolate that such a local government monopoly would inevitably provide poor services, and do so at a higher cost—not because they necessarily want to, but because, as monopolies, they can.

The Politics of Giving People What They Want

In short, public choice theorists—largely relying on free-market principles—have mounted a fairly spirited defense of metropolitan fragmentation in the United States. Not only are small local governments more democratic and accountable, according to this view, but they are also less costly and more efficient. Such arguments have a certain appeal because they are simple and predictable models of behavior. Moreover, public choice advocates can point to the fact that the current fragmented structure of most American metropolises is the result of open and democratic political processes. In other words, it's what we want. As political scientist Gary Miller writes, citizens "voted with their feet for low taxes, low levels of bureaucratic activity, low levels of government spending."[4] Nor is this Balkanized array of insular and independent entities a mere by-product of rapid, unplanned growth. Rather, it is the purposeful result of state and local policy, which are themselves reflections of voter preferences. With over half of all Americans now living in suburbs, dealing with the growing problems caused by fragmentation will be politically difficult. Certainly, public choice scholars—not to mention the millions of Americans who live contentedly in their insulated suburbs—have set the bar pretty high for those advocating for alternative ways of governing urban America.

IN YOUR COMMUNITY

Either in small groups or by yourself, summarize and critique the arguments for and against the public choice school of thought.

Urban Fragmentation: The Case for Metropolitan Government

Many of the problems of the political fragmentation of metropolitan areas have already been mentioned in this and previous chapters, although they have not been catalogued in the defense of any particular reform alternative. During the 1950s, urban planners and some scholars began to question the rapid pace of suburbanization, in particular noticing the impact that suburbanization was having on central cities. Reformers began to argue for an approach that we will be generally referring to as "metropolitan government." As we will see, although metropolitan government can come in many forms, the general idea is to bring governmental coherency and consistency to solving regional problems facing urban areas. However, unlike free-market advocates, these reformers approach the issue of how to structure urban areas from the perspective of social justice. Whereas public choice theorists believe social good will emerge from competition, metropolitan government reformers believe competition has seriously undermined collective approaches to problem solving.

Metropolitan Government and Economies of Scale

Have you ever come back from Costco, Wal-Mart, or any other large retailer with a huge box of your favorite cereal, soap, or some other product? Although you don't normally buy such products in large quantities, you just couldn't help yourself—the items were just so cheap! Why are bulk items so cheap? The answer, economists tell us, is **economies of scale**. The general idea behind economies of scale is that as the volume of any unit increases, the cost per unit decreases. Hence the phrase: "buy in bulk."

Proponents of metropolitan-wide government use this very logic in responding to the public choice perspective's charge that local government services in fragmented urban areas are cheaper and more efficient. Instead, metropolitanists argue that urban areas with large numbers of governments, each providing and maintaining its own garbage, police, fire, streets, parks, planning, and other services are more expensive because they duplicate what other governments are doing. Instead of having thirty-five separate police departments in a large metropolitan area, each with its own fleet of police cars and police stations, jails, bureaucracy, and so on, why not just have one? Second, metropolitanists argue that big cities "can buy wholesale," taking advantages of economies of scale. Large cities can get a better deal on the purchase of a fleet of police cars, fire trucks, or even more mundane items like paper and pencils, while a small city, which lacks the same purchasing power, will spend more money on the same items.

Whether these claims ring true, however, remains a subject of intense debate. Some studies of local government service delivery have found a strong relationship between fragmentation and higher-cost government.[5] In contrast, other studies have found that service delivery in fragmented areas is in fact cheaper and better.[6] Still other studies are more nuanced, asserting that the benefits of economies of scale depend on the type of service in question. In most cases, these savings are probably not major, however, and most small cities seem to make up for such costs with frugality or just making do with a little less. They are usually able to do so because their problems, like crime, are not so severe and they need not offer the range of services most big cities feel obliged to provide. Larger-scale projects that require capital-intensive infrastructure such as water supply, sewage treatment, or solid waste disposal, cost far too much for a single small city to build or manage, whereas big cities provide for them as a matter of course. Fortunately for small cities, this is often an easy problem to solve. They can cooperate to provide the service or buy it from a larger city, although sometimes the larger city denies the service unless smaller ones agree to be absorbed, as Los Angeles did with water and San Jose did with sewage treatment.

The Separation of Needs and Resources

A far more serious and perhaps insoluble problem with the fragmentation of urban areas is the **separation of needs and resources**. As we have seen throughout almost every chapter, communities within metropolitan areas are segregated by race and class, with needy and dependent populations concentrated in declining central cities and inner suburbs, while outer suburbs benefit from stronger tax bases and fewer service needs. Again, the issue here is the way the political boundaries of cities and school districts reinforce these inequalities. The result is that metropolitan areas are polarized, with population groups separated from one another and tax resources isolated from needs. In the book *Place Matters* (2001), the authors argue that "place" does indeed matter: "where we live has a powerful effect on the choices we have and our capacity to achieve a high quality life."[7]

Moreover, metropolitanists believe that many independent jurisdictions do not bear their fair share of regional burdens, including allowing some affordable housing, temporary shelters for the homeless, and community care facilities for addicts, battered women, or the disabled and elderly. A regional government, proponents say, might distribute—or redistribute—both resources and burdens more equitably. But metropolitan fragmentation means more than the unfair distribution of needs and resources. It also means outright competition as each jurisdiction strives to attract projects that will generate more tax revenue than they will cost in services and to avoid or clear their communities of any elements that might be a net tax burden. Critics say the emphasis on costs and benefits of fiscal zoning in land-use decisions may produce tax advantages and private profits, thus satisfying the growth machine, but it exacerbates the separation of needs and resources and other regional problems.

Metropolitanists also say that rather than enhancing democracy, the competitive environment fostered by fragmentation undermines democracy. J. Eric Oliver, author of *Democracy in Suburbia*, argues that there is a great potential for democratic participation in suburbs. However, he finds that "the economic and racial segregation that suburbs promote" undermines "the optimal functioning of America's local democratic institutions."[8] Oliver says that rather than working toward collective solutions to regional problems, the fragmented structure of urban areas creates an environment of competition and isolation.

Externalities

Each government in a metropolitan region makes independent decisions, but often these decisions have an impact on others. A housing or industrial development might cause traffic and air pollution, for example, or the flight pattern of an airport in one city might cause noise problems in another. A suburb might persuade a corporation to move its headquarters out of the central city, netting taxes and jobs for itself, but worsening the disparity between needs and resources. Economists call the spillovers **externalities**: when the impacts of one city's decisions affect others beyond its borders. Externalities may also affect other governments responsible for different services within their borders if, for example, a city zones housing projects where a school or water district cannot provide services.

Externalities are not all negative, however. Positive spillovers occur when cities provide services nonresidents use, such as an airport, shopping center, stadium, or jobs in a business or industrial district. Suburban commuters often enjoy benefits like these (and roads, police protection, and many others) without paying much in the way of direct taxes to support them. But although they pay most of their taxes in the suburbs where they reside, they may pay some sales or entertainment taxes elsewhere, and their presence as workers or shoppers generates business and drives up property values, thus increasing tax revenues.

Whether negative or positive, however, externalities are beyond the control of any but the jurisdiction that makes the decision that generates them, yet they have a regional impact and harm or help other local governments that have no say. Proponents of metropolitan government say that fragmented urban areas exacerbate the potential for negative externalities and minimize incentives to create positive ones. Regional governments, proponents say, would have the opposite effect.

Regional Problems, Regional Solutions?

As we know, cities within a region compete to avoid projects that entail any sort of social burdens (negative externalities) and to attract development that will expand their tax bases (positive externalities). Sometimes their competition for projects such as airports or stadiums can be ridiculously expensive and inefficient. More frequently, their decisions result in externalities that create problems for metropolitan areas that extend beyond the boundaries of any single government.

Metropolitanists say that land-use decision making by individual local governments creates not only imbalances in tax resources, but also hinders finding solutions to regional problems. For example, transportation problems become worse when jobs are in one part of the metropolitan area and housing is in another. Transportation policy transcends the boundaries of individual communities because residents do not confine their activities to a single city, nor is any city self-contained and self-sufficient. Because urban areas are interconnected, highways and mass transit systems must cross boundaries and must be governed with a regional perspective in mind if they are to be successful.

Environmental policy may be an even better example. Imagine what environmental quality would look like in the United States if each local government jurisdiction had its own approach to environmental regulation. An environmentally progressive city might choose to ban automobiles and every other source of air pollution in order to protect its residents. Yet in most cases, such a policy would improve a city's air quality only marginally because of drift from other cities, sometimes dozens, hundreds, or even thousands of miles away. The same applies to pollution of underground water tables, lakes, and rivers. If cities were simply allowed to dispose of their waste by dumping it into a river, what would the impacts downriver be? Of course, this was the general approach to environmental policy in the United States up until the 1960s, when environmentalists began to define environmental contamination as a regional, and indeed national and (now global) problem requiring regional, national, and global solutions. Thus, most urban areas are governed by a special district whose authority it is to regulate environmental quality. These agencies have at their disposal a complex array of local, state, and federal environmental laws in order to carry out their mandate. But the key point is that regional problems require regional solutions. Although this approach may be fairly obvious for clearly regional issues such as the environment and transportation, local governments are less inclined to give up authority over other important areas such as land-use regulation.

Responsibility, Coordination, and Accountability

Ultimately, metropolitanists believe the problem is that nobody is in charge. No government is responsible for what goes on or for solving regional problems. Nor do the many governments within a metropolitan area readily coordinate what they do or cooperate on policies and programs. Each does what it considers best for itself and its constituents, and none accepts responsibility for regional repercussions. Their actions are usually competitive, sometimes contradictory, and almost always uncoordinated, more often exacerbating rather than ameliorating regional problems.

These problems are increasingly serious, however, and they are also increasingly salient to the citizens, who regularly cite traffic and air pollution as two of their top worries in opinion polls on local issues. Yet who can citizens hold accountable for regional problems? In most cases, the answer is no one, because either no one is in charge or the whole system is so confusing that it's difficult to know who is in charge. Their own local governments might be victims of negative externalities rather than their cause and if the actions of one city have negative effects elsewhere, its own residents may benefit too much to complain. Although efforts to regulate traffic and air pollution regionally have met with some success, regional cooperation on other important issues, such as education and land use, is almost nonexistent.

Authors Peter Dreier, John Mollenkopf, and Todd Swanstrom believe that our current system of urban government is now "dysfunctional." They argue that "metropolitan political fragmentation has encouraged unplanned, costly sprawl on the urban fringe. It has imposed longer journeys to work on commuters allowing less time for family life. It has undermined the quality of life in older suburbs, hardened conflicts between suburbs and their central cities, hampered financing for regional public facilities such as mass transit, and encouraged disinvestment from central cities. Countries with strong national land-use regulation and regional governments have avoided many of these problems. Indeed, the United States could have avoided them if we had chosen a more intelligent path for metropolitan growth over the last 50 years."[9]

Although metropolitanists have made a compelling case that fragmentation has its problems, opponents of regional government raise a number of legitimate issues. In addition to concerns about added costs and poor efficiency, they worry that the big and distant institutions it may require will be far less democratically accountable. They say that in most metropolitan areas, where regional agencies have been created to confront some area-wide problems, they have been invisible—unelected, ignored by the media, controlled by developers, or lost in the array of local institutions that govern us, and almost completely beyond public control. When you also factor in over two hundred years of substantial local autonomy, advocates of metropolitan government clearly have their work cut out for them.

In Your Community
Either in small groups or by yourself, summarize and critique the arguments for and against the regional government perspective.

Forging a New Regionalism: Strategies and Solutions

Despite the fear of big government and the loss of local autonomy, regional problems have grown serious enough in some areas to compel the creation of at least some form of regional government. Sometimes state governments have imposed solutions on fractious regions; sometimes individual communities found their own ways of coping; sometimes they even cooperate. Some of their attempted solutions are simple and straightforward, using available institutions and systems; others are more creative, complex, and far-reaching. The following sections discuss several strategies to create metropolitan governments.

Annexation

The most obvious way to solve the problem of fragmentation is to avoid it in the first place. One way to do that would be to allow cities to unilaterally annex adjacent land as they develop, creating one big city rather than the more familiar pattern of a central city surrounded by numerous smaller governments. Metropolitan government advocate David Rusk, in *Cities Without Suburbs* (2003), argues that where cities' boundaries have been "elastic," they were able to easily annex surrounding communities to create regional government. In contrast, Rusk finds that when cities are "inelastic," greater fragmentation has occurred, resulting in wider educational, economic, housing, and other social disparities.[10]

Until the late nineteenth century, liberal **annexation** laws were pretty much the norm. Cities usually went about annexing their suburbs, and quite frequently suburbanites were more than happy to sign on to receive new services such as electricity and sewage. However, as cities became destinations for immigrants, growth began to accelerate on the urban periphery, and in many states, a new and powerful suburban constituency successfully pressed for easy incorporation laws during the early twentieth century. However, in Texas, annexation laws remained fairly liberal, making it a good case study of annexation and its potential for regional government. "If you can't make the neighboring cities help pay your costs," said Fort Worth Mayor Bob Bolen, "then you have to expand your boundaries to the point that you take in the growth areas."[11] In addition to the ability to annex unincorporated areas without their permission, state law gives Texas cities a power known as **extra territorial jurisdiction**, effectively giving cities veto power over land development and new incorporations within five miles of a city's border.[12]

The city of Houston is a good example of annexation's potential to enhance regional government. At various points during the twentieth century, Houston went on annexation binges, gobbling up many of its surrounding suburbs. Today, Houston encompasses over 613 square miles and nearly 2 million residents and is the preeminent city in the region—and a major player in state politics. Annexation campaigns were led by a unified business elite and supported by a widely shared pro-growth consensus. By the 1980s, however, Houston's expansion significantly slowed. Opposition from central city minority groups concerned about annexation's potential to dilute minority voting power in violation of the federal Voting Rights Act, and the rising political influence of unincorporated "leapfrog" suburbs in the state legislature, resulted in increasing opposition to Houston's annexation plans. Currently, you might say there is something of an old-fashioned Texas standoff between central cities and suburbs on the question of annexation. Houston's plan for 2005–7, for example, does not propose the annexation of any new territory.[13]

Still, most researchers believe that Houston and other Texas cities such as San Antonio have managed to somewhat contain the growth of surrounding suburbs and bring about a *relatively* high level of regional coordination. Unlike most major American cities, Houston is still not hemmed in by its surrounding suburbs. Even the city's downtown has seen significant revival since the oil and real estate busts of the 1980s. Moreover, because of its population and political influence, Houston has significant power on regional agencies governing the Port of Houston and mass transit. Still, critics say that issues such as education and land use remain largely local powers, leading to pronounced inequalities among communities. Although Texas is not exactly a shining example of regional government in action, making annexation easier is nevertheless one viable strategy to address fragmentation. One of the advantages of this approach is that it uses an existing institution and that state laws that govern annexation can be changed, given the political will. However, the downside is that the strategy of annexation probably comes too late for most big cities that are already boxed in by independent suburbs.

City-County Consolidation

Where fragmentation already exists, the traditional alternative to annexation is **consolidation**, where central city and county governments are unified into a single entity. Here, a county and one or more of the cities within it merge to form a single government, with a new county council and executive replacing those of the previous county and cities and previous separate departments such as police and sheriff merged into one. In order to achieve consolidation, separate majority approval by the voters in both the central city and the county is usually required. A favorite reform of metropolitanists, the structure exists in cities such as San Francisco (1856), Denver (1904), Jacksonville (1967), Indianapolis (1969), and Louisville (2003) (see Table 4.1). These mergers reduced duplication of services, but most predated suburbanization and involved only one city and one county, thus decreasing the number of governments by only one. New York City's consolidations, however, merged several counties, and latter-day consolidations in Nashville, Jacksonville, Indianapolis, and Louisville merged counties, central cities, and suburbs.

Like a giant annexation, advocates of metropolitan government believe that county-level government can provide the necessary regional consistency, mitigating the problems of fragmentation. Although this reform might be advisable, it is rarely obtained. Central cities are often willing, but in many cases, minority groups worry their political influence will be overwhelmed by suburbanites. Their suburban counterparts are also usually skeptical, preferring to retain their independence, homogeneity, and tax resources. Sometimes "shotgun weddings" occur when one prospective partner has something the other absolutely can't do without, such as water or a sewage treatment facility. In other cases, political will in state capitals has forced such city-county marriages.

Do city-county consolidations work? Metropolitanist David Rusk has found that social inequality is indeed lessened in areas with such regional governments. But some studies are inconclusive about the other claims of metropolitanists regarding the potential for lower taxes, their potential to better align needs and resources, and their ability to bring about area-wide policy coherency.[14] One of the problems in assessing city-county consolidation is that there is no single, generally accepted structure or formula for how they will work. Whether city-county consolidations can bring about the advertised benefits of regional governance really depends upon the type of powers they are given, the amount of public support they have, and the amount of territory they cover. As metropolitan areas grow beyond county boundaries, it may be that the county level is not sufficiently large to provide the necessary regional approach.

Contracts

Another strategy to bring about a regional approach is known as **contracting**. Rather than the radical government restructuring required for a city-county consolidation, or even boundary changes that result from annexation, the potential regional benefits of contracting are more specific to the area of service delivery. The idea works like this: instead of each city providing its own police, fire, garbage, sewage, and other services, cities can obtain such services by contracting out the service to another existing service provider such as the county or another city. Contracting became popularized following its implementation under the **Lakewood Plan**, named after the city in Los Angeles County where it was introduced in the 1950s. The idea of contracting was floated by residents and developers seeking to avoid annexation and taxation by the nearby city of Long Beach. Instead, the community incorporated the city of Lakewood and then purchased services by contract from the county of Los Angeles, which now offers fifty-eight different services, from tree planting to animal control to libraries and fire.[15] The idea of contracting took off, and today, a third of Los Angeles County's eighty-eight cities do not have their own police force, contracting with the county sheriff instead. By providing so many services, Los Angeles County has become a sort of regional government, although its cities may opt in or out service by service at their discretion. The Lakewood Plan has been widely imitated around the country, with over 90 percent of all local governments, mostly in the West, contracting for some sort of service.[16]

But is contracting a viable strategy to bring about metropolitan government? Contracting for services has proven practical and popular because it allows cities to acquire a wide variety of cost-efficient services without surrendering local control. They can sometimes even seek competitive bids from, say, a county, a large city, and a private provider. "The assumption," management expert David Morgan observes, "is that city administrators no longer have to be concerned with enforcing bureaucratic productiveness. Instead they can concentrate on representing consumer interests in negotiating advantageous price and service contracts."[17] Economies of scale are easily and flexibly obtained, and as cities grow, they retain the option of providing the contracted services themselves or finding another jurisdiction to contract with. Moreover, city services can be coordinated because they are provided from a regional perspective.

This is a somewhat idealized version of contracting, however. Cities usually have little choice about which agencies they contract with and consequently have minimal bargaining power, pushing up costs. In some ways, contracting can be the worst of all worlds: a large, unaccountable bureaucracy providing poor services. From a metropolitan government perspective, an even bigger problem with contracting is that the services provided are often the least important from a social justice perspective. In other words, contracting may work for garbage pickup, police services, and sewage, but contracts are usually not available for land use and education. In many ways, contracting compounds regional fragmentation by allowing communities to incorporate cheaply and then use zoning to keep out the poor. As Los Angeles expert Mike Davis points out, the Lakewood Plan was instigated not for service efficiency but for "self-seeking economic advantage," enabling suburbs to "zone out service-demanding low-income and renting populations."[18] Rather than solving the problem of fragmentation, contracting for services may actually facilitate it by enabling small, autonomous cities to survive.

Special Districts

The most common way of dealing with regional problems is through the creation of **special districts**. As noted in chapter 4, special districts are by far the most numerous form of local government. They usually provide a specific service, such as a fire district, which may cover a small part of a city, parts of several cities, or all the cities and counties in a region. Created by states, existing local governments, or the voters, special districts have limited taxing and policy-making powers. The advantage of special districts is that they are a highly flexible way of dealing with regional issues, quicker and far less controversial to establish than multipurpose regional governments. They usually deal only with a commonly recognized and agreed-upon regional problem, with clearly defined responsibilities and strict fiscal limitations. Finally, they mostly do not threaten existing cities and counties and employ only the minimum amount of power deemed necessary to address a specific problem.

However, in terms of their potential to provide regional government, special districts have a number of limitations. The first problem is that most special districts are not truly regional in scope. The vast majority are small, commonly providing such services as transit, water, air quality, sewage, ports, parks, libraries, fire protection, and flood control. There are, of course, exceptions. Perhaps the mother of all special districts is the Port of New York Authority, established in 1921 by an interstate compact between New Jersey and New York. The Authority, with a board appointed by the governors of the two states, manages numerous bridges and tunnels, bus terminals, and the major air and sea ports in the region, as well as the site of the World Trade Center. But this mega-agency is an exception. More importantly, its authority is still limited and does not cover such critical areas as land use and education.

Another more serious critique of most special districts is that although they are intended to deal with regional problems, they inherently do so only on a piecemeal basis. For example, creating one special district responsible for air pollution and another for transportation does not exactly create regional consistency. From a regionalist perspective, issues such as environmental quality, transportation—to say nothing of land use—are interrelated. How can comprehensive solutions to air quality, for example, not take into consideration public transit alternatives? But in some cases where special districts have attempted to expand their authority, they have run into problems. In southern California, for example, the South Coast Air Quality Management District (SCAQMD), a giant special district governing air quality in the five-county Los Angeles region, has overseen a tremendous reduction in air pollution in recent decades. However, when the district attempted to impose a comprehensive transportation plan to meet its air quality goals, it faced litigation from special interest groups claiming it had overstepped its regulatory authority. In other cases, the district's more ambitious plans have been opposed by the area's numerous transit districts, 5 counties, and 160 cities, all of which see SCAQMD as taking their powers.

Special districts may be good at planning and operating regional parks and airports and may even achieve economies of scale in the provisions of some services, such as water supply and sewage treatment. They are less effective, however, at solving regional problems that are difficult to isolate, such as transportation and the environment, or redressing the separation of needs and resources. More damning, most special districts probably augment metropolitan fragmentation by adding yet more, sometimes invisible, layers of government and potential for conflict. In addition, most special districts are appointed by other officeholders rather than being elected, so democratic accountability and representation are minimal. In the end, with a few exceptions, special districts are probably not the answer that regional government advocates are looking for.

Cooperation Agreements

Another, more positive way of dealing with fragmentation is by cooperation. Cooperation can take a number of forms, from consulting one another to minimize negative spillovers of a particular project, to cooperating in a more formal and regional sense by coordinating programs and land-use planning, and reducing competition. Out of necessity, **regional cooperation** on a wide range of issues became more common and more formal in the 1980s. Joint committees of council members, administrators, and/or prominent citizens are often formed to facilitate such cooperation. Some cities banded together through accords known as **joint-powers agreements** to govern agencies that deliver services such as airports and water distribution, or to build facilities such as airports or stadiums, apportioning costs among them. Sometimes administrators lead the way, with fire chiefs, for example, working out mutual aid agreements for cross-boundary emergency assistance such as 911 or fire services. In Wake County, North Carolina, for example, local governments cooperate on economic development, solid waste, and libraries. The city of Albuquerque and Bernalillo County in New Mexico built a shared civic center. In Ohio, Greater Cleveland was formed by the central city, suburbs, and county to share the costs of some large projects. More radically, local governments in the Louisville, Kentucky, and Minneapolis–St. Paul areas agreed to share tax revenues, at least to some extent.

Councils of Governments

But most of these kinds of agreements are between only a few local government agencies. In order to create truly regional cooperation, particularly on land-use planning, local governments in metropolitan areas (and many rural ones as well) have established voluntary **councils of governments**, or **COGs**. The first was organized in the Detroit area in 1954, but other big metropolitan areas soon followed. Originally intended simply to improve communications between local governments, COGs got a boost in the mid-1960s when the federal government, under the Model Cities Program, began to require regional planning and review as a condition of grants to cities to make sure federal dollars were not wasted on duplicate projects in the same region (such as competing international airports). The councils took on this task in most areas, gaining a modest power, official status as a regional planning agency, and federal funding for their operations. Thanks to federal incentives, the number of COGs serving metropolitan areas around the nation burgeoned, reaching 670 by 1980.

Councils of governments are made up of representatives of cities and counties, usually council members, commissioners, and/or county supervisors. Each member government usually has one vote, although some COGs make adjustments to reflect differences in population. The primary function of COGs is to coordinate land-use and transportation planning within their regions, but as voluntary bodies they have no formal power of enforcement other than the goodwill of their members. During the 1960s and 1970s, they gained some authority from federal grant requirements for regional review of local land-use planning. Their ability to withhold federal grants meant that proposed changes to local plans were rarely vetoed by COGs, and projects were commonly revised to minimize any negative regional impact. But the Reagan administration dropped the reviews, denying COGs even this modest power. Subsequent cuts in grants also gave COGs less to do and made them more reliant on membership dues for funding. Many ceased to function.

Even if they had formal regulatory and taxing powers, however, COGs might not take on regional problems with much vigor because their one government/one vote system of representation means suburbs greatly outnumber central cities and the member governments are loath to interfere in one another's affairs. Today, many suburban jurisdictions view their COG as something of a "toothless tiger," with little to fear if they choose to ignore a COG mandate. COGs nevertheless perform useful functions, acting as clearinghouses for information, technical assistance, and sometimes helping with the development of other regional agencies and cooperative programs. Primarily, however, COGs serve as a forum of communication among local governments in each region, a task that may seem negligible, but which is surely a necessary starting point if regional problems are to be addressed. Metropolitan government advocates, of course, hope that one day they will serve a more formal regional governmental purpose. Until then, advocates will have to be content with their informal role.

Federation

An obvious, but largely untried answer to the problems of metropolitan fragmentation is creating a **federation** of local governments, dividing responsibilities between a large, regional government and smaller units along the lines of the state and national governments in the United States. The idea is to identify which services are best provided locally and which are best provided by higher levels. Balancing the need for democratic representation with the need for centralized government and coordination is also critical. In 1953, the province of Ontario, Canada, experimented with metropolitan federation for the city of Toronto and six surrounding independent cities. The top-tier government, known as Metropolitan Toronto, was governed by a regional council, with representation about equally divided between the central city and its suburbs. "Metro" took charge of strategic or large-scale planning, education, transportation, air quality, sewers, water, and police, while the six lower-tier governments maintained responsibility for smaller-scale land use, streets, parks, and other local services. Metro government reportedly helped Toronto build an excellent area-wide education system, good public transport, and affordable housing in mixed-income neighborhoods, although social welfare issues were not given as high a priority as some hoped, presumably because of suburban representation on the regional council.[19]

Then suddenly, in 1996, the provincial government of Ontario announced plans to abolish the federated system and consolidate (it used the term "amalgamate") Toronto and its surrounding municipal governments into one "mega-city." The new city of Toronto came into being on January 1, 1998. The plan came as a surprise to many and was implemented even over the objection of the vast majority of the region's voters. In one fell swoop, the provincial legislature created a city of 2.5 million people with an operating budget of $6.3 billion that exceeded several of Canadian provinces' budgets. The new governing council was originally composed of fifty-seven members, although that number was reduced (again by provincial authority) to a forty-four-member council.[20]

Had Toronto's federation been a failure? Not really, according to most observers. Rather, most scholars explain the amalgamation of Toronto as a strategy hatched by federal and provincial leaders to better position Toronto—Canada's financial center—to compete with the likes of New York, Tokyo, and London in the global economy. Of course, the usual regionalist arguments about greater economies of scale and policy coordination were also part of the discussion. In practical terms, unifying the governments of seven separate cities posed numerous logistical and political difficulties. In addition to budget shortfalls, the new government has had to deal with problems such as ensuring public participation and has instituted programs to enhance civic engagement. Recent polls, however, show that a solid majority of residents now believe the amalgamation was the right choice.[21]

But most experts believe that it is still too soon to say whether the experiment has achieved its goals. Preliminary analysis, however, suggests that amalgamation's promise to produce cost savings by reducing bureaucratic duplication and inefficiency has not been realized. However, it appears that whatever increased costs there were have been used to improve the level of services in many less affluent neighborhoods in the city of Toronto. Moreover, at least one study has found that city services are better coordinated.[22]

No U.S. metropolitan area has tried a Toronto-style federation, but the city of Miami and its suburbs adopted something similar in 1957, with Dade County taking on even more regional responsibilities than the urban counties discussed earlier. Cities there still provide education, police, and other local services, while the county is responsible for mass transit, water, sewage, and some other functions. Cities still retain land-use powers, but the county does strategic planning and sets some standards. As in the Canadian federations, the division of labor is an issue and has generated hundreds of court cases. Miami's experiment has been a qualified success. However, as immigration has radically altered the city's demographics, underlying divisions have been exposed. Some rich suburbs, such as Coconut Grove, have even tried to assert their independence by leading an unsuccessful movement in 1997 to abolish the city's system of government following a financial crisis in the city.

Although two-tiered systems like these have been considered in other metropolitan areas, including Boston, Pittsburgh, and St. Louis, none have yet been adopted. Many reformers believe that—like our national government—federated local government promises to create a the best balance of regional and local needs.

Emerging Systems of Regional Government

Federation and consolidation are rare, but some metropolitan areas have nevertheless moved beyond the ad hoc hodgepodge of contracts, cooperative agreements, special districts, and urban counties to new forms of regional government. Portland, Oregon, and the Twin Cities of Minneapolis–St. Paul are the classic examples of progressive regionalism, and similar plans have been discussed elsewhere. In each of these places, existing cities and counties have been retained, with a new, regional body superimposed over them. These new **multipurpose regional agencies** often combine previous single-purpose special districts into one more comprehensive and efficient unit, although their functions are still limited. Initiatives at the state level have been important in creating opportunities for regional government.

The Case of Portland, Oregon

During the 1970s, amid a period of increasing environmental activism in the United States, one of the first attempts to create a system of state-level land-use regulation emerged. The impetus for reform came from Oregon's environmentally minded Republican governor Tom McCall. During the 1973 legislative session, McCall gave a now-famous speech in which he warned of "grasping wastrels of the land" whose designs for unregulated development he believed threatened Oregon's economy and environment. The result of McCall's leadership was what became known as the Oregon Land Use Act, which required Oregon's cities and counties to develop land-use plans to regulate future growth.[23] The major thrust of the legislation created nineteen state-mandated planning goals to which local governments would be held accountable. In addition, the legislation sought to concentrate future growth within **urban growth boundaries (UGBs)** in land adjacent to incorporated cities. The ultimate goal was to protect Oregon farmland from urban sprawl, while concentrating development in urban cores. The Oregon Land Use Act created a statewide agency known as the Land Conservation and Development Commission (LCDC), which would oversee local plans to ensure compliance.[24]

In an attempt to comply with the new state law, in 1978, Portland area voters created a new government agency called the Greater Portland Metropolitan Service District, or "Metro" for short. Metro essentially combined the functions of Portland's pre-existing council of government, or COG, and an existing regional service agency that had been responsible for some local services. What made Metro unusual was that this was truly a regional government, with its own taxing authority and substantial regulatory powers. Metro is also unique in that it has an independently elected government with a six-member board elected by districts to four-year terms, as well as a separately elected council president who possesses veto power. Today, Metro serves a regional population of 1.3 million covering three counties and twenty-five cities, including the city of Portland. Metro's major functions include the governance of a convention center, park lands, zoos, transportation planning, and solid waste disposal. But what makes Metro unique is that it functions as a regional planning agency that oversees local land-use planning and can override local planning decisions, if necessary. Metro also implements the state-mandated urban growth boundary to protect farmland outside of the growth boundary, while focusing density into urban areas.

Has Portland's experiment with metropolitan government worked in the way that regional government advocates might hope? Yes, with some qualifications. Unlike other examples of regional government, Portland's Metro has some "teeth." In addition to providing a regional perspective for the governance of transportation, environmental quality, landfills, and other services, Metro has substantial authority over land use. Although this has not translated into a perfectly equitable distribution of affordable housing throughout the region, it has probably contributed to less-segregated housing patterns for the region than might otherwise have occurred.

But critics point out that the state-mandated urban growth boundaries have limited the supply of developable land, causing housing prices to become unaffordable. Some believe that this has limited growth in the Portland economy. Also, while Metro has taken on land-use powers, it lacks the authority to govern education, one of the key areas in the separation of needs and resources. Defenders, however, say that metropolitan government reform must be incremental so as not to threaten existing power arrangements, and to retain its public support. Indeed, the state of Oregon's approach to land use appears to have widespread public support. Between 1976 and 1982, the state of Oregon's planning program faced three initiative challenges at the polls, surviving all three.[25]

In sum, the key to Portland's success may be the state government's willingness to become involved in requiring and overseeing land-use planning. But the Portland area did not have to create its regional agency, Metro. The city and its surrounding suburbs each could have come up with their own separate plans to comply with state mandates. Yet, the region chose to take the path of a substantial regional approach to governance, perhaps becoming a model for the rest of the nation.

The Case of Minneapolis–St. Paul

Like Portland, the experience of metropolitan government in Minneapolis–St. Paul sets itself apart from other experiments in regional government in the United States. As in Oregon, state lawmakers took the lead in creating a more regional approach to local government. However, the state legislature did not pass comprehensive state-wide land-use reform, but instead singled out the state's largest urban area, Minneapolis–St. Paul. In 1967, the state legislature created a seven-county area Metropolitan Council, giving it substantial responsibility over transit, land use, redevelopment, and other regional issues. Unlike Portland's Metro, which is locally elected, the Twin Cities Metropolitan Council is appointed by the governor. What also sets the Metropolitan Council apart is its novel approach to **tax sharing**. The Council requires local governments under its jurisdiction to pool their tax resources, requiring them to allocate tax revenue above a certain level to be redistributed to other areas based upon need.

Critics say that Metropolitan Council has not lived up to its promises, particularly in the prevention of sprawl development. Perhaps the most effective advocate for increasing the authority of Metropolitan Council has been Minneapolis state legislator Myron Orfield. Orfield has authored several books and numerous articles, each making the argument that Metropolitan Council can do more to address housing and other regional inequities. But perhaps the major structural shortcoming of the Twin Cities' experiment is the fact that the commitment to regional government is primarily determined by any one governor's philosophical approach to regional government. For example, several housing laws sponsored by Orfield were passed by the state legislature, only to be vetoed by the governor. Direct election of the Metropolitan Council might be the next appropriate step, although some analysts worry that this would only increase the ability of the suburbs to block needed actions.[26]

In the end, regional government, even where it has been tried, has not lived up to the expectations of most metropolitan reformers. Defenders, however, respond that whatever its shortcomings, experiments and regional governments in places like Portland and Minneapolis–St. Paul represent important incremental steps toward a more comprehensive approach to local governance. While they may not have solved every problem, they have certainly injected some regional consistency into decision making. It is important to keep in mind that there are a number of factors that mitigate against the creation of regional government in the United States, not the least of which is our long-standing tradition of local autonomy and fragmented approach to local government. Officials in Portland, Minneapolis, and elsewhere still can only dream about the kinds of authority their counterparts wield in Europe. Can Americans ever be convinced to adopt European-style regional governments for metropolitan areas? A good place to begin in answering this question is understanding how political coalitions for and against metropolitan reform come together.

In Your Community

Of all of the strategies for overcoming metropolitan fragmentation discussed in this section, which seem like they might be effective, and which seem like they would likely be ineffective? Why?

The Politics of Regional Government

As the foregoing inventory of ways of coping with metropolitan fragmentation suggests, any substantive reforms face considerable resistance. Although most metropolitan areas have grappled with the problem, few have made much progress and most make do with partial solutions such as contracting and special districts. The public takes little interest in regional politics despite constant complaints about air pollution and traffic congestion. When asked in referenda, however, the voters almost invariably reject regional government. Perhaps that's why they are so seldom asked and why the issue is usually fought out among elites. But whether the voters or elites make the decision, the key for metropolitan government reformers is to convince the range of stakeholders that reform will serve not only a regional purpose, but their self-interest as well.

Who Favors Regional Government

Over the years, the main **proponents of regional government** have been central city businesses, particularly corporations, downtown interests, larger newspapers, big city politicians, and, more recently, environmentalists. Downtown interests often support regional government in hopes of retaining existing businesses and attracting new development in the downtown area. Major newspapers support regionalism partly because it is the sort of good government issue that newspapers like to crusade on, but also because a single metropolitan government would make their job of covering local news easier, provide bigger stories of wider interest, and cut into readership of their smaller, suburban competitors. Central city politicians campaign for regional government because they covet the tax resources of the suburbs and understandably hope to redistribute some of the burdens of the metropolitan area more widely; some may see regional government as a means of political advancement. Central city interest groups sometimes back their politicians on regionalism as a means of sharing their burdens with the suburbs. Reform or "good government" groups, such as the

League of Women Voters, urban planners, and many academics also often advocate regional government on the grounds of economic efficiency, policy coordination, and social justice.

All of these are fairly traditional proponents of regionalism, but as we saw in Oregon, in the 1970s and 1980s, some new cheerleaders joined them. Environmentalists, alarmed by air and water pollution and disappearing open space, became avid regionalists, seeing metropolitan government as the only hope for sensible conservation and planning. In Oregon, and also in Washington, which has a similar statewide approach to land-use regulation, farming interests seeking to protect an important industry became part of regional government coalitions. Corporations, particularly those with an interest in downtown redevelopment, also climbed on the regional bandwagon. Most showed little interest until recently.

But in the 1980s, many realized that bad regional planning was driving up housing costs and commuting time for their workers, and thus costs and wages for themselves. Some exercised the exit option, abandoning major metropolitan areas for smaller ones or moving their operations offshore. Others settled in to see if they could make their regions work a little better and came to the conclusion that some sort of regional government might help. Big corporate developers who operate on a regional scale sometimes join them, although businesses that are part of suburban growth machines generally do not, preferring to remain big fish in small ponds.

Although regionalism has gotten a boost from larger business interests, it should be noted that these businesses are mostly worried about downtown redevelopment and improved planning and transportation, as well as housing; the redistribution of tax resources, and other social justice concerns remain secondary. And big business is quite content with unelected regional agencies that they can more easily influence rather than having to cultivate separate relationships with many smaller suburban governments. For larger businesses, Metro government may seem like a chance to do some "one-stop shopping."

What then might a coalition for regional government look like? Certainly, the support of big business seems critical, followed by the support of government officials in larger urban areas. An interesting commonality between reform efforts in Oregon and Minnesota is that each of these states had only one dominant metropolitan region that stood to benefit. Add to that support from environmentalists and possibly farming interests, and suddenly, you have put together a potentially formidable alliance in favor of regional government.

Who Opposes Regional Government

Historically, the principal **opponents of regional government** are suburbanites. By now, it should be easy to predict why suburbanites oppose regional government. Suburban citizens wish to protect their homogeneous communities, good schools, property values, and taxes. However, because their support is crucial to any reform, they usually win. They rage about traffic, air pollution, inefficiency, and other regional problems, but when push comes to shove, they protect their own interests. In a survey of Orange County, California, with 2.2 million people and twenty-six cities, political scientist Mark Baldassare found that despite their expressed frustration with such issues, only 28 percent favored city/county consolidation, while 63 percent were opposed and remained "unwilling to give away local power."[27] Officials of suburban governments usually have a more limited understanding of regional governance generally accepting only existing solutions such as contracts, COGs, and special districts. Of course, these arrangements protect suburban autonomy except where limited regional action is absolutely necessary. They balk at more radical (or comprehensive) solutions, protecting their communities as well as their own jobs and powers. However, as Myron Orfield has argued, changes in suburbia may convince some "at-risk older suburbs" to join the regional government coalition.[28] As we saw in chapter 3, many older, inner-ring suburbs are beginning to show signs of inner-city style decay. Convincing at least some suburbs to support regional government may be the next step in putting together successful reform coalitions.

Affluent suburbanites are not the only opponents of regional government, however. Conservative and libertarian antagonists to big government are usually vociferously opposed. Public employees and their unions often oppose advanced forms of metropolitan government because consolidation of institutions may reduce the number of local government jobs. Local growth machines also oppose regionalism because they generally get their way in the current, fragmented setup, and they know that better planning might restrict them.

Perhaps surprisingly, central city minorities that might be expected to support regionalism as a means of tapping suburban tax resources also usually object to regional government. Often with justification, African American and Latino leaders see regionalism as a means of diluting their political power just as minorities are finally becoming majorities and winning representation in big cities. Some have argued that diluting the minority vote was a primary motivation for city/county consolidation in Indianapolis in 1969, when black political clout in that city was growing.[29] As in Indianapolis, metro government has reinstated white majorities almost everywhere. Minority leaders in big cities have concluded that they would rather have power over their decaying, needy communities than share power by being reduced to political minorities once more. They also recognize that proposals for metro government do not always include redistribution of tax resources, better housing opportunities, and so forth. Even if a common tax pool is established, such as in Minneapolis–St. Paul, suburban majorities often succeed in focusing attention on their concerns rather than those of the central city, as some studies suggest was the case in Toronto.[30]

Perhaps the trump card of both suburban and central city opponents to metropolitan regional government is that they can assume the mantle of defenders of local democracy. Metropolitan consolidation would take away public choice, community identity, and local democracy, they say. Moreover, these grassroots groups, including central city neighborhoods, minorities, and suburbanites can legitimately argue that they would be swamped by a big, regional government operating beyond their reach. They would find themselves competing not just with each other, but with regional power holders such as corporations with greater access and means to influence policy. However, reformers might respond, as James Madison famously did in the *Federalist Papers*, that larger governments do a better job of protecting democracy than smaller governments, which are more likely to be taken over by a single faction or interest group.

However, there is nothing inherently evil about larger units of government and more comprehensive regional planning, although there is a great deal wrong when the move to regionalism necessarily disenfranchises the grassroots. But the reality is that the current system of regional governance, with its invisible, unaccountable, mostly appointed bodies, already does that. Stronger regional government does seem necessary and may be inevitable. If so, it should not be imposed by economic elites from the top down, as seems increasingly likely in an age of rapid globalization, but rather constructed from the bottom up in such a way as to assure representation for the least powerful neighborhoods and cities. This will not happen, however, unless grassroots forces, most of whom take little interest in issues beyond their own communities, overcome their parochialism, embrace the benefits of regional government, and involve themselves in shaping it.

Finally, you may have wondered why regional government has caught on—to the extent that it has—in Portland and Minneapolis–St. Paul, while it lags in other parts of the country. Certainly, both of these regions are fairly homogeneous ethnically and economically, and were particularly so during the 1960s when these regional governments were set up. It may very well be that where people share commonalities they are more likely to be open to regional solutions to problem-solving. In addition, the political culture of both Portland and Minneapolis–St. Paul, with large Democratic majorities where many residents trace their cultural roots to socialistic Scandinavian countries, tend to look more favorably upon communal approaches to problem-solving.

In Your Community

Are there any regional governments or organizations in your area? What authority do they have? Do any of them seem successful in solving regional problems?

Regional Government versus Regional Governance

While few areas have moved toward formal, multipurpose regional government, virtually all urban regions in America have institutions and organizations that provide some level of governance, albeit informal and fragmented. The San Francisco Bay Area is an example of **regional governance** without a regional government. The Association of Bay Area Governments (ABAG) is a COG and functions as a regional planning agency. But ABAG has no authority, so its plans cannot be enforced; instead, it serves primarily a forum for the region's local governments and a collector and disseminator of data on the region, including projections of future growth and needs. The Bay Area's Metropolitan Transportation Commission (MTC) has more authority because federal transportation spending in the area must be consistent with MTC transportation plans—but MTC is separate from ABAG, the planning agency. Several additional special districts deal with other regional policies and programs, including air quality, water quality, and land use and conservation along the coast of the San Francisco Bay. The region is also governed by nine counties, multiple transit agencies, nearly one hundred cities, and hundreds of smaller special districts.

Besides the hundreds of governments in the agencies, regional issues are addressed by several private organizations.[31] The Bay Area Council and the Silicon Valley Leadership Group are organizations of the major corporate and business interests in the region, while Joint Venture Silicon Valley brings together business and public sector leaders. These organizations—and similar groups in other metropolitan areas —take an active, advocacy role on regional policy issues, including affordable housing, education, and, perhaps most effectively, transportation, taking leadership on mass transit systems. Although they're far less visible and powerful, the Bay Area Alliance and Urban Habitat are grassroots regional organizations that emphasize environmental and social justice issues.

These organizations, along with the Bay Area's many governments and other, more locally focused organizations and institutions, provide some level of regional governance, if not government. If regional problems are not solved through this system, at least they are considered and sometimes ameliorated—without having the necessity of having a big and distant regional governmental authority. On the other hand, this informal system is fragmented, difficult to move, and invisible to all but those who participate directly. The media largely ignore these regional institutions; citizens and grassroots groups are ill-informed about decisions that affect their lives and their tax dollars. In this system groups representing regional economic interests like the Bay Area Council gain disproportionate power, and decision makers are largely unaccountable to the public. Every decade or so, reformers like the supporters of regional government discussed earlier, suggest moving toward a more unified and visible structure, merging ABAG and existing regional special districts, perhaps even emulating Portland or the Twin Cities. But political reality soon sets in as suburban cities and counties object, and the Bay Area continues to muddle through with regional governance rather than regional government.

The Future of Metropolitan Regional Government

In his most recent book, *American Metro-Politics*, Myron Orfield writes, "[t]he many challenges facing America's metropolitan areas can be attacked effectively only through a coordinated, regional approach."[32] Orfield goes on to argue for a "three-pronged attack" that includes tax sharing, land-use reform, and regional government. But other researchers continue to maintain that the current system is an efficient and flexible adaptation to the complexity of metropolitan areas. Yet as regional problems grow, new pressures to create metropolitan government may emerge. Local governments are already being pushed to act, particularly in the South and West, where rapid growth has intensified the problems and fragmentation has exacerbated them. Transportation and air pollution are key issues, putting regionalism on the agenda of Sunbelt cities that, unlike their counterparts in the Frostbelt, lack mass transit systems. In addition, the need to coordinate regional economic strategies to compete in a global economy has also become an argument of metropolitan reformers. On these and other issues, local governments all over the country are beginning to take collective action, with more formal and informal mechanisms of cooperation starting to emerge. Stronger counties, and special districts and limited multipurpose regional agencies, are also being created. Meanwhile, advocates such as Minnesota's Myron Orfield and other scholars continue to make the case for a **new regionalism**.

Given such fierce local resistance, however, the impetus for stronger regional authorities may have to come from higher levels of government. The federal government under President Clinton showed slightly greater interest in urban problems than it did under Presidents Reagan and George H. W. and George W. Bush. But for the most part, the federal government has stayed out of the issue altogether. The states, which actually created the problem in the first place with their permissive laws of incorporation and annexation, may be the most promising and effective level to initiate reform. Minnesota, for example, initiated the Twin Cities Metro Council, and Oregon, Washington, and eight other states now require comprehensive land-use planning of their local governments, and another six encourage it.[33]

But absent further state intervention, it is likely that the nation will continue the status quo of piecemeal intervention. Texas, as we saw in the case of Houston, gives some of its cities limited "extraterritorial powers" to regulate land use in adjacent unincorporated areas. California has created regional governments for regulation of land along the coast and has witnessed a flurry of legislative proposals over the years to create regional planning bodies and even for a state plan to share development revenues. But none has been enacted. Despite these efforts, however, the suburban majorities of most state legislatures, including Texas and California, seem more interested in maximizing their own benefits under the current system than in redressing the imbalance of needs and resources.

On the question of public education, the courts have shown a willingness to become involved, at least in some states. In California, Texas, Hawaii, and Kentucky, state courts have ordered governors and legislators to resolve spending gaps between rich and poor school districts. Thus far, court-mandated equalization has not yielded the results that reformers want. In many cases, states have simply "equalized down" to a relatively low level of spending rather than bring lower income districts up to the standards of more affluent areas. In addition, many affluent and middle-class Americans have simply abandoned the public school system altogether, perhaps an unfortunate unintended consequence of government intervention.

In a very real way, the future of metropolitan government may simply come down to Americans' willingness to share. Defenders of metropolitan fragmentation often argue that the social good is best served by competition rather than cooperation. Based on free-market principles, the argument is one that carries a fair amount of intuitive weight with many Americans. It may very well be that, as Americans, our affinity for free-market solutions, and our cultural biases against big government and collective solutions may mean that even relatively limited experiments with metropolitan governments are possible only in limited ways, and in certain parts of the country.

Finally, in politics, the status quo often is hard to change. The reality of suburban political power suggests that the future of regional government will reflect its past, with patchwork solutions where necessary, rather than radical change. As the problems of metropolitan fragmentation grow, counties may begin to play a bigger role in some urban areas; cooperative ventures such as COGs may expand; and new special districts may be spawned, some of which will serve important regional functions. But in all probability, the local governments of the foreseeable future will be very much like the ones we see around us today.

Essential Terms

metropolitan government
Metropolitan Statistical Area (MSA)
Combined Metropolitan Statistical
   Areas (CMSAs)
public choice
sense of community
efficiency
economies of scale
separation of needs and resources
externalities
annexation
extra territorial jurisdiction
consolidation
contracting

Lakewood Plan
special districts
regional cooperation
joint-powers agreements
councils of governments (COGs)
federation
multipurpose regional agencies
urban growth boundaries (UGBs)
tax sharing
proponents of regional government
opponents of regional government
regional governance
new regionalism

On the Internet

- The website for the American Planning Association (www.planning.org) contains numerous articles and links on the topic of regional government and new urbanism.
- The San Francisco–based Congress for the New Urbanism (www.cnu.org) is a group of planners, architects, and other professionals who advocate land conservation and new urbanism approaches to planning.
- www.farmland.org is an organization founded to research ways to protect agricultural land from suburban development.
- The Brookings Institution website (www.brookings.edu/metro/metro.htm) has a number of useful studies relating to regional government.
- www.metro-region.org/ is the website for Oregon's regional government, Metro.

Notes

1. Quoted in *The Economist*, October 13, 1990, p. 16.
2. Albert O. Hirschman, *Exit, Voice, and Loyalty: Responses to Decline in Firms, Organizations, and States* (Cambridge, MA: Harvard University Press, 1970).
3. See Vincent Ostrom, Charles M. Tiebout, and Robert Warren, "The Organization of Government

in Metropolitan Areas: A Theoretical Inquiry," *American Political Science Review* 55, no. 4 (December 1961): 831–42. See also Charles M. Tiebout, "A Pure Theory of Local Expenditures," *Journal of Political Economy* 64, no. 5 (October 1956): 416–24; and Hirschman, *Exit, Voice, and Loyalty*.

4. Gary J. Miller, *Cities by Contract: The Politics of Municipal Incorporation* (Cambridge, MA: MIT Press, 1981), p. 8.

5. Drew A. Dolan, "Local Government Fragmentation: Does It Drive Up the Cost of Government?" *Urban Affairs Quarterly* 26, no. 1 (September 1990): 28–45.

6. See, for example, Advisory Commission on Intergovernmental Relations, *Metropolitan Organization: The St. Louis Case* (Washington, DC: U.S. Government Printing Office, 1988). See also Vincent Ostrom, Robert Bish, and Elinor Ostrom, *Local Government in the United States* (San Francisco: Institute for Contemporary Studies Press, 1988).

7. Peter Dreier, John Mollenkopf, and Todd Swanstrom, *Place Matters: Metropolitics for the 21st Century* (Lawrence, KS: University Press of Kansas, 2001; 2nd ed. 2004).

8. J. Eric Oliver, *Democracy in Suburbia* (Princeton, NJ: Princeton University Press, 2001), p. 5.

9. Dreier, Mollenkopf, and Swanstrom, *Place Matters*, p. 176.

10. David Rusk, *Cities Without Suburbs: A Census 2000 Update,* 3rd ed. (Washington, DC: Woodrow Wilson Center Press; Baltimore: Johns Hopkins University Press, 2003).

11. *New York Times*, February 23, 1991.

12. City of Houston Planning and Development Department, "City of Houston Annexation Plan (2006–2008)." Available at: www.houstontx.gov/planning/Annexation/annexation.htm (accessed October 23, 2005).

13. Ibid.

14. Ann O'M. Bowman and Richard C. Kearney, *State and Local Government,* 6th ed. (Boston: Houghton Mifflin, 2005).

15. Miller, *Cities by Contract.*

16. Ronald J. Oakerson and Roger B. Parks, "Local Government Constitutions: A Different View of Metropolitan Governance," *American Review of Public Administration* 19, no. 4 (December 1989): 288.

17. David R. Morgan, *Managing Urban America*, 3rd ed. (Pacific Grove, CA: Brooks/Cole, 1989), p. 30.

18. Mike Davis, *City of Quartz: Excavating the Future in Los Angeles* (New York: Vintage Books, 1992), p. 166 (repr. London: Pimlico, 1998).

19. *Economist*, May 19, 1990, p. 18. See also Bernard H. Ross, Myron A. Levine, and Murray S. Stedman, *Urban Politics: Power in Metropolitan America*, 4th ed. (Itasca, IL: F. E. Peacock, 1991), p. 270.

20. Enid Slack, "A Preliminary Assessment of the New City of Toronto," *Canadian Journal of Regional Science* 23 (2001), pp. 13–29.

21. "Building the New City of Toronto: Three-Year Status Report on Amalgamation, January 1998–December 2000" (report prepared by the Chief Administrative Officer of the City of Toronto, 2000).

22. Slack, "A Preliminary Assessment."

23. Carl Abbott, Deborah Howe, Sy Adler, eds., *Planning the Oregon Way: A Twenty-Year Evaluation* (Corvallis, OR: Oregon State University Press, 1994).

24. Christopher Leo, "Regional Growth Management Regime: The Case of Portland Oregon," *Journal of Urban Affairs* 20, no. 4 (1998): pp. 363–94.

25. Abbott, Howe, and Adler, eds., *Planning the Oregon Way.*

26. Robert E. Einsweiler, "Metropolitan Government and Planning: Lessons in Shared Power," in *The Metropolitan Midwest: Policy Problems and Prospects for Change*, ed. Barry Checkoway and Carl V. Patton (Urbana: University of Illinois Press, 1985), p. 294.

27. Mark Baldassare, "Citizen Support for Regional Government in the New Suburbia," *Urban Affairs Quarterly* 24, no. 3 (March 1989): 467.

28. Myron Orfield, *American Metropolitics: The New Suburban Reality—a Summary* (Minneapolis: Metropolitan Area Research Corp., 2003).

29. Philip J. Trounstine and Terry Christensen, *Movers and Shakers: The Study of Community Power* (New York: St. Martin's Press, 1982), pp. 180–81.

30. Ross, Levine, and Stedman, *Urban Politics*, p. 270.

31. See www2.sjsu.edu/depts/PoliSci/faculty/christensen/gov_bay_area.htm for a list and brief overview of the San Francisco Bay Area's regional governmental and nongovernmental organizations (accessed November 12, 2005).

32. Orfield, *American Metropolitics*, p. 17.

33. Ibid.

Index

About the Authors

Terry Christensen is a specialist on state and local politics who earned his BA at Stanford and his PhD at the University of North Carolina, Chapel Hill. He joined the faculty of the Department of Political Science at San Jose State University in 1970. In 1998 he was named San Jose State University's Outstanding Professor. Christensen is the author or co-author of eight books and frequent newspaper op-ed pieces. Local and national media regularly call on him for analysis of politics in California and Silicon Valley. His most recent book is *Projecting Politics: Political Messages in American Films* (2005), co-authored with Peter Haas. Other recent works include *Recall! California's Political Earthquake* (2004) and the ninth edition of *California Politics and Government* (2007), both co-authored with Larry N. Gerston. Christensen is also experienced in practical politics at the local level as an advocate of policy proposals and charter reform and an adviser and mentor to candidates for local office. He has served on numerous civic committees and commissions. He is currently leading CommUniverCity San Jose, a partnership between the City of San Jose, San Jose State University, and adjacent neighborhoods. Through CommUniverCity hundreds of students are carrying out community service projects selected by neighborhood residents and supported by the city.

Tom Hogen-Esch received his PhD in political science from the University of Southern California in 2002. He joined the faculty of the Department of Political Science at California State University Northridge in that same year. His teaching interests include U.S. and California government, public policy and administration, race and ethnic politics, and urban politics. He has published articles in *California Politics and Policy* (2003), *California Policy Issues Annual* (2003), and *Urban Affairs Review* (2001, 2006). His dissertation, "Recapturing Suburbia: Urban Secession and the Politics of Growth in Los Angeles, Boston, and Seattle," explored issues of governance, social movements, and urban fragmentation. From 1997 to 1999 he held a staff position for the Los Angeles Elected Charter Reform Commission. He is regularly quoted in the local media on Los Angeles and California government, and has made numerous presentations to community groups in Los Angeles.

About the Authors

Terry Christensen is a specialist on state and local politics who earned his BA at Stanford and his PhD at the University of North Carolina, Chapel Hill. He joined the faculty of the Department of Political Science at San Jose State University in 1970. In 1998 he was named San Jose State University's Outstanding Professor. Christensen is the author or co-author of eight books and frequent newspaper op-ed pieces. Local and national media regularly call on him for analysis of politics in California and Silicon Valley. His most recent book is *Projecting Politics: Political Messages in American Films* (2005), co-authored with Peter Haas. Other recent works include *Recall! California's Political Earthquake* (2004) and the ninth edition of *California Politics and Government* (2007), both co-authored with Larry N. Gerston. Christensen is also experienced in practical politics at the local level as an advocate of policy proposals and charter reform and an adviser and mentor to candidates for local office. He has served on numerous civic committees and commissions. He is currently leading CommUniverCity San Jose, a partnership between the City of San Jose, San Jose State University, and adjacent neighborhoods. Through CommUniverCity hundreds of students are carrying out community service projects selected by neighborhood residents and supported by the city.

Tom Hogen-Esch received his PhD in political science from the University of Southern California in 2002. He joined the faculty of the Department of Political Science at California State University Northridge in that same year. His teaching interests include U.S. and California government, public policy and administration, race and ethnic politics, and urban politics. He has published articles in *California Politics and Policy* (2003), *California Policy Issues Annual* (2003), and *Urban Affairs Review* (2001, 2006). His dissertation, "Recapturing Suburbia: Urban Secession and the Politics of Growth in Los Angeles, Boston, and Seattle," explored issues of governance, social movements, and urban fragmentation. From 1997 to 1999 he held a staff position for the Los Angeles Elected Charter Reform Commission. He is regularly quoted in the local media on Los Angeles and California government, and has made numerous presentations to community groups in Los Angeles.